SOCIAL POLICY FOR SOCIAL WORK, SOCIAL CARE AND THE CARING PROFESSIONS

Dedicated to all our students, wherever they may be

Social Policy for Social Work, Social Care and the Caring Professions

Scottish Perspectives

Edited by

STEVE HOTHERSALL AND JANINE BOLGER

Robert Gordon University, Scotland

ASHGATE

Published by
Ashgate Publishing Limited
Wey Court East
Union Road
Farnham
Surrey GU9 7PT
England

Ashgate Publishing Company
Suite 420
101 Cherry Street
Burlington, VT 05401-4405
USA

www.ashgate.com

British Library Cataloguing in Publication Data
Social policy for social work, social care and the caring
professions : Scottish perspectives.
1. Scotland--Social policy. 2. Social service--Scotland.
I. Hothersall, Steve J. II. Bolger, Janine.
361.6'1'09411-dc22

Library of Congress Cataloging-in-Publication Data
Hothersall, Steve J.
Social policy for social work, social care and the caring professions : Scottish perspectives / by Steve Hothersall and Janine Bolger.
p. cm.
Includes index.
ISBN 978-0-7546-7635-5 (hbk) -- ISBN 978-0-7546-7636-2 (pbk)
1. Public welfare--Scotland. 2. Social service--Government policy--Scotland. 3. Scotland--Social policy. I. Bolger, Janine. II. Title.

HV249.S5H68 2010
361.6'109411--dc22

2010015525

ISBN 9780754676355 (hbk)
ISBN 9780754676362 (pbk)
ISBN 9781409412496 (ebk)

Reprinted 2012

Printed and bound in Great Britain by
the MPG Books Group, UK

Contents

List of figures		*vii*
List of tables		*ix*
List of contributors		*xi*
Foreword		*xv*
Introduction		1
Part I	**Context**	**5**
1	What *is* social policy? *Steve J. Hothersall*	7
2	A history of social policy *Steve J. Hothersall*	31
3	Ideology: How ideas influence policy and welfare *Steve J. Hothersall*	51
4	People, policy and practice *Steve J. Hothersall*	71
Part II	**Themes and issues**	**89**
5	Poverty and social exclusion *Janine Bolger and Pedro Morago*	91
6	Risk, support and protection *Mike Maas-Lowit*	109
7	Changing patterns of care *Steve J. Hothersall, Clare Swan and Iain D. Turnbull*	125
8	Welfare rights *Janine Bolger*	151
9	Social policy perspectives on empowerment *Rob Mackay*	175

Part III Policy for practice **203**

10 Health and health inequalities 205
Pedro Morago

11 Mental health 227
Jackie Loxton, Mike Maas-Lowit and Rob Mackay

12 Older people 247
Rory Lynch

13 Disability: A question of perception 271
Jeremy Millar

14 Children and their families 293
Steve J. Hothersall and Patrick Walker

15 Education and training in Scotland 317
Janine Bolger

16 Substance use and social policy in Scotland: The struggle to make sense of things 337
George Allan

17 Social policy in the criminal justice system 367
Anne Shirran

18 Asylum and immigration 393
Clare Swan

19 Housing and homelessness 419
Pedro Morago

20 Conclusions: Onwards and upwards? 435
Steve J. Hothersall and Janine Bolger

Index 439

List of figures

1.1	The court structure in Scotland	16
1.2	An ecological representation of the relationship between society, law, policy and professional practice (after Bronfenbrenner 1979)	22
1.3	The hierarchical relationship between law and policy	25
2.1	A facsimile of part of the Act of 1601	34
3.1	A linear representation of ideological positions	54
3.2	A generalised typology of differing ideologies	56
3.3	Welfare spending 1950–2011	64
4.1	Maslow's Hierarchy of Human Needs	76
9.1	Discourses relating to empowerment	196
16.1	The elements which shape attitudes and trends in society	340
17.1	Scottish criminal justice agencies	368
18.1	The process for seeking asylum in the UK	405
18.2	Applications for asylum in the UK	410
18.3	Asylum settlement figures 1999–2008	411

List of tables

1.1	The devolved powers of the Scottish Parliament	17
1.2	The reserved powers of the Westminster Parliament	17
7.1	Relevant community care legislation	130
8.1	Possible benefit entitlements	154
11.1	Scottish mental health related policy from 2000 onwards	230
12.1	Social policy and legislation in Scotland relevant to older people	256
16.1	Key legislation applying to Scotland	356
17.1	Sentencing perspectives, legislation and associated policy	371
17.2	Notification for registration periods: Sex Offenders Act 1997	380

List of contributors

George Allan qualified as a social worker in 1976 and has worked primarily with adults. He has held front-line practitioner, planning and management posts in the substance problems field in both the statutory and voluntary sectors. He currently lectures on substance problems issues at the Robert Gordon University. George has a particular interest in the effective implementation of the 'Hidden Harm' agenda.

Janine Bolger is a Senior Lecturer in Social Work. Following a period of post-qualifying experience in residential child care in New York and child protection in Manchester, Janine spent nine years as Assistant Principal of a therapeutic community in the Scottish Highlands. She took up a lecturing post at the Robert Gordon University in partnership with the Scottish Institute for Residential Child Care in 2001. She develops materials, tutors and teaches on the BA(Hons) Social Work (Residential Child Care) by Distance Learning. Teaching and research interests are particularly around social policy, social work methods and the development of communication skills in social work practice.

Steve J. Hothersall is a Senior Lecturer in Social Work at the Robert Gordon University, Aberdeen. He is the author, co-author and co-editor of a number of publications including: *Social Work with Children, Young People and their Families in Scotland* (Learning Matters); *Social Work and Mental Health in Scotland* (with Mike Maas-Lowit and Malcolm Golightley: Learning Matters); and *Need, Risk and Protection in Social Work Practice* (with Mike Maas-Lowit: Learning Matters). Steve trained and worked as a registered nurse before becoming a social worker and specialising in child care and child protection. He also trained and worked as a Mental Health Officer. He previously taught at the University of York before moving back to Scotland where he currently teaches on a range of pre-and post-qualifying courses. His main interests are in law, social policy and child care with a special emphasis on attachment theory and social work practice. He is a founding and Board member of the International Association for the Study of Attachment (http://www.iasa-dmm.org/index.php/contact/) and also sits on the Editorial Board of the *British Journal of Social Work*. Steve maintains a practice base as a children's safeguarder and a curator *ad litem*, and in his spare time he indulges his passion for the music of Ludwig van Beethoven.

Jackie Loxton has been a Lecturer in Social Work at the Robert Gordon University, Aberdeen for the past 13 years. Her practice experience is in the field of mental health and children and families. She is currently Course Leader for the Postgraduate Certificate Mental Health Officer Award. Her particular interests are in the field of mental health, adult support and protection, and the involvement of service users in social work education.

Rory Lynch comes from Donegal in Ireland and has been living and working in Scotland for 35 years. He has worked primarily within the fields of single homelessness and mental health where he has carried out international work in the area of the self-evaluation of well-being. He is currently a member of the Distance Learning Programme for Social Work at the Robert Gordon University and has a special interest in human growth and behaviour and social work with older people.

Mike Maas-Lowit embarked on an initial career in residential child care in the early 1970s and then began to develop his interest in mental health social work after graduation from Aberdeen University in 1983. He worked as an Approved Social Worker in the south of England and then as a Mental Health Officer (MHO) in Scotland, where he still lives and works. He has been involved in the development of MHO training since the mid 1980s and, aside from lecturing in social work since 1991, he has written material for and advised the Scottish Government on matters in relation to social work, mental health and law. Since 1993, Mike has also been closely involved as the voluntary chair of Pillar Aberdeen, a small, cutting-edge voluntary agency which offers social support to people whose lives are challenged by poor mental health. He is also co-author (with Steve J. Hothersall and Malcolm Golightley) of *Social Work and Mental Health in Scotland* and co-author and co-editor (with Steve J. Hothersall) of *Need, Risk and Protection in Social Work Practice*.

Rob Mackay is Lecturer in Social Work with the Robert Gordon University, Aberdeen. He has worked for local authorities principally in the areas of mental health and child care and has also worked in the voluntary sector as a practice teacher. He has a long-standing interest in informal networks, peer support and advocacy activities through involvement with a number of voluntary organisations. His teaching and research interests include disability, mental health, social work values and ethics, empowerment, involvement and participation strategies, narrative practice and the European context of social work. Over the past six years, he has been actively engaged with the Robert Gordon University project to promote the greater involvement of service users and carers with students and staff of the social work courses.

Jeremy Millar is a Lecturer in Social Work. The experience of the punk era and fighting the destructive policies of the Thatcher years offered a political education that was practised across a range of social care settings. He has an Open University degree and a MSc in Advanced Residential Child Care. He has, through his teaching and ongoing involvement in models of service user participation, attempted to introduce narratives from the oppressed, marginalised and patronised with the aim of engaging social work students and practitioners in the political nature of their work and a clear understanding of what core social care values stand for.

Pedro Morago worked in Oxfordshire, for three years, with adults with a learning disability and mental health problems, and then qualified as a social worker at Oxford University, specialising in the area of Evidence-Based Social Interventions. After four years working as a Lecturer in Social Work at the Robert Gordon University, Aberdeen, Pedro moved to Teesside University where he is a Senior Lecturer currently teaching Research Methods and Evidence-Based Practice at the School of Health and Social Care. His main area of interest is Evidence-Based Practice in Social Work.

Anne Shirran is a Lecturer in Social Work. Since qualifying as a social worker, she has worked in criminal justice both as a field worker and as a prison-based social worker and team manager at HMP Peterhead. Prior to taking up her current post, Anne was a Practice Learning Facilitator. Her interests include practice learning and research into effective interventions with offenders.

Clare Swan originally studied theology at Manchester University before moving to Aberdeen where she worked in projects supporting people with mental health problems. She undertook the postgraduate course in social work at the Robert Gordon University in 1992, and completed the MSc in 1994. She then worked as a social worker in a community mental health team, and latterly the duty social work team which saw a high number of clients subject to immigration controls. During this time she also worked as a Mental Health Officer and Practice Teacher. She joined the Robert Gordon University staff in 2004. Her main teaching areas are social policy, counselling in social work practice and human growth and behaviour. Clare continues to have an active role in practice learning.

Iain D. Turnbull is a Lecturer in Social Work at the Robert Gordon University, Aberdeen. Previously Development Manager for Angus Drug and Alcohol Action team he has worked in both statutory and voluntary sectors in a range of operational and strategic planning roles. These include having the strategic lead for carers, managing court services in criminal justice social work, working with people with acquired brain injury and, uniquely, working with churches and faith organisations in relation to the development of community care. His interests include substance use problems, social policy and interdisciplinary practice.

Patrick Walker is a Lecturer in Social Work in the Faculty of Health and Social Care at the Robert Gordon University, Aberdeen and with the Scottish Institute of Residential Child Care. His background is in children and families statutory social work. He has also worked in residential social work with local authorities and the voluntary sector.

Foreword

Social policy is critical to the underpinning of social work practice and policy but may seem remote and inaccessible for burgeoning social work practitioners, our students. Social policy is further complicated by its different development in the four countries of the United Kingdom and by the range of policy areas it addresses for different service user groups, children, adults and older people, with a range of policy agendas in relation to poverty, rights, risk, empowerment and patterns of care provision.

This volume, *Social Policy for Social Work, Social Care and the Caring Professions: Scottish Perspectives,* draws on the expertise of staff at the Robert Gordon University, Aberdeen in policy and practice with a range of groups of service users, carers and involuntary service users. Its aim is to engage students and developing practitioners in understanding and potentially challenging the way in which social policy influences social work practice. We believe that this volume will provide an invaluable text for current students and developing practitioners to do just this in the complex and ever-changing world of social work policy and practice.

Professor Joyce Lishman
Head of School of Applied Social Studies
The Robert Gordon University
Aberdeen

Introduction

This book largely focuses on the description, explanation and analysis of social policy in Scotland since devolution in 1999 and reflects the slowly emerging distinctive policy agenda. Integral to the discourse presented throughout this book is consideration of new forms of governance and the emergence of more diverse forms of social policy (Mooney and Scott 2005). The examination of the historical development of a range of themes and issues is intended to assist in contextualising Scotland's progress to date (Stewart 2004), whilst locating this within a broader European and global perspective particularly in relation to the emergence of ideological shifts concerning the nature of the relationship between the state and its citizens and the nature of welfare itself. Throughout the book reference is made to the changing demographics in Scotland and how this has altered the face of current social issues and has thus influenced policy development. The aim is to continue the attempt to integrate the idea of social policy both as a discrete academic discipline and as an interdisciplinary field of endeavour that can provide practical support in understanding how social policy influences social work and social care *practice*. In doing so the hope is that it proves to be a useful aid for undergraduates, postgraduates and to other associated professionals.

The breadth and diversity of social policy is often both confusing and overwhelming to students. Part I of the book looks at what social policy is, how and why it is made and highlights the relationship between social policy and the law. The notion of *need* is discussed at some length and distinguished from concepts of preferences and wants emphasising the fundamental relationship between *people* and *policy*. The political ideology supporting policy development and decisions is examined, as is the relationship between people and the policies in place.

Part II refers itself to specific themes and issues rather than the more usual 'social problems' (which is frequently employed to provide an objective overview of such shared experiences) and considers a range of experiences evident in the public domain that exert considerable influence within society and therefore require to be addressed by reference to policy, however effective that may be seen to be. Beginning with the impact of social exclusion and poverty, we consider their complex and multidimensional forms and discuss the range of policies currently extant that aim to combat such disadvantage. Chapter 6 on risk examines the state's increasing preoccupation with the concept of risk and harm and the need to protect the most vulnerable in society whilst considering the possibility of both beneficial and detrimental outcomes being possibilities of risk taking. Changing patterns of care provision are highlighted in Chapter 7 and recent arguments and developments over unpaid care are discussed in order to explore patterns and developments around the provision of care that have significant effects on the role of the state. The current agenda for welfare support and the systems that fund and deliver it are highlighted in Chapter 8 whilst Chapter 9 considers the theme of empowerment and considers it conceptually as well as within the broad political context, looking at its impact on UK and Scottish social policies over the past 20 years.

Part III provides a comprehensive overview of policy for practice, beginning with a focus on the phenomenon of socio-economic inequalities and the manner in which they can negatively affect service users. Chapter 11 considers and disentangles the two distinct concepts of mental illness and mental health. The chapter on older people looks at the concept of being old in contemporary society, how it is socially constructed according to society's beliefs with regard to the ability and role of 'non-contributing' individuals and the issue of changing demographics.

Chapter 13 explores changing attitudes to people with a range of impairments influenced by a range of factors including poverty, political ideology, scientific advance and the growth in disability rights and the effect on legislation and policy development. Current perceptions also drive the discourse on policy impacting on work with children and families in a direct and indirect manner, which is the subject of Chapter 14.

Chapter 15 on education and training summarises key developments in policy with an emphasis on partnership between central and local government before highlighting disadvantage within educational provision in relation to social class, gender, disability and ethnicity. Chapter 16 on substances looks at how social contexts shape notions of acceptable and unacceptable drug use and questions state and societal responses to this.

Chapter 17 on criminal justice examines the nature of programmes implemented to maximise the protection of the public whilst providing credible alternatives to custody in an attempt to reduce the prison population and satisfy society's need to observe that offending behaviour is being tackled, whilst Chapter 18 looks at the somewhat contentious issue of asylum and migration and necessarily takes a broad UK perspective on this given the control still exerted by the UK government over this area of law and policy.

Housing and homelessness is the focus for Chapter 19, which introduces discussion around how the structure of tenure has evolved in the UK over the last decades. The discussion then focuses on the phenomenon of homelessness, the most severe form of housing need, and its impact on some users of social services. Chapter 20 provides a concluding commentary.

All the contributors to this book have taught in the School of Applied Social Studies at the Robert Gordon University, Garthdee, Aberdeen, which has significantly expanded and developed its social policy teaching over a number of years. In this regard, we would like to acknowledge the contributions (explicit and implicit) of the many students we have taught whose interactions, discussions and debates have encouraged us to produce what will be seen as a core text in social policy studies.

References

Mooney, G. and Scott, G. (eds) (2005), *Exploring Social Policy in the 'New' Scotland* (Bristol: Policy Press).

Stewart, J. (2004), *Taking Stock: Scottish Social Welfare after Devolution* (Bristol: Policy Press).

Part I

Context

1 What *is* social policy?

Steve J. Hothersall

Introduction

In this chapter we shall provide a general overview of the subject area of social policy and look in general terms at what it is, how it is made, why it exists and what it generally looks like. We shall also consider the relationship between social policy and the law and the relevance to and the effect upon professional practice, highlighting some significant themes that will be developed in subsequent chapters.

In the world of social work and related professions and disciplines, policy is *everywhere*. Some would say that over the past 10–15 years there has been a veritable explosion of policy-making. When New Labour came to power in 1997, there was an increased emphasis upon 'government by objectives' tied very much to the 'what works?' agenda and the whole notion of 'modernising government' (Cabinet Office 1999). Within Scotland, as in the rest of the UK, there is still a clear focus around these centralised themes. If you look at the Scottish Government website (http://www.scotland.gov.uk/Topics/), you can see at a glance the differing, broad policy areas to which the Government addresses itself. These policies have an influence upon the lives of all of us, directly or indirectly, so it is worth spending some time becoming familiar with these areas and this is a good place to start. It is also the case that policy development, as one aspect of government, is based on the notion of *collective decision-making* (Scottish Government 2008a).

What *is* social policy?

Social policy is a subject area that appears unfamiliar to most people when you refer to the topic, and yet it affects all of us on a daily basis and it is probably true to say that most of us think or hear about it *every day*. Even giving a cursory glance to a daily newspaper or listening to your favourite radio station, you will invariably come across some reference to social policy. Look at the box and undertake Exercise 1.1.

Exercise 1.1 Policies for everyone!

Think about your own personal situation and make a list of the types of 'policies' that exist in your own home. For example, you might have a policy that says that everyone who comes into the house by the front door must remove their shoes before going into the living room. This is the 'Shoe Removal Policy'. You may also have a policy that says that the last person to go to bed at night must check that all the doors are locked. This is the 'Check the Doors are Locked Last Thing at Night Policy'. And so on.

When you have done your list, think of these as your own 'social policies' for your own social space. Why do you have them? What is their purpose? What would happen if these 'policies' did not exist or were not followed? How would this make life at home?

(This exercise, when done with groups of students, highlights a fascinating (and often hilarious!) range of policies and offers interesting insights into how we all attempt to order our private lives, sometimes in very different ways!).

Now, think about other social phenomenon: the care and protection of children, the treatment of people with a mental disorder, the provision of education and health care. These issues are deemed to be of such importance to us as a society as to require a coherent and consistent response to them so that irrespective of who you are or where you are, you are guaranteed to obtain help or access to a particular service whenever you need it. Ideally, the assistance received should be of high quality, coherently planned and managed and efficiently delivered in accordance with the individual's requirements (needs). Whether these characteristics are present at an individual level is as much about *practice* as it is about policy, but from the broad perspective of policy, dealing with broad-based social phenomena is, in principle, no different from putting in place arrangements for dealing with issues at home. The issue of whether such *collective* and *state-coordinated* responses to such phenomena are the most appropriate will be the subject of discussion in Chapter 3.

The basic function of any policy, social or otherwise (for example economic policy, agricultural policy, defence policy) is to provide what I will refer to (ideally) as a *coherent and consistent response to particular (social) phenomena.* In the examples above regarding your own social space, such phenomena initially referred to removing shoes and locking doors.

Briefly, that is what a social policy is and why it exists. So the next time you listen to the radio, watch the TV or go on-line, make a note of the range of information you find that relates to social policy.

In terms of definitions, social policy can be regarded as referring to the 'actions taken within society to develop and deliver services for people in order to meet their needs for welfare and wellbeing' (Alcock 2008: 2), whereas the *study* of social policy 'is concerned with those aspects of public policies, market operations, personal consumption and interpersonal relationships which contribute to, or detract from, the well-being or welfare of individuals or groups' (Erskine cited in Alcock, Erskine and May 2003: 15). The study of public/social policy used to be referred to as *social administration* and had as its central concern the impact of those policies connected to what used to be referred to as 'the big five'. These were health, education, the personal social services, and social security and housing, which were those areas of governmental intervention that were seen as priorities after the Second World War (see Chapter 2). Respectively, these interventions were designed to address what were perceived as the five giant ills affecting society at that time; respectively disease, ignorance, want, idleness and squalor.

Central to an understanding of social policy is the issue of *public* (state) involvement in *private* life. When we refer to social policy, we are referring to *public* policy, that is, that policy made by government(s), (arguably) on behalf of the people through the (democratic) political process. Erskine (cited in Alcock, Erskine and May 2003: 15) goes on to remind us that social policy 'explores the *social, political, ideological and institutional context* within which welfare is *produced, distributed and consumed*. It seeks to provide an account of the *processes* which contribute to or detract from welfare, and it does this within a normative framework which involves *debating moral and political issues* about the *nature* of the desired *outcomes*' (emphases added), whereas Jones et al. (2004) refer to policy as being 'a set of ideas and proposals for action culminating in a government decision' (p. 596). Thus, to study policy is to study (collective) decision-making.

Hill (2005) reminds us that policymaking is not a simple linear process or one that involves just a few key (governmental) individuals. He suggests the following:

- Firstly, that a *decision network* may be involved in producing action (via policy), which may itself be quite complex and may involve a number of people across a range of different agencies, organisations and departments, many of whom may be unknown to each other.
- Secondly, that policy is often not expressed as a single decision; it is often expressed as a *series* of decisions which, when taken as a whole, represent the policy position on a particular issue. Examples here would be child care policy (Hothersall 2008) and mental health policy (Hothersall, Maas-Lowit and Golightley 2008), both of which cover a range of issues including early intervention, prevention, support, treatment and public education. This should remind us of the need to be aware of the inter-relationships between policies and policy areas and to try to appreciate the influence each may have on the other, particularly when the connections may not be immediately apparent. For example, changes to policy surrounding housing allocations for homeless people may (inadvertently) affect the chances of someone with a learning disability leaving residential care being allocated their own tenancy because the priority for the allocation of houses has now shifted its focus.
- Thirdly, that policy will change over time and may represent aspects of major change or reform as well as *incremental adjustments* to existing policies in response to changing circumstances. It is a fact that many existing policies are founded upon earlier policy positions, which may not always be a good thing. Incremental policy change can be effective but it can also simply 'tinker at the edges' and avoid addressing what may well be deeper underlying issues.
- Finally, that policy 'decisions' may in fact arise as a result of non-decisions or inaction. For example, where the government is seen not to act in relation to certain issues, a response may be forced upon them if things begin to get out of hand. Thus, not doing something initially may result in an untenable situation becoming apparent which forces the government to take action to control the consequences of previous inaction. Some writers would argue that this constitutes a significant proportion of the policy-making activity of governments today (Dery 1999).

Another view taken by Gil (1992) is that the term 'social policy' can be conceived of as having four distinct but interrelated uses:

- As a *philosophical concept* representing the principle whereby political entities and large organisations (in this sense, society) *collectively* seek enduring solutions to the problems that affect them. In this sense, this notion would present itself as the polar opposite of *individualism*.
- As a *product* referring to the conclusions reached by those who concern themselves with the betterment of community and social conditions and social life generally, along with the amelioration of deviance (as defined at any given time) and social disorganisation by reference to the presence of an effective and efficient policy.
- As a *process* which, through its *products* seeks to promote and maintain stability whilst improving conditions. Most extant (current) policies are developments or additions to pre-existing ones and have therefore not gone through the full policy formation process.
- As *a framework for action*, incorporating both *product* and *process*. In this sense, it assumes the presence of well developed policies implemented within a context which is flexible enough to respond effectively to changes in values, structures and the conditions of the so-called 'target group' (Gil 1992: 4).

Gil's commentaries and analyses are quite penetrating, as he makes the point that simply to equate social policies with social welfare is to *fragment* the social world and detach it from the influences of the wider world, particularly the effects of economics and, more recently, the effects of globalisation. He argues that one of the inherent weaknesses of social policy development and analysis is that social policies are often developed simply to absorb the social fall-out of economic and other policies, rather than being the driving force in defining the shape of social organisations and societies. In the West at least, economics is often perceived as the 'Grand Master'. We shall look further at these issues when we consider the relationship between people and policy in Chapter 4.

All governments at various times have recognised the need for a more or less consistent approach to particular (social) issues, often as a means of ensuring that social order does not break down. The historical antecedents of policy are an important element in helping you to understand policy and Chapter 2 looks at this in some depth. Over time, various approaches to the issues of social living and the attendant prospect of social disorder have resulted in the creation of a wide range of policies that are and have been applied to particular situations at particular times with variable effects, and are evident from medieval times to the present day. How differing governments have formulated and subsequently implemented or given effect to policies depends as much upon *ideology* and the nature of government in that society at that particular time as it does upon the perceived and/or expressed needs of the people. In some societies, policies are repressive and implemented with force, often being designed to control the people and express the will (or the whim) of the government, or monarch in some instances. In the West (to be broadly interpreted), democracy as the prevailing form of government attempts to develop policy along the lines of the perceived needs of society as a whole with the needs of the individual being largely assumed to be represented within that general, often state-coordinated response, certainly in the UK and many other developed countries. Inevitably in such an arrangement there will be those who disagree with certain policy approaches to certain issues and will attempt to have their voice heard through the democratic process. At a more acute level, the presence of certain approaches to certain phenomena will, adopting the above 'broad-brush' approach, leave some people marginalised as their requirements (needs) may not quite 'fit' into the policy frame. In these instances, policy makers would claim that they can and will review and modify policy in response to representation regarding these perceived inadequacies. Very often it will be social workers and other professionals who are the best people to highlight the limitations of policy and to bring these to the attention of managers and, ultimately, policy makers. It must be emphasised here that because professional workers are those tasked to implement government policy, they are really the major players in determining how effective policy is *in relation to actually meeting people's needs.*

Policy and the law

The language used to describe policy often confuses many students. Is policy the same as law? Is law policy? What is a 'strategy'? What about government 'initiatives' and 'consultations'? What about 'Rules and Regulations', 'Secondary Legislation' and (Scottish) Statutory Instruments? Often, these terms are used interchangeably, particularly where there are references to the law.

Sources of Scots Law
These can be ranked thus:

1. legislation
2. judicial precedent
3. institutional writings
4. custom
5. equity
   (see Auchie et al. 2006).

Our concern here is with *legislation* and the different types of it that exist. UK Parliamentary legislation is held to be supreme and therefore the most significant legislation within Scotland is still the legislation of the UK Parliament in spite of the presence of the Scottish Parliament; the doctrine of the supremacy of Parliament remains intact. It was the passing of the Scotland Act 1998 that created the Scottish Parliament and granted to it (under section 28) the power to make laws, but only in those areas where it has been granted legislative competency through a range of *devolved* powers (under section 29) (see below).

UK Parliamentary/Scottish Parliamentary Legislation
Government usually initiates these Acts of Parliament/Acts of the Scottish Parliament and once approved and given Royal Assent, they become laws. This type of legislation (or 'statute law') is also referred to as 'primary legislation'.

Subordinate Legislation
Ministers or other executive bodies often make this type of legislation (also called 'delegated' or 'secondary' legislation) by reference to provisions previously laid out in *primary legislation*. This is done because any Act can only really concern itself with the broad principles of the matter being referred to and MPs/MSPs are not experts on the matters being legislated for (for example, child care or mental health). Subordinate legislation, *which has the same force as primary legislation,* is therefore a useful means of utilising expert knowledge and a range of experience to apply to primary legislation *to make it work more effectively*. In some respects, it 'oils the wheels' and makes primary legislation easier to apply in the real world and it can also be enacted very quickly indeed without the need for extensive Parliamentary time or further approval by the Sovereign. The most important examples of subordinate legislation are *statutory instruments/Scottish statutory instruments* (also known as *Rules* and/or *Regulations*) and *Orders of*

Council, although the last of these tend to be used more for matters of constitutional significance.

As an example, the *Looked After Children (Scotland) Regulations 2009* are a Scottish Statutory Instrument (SSI 2009/210) that shall 'revoke and replace both the Fostering of Children (Scotland) Regulations 1996 and the Arrangements to Look After Children (Scotland) Regulations 1996 (collectively referred to as "the fostering Regulations")' and 'should be read with the Support and Assistance of Young People Leaving Care (Scotland) Regulations 2003; and the Residential Establishments – Child Care (Scotland) Regulations 1996, which remain in force' (Scottish Government 2009: 1). These new Regulations are subordinate legislation and as such carry the force of law but they also make the job of implementing the Children (Scotland) Act 1995 easier by virtue of their specifying what should happen in certain situations when a child or young person is 'looked after' by the local authority.

In relation to your practice, the next 'level' downwards, so to speak, is that of National/Governmental *policy* followed by local authority or agency *policy* followed by policies developed by particular branches of the service or a particular team (see the example in Exercise 1.2). A *policy* can be defined as 'a course of action or principle adopted or proposed by a government, party, individual, etc.; any course of action adopted as advantageous or expedient' (SOED 2007).

Law and policy in a devolved Scotland

We now need to look at the political structure within Scotland. Firstly though, we need to look beyond Scotland to the rest of the UK and to Europe as both UK constitutional and other Westminster arrangements, and European rulings are relevant.

The wider picture

The UK has a *constitution*, headed by the Sovereign, which is comprised of lots of rules and procedures, many unwritten (for example, *common law*) and many written (for example, *statute law* and *case law*) which determine how the country is governed and how the different institutions within society relate to each other. This *constitutional law* derives its authority from *convention*, *legislation* and *judicial decisions* and from some other sources like the writings of some institutional writers such as Erskine, Hume and Stair who are considered, certainly within Scots law, to be authoritative.

The Parliament of the UK is comprised of the *Sovereign*, the *House of Lords* and the *House of Commons*. Between them, they provide a government, which generates legislation (laws) and regulations and policies to support these. The subsequent categories of law, *public* and *private* and *civil* and *criminal*, serve to regulate our conduct by providing a framework of rules, which aim to promote cooperation within society. By existing they set up a series of expectations against which society can determine (by and large) whether these expectations have been fulfilled. Criminal law (public law) aims to punish criminal behaviour and impose sanctions on people's liberty (Ferguson and Sheldon 2009; Jones and Christie 2003) if it is felt that their actions were criminal '*beyond all reasonable doubt*' (the standard of proof in criminal law). Civil law (private law) operates in order to arbitrate between private individuals and the (lesser) standard of proof used here to determine whether a wrong has been done against another (delict) is that of 'the balance of probability', that is, it is more likely to be the case than not.

Civil and criminal laws operate UK wide although there are differences in relation to their operation in Scotland as well as laws that are *specific* to Scotland. If you look at Figure 1.1 you will notice that the highest criminal court in Scotland is the High Court; there is no right of appeal to the Supreme Court of the UK in Scotland in relation to criminal matters as there is in England, Wales and Northern Ireland. The names of the courts are also different. In England and Wales there are Magistrates' Courts, County Courts, Crown Courts, the High Court and the Court of Appeal. In Scotland, there are District and Justice of the Peace Courts, Sheriff Courts, the High Court and the Court of Session for civil matters, and ultimately for civil cases only, the Supreme Court of the UK. Judges are also called Sheriffs in the Sheriff Courts. The High Court in Scotland acts as both a *trial court* and an *appeal court* under criminal law, and if it is felt that there has been a miscarriage of justice, there is recourse to the *Scottish Criminal Cases Review Tribunal* which has the power to refer cases back to the Appeal Court for consideration. There are also two different procedures in Scottish Courts: *summary procedure* which means that the Sheriff will hear the case sitting alone, and *solemn procedure* which means that the Sheriff or Judge will sit with a jury of 15 people. As the name implies, solemn procedure is used in more serious matters and in all appeals

In social work and other related professions within Scotland, most (but not all) of the law you will refer to will be civil law and will be dealt with either through the Sheriff Court or the High Court or a tribunal. For example, where a child is allegedly harmed by a parent, redress would be through civil proceedings under the Children (Scotland) Act 1995 to

The Courts in Scotland	
Civil Law	***Criminal Law***
Supreme Court	The High Court of the Justiciary (Solemn Procedure)
Court of Session (Inner House)	Sheriff Court (Summary or Solemn Procedure)
Court of Session (Outer House)	District Court (Summary Procedure)
Sheriff Principal	
Sheriff Court	
(All Summary Procedure)	

Figure 1.1 The court structure in Scotland

protect the child, usually done through the children's hearing (a *tribunal*), but if it was thought that a criminal offence had been committed (sexual assault), then the criminal law would apply in relation to the alleged perpetrator of the deed and would be dealt with, at least initially, through the Sheriff Court. Thus, in complex situations like child sexual abuse, both strands of the law would operate (Hothersall 2008). In relation to Criminal Justice social work, the criminal law is utilised much more and many of its provisions concerning probation orders, drug-testing orders and so on arise from a range of criminal statutes (see Chapter 17).

Legislation and policy in Scotland after devolution

Scotland now has its own devolved Parliament, which came into existence following the granting of Royal Assent to the Scotland Act on 19 November 1998. Prior to this and as a direct result of the Act of Union of 1707, there had only been one Parliament in the UK, located at Westminster which had legislated for England, Scotland, Northern Ireland and Wales since that time, although the general affairs of Scotland (and Northern Ireland and Wales) have had some form of representation through their respective offices. In the case of Scotland this was the Scottish Office, headed up by a UK Government Minister with the title of Secretary of State for Scotland. During the latter part of the twentieth century, however, concessions were made by the Westminster Parliament which granted limited powers to the other countries within the UK and Regional Assemblies were formed in Northern Ireland and Wales, although their powers are not as clearly devolved as those in Scotland are now. This process of *devolution*, which is the delegation of central government powers to another body without the relinquishment of sovereignty, now means that the Scottish Parliament can control some of its own affairs. However, there are a number of matters that the Westminster Parliament and its UK Government have reserved the right to continue to control. We therefore have a range of *devolved* matters which can be controlled through the Scottish Parliament and the Scottish Government, and a number of *reserved* matters which are still controlled from Westminster (see Tables 1.1 and 1.2).

Table 1.1 The devolved powers of the Scottish Parliament

Social work	**Health**
Education and training	Local government
Housing	Planning
Tourism and economic development	Transport (aspects of)
Law and home affairs	Police and fire services
The environment	Sport and the arts
Natural and built heritage	Statistics, records and registers
Agriculture, forestry and fishing	

Table 1.2 The reserved powers of the Westminster Parliament

Constitutional matters	**UK foreign policy**
UK defence and national security	Immigration and nationality
Fiscal and economic policy	Energy
Common markets	Trade and industry
Transport (aspects of)	Employment law
Data protection	Gambling and the lottery
Social security	Equal opportunities
Abortion, human fertilisation, embryology	Genetics and vivisection

(Schedules 4 and 5 of the Scotland Act 1998 detail devolved and reserved provisions.)

In relation to statute law which regulates these specific matters, however, it is important to remember that those that apply only to particular parts of the UK will have a *suffix* attached to them, for example, Children (Scotland) Act 1995; Children (Northern Ireland) Order 1991. The only exception to this general rule that a Scottish Act has a suffix is the Scotland Act 1998. Those Acts that apply to England and Wales and *in some cases the whole of the UK, including Scotland,* will have no such suffix, for example, NHS and Community Care Act 1990. This anomaly requires caution, although each act made by the Scottish Parliament in relation to devolved matters *should* have the suffix 'Scotland' in parentheses in its title (often abbreviated to (S): for example, Mental Health (Care and Treatment) (S) Act 2003).

If you come across a statute with no suffix, then check the *Arrangement of Sections* for the number of the section that refers to the *Extent* of the Act, that is, to which area(s) it does or does not apply. If you don't, you could end up trying to apply a law to a country to which it does not belong or alternatively, *fail to recognise that a particular statute has UK-wide and therefore, Scottish applicability.*

The structure and functions of the Scottish Parliament

The Scottish Parliament is responsible for forming committees and overseeing the work of the Scottish Government. The members of the Government include the First Minister, the Lord Advocate, the Solicitor General and Members of the Scottish Parliament (MSPs) appointed as Ministers. Thus, a Scottish Minister is both a member of the Scottish Government and the Scottish Parliament. MSPs can also be members of the UK and European Parliaments.

The Scottish Government has six Cabinet departments or *portfolios* with responsibility for particular areas of government, some of which have Executive Agencies attached to them, which focus on specific topics and are accountable and report directly to Scottish Ministers.

The current administration has six *portfolios* or Cabinet departments:

- Office of the First Minister
- Finance and Sustainable Growth
- Education and Lifelong Learning (this includes children's services and education)
- Health and Well-Being
- Justice
- Rural Affairs and the Environment

In addition, there are the Law Officers, which include the Lord Advocate and the Solicitor General, who are responsible for the Crown Office and the Procurator Fiscal Service, and although these areas continue to be a part of the Government, they maintain a degree of independence as a prosecution service.

The Government also has a number of Ministerial Offices within the Cabinet portfolios, headed by a Cabinet Secretary and include:

- Culture, External Affairs and the Constitution
- Parliamentary Business
- Enterprise, Energy and Tourism
- Transport, Infrastructure and Climate Change
- Children and Early Years
- Schools and Skills
- Public Health and Sport
- Housing and Communities
- Community Safety
- Environment

It is largely through these Ministerial Offices that most of the major policy initiatives and directives emanate and it is worthwhile visiting the Scottish Government website and following the links to look at these. These Offices also have a number of specialised sections within them that focus on particular areas within the remit of that particular portfolio.

The political and policy-making process in Scotland

The Scottish Parliament does most of its work through the use of *committees*. These hold the Government to account and may inquire into particular issues and report to Parliament. There are a number of standing committees that exist all of the time and these are referred to as Mandatory Committees. These focus upon issues like Audit, Parliamentary Procedures and other matters mainly related to the business of Parliament as a whole. There are also a number of Subject Committees, which Parliament has established, with the aim of addressing specific policy issues within broad subject areas. These include Education, Health and Community Care, Social Inclusion, Housing and the Voluntary Sector and Justice and Home Affairs, amongst others. These committees, be they mandatory or subject related, are able to form sub-committees which can be used to focus upon very specific issues from within the broader topic of inquiry. They can do this by seconding individuals or groups into their midst who may have expertise derived from social work practice, academia, business or some other sphere which it is felt can offer something to the matter under consideration.

With regards to the creation of new or the amendment of existing laws (legislation), section 29 of The Scotland Act 1998 defines the parameters of the Scottish Parliament's power in this regard. Any legislation or subsequent amendments must be consistent with European Union Law and be compatible with the European Convention on Human Rights and Fundamental Freedoms (1950) and the Human Rights Act (1998) (UK). It is important to realise at this point that not all legislation currently in force in Scotland *is necessarily consistent or compatible* as mentioned above. This does not mean that the Scottish Parliament (or the Westminster Parliament) has acted or is acting with blatant disregard for these principles; they could not. Rather, this reflects the incremental and piecemeal development of legislation (and policy) over time. Those aspects that are felt to be out of step, as it were, are and will be amended accordingly, although it is not always as straightforward as that. If the Scottish Parliament feels that its current laws and policies *are* consistent and compatible, then it can appeal to the European Courts for a ruling on these matters.

Where there is a need for new legislation or the need to amend existing laws, then a Bill is introduced before Parliament, although a consultation exercise *must* be undertaken beforehand. A consultation must precede the introduction of any Bill and they are the means through which interested parties may comment and respond to the proposals, including you. There are four main types of Bill:

- *Government Bills* are those drafted and introduced by the Scottish Government. These Bills have to be accompanied by a *Financial Memorandum* and a *Ministerial Statement* explaining the rationale for the Bill, its objectives and its likely (hoped for) impact. Of note is the notion of developing *Child Impact Statements* that are being considered for use in relation to all legislative and policy initiatives to make *explicit* the likely impact upon children (in general) of any initiative, irrespective of its main focus. So, for example there may be a Bill introduced relating to Fish Quotas in the North Sea. The Child Impact Statement may well assess the impact upon children to be negligible; probably correctly. However, a Bill introduced with the intention of regulating child minding arrangements would have a major impact upon children and the possible effects would need to be clearly articulated in order that Ministers, and the public (through *consultations*) can respond in order to influence such matters through the democratic process.
- *Members Bills* are introduced by any MSP who is not a member of the Scottish Government.
- *Committee Bills* are introduced by committees. These Bills may arise following the deliberations of a committee into a particular issue.
- *Private Bills* are introduced by an individual or an organisation.

Each Bill, irrespective of its origin, *must* be preceded by a period of consultation, and consultations can be found via http://www.scotland.gov.uk/Consultations/About.

There is also an important aspect of the devolution settlement referred to as the *Sewel Convention* whereby the Scottish Parliament can adopt a piece of Westminster legislation and apply it to Scotland. This avoids the need to duplicate relevant activity. For information on the key features of the Sewel Convention go to http://www.scotland.gov.uk/About/Sewel/KeyFacts.

The political process and that of policymaking are interconnected. It is through these processes that laws and policy become real and have an impact upon people's lives. But people's lives and experiences and the actions of professionals in the field also affect these processes. Figure 1.2 shows how this happens in general terms. It is important to note that the law applies *directly* to society; it is not all necessarily filtered through policy or practice. However, many laws are quite circumspect with regards to particular issues, offering broad scope for subsequent interpretation by the courts (via *case law* and *precedent*) and other tribunals, and Regulations and Guidance invariably accompanies legislation. For example, the Children (S) Act 1995 (the 1995 Act) is accompanied by four volumes of Regulations and Guidance (Scottish Office 1997a; 1997b; 1997c; 1997d) and the Mental Health (Care and Treatment) (Scotland) Act 2003 is accompanied by a three-volume *Code of Practice* (Scottish Executive 2005). Interestingly, in relation to the Children (Scotland) Act 1995, recent changes to the law relating to the adoption of children under the Adoption and Children (Scotland) Act 2007 (the 2007 Act) have repealed certain parts of the 1995 Act and as a result, Volume 3 of the guidance to the 1995 Act relating to adoption and parental responsibilities orders will have changed and will have to be read differently, largely because Parental Responsibilities Orders no longer exist. New guidance on the 2007 Act comes in several forms, including *Explanatory Notes* (Stationery Office 2007) and a range of *Scottish Statutory Instruments*.

The law can be defined as '(T)he body of rules, whether formally enacted or customary, which a particular state or community recognises as governing the actions of its subjects or members and which it may enforce by imposing penalties' (SOED 2007). Its main practical purpose is quite simply to regulate and in some cases, restrict certain kinds of behaviour within society. Using this definition and understanding of its purpose, we can see how the laws relevant to social work, social care and other forms of human service practice have their broad effect.

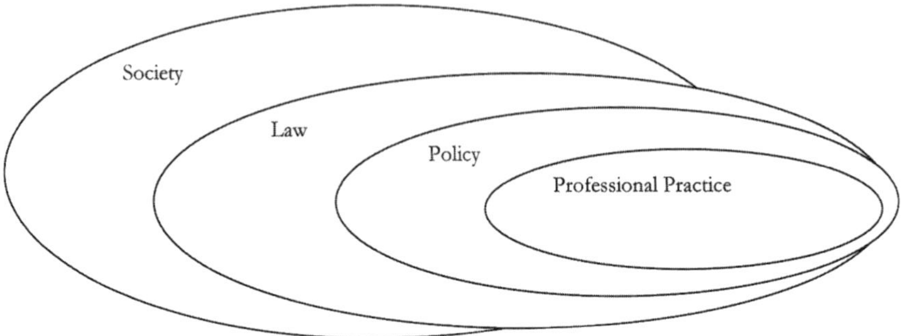

Figure 1.2 An ecological representation of the relationship between society, law, policy and professional practice (after Bronfenbrenner 1979)

The law and policy in action

In essence, the law (usually what we refer to as 'statute law') acts as a set of broad principles to be adopted in relation to particular aspects of life. Laws are given practical effect by policy. (For access to all Acts of the Scottish Parliament, as well as a wide range of other Scottish and UK-wide legislation and other materials, go to www.opsi.gov.uk.) For example, the Children (Scotland) Act 1995 contains a range of differing provisions which focus on issues relating to *Parents, Children and Guardians* (Part 1), which is essentially aimed at regulating, by law and where necessary, certain aspects of the relationships between these groups of people: essentially, it is law relating to issues between *private individuals*. Part 2 of this Act refers to the *Promotion of Children's Welfare by Local Authorities and Children's Hearings etc.* and therefore to what we refer to as *public matters* and has as its focus the regulation of relationships between children, parents and others *where the state, in the form of the local authority*, is seen as having a role to play in these arrangements. This might be necessary because a child is being abused or neglected or it could be the case that a child actually has no one to look after him or her. In these situations, the state, in the form of the local authority, is seen to have a *duty* to become involved because of the generally perceived vulnerability of a child (Smith 2010), and the need to afford them the necessary protections consistent with the promotion of their general well-being, especially in situations when those ordinarily tasked with, and assumed to take on-board those responsibilities, appears to fail to do so, either by omission or commission.

Similarly, the Mental Health (Care and Treatment) (Scotland) Act 2003 'establishes new arrangements for the detention, care and treatment of persons who have a mental disorder. It also refines the role and functions of the (Mental Welfare) Commission and establishes the (Mental Health) Tribunal as the principal forum for approving and reviewing compulsory measures for the detention, care and treatment of mentally disordered persons' (Stationery Office 2005: 3). The 2003 Act is based around a number of fundamental principles (section 1) that have to be adhered to. Their function is generally to *prescribe* certain actions on the part of those implementing their functions under the Act in order to ensure (insofar as possible) that the general approach to the issues relating to the care and treatment of those individuals with a mental disorder is *consistent* and *coherent*, which, as we saw earlier, is one of the principle underpinning themes within policy making, policy implementation and, from your perspective, *professional practice*.

Using the Children (Scotland) Act 1995 as an example, we shall look at how certain policies give effect to this (statute) law, and Exercise 1.2 offers a working example for you to consider.

Exercise 1.2 Law and policy in action

Consider the following scenario: Mary, aged 6, and her brother Ryan, aged 4, have been orphaned. Their extended family is unwilling and unable to care for them. Therefore, the terms of section 25(1) of the Children (Scotland) Act 1995 apply in respect of them:

'25 Provision of accommodation for children, etc.

(1) A local authority shall provide accommodation for any child who, residing or having been found within their area, appears to them to require such provision because –

(a) no-one has parental responsibility for him;
(b) he is lost or abandoned; or
(c) the person who has been caring for him is prevented, whether or not permanently and for whatever reason, from providing him with suitable accommodation or care.'

(Reproduced under the terms of Crown Copyright by Policy Guidance Issued by HMSO.)

The word 'shall' simply means that the local authority is under a legal obligation to provide accommodation, that is, given the presence of certain conditions, they have no choice but to do this. In relation to Mary and Ryan, their circumstances can be seen to be covered by the general conditions laid out under s25(1)a) and c). Notice that I refer to the conditions as being 'general'. Within statute, conditions, or 'grounds' as they are often called, will tend to be rather broad in their purview. This is simply because it would be almost impossible to specify *every possible condition, situation or set of circumstances* which might require the local authority (as the representative of the government or state) to act. Law is generally phrased in such a way and it is here that we can begin to see why we need *policy* in order to make the law work and become *dynamic*.

In relation to all statute law, including the Children (Scotland) Act 1995 and the Adoption and Children (Scotland) Act 2007 there exist a range of *statutory instruments (Rules and Regulations)* (refer to subordinate legislation above) which function to put into action, or *operationalise*, their various provisions. At the time of writing, there are a number of significant changes taking place in Scotland regarding the arrangements for looked after and accommodated children and for those children who require permanency either through adoption or through the new *permanency orders* now available under the Adoption and Children (Scotland) Act 2007. These developments mean that new *regulations and guidance* must be produced to replace earlier versions, which are now rendered obsolete. This is a good illustration of the impact of new legislation on practice and how regulation and guidance is essential to implement such changes correctly (see Scottish Office 1997a; 1997b; 1997c; 1997d; Stationery Office 2007).

This subordinate legislation and other such policies work by offering more detailed and explicit regulation (that is, *you must do*) and guidance (that is, *you should do*) on how the local authority should *interpret* and *implement* the provisions of this or any other Act, although they may be called something else. For example, the Mental Health (Care and Treatment) (Scotland) Act 2003 provides significant guidance in the form of a three-volume *Code of Practice* (Scottish Executive 2005) as does the Adults with Incapacity (Scotland) Act 2000 (Scottish Government 2008b; and see Hothersall, Maas-Lowit and Golightley 2008).

Figure 1.3 offers a pictorial explanation of the way in which the law, referring in this case to the 1995 Act, is put into operation by the provisions of subordinate legislation and policy at a number of different levels, each becoming more specific and more attuned to local practice, each offering more specific guidance on how to interpret differing aspects of the law, initially, then of higher-level (national) policy. It is an iterative process. As we saw above, the 1995 Act states what must happen in the situation where children have no one to look after them, for whatever reason. Volume 1 of the Rules and Regulations to the 1995 Act offers advice to professionals on what kinds of services might be required in order to assist Mary and Ryan (see Annex A and Annex B of Volume 1) whilst Hothersall (2008) offers detail on the issues regarding *providing accommodation* for children, covering such things as the range of accommodation that might be available in a local authority area and the sorts of arrangements local authorities might put in place.

All policy documents will refer back to principle sections of the primary or secondary statute (in this case the 1995 Act) which are intended to be reference points towards other duties and powers of the local authority and which, taken together, aim to provide a coherent overview of how, in this example, to provide a service for children and their families under certain circumstances.

As you look at policy at this level (governmental/national) you will become aware that much of what is referred to is somewhat generalised (although less so than in statute). Policy at this level offers a fairly broad interpretation of statute; it is the function of policy at the next level (that of the local authority and/or the agency or organisation, as these might be the same thing) to be more specific as to the *when* and the *how* in terms of implementation. For example, Northshire City Council is bound by the

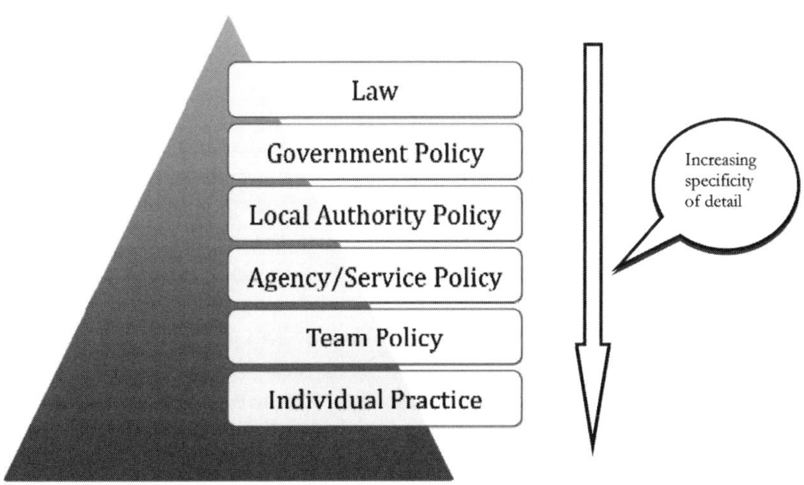

Figure 1.3 The hierarchical relationship between law and policy

terms of the 1995 Act and the associated *Rules and Regulations*. In relation to the accommodation of children under the terms of section 25 (remember Mary and Ryan?), it already has in place a range of services for children (in compliance with section 22 of the 1995 Act and *Scotland's Children: Regulations and Guidance* Volume 1, Annexes A and B and the *Looked After Children Regulations 2009*) and has developed its own Northshire City Council policy which refers to the accommodation of children in *foster care*. This policy would offer more specific guidance on *what* and *how* to respond to a situation like that involving Mary and Ryan. It might for example offer information about the *process* involved in meeting with the children, what details to obtain and from whom, how to ensure that they have sufficient clothing, how to make arrangements to find a suitable foster carer or kinship carer and how best to facilitate this within certain timescales.

This authority-wide policy may then be added to by reference to policy documents at the level of the particular *service* involved. For example, some local authorities will have a *children's services division* or *sector*, which may be sub-divided into *fieldwork services*, *foster care services* and *residential services* for children. The policy you might be working to might be entitled the *Accommodating Children Policy for Fieldwork Services*. This policy would be applied to all *fieldwork services* for children in Northshire City Council's area in situations where children need to be accommodated. This particular policy may then be added to by reference to a further policy document that applies to a particular *team*. It may be that there are particular issues for that team that need to be addressed in order for them to be able to comply fully with the broader Northshire policy. For instance, a particular team may feel that once completed, all relevant documentation appertaining to a particular situation should be given to a particular person or it may impose particular timescales or other requirements on the frequency of visits to children that are in excess of those required by the policy within the service and that stipulated in regulation 46 of the 2009 *Regulations*. So long as each of these so-called *secondary policies* is *consistent* and *compatible* with those from which they are essentially derived, in the same way that *governmental policy* is *consistent*, *compatible* and therefore *compliant* with the law from which it is derived (including European law and other supra-state rulings), all is well.

Finally, at the most personal and intimate level of policy we come to its *integration* and *implementation* by the practitioner. This is the level at which policy *really* affects people, and there are a number of things to discuss regarding this, but first it must be said that effective policy implementation at the practitioner level presupposes that those practitioners have taken the time to study and reflect upon relevant policy at all levels in order that they can then integrate this with their own knowledge, values and skills.

Understanding policy, its genesis, purpose, structure, form and potential effects are but some of the essential pre-requisites for ethical and effective practice, and with this is the need to appreciate the essence of policy and its principle function: the well-being of people, and we shall consider this in Chapter 4.

Chapter summary

This chapter has introduced you to social policy and provided illustrations of the fundamental principles underpinning its existence and you are now probably well aware that social policy is all around us. You have devised your 'own' policies in an attempt to appreciate the basic functions of policy development and application and have then considered these basic principles in relation to two examples of extant social policies in the areas of child care and mental health. You have also seen how the law and its different strands relates to policy and works with it as well as looking at the current arrangements within Scotland for the development of law and policy. The chapter has concluded with a 'working example' of how law and policy come together to provide a service for two children who are orphaned. All of these points will be essential background knowledge for you as you proceed through the rest of the book.

References

Alcock, P. (2008), *Social Policy in Britain* (3rd edn) (Basingstoke: Palgrave Macmillan).

Alcock, P., Erskine, A. and May, M. (eds) (2003), *The Student's Companion to Social Policy* (2nd edn) (Oxford: Blackwell).

Auchie, D., Lauterbach, T., Little, T., McFadden, J., McFadzean, D., McFadzean, C., McManus, F. and Ross, J. (2006), *Introduction to Law and Legal Obligations* (Dundee: Dundee University Press).

Bronfenbrenner, U. (1979), *The Ecology of Human Development* (Cambridge, MA: Harvard University Press).

Cabinet Office (1999), *Modernising Government* (Cmnd 4310) (London: Stationery Office).

Dery, D. (1999), 'Policy by the Way: When Policy is Incidental to Making Other Policies', *Journal of Public Policy* 18(2): 163–76.

Ferguson, P. and Sheldon, D. (2009), *Scots Criminal Law* (3rd edn) (Edinburgh: Tottel Publishing).

Gil, D.G. (1992), *Unraveling Social Policy* (revised 5th edn) (Rochester, VT: Schenkman Books).

Hill, M. (2005), *The Public Policy Process* (4th edn) (Essex: Pearson Education).

Hothersall, S.J. (2008), *Social Work with Children: Young People and their Families in Scotland* (2nd edn) (Exeter: Learning Matters).

Hothersall, S.J., Maas-Lowit, M. and Golightley, M. (2008), *Social Work and Mental Health in Scotland* (Exeter: Learning Matters).

Jones, B., Kavanagh, D., Moran, M. and Norton, P. (2004), *Politics UK* (5th edn) (Essex: Pearson Education).

Jones, T.H. and Christie, M.G.A. (2003), *Criminal Law: Green's Concise Scots Law* (Edinburgh: W. Green & Sons).

Scottish Executive (2005), *Mental Health (Care and Treatment) (Scotland) Act 2003: Code of Practice* (3 vols) (Edinburgh: Scottish Executive).

Scottish Government (2008a), *Guide to Collective Decision-Making* (Edinburgh: Scottish Executive).

Scottish Government (2008b), *Adults with Incapacity (Scotland) Act 2000: Codes of Practice* (6 vols) (Edinburgh: Scottish Government). Available at: http://www.scotland.gov.uk/Topics/Justice/law/awi/010408awiwebpubs/cop (accessed 29 May 2010).

Scottish Government (2009), *Executive Note: The Looked After Children (Scotland) Regulations 2009* SSI 2009/210 (Edinburgh: Scottish Government).

Scottish Office (1997a), *Scotland's Children: The Children (Scotland) Act 1995. Regulations and Guidance, Volume 1 – Support and Protection for Children and their Families* (Edinburgh: Stationery Office). Available at: http://www.scotland.gov.uk/Publications/2004/10/20066/44707 (accessed 29 May 2010).

Scottish Office (1997b), *Scotland's Children: The Children (Scotland) Act 1995. Regulations and Guidance, Volume 2 – Children Looked After by Local Authorities* (Edinburgh: Stationery Office). Available at: http://www.scotland.gov.uk/Publications/2004/10/20067/44723 (accessed 29 May 2010).

Scottish Office (1997c), *Scotland's Children: The Children (Scotland) Act 1995. Regulations and Guidance, Volume 3 – Adoption and Parental Responsibilities Orders* (Edinburgh: Stationery Office). Available at: http://www.scotland.gov.uk/Publications/2004/10/20068/44771 (accessed 29 May 2010).

Scottish Office (1997d), *Scotland's Children. The Children (Scotland) Act 1995. Regulations and Guidance. Volume 4. References and Bibliography* (Edinburgh: Stationery Office). Available at: http://www.scotland.gov.uk/Publications/2004/10/20069/44785 (accessed 29 May 2010).

Shorter Oxford English Dictionary (SOED) (2007) (Oxford: Oxford University Press).

Smith, R. (2010), *A Universal Child?* (Basingstoke: Palgrave Macmillan).

Stationery Office (2005), *Explanatory Notes to the Mental Health (Care and Treatment) (Scotland) Act 2003* (UK: Stationery Office).

Stationery Office (2007), *Explanatory Notes to the Adoption and Children (Scotland) Act 2007* (UK: Stationery Office).

Further reading

For a good introduction to social policy see:

Spiker, P. (2008), *Social Policy: Themes and Approaches* (Bristol: Policy Press).

Web-based resources

Scottish Executive (2005), *Adoption: Better Choices for our Children*. Report of Phase II of the Adoption Policy Review Group (Edinburgh: Scottish Executive). All documentation relating to the review and all relevant policy documents can be found at: http://www.scotland.gov.uk/Topics/People/Young-People/children-families/17972/10958 (accessed 29 May 2010).

Explanatory notes to the Adoption and Children (Scotland) Act 2007 can be found at: http://www.opsi.gov.uk/legislation/scotland/acts2007/en/aspen_20070004_en_1 (accessed 29 May 2010).

For a range of useful fact sheets on the structure and function of the Scottish Parliament and the legislative process, go to:

http://www.scottish.parliament.uk/business/research/ (accessed 29 May 2010).

2 A history of social policy

Steve J. Hothersall

Introduction

Studying the history of social policy invariably leads to commentaries relating to the so-called 'industrial revolution' (circa late eighteenth-early nineteenth century) when large numbers of people began migrating to the towns and cities from smaller and more rural locales in response to the growing need for labour in the factories and mills which had begun to emerge in the wake of technological and economic expansion (Fraser 2003). As a result, the populations of towns and cities expanded at what was probably an exponential rate, and people began to experience living and working together in close proximity to each other. This generated a number of challenges for the governments of the day who had to respond to new demands and expectations based upon the effects of these migrations.

Someone had to take control and set a series of rules within which social life could operate smoothly. For many commentators, the 'New' Poor Law of 1834 is seen as the starting point for the modern history of social policy, although our discussion will take us further back in time because the effects of industrialisation were no different to the effects of earlier socio-economic phenomena in Elizabethan and earlier times, relative to the size of the populations. The effects of enclosures and other agrarian-based issues caused similar difficulties at the time and had similarly necessitated relevant responses. *Any* discussion concerning social policy has to have some reference to history. This is an absolute necessity because where things are today in relation to social life are very clearly products of the past (Berridge 2003). Consider the following:

> History is not a recipe book; past events are never replicated in the present in quite the same way ... [However] ... We can learn from history how past generations thought and acted, how they responded to the demands of their time and how they solved their problems. We can learn by analogy, not by example, for our circumstances will always be different than theirs were. The main thing history can teach us is that human actions have consequences and that certain choices, once made, cannot be undone. They foreclose the possibility of making other choices and thus they determine future events. (Lerner 1997: 199–213 quoted in Hendrick 2005: 11)

To the above we can add that human *inaction* can have consequences in much the same way, as we shall see.

One of the features of social life and, ergo, social policy, is its evolutionary nature. Policies are developed in response to social phenomena and the *Poor Laws* were just such a response. Whilst these laws were in place in the dim and distant past, we shall see that there are, in fact, contemporary parallels. In this respect, an appreciation of how these early attempts to regulate social life worked is important in offering us an insight into the nature of the development of policy. In this regard, social policy can be seen as an *institutionalised response to social and cultural development.*

The Poor Laws

Prior to the Act of Union of 1701, Scotland legislated for itself. The issue of poverty was problematic to the Scots as well as to those in the rest of the UK (and further afield) with responses to it being broadly similar, certainly in terms of hoped-for outcomes. The history of the Poor Laws in Scotland has received far less scrutiny than those that operated in England with the result that most books on social policy refer, almost exclusively, to English legislation, although there are some notable exceptions (Mitchison 2000; Mackay 1907/2008).

In terms of the issues that the Scots and English Poor Laws endeavoured to address, much can be gleaned from those (majority) writings concerning the English system; destitution and poverty tended to have similar effects whichever side of the border you were on and industrialisation created problems in Scotland too. Therefore, commentary concerning both systems will help to give a clear picture of the effects of industrialisation and (often closely associated) destitution and poverty and the attempts by governments to address these.

The (Scots) Poor Law Act 1579 (An Act of the Scottish Parliament 'For Punischment of Strang and Idle Beggars')

The Poor Laws can be seen as early attempts by the state to regulate social life as a response to the potential for social unrest. In this regard, state involvement manifested itself as the provision of *poor relief* for those who could not work as one means of minimising the likelihood of social disorder. In the fourteenth century the state (the Government) passed laws that tried to prevent the practice of people wandering around the countryside in search of work, partly to prevent the spread of the plague but also to try and ensure that the concentration of labour remained within the cities. These laws were to punish *vagrancy*, as this was seen as one factor that contributed to social unrest and increasing levels of crime because of the growing tendency for gangs (bands) of people to roam the countryside and steal from others. These early laws against vagrancy were essentially punitive; people were put in the stocks or locked up and in some cases condemned to death. However, it soon became apparent that a more constructive approach was required.

The first major attempt within Scotland to legislate for the poor occurred with the passing of the Poor Law Act of 1579. As with other parts of the UK, the state recognised the potential for social unrest brought about by the disaffection of the poor, and this had to be responded to. The Act of 1579 remained the basis of Scots' Poor Law, with minor amendments in 1597 and 1672, until the passing of the Poor Law (Scotland) Act 1845. These early arrangements were essentially church-based, drawing funds to finance the system from donations from within the congregations (Cage 1981). However, as secularisation increased and committed churchgoers decreased, this compromised the capacity of the Kirks (Churches) to finance the system. A further factor that placed huge pressure on the Kirk-based system was the split from the Church of Scotland in 1843 of almost half its number to form the Free Church of Scotland. These factors and the increasing lack of fit between the (essentially rural) poor law system and increasing urbanisation raised serious doubts as to the continuing viability of the 'voluntary' system and led to the creation of the Scottish Royal Commission in 1843 to look at these issues which ultimately led to the implementation of the 1845 Act.

In many respects, a rather rosy picture of the operation of the early Scottish Poor Laws exists with local parishes portrayed as benevolent dispensers of comfort and succour. However, some writers question this rather 'rosy' view, arguing instead that the voluntary assessments required of landowners and others in relation to contributions towards the poor-relief fund were often avoided, landowners often being absent and therefore avoiding their liability. As a result, and with a reluctance to *enforce* local rates, the system as it tended to operate, was very harsh (Mitchison 2000).

The 43rd of Elizabeth (The Poor Law Act 1601)

In Elizabethan times, the state became more aware of some of the underlying causes of vagrancy, recognising that individuals were not necessarily solely responsible for their own circumstances. Wider forces beyond their control, notably the effects of economics, were increasingly being recognised as being relevant and prompted the Government of the day to act with more compassion (relatively speaking) and more creatively. The outcome was the development of the Poor Laws, in particular the Poor Law Act of 1601 (Figure 2.1), famously referred to as 'The 43rd of Elizabeth' (Elizabeth being Elizabeth I and '43' referring to the particular year of her reign). Prior to the passing of this Act, the notion of 'setting the poor on work' had been introduced. This meant that if a person was in need of relief (help) via the state because they had no means of their own, they could approach the state for assistance via the early poorhouses, and in return for them undertaking work within these, would receive food and shelter. This option, for those who *could* and *would* work, allowed them to meet their basic needs whilst simultaneously operating in the Government's favour, reducing the likelihood of social disorder and generating income for the poorhouses through the labour of those receiving relief. In respect of those who *could not* work because of disability or infirmity, the state provided for them too through the poorhouses, again recognising that

CAP. II.

An Act for the Relief of the Poor.

BE it enacted by the Authority of this present Parliament, That the Churchwardens of every Parish, and four, three or two substantial Housholders there, as shall be thought meet, having respect to the Proportion and Greatness of the same Parish and Parishes, to be nominated yearly in *Easter* Week, or within one Month after *Easter*, under the Hand and Seal of two or more Justices of the Peace in the same County, whereof one to be of the *Quorum*, dwelling in or near the same Parish or Division where the same Parish doth lie, shall be called Overseers of the Poor of the same Parish: And they, or the greater Part of them, shall take order from Time to Time, by, and with the Consent of two or more such Justices of Peace as is aforesaid, for setting to work the Children of all such whose Parents shall not by the said Churchwardens and Overseers, or the greater Part of them, be thought able to keep and maintain their Children: And also for setting to work all such Persons, married or unmarried, having no Means to maintain them, and use no ordinary and daily Trade of Life to get their Living by: And also to raise weekly or otherwise (by Taxation of every Inhabitant, Parson, Vicar and other, and of every Occupier of Lands, Houses, Tithes impropriate, Propriations of Tithes, Coal-Mines, or saleable Underwoods in the said Parish, in such competent Sum and Sums of Money as they shall think fit) a convenient Stock of Flax, Hemp, Wool, Thread, Iron, and other necessary Ware and Stuff, to set the Poor on Work: And also competent Sums of Money for and towards the necessary Relief of the Lame, Impotent, Old, Blind, and such other among them, being Poor, and not able to work, and also for the putting out of such Children to be Apprentices, to be gathered out of the same Parish, according to the Ability of the same Parish, and to do and execute all other Things as well for the disposing of the said Stock, as otherwise concerning the Premisses, as to them shall seem convenient:

Figure 2.1 A facsimile of part of the Act of 1601
Source: Peter Higginbottom/workhouses.org.uk

this was a way of reducing the likelihood of unrest and of tackling crime and the continuing problem of vagrancy. In this regard, responses to the poor were quite creative in that they effectively marginalised those who *could* but *would not* work from the others, thereby legitimising the use of punishment for some without the fear of huge reprisals from the masses, the rest of whom were being supported. This introduced the notion of the *deserving* and the *undeserving* poor (See Alcock 2006: esp. Chapter 1).

The Poor Law Act of 1601 legitimised a distinction between three groups of the poor. *The impotent poor* (the elderly, the sick, the disabled and so on), who were to be housed in the poorhouses or almshouses, *the able-bodied poor,* who were to be made to work, and later allowed to reside in the work-houses, and *the idle poor,* who were seen as those who *could* work but refused to. This last group tended to head for the open road but when caught, they would be offered the option to work, which if they refused, would lead to them being punished in 'houses of correction' (which were usually a part of the workhouse). This tripartite system of dealing with the poor at a local level was generally seen to be effective from the point of view of the Government. The state also arranged for the children of those people in receipt of relief to be *apprenticed* to a tradesman in order that they could develop a skill that would assist them to earn an independent living at some point later in life.

The description here may appear somewhat rosy. The apprenticeships were not based solely on a concern for the future well-being of children; rather they were focused upon future planning concerning the increased likelihood of having an effective and skilled work-force which could contribute to the economy as well as lessening the number of dependants upon state hand-outs. Conditions in the workhouses were harsh and the implementation of the tripartite system referred to above was very patchy. There were a number of issues which complicated the picture not the least of which was the fact that if people appeared in a locality (parish) and had no means of support, the parish became responsible for them. As this responsibility was funded through local taxation ('rates'), it was in everyone's interests to move such people on so that public money was not used on people who did not belong to the area. These kinds of issues led to massive litigation where local 'overseers', who were responsible for the implementation of these relief programmes, battled their contemporaries from neighbouring parishes to establish who *was* going to be responsible for the relief of such people. Because of this localised squabbling, legal costs probably used up far more of the rates/taxes than the relief itself did. Another consequence of such attitudes was that many families were often forcibly, and cruelly, 'moved on'. Because of such chaos, the Act of Settlement of 1662 was introduced which attempted to define the whole issue of who was responsible for whom. This was yet another example of state regulation over private life, which grew from the inadequacies of earlier legislation and its ineffective implementation.

The Poor Law Amendment Act 1834

The 'old' Poor Laws had evolved into something unworkable. Because of the complexities of administering the system and the cost of building, maintaining and regulating the workhouses, a series of compromises had evolved which led to the increasing use of what came to be known as '*outdoor relief*'. This meant that people were offered a series of allowances, in cash or in kind, rather than having to go into the workhouse. One example of this was the introduction, around 1790, of child and family allowances along with a number of other *supplementary benefits*. These emerged in response to the effects of economic forces upon rates of employment. Because of changing economic forces, wage levels could drop below that of the level of relief offered to the pauper in the workhouse resulting in a situation where, through no fault of their own, labourers could find themselves worse off than their contemporaries in the workhouses. Thus, in order to avoid the potential for social unrest created by this situation, the Government allowed parishes to administer outdoor relief in the form of allowances and supplementary benefits until wage levels rose again in the wake of changes in economic conditions. One unintended consequence of this, however, was that labourers, finding themselves supported through hard times by these supplementary benefits, were sometimes less likely to return to full employment once it became available, preferring instead the easier existence afforded them by the provision of allowances. Furthermore, the availability of allowances for children encouraged people to have larger families, thus increasing the burden on food supplies. These and a range of other factors were instrumental in the Government recognising that it needed to change things as the cost of allowances and benefits was becoming increasingly prohibitive. In effect, the allowance system had steered the Poor Law into dealing with *poverty*, something it was never meant to do; its role had been to deal with *destitution*. The allowance system had also ignored the principle of 'setting the poor on work', a fundamental principle from 1601, so things had to change.

As industrialisation progressed, the focus of the earlier poor laws came to be less and less appropriate. Industrialisation became the driving economic force of the time and as a result, mass migration to the cities began. These factors, coupled with the issues referred to above led to the Poor Law Report of 1834, which suggested three main things: the principle of '*less eligibility*', the introduction of a '*workhouse test*' (eligibility criteria) and *administrative centralisation* for any system of relief. Central to the new system was the principle of 'less eligibility' which, simply put, meant that the allowance system was to be replaced with a system which provided relief at a standard *below* that of the poorest labourer. What this meant was that anyone who was not working *would* receive help from the state but it would be at a level *lower* than that received if working. It also meant that any relief offered would be within the workhouse itself. There was to be no more 'outdoor relief' under the terms of the *Outdoor Relief Prohibitory Order 1844*. Thus, the workhouses (known colloquially as 'Bastilles') were now seen as a deterrent to idleness and something to be avoided. The 'workhouse test' was the means by which the principle of 'less eligibility' was operationalised. One other important principle central to the workings of the new Poor Laws was that of *utilitarianism*. The principles underpinning utilitarianism are disarmingly simple: any action undertaken should aim to maximise 'pleasure' (generate a positive outcome) and minimise 'pain' (negative outcomes) *for as many people as possible*, the general maxim being 'the greatest good for the greatest number'.

On the surface this looks like a useful position to adopt, certainly in relation to policy implementation. However, the (often unexplicated) consequences of such a view are that there will always be those who fall into the 'smallest number' and who do not benefit. If you are in the 'greatest number', then you benefit and there is no problem as far as you are concerned. However, being in the minority group can generate huge problems, particularly if you are marginalised in some other way to begin with.

This view effectively meant that whilst any scheme or system would have its victims, so long as the majority benefited, then the minority would simply have to suffer.

Exercise 2.1 Principles of the past – principles for the present?

Can you think of any examples where principles from the past are present today in some form or another? For example, 'less eligibility', 'the workhouse test', 'setting the poor on work', utilitarianism.

In responding to Exercise 2.1 you might think about some of the 'welfare to work' initiatives introduced by New Labour during their tenure in office. Chapter 3 outlines some of these and later chapters will give particular mention to many of these issues.

The conditions within the workhouses were harsh and as industrialisation developed and the effects of economics became more and more relevant to everyone's daily life, factory owners began to treat workers very badly, many being dismissed for no good reason. These attitudes on the part of employers meant that many perfectly good workers were forced to rely upon the workhouse and this generated a great deal of unrest and a number of riots within many towns and cities. Whilst the *principle* of less eligibility could, all other things being equal, be seen to have *some* merit from a governmental perspective, workers who were effectively forced into the workhouse because of the greed of employers was something people were not prepared to tolerate. As a result of the fear and dread associated with the workhouses, people would instead work for terribly low wages, for hours on end and endure the most appalling working conditions. As Fraser (2003) notes, the principles of 1834 made the task of marrying deterrence and humane relief within the same system virtually impossible (pp. 59–60).

The Poor Law (Scotland) Act 1845

The 1845 Act for '*The Amendment and Better Administration of the Laws Relating to the Relief of the Poor in Scotland*' was *specific* to Scotland. The 1834 Poor Law Amendment Act referred to above did not apply north of the border. The Act of Union of 1707, although dissolving the Scottish Parliament at that time and transferring legislative power to Westminster (until it was restored in 1999), had allowed Scotland to retain its own distinctive judicial system. Westminster, partly to distance itself from Scotland's problems and in recognition of its particular geography and demography, saw the Scottish Act as purposive. In terms of broad principles, the 1845 Act differed from the operation of the English, Welsh and Irish Act in that the able-bodied were exempt from relief and outdoor relief was encouraged in opposition to the enforced use of workhouses (poorhouses in Scotland) across the rest of the UK. Attendance in the poorhouses in Scotland was voluntary with outdoor relief being a viable alternative. These factors suggest that the operation of the poor laws in Scotland were less punitive. Whilst this may have been the perceived case at the macro-level, at the micro- (individual) level, the operation of the poorhouses was in reality no different in Scotland to the rest of the UK – harsh.

In order to help with Exercise 2.2 below, think about the various 'eligibility criteria' that exist for certain services. In relation to notions of 'deserving' and 'undeserving', someone who uses hard drugs may be seen as less deserving than someone else in similar broad circumstances *who does not use hard drugs*. In terms of implications for practice, you may want to think about whether you could be faced with a situation in which a limited resource can only be given to one person: one who uses hard drugs let us say, and a person who doesn't. Who would you give it to?

Exercise 2.2

Can you think of a contemporary situation where you have come across the notion of people who are deemed as either 'deserving' or 'undeserving'? In what context did this arise? What language was used to describe these categorisations? What might be the implications of such notions for professional practice? Can you think of a practice example where such categorisations operate today, and can you think of a situation where this distinction might actually be justified or useful?

Victorian society and industrialisation

In many respects, it was the recognition of the fact that whilst the ideas underpinning the Poor Laws were intended to be beneficent, their articulation through indoor relief and the workhouses/poorhouses compromised the principles to such an extent that they became subverted and tarnished because of the cruelty of the workhouse system. Through the Poor Laws, there was a clear distinction drawn between *pauperism* and *poverty*. The Poor Law Amendment Act of 1834 and its various amendments sought not to concern itself with poverty. Rather, it was the nature of pauperism with its associated costs to the state that meant efforts were to be focused on reducing costs to the ratepayer, hence the workhouse test and the principle of less eligibility. These were essentially money-saving options. As the Act of 1834 was implemented, the inherent tensions at the interface of poor relief and industrialisation, along with the added impact of the economic forces spurred on by the growth of capitalism, meant that its implementation and subsequent effectiveness was soon compromised. People were beginning to recognise that whilst *pauperism* might be being reduced, largely because people would rather starve than face the workhouse, *poverty* remained and was a huge, and rising, problem. The rise of industrialisation and the capitalist mode of production brought into stark relief the fact that hard-working people were sometimes forced onto hard times because of the demands and vagaries of economics. People simply *refused* to accept poor relief and as time progressed, the scale of this problem became immense. In an effort to ease some of the tensions, the *Outdoor Labour Test Order (1842)* was given effect whereby in certain circumstances allied to harsh economic conditions (depressions) outdoor relief in the form of allowances *was* given in return for work. This was a clever move by the government of the time as it merged the principle of less eligibility with the workhouse test and to some extent reinstated the principles of the 1601 Act of 'setting the poor on work'. This principle, enshrined in the 43rd of Elizabeth, and for all its faults, had as a central feature an appreciation of the need for people to feel that they are were of use and could actually *do* something. The implementation of the labour test is a good example of how law and policy can be seen to respond to particular phenomena, in this case, the particular features of industrialisation and capitalism.

As the Poor Laws were designed, in principle at least, to deal with *extreme* cases of hardship (that is, pauperism) largely through deterrence, there was no apparent mechanism available to deal with the rising tide of poverty and its associated hardships which, by default, were no less great in many circumstances than those experienced by the 'pauper'. As a result, charitable activity began to increase. Based as it was on Victorian wealth, the spirit of philanthropy blossomed as many families found themselves in intolerable situations, often through no fault of their own, the vagaries of industrial capitalism beginning to show itself, full-force. Alongside charity, the government and its officers were keen to emphasise the value of 'thrift', a now characteristic 'Victorian Virtue'. This, alongside an increasing awareness by the government of the need to begin to take a rather more 'holistic' approach to the whole issue of need, resulted in a focus upon a range of other factors. Notable amongst these was health, particularly *public* health, housing, education and, of great interest, the provision of public spaces for the masses to enjoy in the form of parks, gardens, zoos, museums and theatres.

The role of charitable organisations and the emergence of social work

During the Victorian era, with the blight of the workhouses and poorhouses and the general refusal of the state to offer outdoor relief and the ever-increasing impact of poverty upon people's lives, the role of charitable activity soon became very noticeable. The roots of this activity and its motivation are still very much open to debate, as

> (T)he whole concept of charity presupposed a class of superior wealth with the means to dispense bounties, and in the Victorian period it equally presupposed a class of superior attitudes and values. Charity was a means of social control, an avenue for the inculcation of sound middle-class values .... (Fraser 2003: 139)

There were many charitable efforts in place, operating up and down the whole of the UK, but particularly concentrated in the cities. In the clamour to 'do good', there was much duplication of effort and significant abuses of charitable effort by those in receipt of it and, overall, a lack of effectiveness in terms of providing as much assistance to as many as possible. The prevailing spirit of Victorian philanthropy, excellently portrayed in Robert Tressell's novel *The Ragged Trousered Philanthropist*, was one that ultimately tended to degrade recipients and in some respects it was felt that the whole ethos was beginning to undermine the need to encourage, promote and support self-help and independence, rather than to diminish it. It is worth quoting a contemporary view of the time that encapsulates the perceived 'problem' of charity:

> The number and extent of our charitable institutions and the large amount of indiscriminate relief are a growing evil. If habits of self-respect and an honest pride of independence are the safeguard of the working classes and a barrier against inroads of pauperism it will follow that any public institutions which lead them directly to depend upon the bounty of others in times of poverty and sickness and which tend to encourage idleness and improvidence are not public charities but public evils. (McLeod 1958, quoted in Fraser 2003: 141)

Exercise 2.3

Look at the type of language used here to describe the types of virtues, behaviours and attitudes seen to be valued. Make a note of these. Now look at the *Report of the 21st Century Social Work Review, Changing Lives* (Scottish Executive 2006), available at http://www.scotland.gov.uk/Publications/2006/02/02094408/0 and note the types of words used to describe virtues, behaviours and attitudes there. For example, are there any parallels to 'building capacity'? You might want to spend some time browsing through a thesaurus as you attempt this task.

In response to these general perceptions, groups were formed to oversee and manage charitable effort. In 1819, Thomas Chalmers developed the very first such group in the UK, based in Glasgow. In 1869 in London, *The Charitable Organisation Society* (the COS) was formed. This group is generally seen as the forerunner of modern social work, though the aims of both this group and that of Chalmers were similar: to distribute charitable effort more efficiently and effectively. In terms of aims, those of both groups and its members were laudable, as were their activities, in principal at least. In terms of the COS, because of poor administration and a rather unfortunate attitude towards the provision of assistance, the organisation became very unpopular, to some extent subverting its own aims.

The idea of visiting the applicants for charitable donations arose because charitable effort was largely chaotic. It was also the case, as we can see from the comments above, that the whole ethos of charity was seen as undermining the Victorian virtues of thrift, self-help and independence. Some writers were of the view that it was beginning to replicate the worst outcomes of Poor Law relief whereby people were 'happy' to partake of relief rather than work (prior to the workhouse test). Thus, a system of *investigation* was developed which aimed to target resources more effectively. The aim was, broadly, to 'educate and reform the recipients of charity so that they might become once more independent, self-respecting individuals' (Fraser 2003: 142). Some of the methods and practice principles of the COS. are still with us today in the form of *casework* and *initial assessment*, and these formed the basis for what we now regard as the profession of social work. Its social philosophy, however, was one borne within the ethos of self-help and strict individualism, a view often challenged and one that perhaps does not sit so comfortably with the realms of modern social work practice, although there are still echoes of this view to be found within the profession, dependent upon the prevailing ethos of the time.

Victorian society had enjoyed what might be regarded nowadays as an unparalleled expansion of wealth. Those people in the working classes were recognised by the industrialists (and the Government) as valuable assets in terms of the capitalist cause. It is worth remembering that without the working classes, the capitalists could not amass their wealth. Therefore, and once again we see this, the need to minimise the potential for social unrest became an imperative (although not one articulated as such). Furthermore, the *social* impact of the industrial revolution (a term coined by one of the great reformers of the nineteenth century, Arnold Toynbee) was beginning to be seen by all. There were concerns over public health and sanitation, squalor, disease (largely because of outbreaks of cholera), public ignorance as to the real state of the nation, air pollution, industrial injury and death as well as the use of children for labour.

The (re-)discovery of poverty

A major issue underlying many of the concerns referred to above was the extent and impact of poverty. As we saw above, early attempts through the Poor Laws to respond to need focused upon destitution; poverty was, to some extent, seen as a necessary, and some would say, natural condition of the working classes. However, the work of Charles Booth (*Life and Labour of the People of London*, 1903) in the 1880s in London and that of Benjamin Seebohm Rowntree in York in 1899 (*Poverty: A Study of Town Life*, 1902) brought to light the nature and extent of poverty at that time. These reports, Booth's running to a massive 17 volumes, revealed for the first time the true extent of poverty and made comment on what they thought caused it, as well as distinguishing between different types of poverty, thus prefacing a whole era of poverty research (see also Townsend 1954; 1979). These two reports were instrumental in placing the issue of poverty on the political agenda at the turn of the century.

It is also worth noting that these studies by Booth and Rowntree were groundbreaking insofar as research methodologies were concerned. Both undertook to examine and report upon poverty in a systematic way and Rowntree undertook two follow-up studies (1942 and 1951) in York, thereby demonstrating the importance of longitudinal research.

These and other matters were the subject of a number of measures over the years leading up to the beginning of the twentieth century. The period between 1905 and 1914 was the era of the great Liberal reforms, which heralded the creation of the welfare state, and it is to these we now turn.

The liberal reforms 1905–14

By the turn of the twentieth century, a number of laws and other policy initiatives had emerged which sought to address many of the ills of late Victorian society and the expansion of capitalist labour. These included improvements in arrangements concerning child labour, the development of a hospital system that grew from the earlier introduction and subsequent expansion of poor-law hospitals, and improvements to public health (legislated for from 1848). There were a number of Factory Acts aiming to improve workplace safety, and legislation regarding secondary and technical education was introduced from 1902. Similar developments dealt with the provision of public housing (from 1851), unemployment (beginning with the Unemployed Workman's Act, 1905) and concerns for the condition of the elderly that led to the provision of old age pensions (which had been introduced in Germany in 1889) rather than relief from the workhouse.

From an ideological perspective, the growth of industrialisation mirrored the ideology of *individualism*; the intervention of the state, often through the Poor Laws, was seen as a last resort and therefore *minimalist*. As the awareness of the impact of industrialisation upon public health for example became clearer, as well as the effect of economics in relation to poverty, a more *collectivist* attitude towards welfare and well-being began to emerge. The Liberal reforms were the beginnings of a growing social awareness and a refinement of the 'social conscience' after what might be seen to have been the barbarism of industrialisation. At the turn of the twentieth century, social reform was very much the order of the day and in its midst were to rise a number of great historical figures, two of which were Lloyd George (Liberal) and Winston Churchill (Conservative).

Running alongside these reforms, and to some extent informing them, was the Royal Commission on the Poor Law, which had been set up in 1905 and reported in 1909. This 'think-tank' had as its remit to consider the apparent failings of the system of poor relief that had evolved (again) into something unworkable and unmanageable.

The 'Minority Report' of the Royal Commission 1909

Within the context of the work of the Royal Commission on the Poor Law, there were two reports produced; the main or *Majority Report* was that of the Commission. This made a number of proposals, many of which were not implemented. A number of people who formed part of the Commission were in total disagreement with the others and dissented, producing a *Minority Report*. This report was to have an impact upon subsequent policy development in reality beyond that of the Majority Report, and was authored in the main by Beatrice Webb. She, along with her husband Sidney Webb, was later to form the Fabian Society (http://www.fabians.org.uk/) and be instrumental in the creation of the London School of Economics.

The recommendations of the Minority Report were seen by some as being revolutionary. In fact, most of them were fairly sensible. One of the report's main thrusts was that destitution was a major problem and that this should be the subject of *prevention*, rather than relief. Essentially, the Minority Report called for the development of a Ministry of Labour to deal with issues of (un-)employment, the establishment of Labour Exchanges, proper care for children and the aged, including incomes for the elderly in the form of pensions, the provision of social insurance against sickness, disablement and unemployment and the relaxing of the rules regarding other forms of relief where these existed. The Minority Report also called for the establishment of a range of agencies under the aegis of local councils to deal with particular social problems (the beginnings of social work and other departments).

The tenure of the Liberal government during this time brought major changes to the way in which social policy was conceived, implemented and subsequently developed. The notion of *social insurance*, a concept whereby there was some kind of safety net in place for people when things went wrong, was borne out through the Liberal administration. In the so-called 'People's Budget' of 1909, taxation, the imposition of duties on alcohol, tobacco and petrol, and land taxes were the means used to fund old age and other types of pensions for the sick and disabled, as well as to provide for those who found themselves unemployed through no fault of their own. Thus, progressive *economic* policies were the means by which progressive *social* policies were developed and implemented. This was a theme referred to in Chapter 1.

The emergence of the welfare state (1914–48)

The inter-war years saw further developments in relation to policy, particularly with regard to unemployment and national health insurance. The advent and impact of the Second World War generated a level of determination to overcome significant adversity and promoted the spirit of *universalism* to new heights. The Second World War, as a *total war*, tended to reduce social distinctions. This was something that affected everyone and required a contribution from everyone. As a result, the welfare of all, not just the military, was the concern of government and social policy began increasingly to reflect this.

The (elaborate) series of social services, which had emerged somewhat piecemeal over the preceding years, were still tainted by the shadow of the Poor Laws and still only responded to those who had what were seen to be *exceptional* difficulties, although what was regarded as exceptional was becoming relative, given the privations of the war. The demands placed upon the nation as a collective entity because of the Second World War brought into stark relief the effects of the (relative) indifference to the nation's well-being in peacetime by Government, and it was agreed that such an attitude was counter-productive. National complacency received a shock, not the least of which arose from the effects of the evacuation of huge numbers of children from the towns and cities into the countryside and other safe-havens to avoid Nazi bombings. The poverty of these children, as well as the effects of poor nutrition and poor parenting all served as a wake-up call for the country.

The coalition Government during the war years introduced a range of measures including the Determination of Needs Act 1941, which abolished the (dreaded) 'Household Means Test'. This test had previously demanded that the means of all family members be taken into account in relation to any determination of need where assistance (in cash or in kind) was requested. This meant that many young men, in order to help the family out, would leave the family home in order that their means were not considered as part of the families, or would give false addresses to the 'means test man'. Such a policy was seen as divisive and not supportive of harmonious relationships between families and the state, the test itself seen as a force that had the potential to split families up. Other measures introduced from 1940 included free school meals and free milk for all school children, free milk for mothers and babies and a wide-ranging programme of free immunisations (especially against diphtheria, which actually killed more children than the bombs did). Another development, and one that has since proven itself a major strand of welfare provision across the UK, arose from the enhancement of the provisions of the Maternity and Child Welfare Act 1918. This Act allowed local authorities to set up 'home help' schemes for pregnant women, which many did. In the mid-1940s the government allowed for an extension of this provision to older people and to those who were ill at home. This 'home-help' service, along with the introduction of supplementary pensions for older people, provided a much needed and highly valued service.

The post-war reconstruction was central to the thoughts of most people at the time and in some respects the cessation of the Second World War provided a platform for a number of reforms. Moreover, it was the effect that the force of the war had had upon the population that led, largely, to the introduction of the welfare state. The war effort had emphasised the value of a *collective* approach in responding to common problems, and this view was carried forward into the passing of a number of significant pieces of legislation that essentially created the welfare state. One writer refers to its emergence as being the result of 'a whole series of fits of conscience' (Bruce 1966: 259).

The Beveridge Report (1942)

The responses of the government to the range of emerging social issues and problems referred to above serves to illustrate how the impact of common difficulties on a large scale can bring about major policy changes with desirable effects. However, these responses are often piecemeal and this was the case in relation to the reforms mentioned above, although thematically they were all clearly connected. It took the attentions of the *Interdepartmental Committee on Social Insurance and Allied Service,* chaired by Sir W.H. Beveridge to pull these themes and issues together in their survey of the state of the nation's welfare services at this time. The *Beveridge Report* was published in December 1942 and it was this which identified the so-called 'five giant ills of society' – want, disease, ignorance, squalor and idleness – which were subsequently to be responded to by national schemes and systems of *social insurance and social security* (want), a *national health service* (disease), *compulsory education for children* (ignorance), a *national programme of house building by local authorities with attention on public health matters* (squalor) and a *system of labour exchanges and allowances to deal with unemployment* (idleness).

In order to implement these measures, a range of new legislation was introduced, the main ones being:

- The Education Act 1944 (The Butler Act)
- The Family Allowances Act 1945
- The National Health Service Act 1946
- The National Insurance Act 1946
- The National Insurance (Industrial Injuries) Act 1946
- The National Assistance Act 1948
- The Children Act 1948

The Beveridge Report was hailed as a major milestone in social policy, and formed the basis of what we today would refer to as 'the welfare state'. The post-war Labour Government of 1945 implemented the recommendations of the Committee, with the newspapers of the day proclaiming:

> Beveridge tells how to BANISH WANT. Cradle to grave plan. All pay – All benefit ... from Duke to Dustman. (*Daily Mirror*, 2 December 1942)

Subsequently, there has been condemnation of the report, its recommendations and the actions of the Government of the day (Abel-Smith and Townsend 1965; Barnett 1986). At the time, with peace breaking out across Europe and the rest of the world, people understandably saw this as a great development relative to the hardships of earlier years. However that may be, and however we interpret those attempts today, we cannot minimise their importance in terms of the development of social policy.

Welfare consensus 1951–79

The period from 1951 to the advent of the reign of Margaret Thatcher as leader of the Conservative Party and Prime Minister in 1979 is seen as the last great period of welfare consensus. From an ideological perspective, all political parties during this time tended to agree, in general, that state intervention in certain areas of private life, along with the public (governmental) regulation of large sectors of the economy (nationalisation of railways, gas, electricity and water, telecommunications, coal and so on) should be the norm. Such a position tended to eclipse the usual ideological positions adopted by the respective political parties (see Chapter 3). However, this tradition of liberal ideas came to a halt when Mrs Thatcher came to power and adopted a neo-liberal approach to policymaking and welfare, which emphasised the role of the free market, individualism and minimum state intervention.

The policies of the Thatcher era led to the privatisation of most publicly owned services (railways, utilities, telecom, transport, coal and steel industries) and the development of a 'mixed-economy' of welfare which allowed for the purchase of tiered services by individuals who could afford these, thus heralding what can be seen to be a two-tier system of welfare and health provision today, and one perpetuated by New Labour since 1997.

Such a trend can be seen to have permeated social work practice through a number of developments, including the NHS and Community Care Act 1990 (Care Management) and the Community Care and Health (S) Act 2002. These underpinning ideological themes are discussed in detail in Chapter 3 where we also discuss the impact of the 'third way' of New Labour and briefly consider the relevance of the emergence of the new Conservative/Liberal Democrat coalition Government elected in May 2010 (see Powell 2008; Lowe 2005).

Chapter summary

All of the above in relation to the historical antecedents of social policy allows us to see how policy has *developed* and *evolved* in response to the demands placed upon societies and the responses of governments. These demands are clearly influenced by a range of other factors, not the least of which is economics. Furthermore, the growth and development of policy can often be seen to arise in a piecemeal fashion with no particular strategy behind it. However that may be, the policy we have today is invariably aligned to earlier attempts at regulation across the boundary of the *state* and the *individual*. These issues are important in helping us to understand how certain practices came into being and how trends in society can become policy themes that may persist for generations.

References

Abel-Smith, B. and Townsend, P. (1965), *The Poor and the Poorest: A New Analysis of the Ministry of Labour's Family Expenditure Surveys of 1953–4 and 1960* (London: Bell).

Alcock, P. (2006), *Understanding Poverty* (3rd edn) (Basingstoke: Palgrave Macmillan).

Barnett, C. (1986), *The Audit of War: The Illusion and Reality of Britain as a Great Nation* (London: Macmillan).

Berridge, V. (2003), 'Public or Policy Understanding of History?', *Social History of Medicine* 16: 511–23.

Bruce, M. (1966), *The Coming of the Welfare State* (3rd edn) (London: Batsford).

Cage, R.A. (1981), *Scottish Poor Law* (Edinburgh: Scottish Academic Press).

Fraser, D. (2003), *The Evolution of the British Welfare State* (3rd edn) (Basingstoke: Palgrave Macmillan).

Hendrick, H. (ed.) (2005), *Child Welfare and Social Policy: An Essential Reader* (Bristol: Policy Press).

Lowe, R. (2005), *The Welfare State in Britain Since 1945* (Basingstoke: Palgrave Macmillan).

Mackay, G.A. (1907/2008), *Practice of the Scottish Poor Law* (London: BiblioBazaar).

Mitchison, R. (2000), *The Old Poor Law in Scotland: The Experience of Poverty* (Edinburgh: Edinburgh University Press).

Powell, M. (ed.) (2008), *Modernising the Welfare State: The Blair Legacy* (Bristol: Policy Press).

Scottish Executive (2006), *Changing Lives: Report of the 21st Century Social Work Review* (Edinburgh: Scottish Executive).

Townsend, P. (1954), 'Measuring Poverty', *British Journal of Sociology* 5(2): 130–37.

— (1979), *Poverty in the United Kingdom: A Survey of Household Resources and Standards of Living* (Harmondsworth: Penguin).

Further reading

For a detailed discussion of the Poor Laws, see Fraser (2003), especially Chapter 2. Lowe (2005) offers an excellent account of the broad development and operation of the welfare state from 1945 up to the present day with a focus more upon the 'modern' history of welfare, including useful commentary on Thatcherism and New Labour. You may also wish to read some of Charles Dickens' novels, which give some insight into the lives of people at this time, particularly *Oliver Twist, Bleak House, Our Mutual Friend, Little Dorrit* and *Hard Times* or Arnold Bennett's *Clayhanger* with more contemporary writing on the same issues by Michel Faber in *The Crimson Petal and the White.*

Web-based resources

http://users.ox.ac.uk/~peter/workhouse/index.html (accessed 29 May 2010).

http://www.historyandpolicy.org/ (accessed 29 May 2010).

3 Ideology: How ideas influence policy and welfare

Steve J. Hothersall

Introduction

As we saw in the previous chapter, centralised, state-coordinated responses to particular issues within society have been evident since the earliest times. Often, whether the state became involved was as much about whether an issue was felt to be one likely to generate social unrest if not dealt with, rather than about governments being worried about the well-being of their citizens. Whatever form the response may have taken (or not) reflected in some way the ideas of the people in charge: these ideas we refer to as *ideologies* and in this chapter we shall look at a range of these as well as considering how relevant these might be today.

We might at this point remind ourselves about the purpose of welfare within modern society. In the UK and in many other European countries at least there has been a tendency for the state to be the central 'provider' of welfare services to the population, although the extent to which welfare services are connected to market forces tends to vary. At the cessation of the Second World War the UK Government and its political opponents from across the party-political and ideological divide agreed that the country and its citizens needed help to recover from, amongst other things, the effects of two world wars. It was agreed at that time (1940s) that a *collective approach* to promoting and supporting the welfare and well-being of citizens could best be effected by the state taking the lead in organising and delivering a range of services which we referred to in the previous chapter as those designed to address the 'five giant ills of society'. The argument was that the state should shoulder the burden and absorb the costs of providing these services so that everyone could benefit from them. This was the point at which large-scale, state-sponsored and centralised welfare services began. Prior to this, there had been much more of a reliance on the role of the family and small, voluntary and/or charitable efforts to provide help in times of need, and schooling for example was provided via the church or trade associations. In the 1940s this all changed and up until the 1970s it was generally felt that the collective arrangement of the 'welfare state' was working and would in fact continue to work to provide collective welfare for all citizens, despite its increasing shortcomings. However, as we saw earlier, the prevailing ideology of *collectivism* based on ideological consensus appears to have broken down in the face of the neo-liberal policies of the 1970s onwards, to be replaced by an increasing preference for *individualism*. It is *ideology* that underpins such apparently differing approaches to providing welfare through social policy and as an example, the short account above reflects the influence of the two major ideological positions within UK politics, essentially the *left* and the *right*, although as we shall see, there are many other influential views.

Welfare regimes: Three worlds of welfare?

Esping-Andersen (1990) suggests that different nation-states have different types of welfare systems which reflect their underpinning views on the nature of the relationship between the state and its citizens. He constructed a three-part typology to describe what he considered to be the main forms of welfare regime across Europe. His central theme was the degree to which welfare services were seen as a *commodity* and how much therefore they were connected to market systems. The level or degree of *commodification* indicates the extent to which welfare is seen as a right or as a commodity. His typology identifies three predominant regimes:

Social democratic: these arrangements are highly *decommodified* in that welfare services are provided by the state for all citizens irrespective of income, status or any other particular characteristic and welfare services are *universal*. Many of the Scandinavian and Nordic countries would fall into this particular typology (Benner 2003; Greve 2007).

Conservative: these arrangements are usually highly decommodified, but not necessarily universal. Their availability is often linked to things like a person's particular status within society; for example, married women with young children would receive more generous welfare benefits than a single parent because their *married status* is thought to promote family stability. France and Germany would be typical of these types of regime (Palier and Martin 2008).

Liberal: these types of regime are highly *commodified* and welfare is therefore seen as something that people can purchase for themselves. The USA would be a typically commodified regime. Those who do require welfare but cannot afford it are subjected to means testing in order to determine their eligibility and as such, these types of regime often lead to highly stigmatised welfare provision. Recent attempts in the USA to *decommodify* aspects of health care by the Obama administration have resulted in some interesting debates (Clinton and Obama 2006; Marmor, Oberlander and White 2009).

Exercise 3.1

On the basis of your reading of previous chapters and the above accounts of welfare regimes, which of the three regimes most closely resembles that of the UK in 2010?

You might have found yourself thinking it was nearer to the Social democratic model, but then perhaps you changed your mind and thought it was nearer to the Liberal model, but then .... This is what you should have thought because the UK system has shifted *towards* a more Liberal model although it still retains elements of the Social Democratic model, with a sprinkling of Conservatism in terms of the way tax breaks and occupational benefits are used to provide welfare services (or to facilitate access to them by private purchase) differentially depending upon occupational status.

The descriptions above of different approaches to what constitutes welfare and how it might be provided are all influenced by particular *ideas* concerning the role of the state in relation to its citizens and these ideas or *ideologies* can be very influential.

Ideology: What it is and what it does

> An ideology is a more or less coherent set of ideas that provides the basis for organised political action, whether this is intended to preserve, modify or overthrow the existing system of power. All ideologies therefore ... offer an account of the existing order, usually in the form of a 'world view' (and) advance a model of a desired future, a vision of the 'good society' ... and explain how political change can and should be brought about .... (Heywood 2007: 11–12)

Ideology refers to a set of underpinning ideas and values that inform thought, language and subsequent action. In relation to social policy, *such ideologies are indicative of the extent to which the state should have a role in organising, controlling and providing welfare to its citizens*. Historically, differing ideologies have informed this debate to varying degrees and certain views have been either more or less pervasive or penetrative depending on time, place and space. Simplistically, discussions around ideology and its capacity to inform and influence welfare provision have tended to be represented by a left/right schism which has tended to become more apparent the more that the 'welfare state', typified by reference to the reforms of the Liberal government from 1905 to 1914 and the post-war Beveridge reforms, has been seen not to deliver on its stated aims of tackling the 'five giant ills of society', today perhaps exemplified by incontrovertible evidence of continued poverty and increasing and more diverse forms of inequality (Wilkinson and Pickett 2010).

Classifying ideology

There are many ways in which ideology can be classified, but the basic formulation is as noted in Figure 3.1.

Left >>>>>><<<<<<< Centre>>>>>><<<<<<<<<Right

(Collectivists>>>>>>>>>>> Reluctant Collectivists>>>>>>>>>> Anti-Collectivists)

Figure 3.1 A linear representation of ideological positions

This simplistic arrangement sees those on the left as being pro-welfare and in favour of the *public* provision of services. The left also prefer a *collectivist model* of welfare provision which means that such provision would be available to everyone and provided on an *institutional basis* through certain structures, such as the National Health Service or state-run schools.

Those on the right of the spectrum are generally opposed to state welfare provision and favour an individualistic or *anti-collectivist* approach within the context of a free-market economy where the 'hidden hand' of economics largely determines the relative cost and availability of all services. Within the context of right-wing ideologies, welfare provision in and for times of need is seen as something for which individuals make their own arrangements and purchase (private) pension schemes, (private) health care and (private) schooling.

These positions have many variants, from strong to weak. Those positions occupying the centre ground are those that see a mixed economy as being viable and permissible within certain limitations. A *mixed economy* refers to the presence of state provision of certain, fundamental services (for example, basic health care, basic schooling for all children), along with the presence of privately-funded services which people can opt into if they so wish and if they can afford to pay for these themselves.

These ideological positions clearly reflect differing views on the role of the state and depending on a number of factors, some ideological influences may be more visible than others. Their 'visibility' or felt presence is likely to be a function of the degree to which they are shared between those who hold political power at any given time and, following the strict observance of the basis of democratic principles, should also reflect the views of the majority of citizens. According to George and Wilding (1994), any major ideological perspective is likely to be *coherent, pervasive, extensive* and *intense. Coherency* refers to the internal logic and theoretical consistency of the perspective; it should make sense. *Pervasiveness* refers to the need for any perspective to be relevant and in-tune with current happenings as well as being *extensive* in that it has wide appeal with an *intensive* level of support. However, some writers, notably Fukuyama (1989) argue that '... (E)conomic and political differences (will) progressively diminish as all societies, at different rates, converge on an essentially liberal model of development' (in Heywood 2003: 66). Western models of liberal democracy, it is argued, will soon therefore be the dominant ideology, effectively replacing ideological distinctions because of the pervasive effects of capitalism and the model of individualism valued in many societies. From the perspectives of welfare-oriented professions, such a development may threaten the perceived values of collectivism and redefine notions of what should constitute a coherent and effective *ideology of welfare*. This of course presupposes that a *collectivist* model of welfare is the best model to adopt and that view of course depends upon your ideological position.

Political ideologies

In this section we shall look at a range of political ideologies (as represented in Figure 3.2) and discuss some of their main components; the categorisations used are those adopted by Heywood (2002), who provides a very good account of the whole issue of political ideology (Heywood 2007).

Liberalism

Most commentators would argue that any account of political ideology must begin with an account of liberalism. Liberalism is, effectively, the ideology of the industrialised West and can be conceived as a *meta-ideology* in that it has the capacity to embrace a broad range of competing, and sometimes rival values

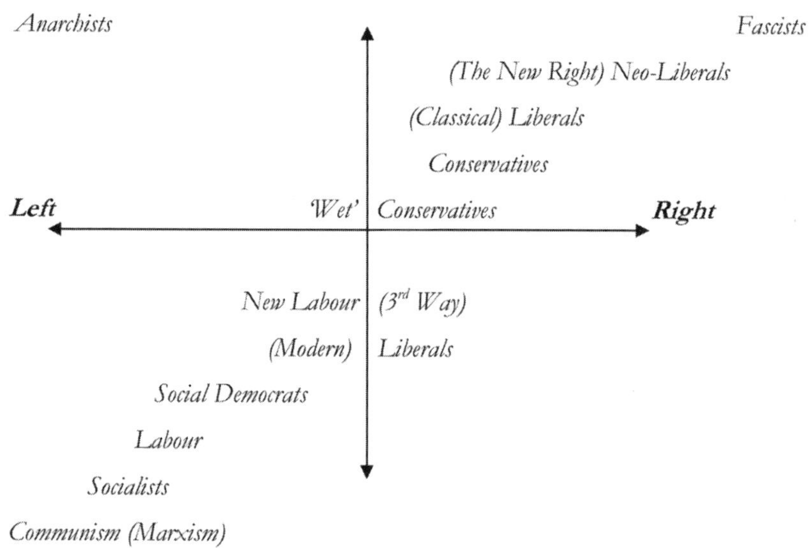

Pro-welfare/Collectivism<<<<<<<<<<<

Figure 3.2 A generalised typology of differing ideologies

Note: These typologies work because of 'ideal types'. Within the extreme positions, we can see what appear to be inconsistencies. For example, fascism would see no place for outright independence and the claims by Russia for the adoption of communism based upon Marxist ideology are clearly seen to be untrue.

and beliefs. Although closely associated with the events of industrialism, liberalism as a creed arose following the breakdown of feudalism, which this particular doctrine eschewed. The early liberals certainly associated themselves with the (aspirant) middle classes and the capitalistic creed and were initially opposed to any form of state intervention. This became known as *classical liberalism* and supported clear distinctions within society based upon privilege. However, as the industrial revolution advanced and the effects of *laissez-faire* capitalism were seen to be no respecter of place or person or status, a change in attitude emerged regarding the potential value of the *moderating* effects of state control and intervention. As a result, a form of liberalism we might refer to as *social liberalism* emerged, and although seen by some as a weaker form of classical liberalism, people had begun to acknowledge that, unchecked, laissez-faire capitalism could destroy those who were weaker and less able to compete in an open market. It appeared that the spectre of feudalism was operating within the guise of capitalism, the master now being market forces as opposed to the Lord of the Manor. Thus, the shift towards a more empathic doctrine was, some would say, inevitable. As a result, social liberalism looked more favourably upon state intervention in relation to welfare and aspects of economic regulation.

In recent years, there has been a growth in *new right* philosophies. Perhaps exemplified in the UK by the tenure of Margaret Thatcher as the leader of the Conservative Party and Prime Minister from 1979 to 1990, and in the US by Ronald Reagan, such views incorporate elements of *neo-liberalism* and *neo-conservatism*. These views are seen to favour a move *away* from state intervention and a renewed focus on the role of the free market economy, thus resembling classical liberalism, although these views would claim to be more theoretically informed by reference to major economic theorists, notably the work of Friedrich von Hayek (1960/2006).

Liberalism has at its core a number of fundamental principles that can be seen to operate in both strong and weak forms. Its central principle is that of *individualism*. This represents the view that the human individual is far more important than the collective or group, with emphasis given to the importance of allowing individuals to develop and flourish in their own way. This is aligned to other important values within the liberal tradition, those of *individual freedom* and *liberty*, which are given precedence over other values of *justice, equality* and *authority* that are perhaps more in keeping with socialist values, and are seen to work by reference to the capacity of individuals to *reason* and thereby make reasoned judgements for themselves. In addition, liberalism would support the view that whilst all of us are born equal, at least in terms of *moral worth*, it is individual effort which generates success and therefore legitimates the idea of a *meritocracy* and, inevitably one could argue, *inequality* (Young 1970; Dench 2006).

In terms of the evolution of a more socially aware and welfare-oriented liberalism, the post-war Liberal Government reforms (see Chapter 2) were perhaps a good example of this.

Conservatism

As a political creed, conservatism as 'the desire to conserve', arose in response to the (radical) change that followed the French Revolution. If we look to dictionary definitions, we see an emphasis upon *moderation, caution* and *conventionality*. The forces of liberalism, socialism and nationalism were seen as being destabilising influences on the 'traditional' social order of the day, which was that of authority, hierarchy, a wealthy and propertied class and stability grown from predictability, obligation and a sense of duty.

These principles, along with that of pragmatism are essentially the defining features of conservatism. The writings of Benjamin Disraeli (1804–71) and his notion of 'one nation' built upon the idea that the privileged in society had an obligation towards the less fortunate, but exemplifies the need to preserve so-called 'traditional values'. However, one can argue that the need to ensure 'one nation' was more about minimising the likelihood of social revolution; the idea here was that *reform from above* was better than *revolution from below*. Here we see a key idea connected to the use of pragmatism ('what works' in a policy sense) being used to shape and implement an ideology. In some respects, conservatism sits mid-way between free-for-all laissez-faire capitalism, in which only the strong survive, and the notion of a socialist oriented 'nanny state' in which the government is responsible for almost everything, with it being located to the right of centre on the political spectrum. Thus, the importance of social reform is a key message of conservatives because such activity is consistent with the maintenance of tradition, order and the upkeep of the traditional values of obligation and duty and the avoidance of social breakdown. In 2010, conservatives can often be heard to refer to our 'broken society', a euphemistic reference to conservatism's healing power through tradition (Kenny 2009).

The late 1980s and early 1990s saw Margaret Thatcher's policies bring the *New Right* into focus, representing a further shift along the political spectrum *away* from her so-called conservative roots. This was seen as a reaction to what some conservatives had perceived as a slide towards the centre ground ('wets'). The results of such views, tinged to some extent with *neo-liberal* thinking have been quite startling. The policy actions of Thatcher in the UK and Reagan in the US have had worldwide implications with significant shifts away from state-controlled forms of welfare organisation to market-oriented forms taking precedence, both practically and ideologically. Within social work, this is probably best represented by the emergence of a 'contract culture' whereby social work and other related services are offered by local authorities to private and other organisations for tender, and the service provider that can convince the state that it can provide the service(s) the cheapest will usually win the contract (Harris 2003). Somewhat perversely, it is usually the *lowest bidder* that takes control of delivering services.

Socialism

As a political creed, socialism (a term first coined by Henri de Saint-Simon (1760–1825), a French utopian socialist thinker and intellectual) arose in response to the impact of increasingly industrialised and mechanised methods of production upon artisans and latterly factory workers with the aim of minimising exploitation by the capitalists. Here again, both weak and strong forms can be seen. In its early days, socialism tended to have a clear revolutionary feel about it with this being represented at one extreme by *Marxism*, with a more 'reformist' brand of ethical socialism evolving into *social democracy*. The aims of these groups did not really differ from each other very much; rather, it was the means by which the ends could and should be achieved which offered clear differences, specifically referring to either *revolution* or *reform*, but this was especially so in terms of the differences between socialism and other political creeds, particularly those representative of unbridled individualism with money and profit at the heart of their thinking.

The main elements of socialism include notions of community and the importance of common humanity and the centrality of the *group* or the *collective* (society). Connected to this are ideas of *fraternity*, *social equality* and the reduction or eradication of *class differences*, with the belief that material benefit and assistance should be distributed to whomsoever purely on the basis of need (see Chapter 4). This latter principle is predicated upon the earlier assumptions concerning equality and the role of the group in relation to well-being, thus offering some indication of a sense of coherence to the philosophy as a whole, which essentially advocates the public and/or collective ownership of the means and distribution of production with the aim of creating an egalitarian society.

The particular 'brand' of socialism would determine where it might be located on the political spectrum (see Figure 3.2). Looking at the matrix in Figure 3.2 we could quite easily move some of the creeds to the left or to the right depending upon how we interpret their principles. However we choose to do this, it is the underlying principles of the ideology that affect not only how society ought to be structured (in this case, based on *equality* as an organising principle) but also how society should respond and relate to its citizens and *vice versa*.

The so-called 'third way' of the recent Labour government and to some extent (because of Westminster influence, see below) the Scottish Nationalist Party (SNP) within Scotland, is an approach which represents a blend of different ideological components essentially based around a 'what works' or pragmatic *conservative* view with elements of social democracy. Notions of socialism as represented by top-heavy state control and intervention are superseded by a 'dynamic market economy', which, interestingly, utilises some of the principles around social justice in its lexicon when it refers to the value of individual skills. However, state intervention *is* seen as being viable in the form of economic controls that would aim to offset the worst excesses of the laissez-faire approach of capitalism and other neo-liberal philosophies. However, it is debatable whether there was enough state intervention in place to control the economy before the major banks collapsed during the 2000s, heralding the beginnings of a worldwide economic recession.

The 'third way' was clearly an approach that incorporated a number of principles drawn from liberalism, conservatism and socialism. The major values enshrined by the third way approach were *opportunity, responsibility* and *community* and are representative of *New Social Democracy* (NSD). In essence, the third way had a focus on the need to eradicate what many now saw as an inadvertent consequence of the Beveridge system; that of *passivity* and *dependency*. Rodger (2000) argues that there is a new face to conceptions of welfare today and that there is a new moral framework developing within which future welfare will sit. One can easily transpose the notion of a new moral framework into the emergence of a new *ideology* of welfare. By this argument, the 'old' moral framework of universal social insurance in the form of collective and institutionalised welfare provision *à la* Beveridge is being replaced by what Rodger refers to as the 'privatisation of responsibility' (p. 3), a strong theme evident in much of New Labour social policy during their time in power from 1997 and a theme clearly detectable in each of the chapters in this book. What Rodger is referring to is the increasing tendency for policy to move the responsibility for welfare provision *away* from the state and *towards* the individual who is increasingly expected either to meet their own welfare needs or for those who clearly cannot, for them to receive welfare and assistance on a *conditional* basis. For Rodger and others, this signals a move *away* from a welfare *state* and a corresponding move *towards* a welfare *society*. This renegotiates the 'social contract' between the state and its citizens and perhaps for some amplifies (and exemplifies?) Rousseau's claim that 'L'homme est né libre, mais partout il est dans les fers' ('Man is born free, but everywhere he is in chains') (Rousseau 1762/1998: 5).

Nationalism

At the outset it has to be said that the notion of *nationalism* has been somewhat tarnished because of the advent of radical and extreme forms of the creed in the shape of Hitler and Mussolini and their variant of it, fascism. The idea of nationalism is linked to the growth of industrialisation and other nationalist movements in the eighteenth and nineteenth centuries, and central to the ideas underpinning it is the definition of what actually constitutes a nation, which is not identical to the idea of a *state,* although the two are often used together when we refer to a *nation-state* (Delanty and Kumar 2006). A nation can be seen as being comprised of a body of people who share a real or imagined history, culture, language and value-base who usually co-exist in one geographical area. The underlying and most straightforward aim of nationalism is to achieve self-determination. However, there are, typically, a number of variants on the broad theme of nationalism and it is difficult to find agreement on what it actually is. In a general sense, the most benign form it can take is that referred to as *civic nationalism* which focuses on *cultural* rather than hereditary ties between people and as such promotes the development of common cultural values and allows people from different origins to assimilate into the culture thus accommodating multi-racial, multi-ethnic and multi-religious elements.

One of the central tenets of nationalism is that humankind is *naturally* divided into nations that have distinctive characters and identities. The notion of *Gemeinschaft* (Tönnies 1887/2001) is a relevant concept here. However, some authors believe that the very idea of a nation is in fact a myth (Hobsbawm 1992) and that it is the myth itself that creates nations rather than the other way around; it is for some a 'virtual' concept.

Fascism

This ideological position is associated mainly with dictators like Hitler and Mussolini. It is regarded as being an inter-war phenomenon arising because of a number of forces including the collapse of democracy in Europe at that time. As an ideological position it extols the virtues of strong leadership, brought about by personal rule (Mussolini, Hitler), and recognition of the power of unity. In this regard, the rise of industrialisation, inter-war economic decline and fears of social revolution from the lower-middle classes brought on by the impact of the Russian Revolution led to the growth of fascist support.

The main tenets of fascism propose that the individual is nothing, identity gained only through unity with the national community and the common cause. Its values are power, leadership, struggle and war, all of which are deemed important for the glory of the nation or the race. Fascism is anti-liberal, anti-individualist, anti-capitalist and anti-communist, often seen therefore as based upon what it *opposes* rather than what it supports. Fascism tends to represent a darker side of political thought; established ideals such as freedom, progress and democracy are transmuted into submission, struggle and dictatorship respectively. It does, however, see itself as a creative philosophy, using the notion of 'creative destruction' to embody this aim. This notion could be seen to be operative in Hitler's Nazi Germany where he espoused the view that the complete destruction of the Jewish race (the 'Final Solution') would lead to the rise of Aryan supremacy and thereafter a better life.

It seems that fascism breeds in conditions of economic uncertainty and political instability. The politics of hatred and resentment appear to dwindle in the face of coherence and consistent approaches to social issues. In the twenty-first century, the possibilities for fascism to re-emerge should not be discounted, although it is unlikely that the virulence associated with their growth in the years following the First World War would be repeated.

Anarchism

The central theme within anarchism is a belief that *all* forms of political authority, particularly as represented by the state, are evil and unnecessary. The term anarchy means, literally, 'without rule'. The notion subscribed to is one of a stateless society within which individuals manage their own affairs through negotiation, voluntary agreement and cooperation. In respect of these ideals, anarchism represents forms of ultra-liberalism and ultra-socialism. The anarchist tradition draws on socialist ideas of collectivism and the value of social solidarity with its virtues of sociability and gregariousness. One of its major drawbacks is the issue around the emphasis upon individualism combined with the lack of any form of state regulation. History would suggest however that humans are largely incapable of continued voluntary cooperation and that some form of 'rule' would be necessary. Ideas around anarchism are anathema to the ethic of humanism and posit the very real possibility that those unable to manage their own affairs have no place in such a society. It is therefore difficult to see anarchism as a coherent ideology given that it appears to be representative of internal contradictions rather than cohesions.

Feminism

Feminist political theory has existed for millennia but the first articulation of a coherent political theory of feminism did not arrive until Mary Wollstonecraft's *A Vindication of the Rights of Women*, published in 1792. Although diverse in its doctrine, feminism's unifying feature is a desire to enhance the social role of women. Within its gambit, we can identify three distinct strands. Firstly, liberal feminism, which has as its focus the reform of the public sphere in relation to the legal and political standing of women. Secondly, there are socialist feminists who focus on the issues relating to the subordination of women in relation to issues around the ownership of the means of production (widely interpreted) with a focus on the domestic sphere and the role played by women here. Finally, there are the radical feminists who believe that only a revolution will remedy the perceived problems of patriarchy that is seen as institutionalised across many cultures.

Environmentalism/ecologism

Although seen as a relatively nascent ideology linked to the emergence of the Green movement, environmental politics can be traced back to the nineteenth century as a reaction to the threat of industrialisation. It therefore reflects concern over the pace of economic development and the technological changes associated with this, particularly in terms of the technologies of mass-production.

One of the significant aspects of this ideology is its rejection of the *anthropocentric* attitude adopted by other ideological positions that see the planet (simply) as a resource for humankind. Ecologism adopts an *ecocentric* view of the world, seeing humankind as but one of a range of species on the Earth using its resources, albeit in a much more aggressive fashion than any other living organism. There are weak and strong versions of this ideology, represented as light or dark Green depending on the position. The 'lighter' proponents suggest that by appealing to self-interest and common sense, the damage to the planet can be minimised. The 'darker' side suggest that nothing short of a fundamental re-ordering of political priorities, where the needs of the ecosystem have paramountcy over the needs of individuals will do to ensure that the planet survives.

Religious fundamentalism

Many ideological positions are grounded in a number of different religious creeds. Protestantism, for example, and its views on self-help and individual responsibility found expression in classical liberalism, whereas the notion of ethical socialism can be seen to express views embedded in both Christianity and Islam. However, *religious fundamentalism* has a different emphasis in that all other things, including politics and personal and social experiences are to be subsumed within the particular religious doctrine being espoused. Thus, social and political life is to be organised around essential religious principles.

There are contrasting and contested views around where such ideologies come from. One view holds that fundamentalism is essentially a reaction to increasing secularisation, symptomatic of the need to find new ways to cope with the changes brought on by modern living. In this regard, it is seen as being aberrant. The second would hold that such fundamentalism is in fact normative, a consequence of the failure of secularisation and therefore of major and enduring significance, and therefore, not an aberration.

There are many forms of fundamentalism across the world; despite what the media hype may lead us to believe, it is not all Islamic. Fundamentalism can arise from within all religious creeds including Christianity (especially in the US), Hinduism and Judaism and each in their own way have shown themselves to be capable of behaviours to support their views which would generate concern.

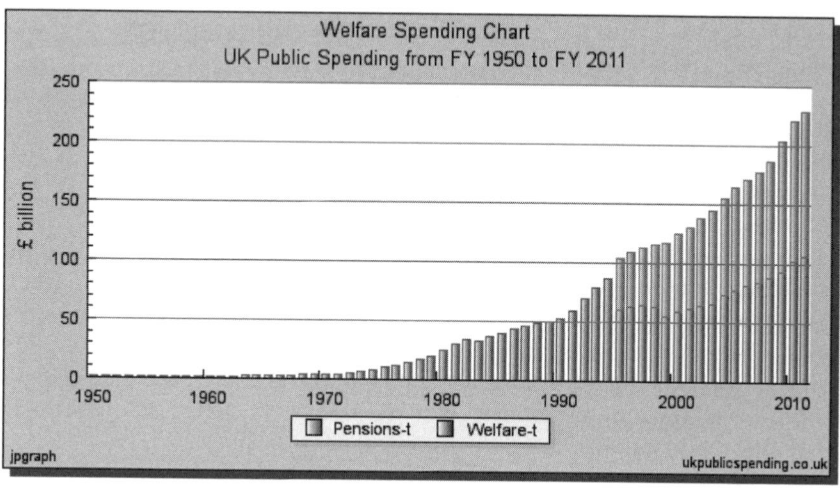

Figure 3.3 Welfare spending 1950–2011

Source: Reproduced with kind permission of Christopher Chantrill (www.ukspending.co.uk).

The end of ideology, the end of history or the beginning of something else?

There has been a lot of debate about whether the stock of political ideologies has run its course. Bell (1960) argued that ethical and ideological questions had become irrelevant because most Western powers competed for power simply on the basis that under capitalism, they were able to offer higher levels of economic growth and material wealth, thus eclipsing debates about ideology by reference to self-interest and comfort. Alternatively, this has been interpreted as not so much about the end of ideology as the emergence of a (lengthy) period of (welfare-based) consensus where ideological debate diminished. Fukuyama (1989) on the other hand argues that there is not so much a dying off of ideology but that we are beginning to experience the emergence of a *meta-ideology* in the form of *liberal democracy*, arguably the form to which most (Western) powers appear to have gravitated. Other writers, notably Giddens (1994), argue that conventional ideologies are becoming less and less relevant because as we move away from modernisation and into a period of *post-modernity* characterised by globalisation, increasing fragmentation, consumerism and individualism, different ideological positions begin to lose their relevance as we are all enveloped into a meta-ideology which supports those features referred to. We must therefore rethink our notions of ideology (Heywood 2002: 41–66).

The Modernity Debate

In many debates in the social sciences today we see references to 'modernity', 'anti-modernity' and 'post-modernity'. What do these mean and what is their relevance to social policy and professional practice?

Essentially, a modern society is one that has utilised its stock of human knowledge to best effect in informing how best to manage society. By applying rationally based scientific evidence, drawing on past experiences (good and bad) and by systematically applying all of this to the good of society *now* is regarded as the epitome of a modern society, hence *modernity*. The Beveridge welfare state, with its focus on the centralised control of collective resources applied rationally through specially- and specifically-created institutional models (for example the National Health Service), with the state (the government and its agents) taking the lead role in administering these *social* services, thereby taking the burden of providing for oneself and one's family in times of hardship, is perhaps the most obvious example of *modernity* in relation to welfare.

In contrast, *anti-modernity* (or *traditionalism*) sees such *modern* approaches as being unnatural and argues that the essence of a welfare state lies not in centralised and collective provision by a (faceless) state but in *human relationships*. The anti-modernist view would hold that individuals are quite capable and willing to take responsibility for their own welfare, and for that of their family and others. This view emphasises characteristically human and individual virtues like self-reliance, charity and public spiritedness, and argues that these are sufficient to provide the motivation for an effective welfare system that is underpinned by the presence of welfare services that individuals can obtain through the market as and when they require them. They see a centralised state apparatus as undermining self-reliance (the so-called 'nanny state') and promoting *passivity* and *dependence*. The anti-modernists would claim that forms of social living in the past have been proven to be effective and would cite the functionalist role of the (patriarchal) family as the core of an effective social system (Parsons and Bales 1956; Parsons 1952), and the community and charitable organisations and their efforts in the past as evidence that such arrangements work.

The *post-modernist* position would suggest that neither *modernism* nor *traditionalism* is nowadays sufficient to provide a coherent account of how welfare should be organised and delivered. They point to the apparent failures of modernism, particularly in the form of the Beveridge welfare state, citing continued and in some cases increased levels of inequality and unmanageable bureaucratic systems failing to deliver within reasonable expenditure levels. Welfare spending has continued to increase year on year (see Figure 3.3) and it is still to be seen whether recent and future welfare reforms will impact upon this trend (Brewer 2007; Gregg 2008). Postmodernism would therefore propose a completely new and different approach to welfare, although the descriptions of what this might look like are far from clear. Nonetheless, one of the main features is the rejection of centralised planning and control which is seen as 'clumsy and divisive' (Rodger 2000: 30), perpetuating unhelpful distinctions based around the old Poor Law notions of 'deserving' and 'undeserving'. Leonard (1997) suggests that postmodern welfare should be based on community participation and definitions of what constitutes welfare predicated on the views of those likely to require it and to consider *how* it might be delivered within culturally diverse societies. Rojek, Peacock and Collins (1988), in their postmodern critique of social work practice, emphasise the importance of understanding constructs like 'welfare' and 'social work' from the perspective of the user: welfare services define the nature of the relationship between people and therefore construct particular identities for them which in turn generate certain *prescribed* expectations which available services then respond to, subject to their own terms and conditions. In this way, welfare does not in fact respond to real need; rather, it responds to a preconceived notion of what needs the state or the welfare provider allows you to have. Postmodernism is described by Pinch (1997) as 'A broad trend in social thinking that rejects the idea that there is one superior way of understanding the world' (p. 146).

How many ways to welfare: From a welfare state to a welfare society?

The welfare system within the UK can be seen to have had three relatively distinct phases. The 'first way' was that personified by the establishment of the Beveridge welfare state based upon post-war consensus (see Chapter 2). Here, what are generally regarded as the fundamental principles of the 'welfare state', social insurance for all with a 'safety net' in place for everyone in case of hardship, were generated and implemented through the creation of an institutional model of welfare. The 'second way' is generally regarded to have begun in 1979 when Thatcher's neo-liberal, market-oriented policies moved away from the social insurance principle and focused instead on the primacy of the individual and the regulatory effects of the free market in the context of the controlling forces of supply and demand. Any welfare provision was residual and minimalistic. The ascension to power of New Labour in 1997 heralded what became known as the 'third way', typified by 'active' and conditional welfare policies that aim to reverse the perceived trend for passivity and (welfare) dependency by offering citizens 'incentives' to return to the labour market, thereby enjoying full and active citizenship. In terms of the newly elected Conservative/Liberal Democrat coalition government, it is as yet too early to discern what their particular approach to this issue will be although it is likely that the same themes will occupy them.

These differing 'ways towards welfare' are seen by some as representing a shift *away* from a welfare *state* towards a welfare *society*. Rodger (2000) cites Robertson (1998) who, following Schottland (1967), refers to a welfare state as being a *legal state* in which a citizen is entitled to (welfare and other) goods and services *as of right*, guaranteed by statutory rights. A welfare *society* on the other hand is 'a social system in which welfare assumptions are an organic part of everyday life' (in Rodger 2000: 8). What this means is that where there is centralised control of collective resources, the role of the state is one of an administrator that not only 'dispenses' welfare, but regulates it too by reference to its own mandates in the form of statutes, designed to delineate the parameters of the extent of its obligations to its citizens. In some respects it is a circular process with ideological assumptions regarding welfare being prescribed and proscribed by legalities. A welfare *society* is, according to Robson '… what people do, feel and think about matters which bear on the general welfare', and that 'unless people generally reflect the policies and assumptions of the welfare state in their attitudes and actions, it is impossible to fulfil the objectives of the welfare state' (in Rodger 2000: 9). This latter point bears heavily upon some of the current concerns about how welfare is delivered as well as *to whom* it tends to be delivered. There is an increasing sense that many people feel quite ambivalent about a system for which everyone pays through their taxes, but one which seems to support a significant minority of people *who do not contribute* through their taxes, because they are not in the labour market. New Labour themes of 'activity' and welfare conditionality (Dwyer 2008) sought to address these concerns whilst also serving to marginalise even further some of the most vulnerable people in our society, illustrated by the concerns around some aspects of New Labour's welfare reforms, for example the review of the criteria for incapacity benefits (Powell 2008) so the balance has to be correctly struck and this is one area which the new Conservative/Liberal Democrat coalition government has begun to focus upon.

In essence, the future of welfare appears to depend upon the integration of principles of social justice, social insurance and social cohesion propounded and institutionalised by the Beveridge welfare state in a form of delivery that utilises social conscience and notions of community spirit and 'civil society' in a socio-political context that has to embrace many changes, including devolution (Stewart 2004) and globalisation. However, what does appear to be very clear is that some form of organising principles for welfare need to be found as the need for welfare, be it in the form of a state or a society, is likely to continue to exist, as states of welfare, as well as welfare states it seems (Brooks and Manza 2006; Greve 2008), do persist.

Chapter summary

This chapter has considered the influence of ideas, ideologies, on the development and implementation of social policy. We have considered a range of differing ideologies and looked at some of their main features. We have also taken a critical look at some emerging debates that appear to question the validity of specific ideological positions in terms of forming and framing welfare and which consider whether we are witnessing a radical shift in conceptions of society and, therefore, on how welfare ought to be developed and delivered in the future.

References

Bell, D. (1960), *The End of Ideology* (Glencoe, IL: Free Press).

Benner, M. (2003), 'The Scandinavian Challenge: The Future of Advanced Welfare States in the Knowledge Economy', *Acta Sociologica* 46(2): 132–49.

Brewer, M. (2007), *Welfare Reform in the UK: 1997–2007* (London: Institute for Fiscal Studies).

Brooks, C. and Manza, J. (2006), 'Why do Welfare States Persist?', *The Journal of Politics* 68: 816–27.

Clinton, H.R. and Obama, B. (2006), 'Making Patient Safety the Centrepiece of Medical Liability Reform', *New England Journal of Medicine* 354(21): 2205–8.

Delanty, G. and Kumar, K. (2006), *The Sage Handbook of Nations and Nationalism* (London: Sage).

Dench, G. (ed.) (2006), *The Rise and Rise of Meritocracy* (London: Wiley Blackwell).

Dwyer, P. (2008), 'The Conditional Welfare State', in M. Powell (ed.), *Modernising the Welfare State: The Blair Legacy* (Bristol: Policy Press): 199–218.

Esping-Andersen, G. (1990), *The Three Worlds of Welfare Capitalism* (Cambridge: Polity Press).

Fukuyama, F. (1989), 'The End of History', *National Interest,* Summer.

George, V. and Wilding, P. (1994), *Welfare and Ideology* (London: Harvester Wheatsheaf).

Giddens, A. (1994), *Beyond Left and Right: The Future of Radical Politics* (Cambridge: Polity Press).

Gregg, P. (2008), 'UK Welfare Reform 1996 to 2008 and Beyond: A Personalised and Responsive Welfare System?', Working Paper 08/196: Centre for Market and Public Organisation, University of Bristol.

Greve, B. (2007), 'What Characterise the Nordic Welfare State Model', *Journal of Social Sciences* 3(2): 43–51.

— (2008), 'What is Welfare?', *Central European Journal of Social Policy* 2(1): 50–73.

Harris, J. (2003), *The Social Work Business* (London: Routledge).

Hayek, F.A. (1960/2006), *The Constitution of Liberty* (London: Routledge).

Heywood, A. (2002), *Politics* (2nd edn) (Basingstoke: Palgrave Macmillan).

— (2003), *Political Ideologies: An Introduction* (3rd edn) (Basingstoke: Palgrave Macmillan).

— (2007), *Political Ideologies: An Introduction* (4th edn) (Basingstoke: Palgrave Macmillan).

Hobsbawm, E.J. (1992), *Nations and Nationalism since 1780: Programme, Myth, Reality* (2nd edn) (Cambridge: Cambridge University Press).

Kenny, M. (2009), 'Taking the Temperature of the UK's Political Elite', *Parliamentary Affairs* 62(1): 149–61.

Leonard, P. (1997), *Postmodern Welfare: Reconstructing an Emancipatory Project* (London: Sage).

Marmor, T., Oberlander, J. and White, J. (2009), 'The Obama Administration's Options for Health Care Cost Control: Hope versus Reality', *Annals of Internal Medicine* 150(7): 485–9.

Palier, B. and Martin, C. (eds) (2008), *Reforming the Bismarckian Welfare Systems* (Oxford: Blackwell).

Parsons, T. (1952), *The Social System* (London: Tavistock).

Parsons, T. and Bales, R.F. (1956), *Family Socialization and Interaction Process* (London: Routledge and Kegan Paul).

Pinch, S. (1997), *Worlds of Welfare: Understanding the Changing Geographies of Social Welfare* (London: Routledge).

Powell, M. (ed.) (2008), *Modernising the Welfare State: The Blair Legacy* (Bristol: Policy Press).

Robertson, J. (1988), 'Welfare State and Welfare Society', *Social Policy and Administration* 22(3): 222–34.

Rodger, J.J. (2000), *From a Welfare State to a Welfare Society: The Changing Context of Social Policy in a Postmodern Era* (Basingstoke: Palgrave Macmillan).

Rojek, C., Peacock, G. and Collins, S. (1988), *Social Work and Received Ideas* (London: Routledge).

Rousseau, J.-J. (1762/1998), *The Social Contact or Principles of Political Right* (Hertfordshire: Wordsworth Classics of World Literature).

Schottland, C. (1967), *The Welfare State* (New York, NY: Harper).

Stewart, J. (2004), *Taking Stock: Scottish Social Welfare after Devolution* (Bristol: Policy Press).

Tönnies, F. (1887/2001), *Gemeinschaft Und Gesellschaft* [*Community and Civil Society*] (New York, NY: Cambridge University Press).

Wilkinson, R. and Pickett, K. (2010), *The Spirit Level: Why Equality is Better for Everyone* (London: Penguin).

Young, M. (1970), *The Rise of the Meritocracy* (Harmondsworth: Penguin).

Further reading

Heywood, A. (2007), *Political Ideologies* (4th edn) (Basingstoke: Palgrave Macmillan). This text provides a thorough grounding in political ideologies and is very accessible.

Rodger, J.J. (2000), *From a Welfare State to a Welfare Society: The Changing Context of Social Policy in a Postmodern Era* (Basingstoke: Palgrave Macmillan). This book offers an excellent account of some of the critical debates in policy studies concerning the future of welfare. Very well written and very accessible indeed.

4 People, policy and practice

Steve J. Hothersall

Introduction

This chapter will introduce to you a fundamental issue within policy studies: *people*, and their relationship with and to policy. People are what social policies are all about, or at least they should be. In many books on social policy there is a lot of general discussion about the policies themselves: the general shape they take, what they aim to achieve (often referred to in terms relating to increases in this or reductions in that) and lots of other details about their structure and content, but there is often little reference to fundamental issues regarding *basic human need*, and how this relates to social policy initiatives. We feel that an understanding of the intrinsic relationship between people's needs and policy is essential in order to appreciate not only the relevance of policy to people's lives but importantly for you, the importance of policy in relation to your *professional practice*. We also need to think about the kinds of effects (both good and bad) that policies may have upon all of us, both in terms of specific policy initiatives but also in terms of the (usually unintended) *interaction* between different policies and policy areas.

It is, however, important to bear in mind that the profusion of policy initiatives should not be seen to represent a diminution of the central importance of *relationships* in terms of getting things done. We can try to legislate for everything (and some would argue that that is exactly what government(s) are trying to do) and *prescribe* what should be done, how, in any given circumstance. If we see policy as the master and interpersonal relationships and our intellect as the servants, then such a technical-rational approach to managing social life will strip away the importance of using *yourself*. Law and policy can be, and at times are, (rightly) prescriptive, but much of it is open to interpretation within certain parameters, thus allowing for the interjection of interpersonal and people skills (Thompson 2009) and the use of judgement and discretion in terms of implementation (Lipsky 1980). Policy aims both to determine and to guide practice within certain parameters; but your actions as an individual can be the most important factor between something being done well and with passion, or something being done dispassionately with no regard for feelings. Clearly, this view does not imply that we should only regard policy if it suits us; on the contrary, policy is there for a purpose and has to be acknowledged. However, giving effect to the requirements of policy is essentially about interpretation, understanding and the effective *use of self*. We shall consider these aspects as we progress because if we lose sight of the importance of *people* in our study of policy, we lose sight of the *social* in social policy.

People and policy

It should now be clear to you that the fundamental purpose of social policy is to provide a *coherent, consistent and collective response to a range of differing social phenomena*. By definition, the term *social* refers to people individually and collectively, and here we shall consider why social policies are an essential part of our lives; we need them. Some will suggest that social policy is no more than a form of *social engineering*, and in reality it is, but such engineering is an essential element contributing (in large measure) to the provision of a relatively stable, ordered and, importantly, *secure* social life for most, if not all of us.

A further point to consider is that when we talk of *social* policy, we should not forget about the *social effects* of other types of policy that do not readily spring to mind as being social. For example, *defence policy* would not routinely be included in a text on social policy and would not usually occupy a practitioner's thoughts. However, in relation to the broad study of social policy, we must remember that all policies, even defence policies, have a social element to them and can and do impinge, to a greater or lesser extent, upon people. In times of war, defence policy will have huge effects on areas of people's lives normally the province of social policy proper. For example, during the Second World War, defence policy dictated that a generalised 'blackout' be enforced during the hours of darkness in all cities and towns (see Chapter 2) where all windows had to be covered and lights were not to be used unless essential. This had a huge impact upon the way people led their lives, so what was essentially a policy focused upon the defence of the country became, *de facto*, a social policy. Similarly, agricultural policy may seem a long way from social policies that focus upon children or the elderly, but restrictions on what farmers might grow, how much of it and controls regarding to whom they might sell it and for how much can result in food prices increasing with the effect that low-income or vulnerable groups of people will be particularly affected. Subsequently, changes in consumer behaviour because of increased food prices may have an effect upon health because people buy cheaper foods that contain more saturated fat. This may lead to additional demands upon health care.

The issue here, and central to our thinking about a coherent and consistent *theoretical approach* to policymaking, analysis and implementation, is the *aggregate effects* of other policy areas and individual policies within them. One of the failings of current policymaking and analysis is the lack of awareness of such aggregate effects, and it would appear that little time is spent mapping out the consequences, in particular the *unintended* consequences, of policy and particularly of policy which may appear, superficially at least, to be remote from the social sphere. Having said that, if you refer to earlier comments regarding changes in policy regarding people who are homeless and the possible effects this may have on the allocation of social housing to other service-user groups, sometimes the distance between policy areas is not all that great, so we do need to be aware of how small changes in one area can cause major issues in another, the so-called 'butterfly effect' as demonstrated in chaos theory and the like.

Appreciative of these (social) facts, but aware also that the expectation here is not for practitioners to be mindful of every aspect of policy in the world (as that would be impossible and totally unrealistic) we shall now discuss the intricate relationship between people and policy, using the fundamental theme of *need* to guide us. In the process we shall try to develop a *theory of social need and social policy*, and establish some fundamental principles regarding the interface between people and policy to guide us in both our thinking and our practice.

Conceptualising people and what they need

Texts on social policy tend to focus on just that: policy, without really offering what we would see as a viable context to facilitate an understanding of what policy is actually all about. In relation to social policy, this is *human need*, and more specifically, *basic* human need.

All of us, irrespective of where we live and the shape and form of the society within which we live have the same *basic* needs. Since time began, people have always needed water, food, some form of clothing to protect them from the elements, some form of shelter, and they have also needed to ensure that they continue the species by reproduction. Race, religion and politics do not change these in their essential forms, although their superficial shape may differ (for example, in extremely hot climates, the need for water is more acute than it might be in a colder clime, where the type of shelter required may differ from that in the hotter climate in that it is expected to provide warmth and not just shelter from the sun), and how and whether they are provided, in what quantity and to what groups at any given time they may (or may not) be given. What is beyond question, however, is that these needs must be met and because we all share them, wherever we are, people decided (eventually, and particularly when they began living in *groups*), that it might be a good idea to manage these essential resources and attempt to address these essential needs *collectively*. Within most societies, although by no means all, collective action as a corollary of group living came to be seen as the most effective way of managing these resources and in order to do this as efficiently as possible and to minimise the likelihood of disagreements over who should have what, in what quantities and so on, sets of rules or *policies* were drawn up to which everyone was expected to comply.

Moving beyond these basic needs, we have next to consider what other sorts of needs we have as human beings and how these might be met, and by whom. The issue regarding the *type of need being addressed* is important in terms of thinking both about *how* it ought to be met and *by whom*. Basic needs, common to all are arguably best met by a common approach so that everyone gets enough to satisfy their needs. However, as the nature of the need becomes less relevant to survival, the question then begins to emerge as to whether the needs referred to are those which should be met for all by all, or whether we as individuals should have responsibility for meeting these ourselves without expecting some 'collective', usually in the form of governments, to do this for us, as is certainly the case in some countries. We touched upon some of these broad themes in Chapter 3, particularly in relation to whether current arrangements to address social need through a collective and centrally organised and institutionalised system (the welfare state) was the best way of doing this.

Theories and conceptions of need

In order to appreciate fully the role social policies play in society, we need to attend to differing conceptions of need and how differences in these may influence how they come to be addressed, and importantly whose responsibility it might be to do this. As we saw in Chapter 2, the way in which need has been addressed within society has changed over time. We saw earlier that following the Second World War, for example, the government decided that it should take the primary responsibility to meet a range of differing needs, including education, housing and health care, on a collective basis, effectively marginalising those systems previously charged with these roles and tasks, notably the family, the Church and charitable organisations (Fraser 2003). In the 1980s and early 1990s, this collective approach was felt to be too costly and too patriarchal, the state, through its 'collectivism', seen by some to be denying the individual their opportunity to do as much for themselves as possible. These arrangements are representative of differing views, or *ideologies* of welfare and Chapter 3 has already looked at these. Suffice to say that need is omnipresent, so how it is defined, addressed and paid for is very much a factor to occupy us. Below are three formulations of need that we can use to appreciate its complexities within society.

A hierarchy of human needs

One broad-based theory of human need developed by the American psychologist Abraham Maslow (1970) suggests that there are essentially five categories into which our needs can be grouped, subdivided into '*deficiency*' needs and '*being*' needs, which are seen as being ranked hierarchically, as in the 'famous' triangle (Figure 4.1).

Maslow's thinking was firmly located within the tradition of humanistic psychology that posits (somewhat optimistically perhaps) that the paramount internal drive is the motivation to achieve one's fullest potential. This ultimate goal was that of 'self actualization' and refers to the satisfaction of the need to understand, to give and to grow as a person. Hence, 'needs' in Maslow's scheme are sometimes referred to as 'motives' or 'motivators'.

Maslow said that each level of need must be sufficiently satisfied before we can 'progress' upwards to meet the needs on the next level. So, our need for oxygen, food and water, sleep, the elimination of waste and reproductive sex takes priority over other needs when these arise. Next we concern ourselves with ensuring that our 'safety' needs are attended to; being safe, feeling safe and ensuring others are safe, particularly our progeny. Thereafter, the other needs within each of the levels are attended to. However, we don't consciously think 'I need to meet all my physiological needs this morning then I can look at the others after lunch.' We simply 'get on with it' until a certain 'need' effectively tells us that it must be met. In relation to basic physiological needs, if you need sleep, this will override anything else you may want to do or be doing at any particular time. In relation to level two, the safety needs, these can be compromised if level one needs are not met. If you are in need of food (and here we must acknowledge that we are talking about a *real* need for food which many of us will not be familiar with – near starvation), we would engage in some fairly dangerous activities to satisfy it and compromise our safety needs in the process as the

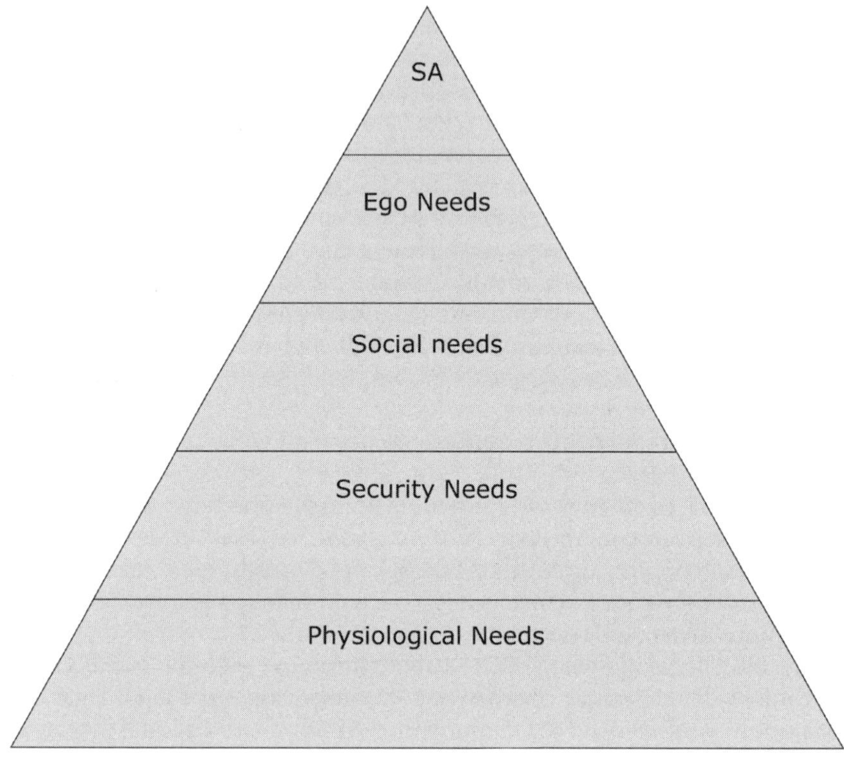

Figure 4.1 Maslow's Hierarchy of Human Needs

Note: SA = Self-actualisation.

need for food is paramount. You might however be in level five and enjoying reading your copy of Dostoyevsky's *Netochka Nezvanova* or listening to the *Arietta* of Beethoven's piano sonata opus 111, all other needs having been satisfied, when you feel the need to go to the toilet. Everything else stops whilst you attend to this. Similarly, whilst enjoying your book or your music, you receive a message that suggests your loved one is unwell; immediately, those needs around love and belongingness are activated and motivate certain goal-directed behaviours that continue until the need is satisfied; in this case when you have all the information regarding what is happening to your loved one. In all of these situations, you go straight from level five to level three or below in an instant and have to meet the needs which have arisen there before you can return to your previous activities.

In essence, Maslow's theory argues that each level of need must be met if we are to be able to function effectively and enjoy a 'rounded' existence. In reality, there are many people across the world that never progress beyond meeting those needs at level one. In the UK, there are many who do not go much beyond level two; these may be people you work with who may be homeless or otherwise alone. There are also those people who cannot attend to their basic needs themselves without assistance. Think of someone with motor neurone disease, for example; Professor Stephen Hawking, the Cambridge cosmologist has suffered from this degenerative condition for many, many years and whilst he spends his days thinking about the origins of the universe (clearly a level five activity), he is totally dependent upon others to meet all his other needs. If they did not attend to these routinely and regularly, he would be unable to focus upon other, such lofty matters.

In the field of social work, social care, nursing and other related disciplines, we encounter many individuals who are dependent upon others to meet their lower-level needs. For example, someone may not have enough income to allow them to provide sufficient food, warmth, shelter and so on for their family, so they may require state assistance in the form of welfare benefits to achieve this. A young child may be the victim of sexual abuse by an adult and therefore requires someone to help them meet their safety needs, and someone who has experienced the loss of a spouse in some way may need help and support in meeting their needs around love and belongingness. It may be that they all have friends and/or family who can help them, or they may not. If they do not, the question then becomes one of *who* should do this and *how*, and *for how long*? Should the state provide assistance and services? If so, what form should these take? Who should pay for it? Is it a priority for the social work/social services department *relative to their other operational priorities*? The issue here is what kinds of needs are to be met by whom under what circumstances. The writings of Bradshaw (1972) offer a framework for conceptualising need in a broad-based welfare context and help us to understand how a phenomenon (that of being in need) comes to be *socially determined* by reference to norms, values, expectations and, importantly, *resources*.

A taxonomy of social need

In his seminal paper, Bradshaw (1972) proposed that when human need manifests itself, it is defined in certain ways depending upon a number of factors. He does not discuss whether there are 'universal' needs or whether some needs are more important than others *per se*; rather, he suggests that the ways in which need *as a concept* is dealt with varies according to who is *experiencing* it and who is *defining* it. If you refer back to the discussion in Chapter 3 on postmodernism and the views of Rojek, Peacock and Collins (1998), you will see parallels with the ideas presented here. Implicit here of course are *subjective* determinations of what need *is*, *who* has a need and *how* it should be responded to, which ultimately raises the issue of how needs are to be prioritised.

In his opening to the paper, Bradshaw states:

> The concept of social need is inherent in the idea of social service. The history of the social services is the story of the recognition of social needs and the organisation of society to meet them. (1972: 640)

Bradshaw notes that the genesis of social services (in the broad sense) represents one manifestation of a collective means of responding to human need. The issue Bradshaw tackled was how to understand how needs manifest themselves within society and how, on the basis of this, we ought (or ought not) to attend to them. There are obviously many competing needs to be considered simply because, as T.H. Marshall astutely observed, '(W)elfare ... is a compound of material means and immaterial ends' (in Timms and Watson 1976: 51–2), and as such, this issue is very much a live one for policy makers today, particularly in times of economic recession. Bradshaw's taxonomy presents four constructions or *classifications* of need that have implications for policy makers, service providers and, ultimately, service users.

> *Normative need*: This is what the professional or other person with expertise in an area or subject defines as need in any given situation. This definition would usually be supported by reference to some generally agreed upon standard regarding the need in question. For example, you might be said to be depressed when you reach a particular score on the Beck Depression Inventory (Beck et al. 1961) or you might be said to be in need of nourishment when your weight and other indicators register below a set (or *normative*) standard. Nowadays, most social work and social services departments utilize differing forms of 'eligibility criteria' to determine whose needs are the greatest based on the outcomes of an assessment and a point-scoring system, usually mapped against some normative measure similar to those referred to above. For example, if you are 90 years old, live alone, have limited mobility and have no family or other social support, you are more likely to be seen as having a greater need for assistance than a 90-year-old person living alone with no mobility issues who has family living in the same street who pop in and see them two or three times a day, seven days per week.

Such classifications of need are open to claims of paternalism, and the standards to which people refer (and perhaps *defer*) in order to make a judgement about the level of need may conflict with other normative measures used by service providers, and these measures are also likely to change over time. Eligibility criteria are regularly reviewed (although usually more in the context of *resource* management than *need* management) and may appear to the recipient to be either more or less generous or facilitative depending on whether the person obtains what they think they need or not. This leads us to the next classification, that of *felt need*.

> *Felt need*: In this classification, need is equated with *want*. It is argued that this is usually inadequate as a 'true' measure of need because of the element of subjectivity inherent within it. Some may say 'Yes, I need it' whereas others may say they don't (even though they do) because this could signal for them a loss of independence. Doyal and Gough (1991) consider the issue of *need* versus *want* and we look at this later.
>
> *Expressed need*: This is *felt need* turned into action. Here, unmet need is determined to exist by reference to those who are requesting the service. The greater the number of requests for a certain thing, the more likely it is that this particular need will be seen as more of a priority than those needs not articulated. In this way, if no one is asking for a particular thing, then no one is in need of it. This raises issues concerning those people who, by themselves, are *unable* to express felt need, for example someone with a profound learning difficulty, so as an accurate measure of need, *expressed need* is perhaps unreliable.
>
> *Comparative need*: Here, the measure of need is taken by reference to the characteristics of a particular group *who are in receipt of a service* (that is, they have an identified need), and is then applied to other groups with similar characteristics *who are not in receipt of a service.* This latter group is then said to be in need, based on this comparison. Such determinations are used to compare not only individuals, but also areas of need across communities and society in general. Need determined by reference to this measure is essentially the gap between what people receive in one place as opposed to similar people in another area. However, as an accurate measure of need it too can be flawed, as the level of analysis may apply only to a few individuals there, even though the larger group may *appear* to be in need.

A theory of universal human need

Doyal and Gough (1984; 1991) in their formulations concerning need first of all contend that there has to be agreement on what constitutes *universal, basic human needs*. Once this exists, we can then move on to think about how best to meet them. They propose that universal, basic human needs (or *primary needs*) are *those that must be achieved (or met) if an individual is to achieve any other goal*. These relate to *survival* and the maintenance of adequate levels of *health* and the ability to exercise *autonomy* and to *learn*. These can only be met they argue, if four *social* pre-conditions exist, namely *production, reproduction, culture/communication* and *political authority*.

This theory is rather convoluted in places but in essence it maintains that we all need certain things like water, food and shelter that are essential to basic survival and which allow us to maintain an adequacy of health. What is meant by 'adequacy' refers to that level of health necessary for us to be able to function towards meeting our other basic and ultimately higher needs. If we were so unwell that we could not do anything for ourselves, or were disabled to such an extent that we were dependent on others, then we would be unable to obtain food or water and so on and would then be unable to address other needs which could result, ultimately, in our death.

In relation to the social pre-conditions, *production* refers to the requirement of society to produce sufficient goods (water, food and so on) for all of us to use; *reproduction* is largely self-explanatory whereas *culture/communication* refers to the necessity for modes of being and a shared language or other means of communication to allow for the expression of need and the presence of culturally sanctioned means of addressing these. *Political authority* refers to the capacity of a society to endorse its means of production and distribution, with due reference to appropriate sanctions and law enforcement where the activities of others have the capacity to compromise the well being of others.

Following on from their rather absolutist position on defining universal basic needs, Doyal and Gough then use the notion of 'historical progress' effectively to denote the role of time, place and space in relation to discussions about how needs change over time, thereby acknowledging their *relative nature* in terms of form. What Doyal and Gough then discuss, at some length, are the various issues raised by the *relative* nature of need in terms of *how much* of a thing an individual requires, along with issues around the *subjective* presentation of need in the guise of 'wants'.

Doyal and Gough argue that there are certain needs that are common to *everyone*, irrespective of who they are and where they live, although we should note that they do not (and I would say, cannot) specify *how much* or the *particular form* such a requirement should take, as this must be culturally and historically *specific* and therefore *relative*. It is important to think about this because there is a danger of seeing the argument for universal human needs as one based around a certain degree of *absolutism*. For example, you may be familiar with the work of Townsend (1954; 1979) in relation to poverty and his notions of *absolute* and *relative* poverty. The former categorisation was an attempt to identify and fix a rock-bottom level of goods and services which all of us required in order to be able to function; a drop below this would be incompatible with continued well-being (and possibly life). Current social security levels ('subsistence') are based on this thinking, as are eligibility criteria for access to many services. However, what may have been regarded as absolute a number of years ago will have changed. For example, central heating is today generally regarded as a 'basic' feature of a home, as is an inside toilet. Some would argue strongly that another 'basic' requirement is a mobile phone. We can argue about *what* and *how much of it* is felt to be essential, but ultimately, we *cannot* fix an absolute level of anything, as this will vary from individual to individual (even at minute levels). However, what we *can* say is that there are certain things that we *all* need, but that their particular form, structure, quality and quantity would of necessity be individually, geographically, culturally (socially) and historically *relative* and therefore *subjective* in relation to these conditions. Thus, arguments around absolute and universal *levels* of need are difficult to sustain because there will always be a degree of subjectivism at play in the sense that these represent the requirements of geography, culture and historical time, although these subjective *elements* should be differentiated from those subjective *demands* which present as *wants*, as a 'want' (as opposed to a 'need') is something which would be regarded as exceeding the basic amount, even though, by definition, we cannot say for certain what that basic, rock-bottom requirement is in terms of how much of it is required.

A useful element of this approach to thinking about need is the way in which needs are seen as functioning in differing ways, depending on a range of other factors. Doyal and Gough refer to needs as *goals*, needs as *wants* and needs as *strategies*.

- *Needs as goals*: the 'need' motivates particular, goal-oriented behaviours (or 'drives' at the basic physiological level) that only cease once the need has been satisfied (or the drive reduced). This suggests that such needs are generalisable to everyone because they are seen as the *necessary pre-requisites* for the accomplishment of other things. Water would be a prime example, as without this we would at best be severely hampered in our efforts to do anything, and at worst, and ultimately, we would perish.
- *Needs as wants*: this implies a different conception of a need and brings in the issue of *preferences*. These are not necessarily generalisable to everyone as they involve a personally subjective determination as to their importance *to that individual* (or group of individuals). For example, you might feel that you need a new plasma TV, but this type of need does not fall within the category of being a necessary

pre-requisite for the meeting of other, essential needs. It is therefore a 'want', which may in itself add value to your life, in your opinion, but your lack of a plasma screen TV would fail the 'needs test' on a number of grounds, not the least of which would be the fact that it does not accord with what Doyal and Gough, citing Nevitt (1977) see as the essence of social needs, which are:

> ... demands which have been defined by society as sufficiently important to qualify for social recognition as goods or services which should be met by government intervention. (Nevitt 1977: 115 in Doyal and Gough 1991: 10)

Interestingly, in this technologically advanced age, broadband internet access appears recently to have acquired that status to which Nevitt refers, as the former Scottish Executive appears committed to ensuring that everyone in Scotland has access to this service (Scottish Executive 2002), and the Scottish Government is introducing policy to this effect. This is an example of Bradshaw's notion of comparative need and is another illustration of how notions of need and their relevance to society change over time.

- *Needs as strategies*: this would refer to the means we might adopt in order to meet other needs (goals or wants). You might for example say 'I need to see a doctor' in order that you can then meet other needs like getting rid of your headache so that you can go back to work, and so on. The need for assistance organises your behaviour in particular ways, much like the innate ability we have to *attach* to other human beings in such a way as to ensure our survival across the lifespan (Cassidy and Shaver 2008).

These three formulations on need have within them a number of common themes and we shall summarise these and consider a number of other features that we shall apply in the context of social policy and policy development to emerge with a *theory of human need and policy*.

Integrating need and policy

From the above discussion we can see that it is the issue of how to meet human need, or certain aspects of it, that lies at the heart of social policy. It is, as we have already said, the means by which society aims to address particular aspects of need for certain or for all people, depending on what is regarded at any given time as being *essential* to the capacity to survive (at its most basic) and to facilitate the pursuit of other, 'higher' goals once those appertaining to basic survival have been met. Implicit within this statement, if it is accepted, is the assumption that the state (as the government, and the collective body overseeing policy development and implementation) accepts responsibility only for meeting *some* of our needs, namely the basic or primary ones. What about the 'higher-order' needs? Is the availability of education until the age of 18 for everyone an example of collective action towards meeting higher-order needs? At what point on Maslow's hierarchy should collective action stop and everyone then become individually responsible for their own needs, or should individuals be wholly responsible for meeting their own needs and those of their family? This could be done by purchasing services from institutional providers if it was felt that the latter option was the most preferred (refer to Chapter 3 to remind yourself of these issues). The answer to this appears to lie in the conception we have within society as to what is essential for life, how these necessities are to be provided, by whom, and to whose cost, but beyond this in our particular society, what is essential for a reasonable *quality* of life?

Towards a theory of socially relevant policy

> Social policies are guiding principles for ways of life, motivated by basic and perceived human needs. They were derived by people from the structures, dynamics and values of their ways of life and they serve to maintain or change these ways. Social policies tend to, but need not, be codified in formal legal instruments. All extant social policies of a given society at a given time constitute an interrelated, yet not necessarily internally consistent, *system* of social policies. (Gil 1992: 24: emphasis added)

A conceptual approach to policy making, implementation and evaluation must take account of the inherent nature of the human condition. The satisfaction of innate basic human needs will always be a priority, whether perceptions concerning what these are alters; we may discuss and debate their shape and form, but the needs themselves, however we choose to describe them, will always demand satisfaction. In a similar way, we must recognise that society itself *constructs* specific forms of need by way of increasing expectations that arise on the basis of experience. Policy has a role to play in ensuring that these are not elevated, in terms of policy responses, to a status beyond that demanded and required of basic needs. Within societies where basic needs are ignored or relegated to a secondary status, consciously or not, responses to alternative, socially constructed 'needs' can take priority. For example, if the basic requirements for access to adequate food or housing were to be effectively ignored whilst policies aimed at wealth creation were the priority in the form of tax breaks, then *wealth* as a specific social construct would be elevated to a status above that of basic needs. Arguably, all social policy should, as a minimum, ensure that it addresses all areas of basic needs before it then focuses on other areas.

Perhaps differing political parties should agree upon the basic social policy infrastructure for society and leave this *in situ*. This would require a commitment to overcoming the impact of differing political ideologies where these are likely to generate schisms in relation to fundamental issues. Subsequent policy development, irrespective of ideological concerns, should not encroach upon agreed minimums, as happened with the advent of the Thatcher regime in the 1980s; this was the formal end of the 'post-war consensus' as we saw in Chapters 2 and 3. Rather, energy should be invested in developing a more systematic and systemic approach to policy, working on the relationships between differing policy domains, with the explicit goal of achieving *increased integration* of all areas, which should present itself as a 'functional map' of the social condition. This we might think of as idealistic, but the aim would be to increase the level of integration between areas such as economics, defence and so on in order that these can be tested in terms of their impact upon society, even in those ways that may in reality be minimal. To assume a minimal impact is not the same as trying to predict it and work with potential consequences. Current policy development waits until there has been an effect, usually negative, and then attempts to ameliorate this by developing a policy response; it is *reactive* where it should aim to be *proactive*.

If we accept that policy should be systemic in its scope *and* systematic in its approach and application, there should be no reason to keep artificial divisions alive between policy domains, as all policies have social effects and societies have long recognised the need to compromise for the greater good, certainly where being able to meet basic needs more effectively in the longer term is a clear possibility. Policy as a *strategy* therefore needs to have a broader time frame around it rather than one based on political expediency and funnelled into four-or-five-year time frames as dictated by the current cycle of general elections. Thus, energy devoted to economic growth through policy development in relation to agriculture for example (natural resources) should be seen as a *socially relevant* policy, rather than as an agricultural or non-social policy. Whilst this might appear to represent an exercise in semantics, if we are to see policy as systematic in its approach, and *systemic* in its aims, then there would be less concern about and divisiveness over resource allocation for policy development across different spheres. So long as those policies designed to address basic need are *in situ*, there is no reason why resources could not be diverted and directed at other areas for as long as is required. The problem is often that governments *take resources back* from already established policy areas where the priority is seen to be elsewhere. The net effects of this are *cutbacks,* and where cutbacks erode the basic policy fabric of a society, and by this I mean those policies designed to address basic needs, tensions increase and, as Gil (1992) argues, this equates with a form of 'structural violence', comprising essentially of repressive policy regimes designed often to benefit one group at the expense of another, usually 'weaker' group.

This raises the issue of *social justice* or fairness within society and the importance of values. There are differing organising principles one can apply to a society, and one of these is social justice or social *equality*. The converse would be a society based upon social *inequality*. In our society, we have a mix of these things but generally the view is of an *unequal* society (Wilkinson and Pickett 2010) that values wealth and individualism above that of shared concern for others and a shared approach to social life. However, a shared and collective approach in the form of the Beveridge welfare state appears to have been found wanting. Its stated aims of, amongst other things, promoting the social insurance principle and therefore offsetting the worst effects of capitalism appear to be failing. Perhaps collectivism *via the state* is not the best model to pursue, although a *society (and even a global) concern for the welfare of everyone has to remain a priority*.

Another fundamental issue to be considered in relation to the development of a coherent theory relating to human need and *socially relevant policy* is that of *rights*. It was Rawls (1971) who offered a significant account of the issue of rights in the context of the relationship between a state and its citizens. He argued that all citizens have a *right* to what he referred to as 'basic goods and services', those things that in essence equate with basic needs. The issue of having a *right* to these things is however rather problematic. None of us have an inalienable right to anything *unless that right is recognised and given practical effect by the accepted laws of that society*. There exists the United Nations Declaration on Human Rights which makes a number of statements (in the form of 'Articles') regarding what every one of us has a *right to* (expressed in either positive form – a right to receive something, or in negative form – a right *not* to receive or be forced to accept something, for example torture), but these rights are only enforceable if the nation-state concerned accepts them into their constitution. Since New Labour came to power in 1997 there has been an increasing trend for pre-existing rights-based policy measures to be reframed as being *conditional* on certain behaviours (Dwyer 2008). This conditionality was designed to reduce some of the perceived negative effects of the current UK welfare regime that were seen to promote passivity and welfare dependence. However, how far reforms in these areas can and will go remains to be seen (Brewer 2007; Gregg 2008).

As we saw in Chapter 3, differing conceptions of what welfare is and how it should be addressed are becoming more complex because of the apparent decline of nation-states with the advent of devolution and globalisation. However, these themes and issues must be addressed, as human beings will always have needs that must be met, so the issue of whether there will be needs that require to be met is really a redundant notion. What is not redundant is the requirement to ensure that someone at some level addresses these. And it may well be that future arrangements to address social need will in fact require to have some form of centralised authority to guarantee that social justice is seen to be done, as left to our own devices, (selfish) human nature tends to become somewhat inward looking, particularly when we least expect it and usually when someone else and not us (or our loved ones) requires some assistance. We must always remember that all of us, without exception, will at some point require some help from someone else, and it would be a terrible thing if there was no one there when you needed them, even if the only person available was a paid worker or a faceless bureaucrat. I know what I would choose.

Chapter summary

This chapter has looked at the important relationship between human need and social policy. It has outlined differing conceptions of need and looked at some of the implications of these for practice. We have also considered, quite broadly, how and why social policy requires to be integrated with other areas of social life and how functional arrangements to ensure that human need can be met in extreme circumstances must always be visible to all of us should we ever be in a position where we have no one to turn to.

References

Beck, A.T., Ward, C.H., Mendelson, M., Mock, J. and Erbaugh, J. (1961), 'An Inventory for Measuring Depression', *Archives of General Psychiatry* 4: 561–71.

Bradshaw, J. (1972), 'The Concept of Social Need', *New Society* 19(496): 640–43.

Brewer, M. (2007), *Welfare Reform in the UK: 1997–2007* (London: Institute for Fiscal Studies).

Cassidy, J. and Shaver, P.R. (eds) (2008), *Handbook of Attachment: Theory, Research and Clinical Applications* (2nd edn) (London: The Guilford Press).

Doyal, L. and Gough, I. (1984), 'A Theory of Human Needs', *Critical Social Policy* 4(1) 10: 6–38.

— (1991), *A Theory of Human Need* (Basingstoke: Macmillan).

Dwyer, P. (2008), 'The Conditional Welfare State', in M. Powell (ed.), *Modernising the Welfare State: The Blair Legacy* (Bristol: Policy Press): 199–218.

Fraser, D. (2003), *The Evolution of the British Welfare State* (3rd edn) (Basingstoke: Palgrave Macmillan).

Gil, D.G. (1992), *Unraveling Social Policy* (revised 5th edn) (Rochester, VT: Schenkman Books).

Gregg, P. (2008), 'UK Welfare Reform 1996 to 2008 and Beyond: A Personalised and Responsive Welfare System?' Working Paper 08/196: Centre for Market and Public Organisation, University of Bristol.

Lipsky, M. (1980), *Street-Level Bureaucracy: The Dilemmas of Individuals in Public Service* (New York, NY: Russell Sage Foundation).

Maslow, A. (1970), *Motivation and Personality* (2nd edn) (New York, NY: Harper and Row).

Nevitt, D. (1977), 'Demand and Need', in H. Heisler (ed.), *Foundations of Social Administration* (Basingstoke: Macmillan).

Rawls, J. (1971), *A Theory of Justice* (16th edn) (Cambridge, MA: Harvard University Press).

Rojek, C., Peacock, G. and Collins, S. (1988), *Social Work and Received Ideas* (London: Routledge).

Scottish Executive (2002), *Connecting Scotland: Our Broadband Future: Making It Happen* (Edinburgh: Scottish Executive).

Thompson, N. (2009), *People Skills* (3rd revised edn) (Basingstoke: Palgrave Macmillan).

Timms, N. and Watson, D. (eds) (1976), *Talking about Welfare: Readings in Philosophy and Social Policy* (London: Routledge).

Townsend, P. (1954), 'Measuring Poverty', *British Journal of Sociology* 5(2): 130–37.

— (1979), *Poverty in the United Kingdom: A Survey of Household Resources and Standards of Living* (Harmondsworth: Penguin).

Wilkinson, R. and Pickett, K. (2010), *The Spirit Level: Why Equality is Better for Everyone* (London: Penguin).

Further reading

Hothersall, S.J. and Maas-Lowit, M. (eds) (2010), *Need, Risk and Protection in Social Work Practice* (Exeter: Learning Matters). This text offers a useful account of the whole issue of need and its significance in social work and related practice.

Rose, N. (1999), *Governing the Soul: The Shaping of the Private Self* (2nd edn) (London: Free Association Books). This provides an in-depth sociological analysis of the links between political power, people and policy. This can be heavy going at times, but worth spending time with.

Part II

Themes and issues

5 Poverty and social exclusion

Janine Bolger and Pedro Morago

Introduction

This chapter will explore definitions and measurements of poverty, the impact of social exclusion and will then examine a range of policies and strategies adopted by the Government in an attempt to improve the lives of some of the most vulnerable people in society.

Poverty

Any definition of poverty, by its very nature, is influenced by value judgements and belief systems. This is because the term poverty has a moral imperative attached, that is, that something should be done about it because it is deemed to be unacceptable. The term is critical of the state and of the *status quo* and carries with it a demand for action.

There is no single universally accepted standard of poverty, instead we are left with present debates around poverty centred on the notion of:

- *Absolute poverty* (Booth 1889; Rowntree 1901). This definition is one of a standard based on subsistence, that is, the minimum necessary to ensure that life is maintained (An Introduction to Social Policy 2006).
- *Relative poverty* (as described by Townsend in his studies undertaken in Bethnal Green during the 1960s and 1970s. See Townsend Centre for International Poverty Research, n.d.). Under this definition individuals, families and groups within the population can be said to be in poverty when they lack the resources to obtain the kind of

> diet, participate in the activities and have living conditions and/or amenities customary, encouraged or approved in the societies to which they belong. This also takes into account changes over time and the wider impact of poverty (Scottish Poverty Information Unit 1999). However, one problem with this definition is that in an affluent society it could become hard to tell the difference between those who are in poverty and those who are simply less well off. Critics argue that relative definitions relate to inequality (descriptive) rather than poverty (prescriptive). Inequality, however, may be undesirable but it does not necessarily imply the need for change in the same way that poverty does.

The relative approach is the most preferred and utilised of the definitions given.

There is a close relationship between relative poverty and the notion of *social exclusion*. Tony Blair explained social exclusion as 'a short-hand label for what can happen when individuals/areas suffer from a combination of linked problems such as unemployment, poor skills, low incomes, poor housing, high crime environments, bad health and family breakdown' (Institute for Volunteering and Social Exclusion 1997: 19). The risk of long-term poverty and social exclusion is highest in Scotland. Those in social housing are more likely to live in poorly-served housing estates. The risk of becoming isolated and depressed is high (Scottishpolicynet 2004). Social exclusion is certainly complex – the causes are connected and its effects become subsequent causes of further exclusion, that is, poverty is both a cause and an effect. In short Social exclusion deals with the relational aspects of disadvantage rather than distribution.

Another area which requires some consideration is around the measurement of poverty. Although there is no uniform measurement one of three methods are usually employed:

1. Households below average income (HBAI) or 'low income', which is currently measured at 60 per cent of the median (mid-point) average income (this can be a useful indicator of 'economic distance', that is, the adequacy of income relative to other social standards). This information is compiled by the Department for Work and Pensions (formerly the responsibility of the Department of Social Security) and used in their annual review of distribution. This includes people on benefit and those in work (New Policy Institute 2005).
2. Income Support – a means-tested benefit payable to those who are on a low income (Department for Work and Pensions 2006). The number of people in receipt of Income Support is taken as a measure of those living on or below the subsistence level or 'safety net' set annually

by the Government. Living standards are measured by incomes after housing costs (rent/mortgage interest) have been paid. However this is not to say that Income Support actually meets the needs of individual people in poverty. Income related measures of poverty do not take into account regional variations, for example in the costs for fuel, heating, clothing and so on. This has huge implications for Scotland with its colder climate. We gain information on Income Support from the Census and from the Scottish House Condition Survey (available since 1993) and from the Department for Work and Pensions. However, there will be people who are entitled to claim benefits but do not and are therefore excluded from the figures. There are also many families dependent on other benefits who may only be marginally better off.

3. Sometimes a third method based on 'deprivation' is utilised. This gauges what people think of as essentials and then measure how many people are unable to afford such items through the use of the Townsend Deprivation Index (1981).

Any attempt to define a poverty line can be said to ignore the variability of people's circumstances and ignores the lived experience of poverty. 'Yet using a single criterion of poverty can be problematic, because such definitions fail to take into account variations in human needs within and between societies' (Giddens 2001: 311). The major difficulty when assessing the extent of, and trends in, poverty are around the funding of adequate, comprehensive and robust statistical data, for example, many groups who face a disproportionate risk of poverty such as people with disabilities, ethnic minority groups and so on are often not identified in statistics because they are rarely separated out by gender, ethnicity, impairment and so forth. It has already been acknowledged that there is no agreed definition or measurement of poverty and neither is there one simple cause of poverty. Any one of us might experience poverty through marital breakdown, mental health problems and unemployment. It is this relationship with employment, however, which can be most commonly linked to the experience of poverty.

The situation in Scotland

In 2008 the total population of Scotland was estimated at about 5,168,500 (General Register Office for Scotland 2009). Over recent years fewer people have moved from Scotland to the rest of the UK and more people moved to Scotland. The number of asylum seekers has not fluctuated contrary to popular belief (see Chapter 18). In line with current trends there have been more deaths than births in Scotland.

The Family Resource Survey is a continuous survey carried out jointly by the Office for National Statistics and the National Centre for Social Research for the Department for Works and Pensions. It suggests that there are indications that Scotland has above average numbers of people living in households on *absolute low incomes*; that is the measurement of whether incomes are rising in real terms (Lindsay and Dobbie 2009). For example, in 2006/7, approximately 12 per cent of working age adults lived in low income families; 6 per cent of pensioners; 11 per cent of children under the age of 16 (Lindsay and Dobbie 2009). According to the Child Poverty Action Group (CPAG) in 2006, however, 30 per cent of children in Scotland were still living in poverty (Green 2009).

In 2006/2007 in Scotland, 840,000 individuals (approximately 17 per cent of the population) were living in *relative low income poverty* (Scottish Government 2008).

> In August 2004, 536,800 people of working age in Scotland were claiming a key benefit, approximately equal to 17 per cent of the working age population. 212,700 aged under 16 were living in households where benefits were being claimed (approximately 22 per cent of all under-16s). Although the number of claimants has increased by around 7 per cent in the last five years, it is estimated that approximately 130,000 people are eligible for but not claiming Income support.
>
> (Scottish Executive 2005).

As already stated, in the UK there is *no one agreed measurement of poverty*. A good poverty assessment strategy requires the development of an agreed poverty line that would highlight the point at which the government and electorate agree that action is necessary. A breakdown of that measure by geographical variation would allow the monitoring of an area-based policy and a breakdown of individual circumstances (gender, age, family composition and so on). This would offer a greater understanding of the *process* of poverty and social exclusion and would offer a comparison over time or following policy change. This would assist in monitoring the impact of policy and could offer a clearer understanding of key factors and their reduction.

The contribution of politics

There has been a general growth in inequality in recent years as a result of a number of changes in the political, economic and social context (Wilkinson and Pickett 2010). A Conservative government was elected to power in 1979 where they remained for a further 18 years. Their philosophy supported the 'natural efficiency' of markets and as a result they applied a policy of deregulation in order that markets might be opened up and nationalised industries might be privatised to increase efficiency. Such principles were also applied to social policy in order to drive economic change. Monetarist policies were promoted by the Conservatives, which supported their belief that control of the supply of money is the key to achieving low inflation and economic growth. They thought that such state intervention would create wealth, which would then trickle down through the class structures. Unfortunately this was not the result. The Government, however, believed that it was not poverty that was being identified. They felt that society was experiencing an inequality that was present in all societies (Philip 1999).

Theories around those in poverty being responsible for their own position became popular. The Conservative Government argued that the benefits system created dependency. Within the same economical/political context we saw a rise in home ownership amongst low-income households coupled with high interest rates (1980s/1990s). On the basis of this, real incomes in the poorest households were only a little higher than they were in the 1960s. When in rented accommodation housing costs would have been met through central/local government subsidy. By the 1990s many of the 'new poor' were meeting high mortgage repayments on the strength of low earnings.

In looking more specifically at the situation in Scotland then, why does there appear to be a greater problem of poverty here than in the rest of Britain? It is likely to be as a result of the industrial and occupational structure of the economy; the highly uneven and uncontrolled character of economic development and the fact that inequalities in wealth are greater in Scotland than in the rest of Britain. For example, the top 1 per cent of Scots own one quarter of the personal wealth, the top 5 per cent own half and the top 10 per cent own four fifths. Five hundred individuals and/or companies own half of Scotland's land while company shareholdings are concentrated with the minority. Even after tax the top 10 per cent of income earners take home more than the bottom 50 per cent.

If we look at the industrial and occupational structure in more detail we can consider at least two reasons why poverty is deeply rooted. Over the last half century there has been a huge decline in heavy industry (shipbuilding, coal, iron, steel, heavy engineering and textiles). This has resulted in a highly skilled workforce experiencing insecure employment/unemployment and a drop in living standards. One in three skilled jobs have been lost and there has been a huge decline in skilled opportunities. In 1974 in Scotland less than 4 per cent of the workforce was unemployed. By the 1980–82 recession unemployment had risen to 14 per cent. Despite the recent economic downturn in April 2009 unemployment in Scotland stood at 6.6 per cent, still below the UK average of 7.2 per cent (Scottish Government 2010).

With the disappearance of heavy industry, the new occupational structure has developed in a haphazard way. A quarter of a million Scots, whose fathers were manual workers, have moved into white-collar work. In addition, nearly one in five Scottish workers are employed in semi-skilled or unskilled occupations. This is concentrated among working women in general, many of whom are also part-time employees. Despite the current economic crisis there has been a growth in employment through the Scottish public sector (Scottish Government 2009).

Low income by work status has worsened over past years (Joseph Rowntree Foundation 2004). In 1997 44.5 per cent of all Scottish workers were considered to be low paid. The Low Pay Unit criteria in 2003 indicated that those paid less than £7.58/hour should be considered as experiencing low pay. Women, part-time workers and manual workers are most likely to be low paid. Scotland seems to have turned into a low pay economy (Scottish Low Pay Commission Report 2009). In addition there has been an increase in the number of self-employed people experiencing poverty partly, it would seem, because when alternative work is not available some people work for themselves. The Low Pay Commission Report (2009) suggests that the number of jobs paid at minimum wage level have remained the same over the past few years and that job losses in low paying industries have been in similar proportions to those within the UK economy as a whole (Scottish Low Pay Commission Report 2009).

Vulnerable groups and demographic issue

The risks of poverty are not spread evenly but are dependent on a range of factors. These include geographical location, discrimination, additional costs of a child or those imposed by disability and access to services/employment, unequal access to the labour market and so on. Discrimination appears to limit opportunity while the cost of accessing these opportunities remains high.

There is a general perception that ethnic minorities own their own businesses and houses and are therefore quite wealthy. Minority groups constitute about 1.3 per cent of the population in Scotland and poverty rates vary between ethnic groups, for example, more than half of Pakistanis and Bangladeshis are poor which equals four times that of the rate for white people (The Poverty Alliance 2009). These people are three times more likely to be unemployed than the white population and, when in employment, tend to work in sectors where low wages and low status are common (The Poverty Alliance 2009).

Young people are also more likely to be in low paid jobs or on training schemes. Sixteen and 17 year olds have no automatic entitlement to benefits (severe hardship payments are discretionary, Income Based Job Seekers may be paid if a number of criteria are satisfied) whilst 18 to 24 year olds can claim reduced rates of Income Support (New Policy Institute 2005) (see Chapter 8).

Those living in rural areas suffer a higher cost of living and may have limited access to work, and the take up of benefits in rural areas is extremely low. Low-pay employment is prevalent in rural areas, and accommodation and transport is expensive (EKOS 2009). However, it should be noted that, people from rural areas represent only approximately 15.7 per cent of poor households (EKOS 2009).

The elderly and lone-parents, too, are more likely to live in poverty. The likelihood of experiencing poverty varies across the life-cycle and over time. Unemployment, as previously stated, is likely to be linked with poverty in most cases. The cause of unemployment will be different for individuals. Significant demographic changes over the last 20 years have altered the shape of the family and of the households in which we live (Joseph Rowntree Foundation 2004). There have been some significant changes in the demography of Scotland. There has been an increase in the older population, which trebled in the 1900s. There are now approximately 900,000 over 65s in Scotland. This means that 40 per cent of the Health and Social Security budget in Scotland is spent on older people who are more likely to have a limiting long-standing illness or disability. A high proportion of these elderly people, 34–40 per cent, do not claim the benefits to which they are entitled and which are roughly equal to £4.1 bn (BBC 2006; and see Chapter 8).

Alongside this increase in life expectancy we have seen a slight increase in birth rates in Scotland over the past three years, although it is not clear yet whether this will be a permanent phenomenon (Scottish Government 2009). There is a projected fall of 8 per cent in the number of households with two or more adults and children by 2024. Nearly 40 per cent of births are registered to mothers over the age of 30 years and over one third of births to unmarried parents (General Register Office for Scotland 2008). The divorce rate in Scotland fell by 3 per cent in 2005, the lowest for 22 years (National Statistics 2007).

The relationship between benefits and poverty

Benefits have declined in relation to incomes because benefits are tied to prices rather than average incomes and this has reduced their effectiveness. Restrictions on eligibility for benefits have been tightened, for example, in 1998 the majority of 16–18 year olds lost the right to Income Support whilst 1996 rules had already introduced policy which effectively prevented asylum seekers from receiving a range of benefits (see Chapter 8). As a result of demographic changes there has been an increase in the number of people who rely on benefits, for example the elderly and lone parents.

There are increasing numbers of people reliant on means-tested rather than contributions-based benefits, for example retirement pension, bereavement payments, widow's pension and so on. Benefits play a large part in helping to reduce income inequality. Cash benefits make up 58 per cent of gross income for the poorest fifth of households (National Statistics 2008/9).

The relationship between taxation and poverty

Since the 1980s, governmental policy has favoured the better-off with the top rate of taxation reduced from 84 to 40 per cent (HM Revenue and Customs 2006). Tax concessions have also favoured the wealthier. In 1996/97 tax relief on occupational/personal pensions amounted to nearly £13 billion. There has been a shift from tax on income (direct) to tax on expenditure (indirect), for example VAT on fuel. The burden of tax has been moved from the rich to the poor, for example, by 1995 the poorest fifth paid more of their income in tax – proportionally – than the richest fifth. In 1985–95 tax changes reduced the net incomes of the poorest 10 per cent by an average of £3 per week whilst the richest gained approximately £31.50 per week

Social exclusion

Background and definition

The term *social exclusion* was originally used in the 1980s in France to indicate a process of rupture of social bonds through which people become excluded from participation in society (European Foundation 1995). Such a way of understanding social disadvantage gained increasing popularity over the 1990s in most countries within the European Union, amongst them the UK. In fact, one of the first initiatives of New Labour's Government was the creation, in 1997, of the Social Exclusion Unit, which defines social exclusion as a situation of disadvantage derived from a combination of adverse factors such as unemployment, discrimination, poor skills, low income, poor housing, high crime, ill health and family breakdown (Social Exclusion Unit 2004). Although such a definition has the merit of including most of the major dimensions of social exclusion, it should not be regarded as exhaustive since there are other factors – for instance, stigmatism, the lack of accessible and affordable transport and low educational attainment – that can also contribute to the exclusion of individuals and communities.

The nature of social exclusion

Social exclusion has a multi-dimensional and dynamic nature. It is multi-dimensional because it focuses on the fact that socially excluded people are exposed to multiple and interconnected adverse factors. For example, factors such as poverty, homelessness, unemployment, stigma, discrimination, depression and isolation are all significantly higher among individuals with HIV compared to the general population (Culhane and Gollub 2001; Culhane et al. 2001). In addition, social exclusion has a dynamic nature because its different dimensions are constantly operating and reinforcing each other. The consequence of this process is that individuals or communities exposed to such dimensions enter what is known as the *cycle of disadvantage* – in which deprivation leads to exclusion and exclusion leads to increased deprivation, which in turn leads to increased exclusion and so on – which gradually prevents those affected from participating in society and leaves them with little chance and hope of overcoming their situation.

Differences between poverty and social exclusion

Although the term social exclusion is gradually replacing definitions of poverty in the political and academic discourse, both terms are not interchangeable. In other words, social exclusion should not be seen as a new label for poverty since there are significant differences between them. What are those differences?

Firstly, notions of poverty generally involve a one-dimensional approach to need and deprivation, based on the measurement of material or financial disadvantage. Even the concept of *relative deprivation*, which has the merit, as we have seen, of going beyond subsistence criteria, is defined in relation to goods or services that can be purchased. Social exclusion, however, adopts a multi-dimensional approach which, besides material disadvantage, also considers societal factors such as discrimination, lack of opportunities for participation and lack of networks.

The second major difference between both terms is closely related to the first one: because poverty focuses on material needs, it seems to assume that the provision of sufficient material goods and resources to everybody would eradicate poverty. Conversely, social exclusion's analysis is more dynamic, with a strong focus on the processes and constant interrelation of factors through which people and groups become detached from society.

Finally, while poverty approaches often measure the resources of individuals or households, social exclusion can also be applied to communities. For instance, the existence of factors such as crime, pollution, heavy traffic and lack of community services in a particular area is likely to have a negative impact on all neighbours, regardless of their income and resources.

Usefulness and limitations of the social exclusion approach

One of the main advantages of the notion of social exclusion derives from its multi-faceted nature: because social exclusion focuses not only on material disadvantage but also on societal and cultural factors, policies to combat social exclusion therefore imply (i) tackling the multiple dimensions of deprivation which contribute to people's marginalisation; and (ii) the promotion of social integration and participation of individuals and groups in society. Such an approach is particularly relevant for understanding the disadvantage experienced by traditionally excluded population groups like individuals with disabilities and ethnic minorities. However, social exclusion is a rather broad notion, which, due to its multi-factorial nature, may be difficult to precisely define for methodological purposes. Thus, the breadth of the concept – especially in relation to its social and cultural dimensions – can make it difficult to assess accurately the success of strategies aimed at combating deprivation.

The fight against poverty and social exclusion

New Labour did not overtly accept the stigmatisation of groups perceived as belonging to the 'underclass'. However, they did accept to some extent the 'dependency' argument and have replaced the language of rights with an emphasis on obligations and responsibility to the wider community. Since May 1997 there has been a range of programmes to promote opportunity and tackle social exclusion and poverty. There is now a social exclusion strategy steered by the Scottish Social Inclusion Network. It has been recognised that action needs to be comprehensive and co-ordinated. Projects have focused on inclusion through employment, education, housing and health care. Different agencies and organisations are involved: central Government and its agencies, public bodies such as Scottish Enterprise and Scottish Homes all direct and fund programmes. The voluntary sector and community activity support vulnerable people. Community groups and organisations take action directly, for example through credit unions, playgroups, community based housing associations and through putting pressure on other service providers. The Government and the Scottish Social Inclusion Network put forward a 'Vision' stating:

- 'every child has the best start in life
- opportunity for work for all
- decent quality of life for those who are unable to work
- encouragement for all to participate in life to the maximum of their potential' (Scottish Executive 1999: 1).

Increased participation in the labour market

Action has been taken in a variety of forms through a range of New Labour's welfare-to-work initiatives. Strategies such as New Deals for Young People and New Futures Funds have resulted in increased employment by supporting individuals into jobs and to increase their long-term employability. Through the National Minimum Wage over 110,000 Scots aged 22 years and over benefitted from an increase to £5.73/hour in 2008 (Citizens Advice 2008) whilst 18–21 year olds now receive the development rate of £4.77. Workers under the age of 18 years who are no longer of compulsory school age receive a minimum wage of £3.53/hour (Scottish Government 2009). However, 41,000 workers in Scotland are still paid below the National Minimum Wage (Scottish Government 2009).

The New Deal programmes have helped over 56,000 Scots into work whilst the proportion of children living in a workless household in the UK has fallen.

Under the UK's ten-year National Child Care Strategy all 3–4 year olds were entitled to 15 hours free provision by 2010 and from September 2008 2,500 schools provided morning and early evening child care and activities to assist working parents (House of Commons Library 2005).

Tackling poverty at both a national and a local level

Pension Credit guarantees pensioners £124.05 (or £189.35 with partner) weekly for 2008/2009. This has helped in excess of 900,000 Scottish pensioners. Winter fuel payments have also increased to between £100 and £200 (up to £300 if over 80 years of age) per eligible household for 2008/2009 and free television licenses have also been made available for those aged 75 years or more. Furthermore, there has been a record increase in child benefits and the introduction of the Children's Tax Credit has helped over 400,000 Scottish families. Around half a million fewer pensioners are living in households of absolute low income (since 1996/97), Working Tax Credit has been thought to help over 114,000 Scottish families by guaranteeing income levels, and the New Deal programmes for lone parents, people with disabilities and so on has helped support people, on a voluntary basis, back into work (Department for Work and Pensions 2006).

The Government have also realised that they need to ensure that children are adequately prepared for school so that they can maximise their use of what is on offer. In order to achieve this, affordable nursery school / day care placements have been provided under the National Childcare Strategy and Sure Start Schemes offer support for families with children under the age of four years.

To reduce the numbers leaving school unqualified or ill-equipped to cope with approaching adulthood, early intervention schemes and new community schools, family literacy classes and alternatives to exclusion programmes have been developed. And in order to widen participation and increase the demand for lifelong learning, over 40,000 additional places in further education have been created (Opportunity Scotland 1998).

In an attempt to tackle specific barriers, for example ill-health and homelessness, to reduce inequalities in health and to re-generate deprived communities action has been taken through the 'Working Together for a Healthier Scotland' (Scottish Government 1999) which aims: to tackle health inequalities through multi-agency working; to improve Scottish housing through new housing partnerships that have been developed to empower communities and provide investment; to tackle exclusion facing deprived communities and vulnerable groups though Social Inclusion Partnerships (SIPs); and, through consultation papers such as 'Supporting Families', to make provision for strengthening marriage/adult relationships, helping balance home and work, reducing serious family problems and improving family prosperity.

Action is also being taken to eliminate discrimination through Family Mediation in Scotland, involving a broadened service to demonstrate cultural sensitivity in supporting families from ethnic minority groups. Furthermore, support and encouragement for the contribution of business to community life is being demonstrated through the new community schools and SIPs. It is also noticeable that there is a much greater impact when Government initiatives complement other initiatives from local authorities, health boards and so on. Moreover, the Scottish programme to promote inclusion stands alongside efforts at the UK level, for example through welfare reform.

Tackling social exclusion

Social exclusion became a core policy concept in the UK when New Labour came into office. One of the first initiatives of Tony Blair's cabinet was to establish in December 1997 the Social Exclusion Unit, the main objectives of which are to combat the cycle of disadvantage and promote opportunities, participation and inclusion for all. The Social Exclusion Unit operates across a range of areas such as children and young people, crime prevention, employment, health, homes and neighbourhoods, and transport, and its progress was reviewed in the report *Breaking the Cycle* (Social Exclusion Unit 2004).

In Scotland, the Government's plans to tackle social exclusion crystallised with the creation, in the summer of 1998, of the Scottish Social Inclusion Network. The network – made up of representatives of the Government and other Scottish organisations, as well as of professionals with expertise in this area – aims to improve the liaison between relevant agencies and to support the government to develop its social inclusion programmes. The first major initiative of the partnership between the Scottish Executive and the Scottish Social Inclusion Network was to launch the document *Social Inclusion – Opening the Door to a Better Scotland: Strategy* (The Scottish Office 1999), which sets out the general strategy for promoting social inclusion in Scotland. In order to achieve its ultimate goal of social inclusion, the plan established a set of objectives such as increased participation in the labour market, action against poverty, improved educational attainment, wider participation in lifelong learning, action against discrimination and other barriers to participation, reduction in health inequalities, and promotion of participation in the community.

The progress made in the above areas is examined in the report *Monitoring Poverty and Social Exclusion in Scotland 2008* (Kenway et al. 2008) which shows that, despite the relative success of the strategies to combat income poverty, social exclusion is still a cause of major concern in Scotland. For instance, the situation of particularly deprived areas with large numbers of working-age adults claiming out-of-work benefits has not significantly changed in the last years. In addition, socio-economic inequalities arising from situations of social exclusion are probably making a strong impact on the Scottish population's life expectancy, which is still lower by up to three and five years for women and men, respectively, compared to other developed countries.

Chapter summary

In theory, transferring money and resources from the rich to the poor eliminates poverty. Obviously this is not feasible as it would conflict with other public policy and eliminate incentives to work. There would also be a distinct possibility that people would not reveal the true nature of their worth. An alternative way forward might be to carry out further tax and social security reforms. The Government has focused on welfare-to-work making work 'pay' through tax credits and the national minimum wage. There is possibly some scope to bring the national insurance structure in line with income tax to ease the administration burden on employers and to encourage the hiring of more employees. In addition, social exclusion analyses show that deprivation and marginalisation cannot be eradicated with the provision of basic material goods and resources alone. For example, employment policies may not suffice in order to eliminate social exclusion if certain sectors of the population – particularly those with lower educational attainment and skills – can only access low-paid jobs and are not provided with affordable housing, transport and child care, among others services. Therefore, combating deprivation requires a strategic course of action which addresses every single dimension of disadvantage and pays particular attention to the redistribution of wealth and opportunities for participation.

References

An Introduction to Social Policy (2006). Available at: http://www2.rgu.ac.uk/publicpolicy/introduction/needf.htm (accessed 31 May 2010).

BBC (2006), 'Billions in Benefits "Unclaimed"'. Available at: http://news.bbc.co.uk/1/hi/business/4666396.stm (accessed 31 May 2010).

Booth, C. (1889), 'Poverty Map'. Available at: www.umich.edu/~risotto/ (accessed 29 May 2010).

Citizens Advice (2008), 'Minimum Wage Boost for Low Paid Earners'. Available at: http://www.citizensadvice.co.uk/en/Old-News/Minimum-wage-boost-for-low-paid-workers (accessed 31 May 2010).

Culhane, D. and Gollub, E. (2001), *Connections between AIDS and Homelessness*, Leonard Davis Institute, Issue Brief, 6(9): 1–4.

Culhane, D., Gollub, E., Kuhn, R. and Shpaner, M. (2001), 'The Co-occurrence of AIDS and Homelessness: Results from the Integration of Administrative Databases for AIDS Surveillance and Public Shelter Utilisation in Philadelphia', *Journal of Epidemiology and Community Health* 55: 515–20.

Department for Work and Pensions (2006), 'Income Support'. Available at: http://www.direct.gov.uk/en/MoneyTaxAndBenefits/BenefitsTaxCreditsAndOtherSupport/On_a_low_income/DG_10018708 (accessed 31 May 2010).

EKOS (2009), 'The Experience of Poverty in Rural Scotland', Research Findings No. 3/2009. Available at: http://www.Scotland.gov.uk (accessed 31 May 2010).

European Foundation for the Improvement of Living and Working Conditions (1995), *Public Welfare Services and Social Exclusion: The Development of Consumer Oriented Initiatives in the European Union* (Dublin: The Foundation).

General Register Office for Scotland (2008), 'Life Expectancy in Special Areas (Urban/Rural, Deprivation and Community Health Partnership) Within Scotland 2004–2006'. Available at: http://www.gro-scotland.gov.uk/statistics/publications-and-data/life-expectancy/life-expectancy-in-special-areas-2004-2006/index.html (accessed 10 June 2010).

— (2009), '2008-Based Population Projections for Scottish Areas'. Available at: http://www.gro-scotland.gov.uk (accessed 31 May 2010).

Giddens, A. (2001), *Sociology* (Cambridge: Polity Press).

Green, A. (2009), *Welfare through Wellbeing*. Policy Network. Available at: http://www.policy-network.net (accessed 31 May 2010).

HM Revenue and Customs (2006), *Budget 2006*. Available at: http://www.hmrc.gov.uk/history (accessed 31 May 2010).

House of Commons Library (2005), *The Childcare Bill*, Research Paper 05/81. Available at: http://www.parliament.uk/documents/commons/lib/research/rp2005/rp05-081.pdf (accessed 29 May 2010).

Institute for Volunteering and Social Exclusion (1997), *Volunteering for All*. Available at: http://www.ivr.org.uk/social exclusion/fullreport.pdf (accessed 31 May 2010).

Joseph Rowntree Foundation (2004), 'Progress on Poverty 1997 to 2003/4'. Available at: http://www.jrf.org.uk/publications/progress-poverty-199720034 (accessed 31 May 2010).

Kenway et al. (2008), *Monitoring Poverty and Social Exclusion in Scotland 2008*. Available at: http://www.jrf.org.uk/publications/monitoring-poverty-and-social-exclusion-scotland-2008 (accessed 29 May 2010).

Lindsay, K. and Dobbie, L. (2009), 'Poverty and Inequality in Scotland: Ten Years of Devolution'. Available at: http://www.povertyinformation.org (accessed 29 May 2010).

Low Pay Commission Report (2009), *National Minimum Wage*. Available at: http://www.lowpay.gov.uk/lowpay/report/pdf/7997-BERR-Low%20Pay%20Commission-WEB.pdf (accessed 29 May 2010).

National Statistics (2007), 'Divorce Rates Lowest for 22 Years'. Available at: http://www.statistics.gov.uk/pdfdir/divorce0807.pdf (accessed 10 June 2010).

— (2008/9), *The Effects of Taxes and Benefits on Household Income*. Available at: http://www.statistics.gov.uk/pdfdir/taxbhi0610.pdf (accessed 10 June 2010).

New Policy Institute (2005), 'Should Adult Benefit for Unemployment Now Be Raised?'. Available at: http://www.npi.org.uk/publications/index.htm (accessed 31 May 2010).

Opportunity Scotland: A Paper on Lifelong Learning (1998). Available at: http://www.scotland.gov.uk/library/documents-w1/lllgp-01.htm (accessed 31 May 2010).

Philip, L. (1999), *Rural Poverty in Scotland*, Scottish Poverty Information Unit, Briefing Sheet. No. 10.

Rowntree, B.S. (1901), *Poverty: A Study of Town Life* (Harlow: Longman).

Scottish Executive (1999), *Social Inclusion: Opening the Door to a Better Scotland*. Available at: http://www.scotland.gov.uk/library/documents-w7/sima-04.htm (accessed 31 May 2010).

—— (2005), 'Scottish Executive Consultation: Future European Structural Funds Programmes in Lowlands & Uplands Scotland 2007–2013'. Available at: http://www.scotland.gov.uk/Publications/2006/10/20155513/25 (accessed 29 May 2010).

Scottish Government (1999), *Working Together for a Healthier Scotland* (Edinburgh: Scottish Government). Available at: http://www.scotland.gov.uk/library/documents1/chap5.htm (accessed 29 May 2010).

—— (2008), *Scottish Economic Statistics*. Available at: http://www.scotland.gov.uk/Resource/Doc/258934/0076785.pdf (accessed 22 December 2009).

—— (2009), *Scottish Budget: Draft Budget 2010–11* (Edinburgh: Scottish Government). Available at: http://www.scotland.gov.uk/Resource/Doc/284860/0086518.pdf (accessed 29 May 2010).

—— (2010), *Scotland's Economy Returns to Growth*. Available at: http://www.scotland.gov.uk/News/Releases/2010/04/21101531 (accessed 6 April 2010).

Scottish Office (1999), *Social Inclusion – Opening the Door to a Better Scotland: Strategy* (Edinburgh: The Scottish Office).

Scottish Poverty Information Unit (1999), *Poverty in Scotland*. Available at: http://www.scottish.parliament.uk/business/research/pdf_res_notes/rn99-07.pdf (accessed 22 December 2009).

Scottishpolicynet (2004), *Three Nations*. Available at: http://www.scottishpolicynet.org.uk/scf/publications/paper_3/chapter3.shtml (accessed 31 May 2010).

Social Exclusion Unit (2004), *Breaking the Cycle: Taking Stock of Progress and Priorities for the Future* (London: Office of Deputy Prime Minister).

The Poverty Alliance (2009), *Ethnicity, Gender and Poverty in the United Kingdom*. Available at: http://www.vhscotland.org.uk/library/vol/Briefing11_Gender_Ethnicity_Poverty_Final.pdf (accessed 31 May 2010).

Townsend Centre for International Poverty Research (n.d.). Available at: http://www.bris.ac.uk/poverty/background.html (accessed 10 June 2010).

Townsend Deprivation Index (1981). Available at: http://www.blackacademy.net/content/3264.html (accessed 22 February 2010).

Wilkinson, R. and Pickett, K. (2010), *The Spirit Level: Why More Equal Societies Almost Always Do Better* (London: Penguin).

Further reading

Age Concern Scotland, http://www.ageconcernscotland.org.uk (accessed 31 May 2010).

Meeting the Childcare Challenge: A Childcare Strategy for Scotland (1998), (Edinburgh: Stationery Office).

Palmer, G., Carr, J. and Kenway, P. (2005), *Monitoring Poverty and Social Exclusion in Scotland 2005* (York: New Policy Institute and Joseph Rowntree Foundation).

Performance and Innovation Unit (2001), *Ethnic Minorities' Economic Performance* (London: Central Cabinet Office Publications).

Scottish Executive, http://www.scotland.gov.uk (accessed 31 May 2010).

Scottish Low Pay Unit, http://www.lowpay.gov.uk (accessed 31 May 2010).

Scottish Office (2004), *Social Inclusion – Opening the Door to a Better Scotland.* Available at: http://www.scotland.gov.uk/library/documents-w7/sima-03.htm (accessed 31 May 2010).

Towards a Healthier Scotland (1999), The Scottish Office, The Stationery Office.

6 Risk, support and protection

Mike Maas-Lowit

Introduction

To paraphrase Bradshaw, in the opening discussion of his 'A Taxonomy of Social Need' (1972), *risk is the vernacular of need* (and see Part I). In other words, risk is a quality that arises out of the general context of human beings having needs. It arises because we are compelled to meet those needs in order to survive. Risk is a problematic concept which we often misleadingly reduce to one of its dimensions – the risk that bad things may happen. Most evidently, gamblers do not gamble on the risk of losing. They gamble on the opposite – the risk of winning. This is important to remember at the door to any examination of risk. Risk is the chance occurrence of not just detrimental things happening, but also of potentially beneficial things happening. Otherwise, why would we take risks in pursuit of our needs?

Aldberg et al., quoted in Titterton (2004: 25), helpfully capture all of this in their definition: risk is 'the possibility of beneficial and harmful outcomes and the likelihood of their occurrence in a stated time-scale.'

For purposes of clarity in the ensuing discussion, note the various components of this definition:

- '*Possibility*' suggests that we are dealing with uncertainty because risk deals with *what may happen in the future*. Therefore, risk assessment is never an exact science.
- '*Beneficial* and *harmful outcomes*' suggests two edges to risk assessment. Note that the definition does not say '*beneficial* or *harmful*'. One reason for this is because that which causes us harm may also be beneficial to us, in the sense that we may learn from exposure to harm.

- *'The likelihood of occurrence'* suggests that risk is not one-dimensional (in the sense that it is only about what beneficial and harmful things may happen). It is two-dimensional, in the sense that it also contains a dimension of how likely it is to happen. For example, I am at risk of suffering the harm of being hit by a meteorite before I finish typing this sentence, but the likelihood is extremely low.
- *'In a given time-scale'* implies that risk is only meaningful if it is framed in time. There is a 100 per cent certainty that I will die, but it is only meaningful in terms of risk management if I examine the specific dangers involved in any action within a set time-scale.

In this chapter we will examine the public's and governments' growing preoccupation with risk and the need to protect certain groups and individuals who are considered to be vulnerable. Note how, in the foregoing sentence, we are already distorting the *beneficial and harmful* aspect of the definition, by veering towards a negative conception, where only *harm* is considered. We will look at the broad culture in which policy has developed around this subject. In this we will redress the tendency of governments, policy makers and professionals to render risk to its harmful aspect alone by examining it from both sides (both the beneficial and the detrimental). We will consider that governments, professionals, societies and all of us increasingly attempt to devise structures in which to manage risk. We will then look at examples of the specific policy on risk assessment and management, the most relevant to this book lying generally very close to various pieces of legislation in areas of child protection, mental health, adult support and protection and criminal justice. Note, in the above discussion we make reference to both the *assessment* and *management* of risk. Much of the debate about professional practice is preoccupied with risk assessment. However, there is no point in quantifying risks in an assessment process unless it is going to be followed up by a plan to manage those identified risks.

A particular focus will be upon that which is good or beneficial and that which is bad or problematic in the unavoidable incremental growth of risk as a preoccupation of governments and services. We ask the reader of this chapter to keep all three elements (good, bad and unavoidable) in mind, so as not to misunderstand our message: there are people living in any large and complex society who are less able to protect their interests than the majority. Such people are more likely to be vulnerable to abuse, neglect, exploitation and harm. As per the above definition, this *likelihood* is one of the dimensions of *risk* and, as such, it is a good thing that *risk* has become a standard part of the furniture of modern policy and practice: to the extent that the concept of risk is applied to strategies which enable vulnerable people to become less vulnerable, it is a positive entity. It protects those who cannot protect themselves and it strives to make us more equal. Nothing said in this chapter which is critical of our growing preoccupation with risk should detract from this perspective. Furthermore, nothing we say, implying problems arising out of the relationship between government, services and the media in relation to delicate matters such as the death of Baby Peter (see below), should diminish the tragedy that such a death represents or the proper findings of fault in any enquiries into it.

The risk of failing to manage risk successfully

The thesis of this chapter is that of failing to manage risk successfully and a particular focus will be upon that which is good or beneficial and that which is bad or problematic in the unavoidable incremental growth of risk as a preoccupation of governments and services.

As we begin to expound upon this thesis, it may help to explain it at length. Any reader who is unfamiliar with policy making in big or small government contexts will not immediately recognise that all policy has to be risk assessed. That is to say, whatever the policy, it must be put through a process whereby its potential benefit and harm, not to the recipients of the policy but to the policy-making body itself, has to be assessed.

To use a very local example, at the time of writing this chapter, Aberdeen City Council has to make some extremely difficult decisions about funding public services. In order to manage a large deficit in its budget, it will have to make what it calls *efficiency savings*. Effectively, this means restricting the money it commits to fund a range of organisations which meet the needs of the citizens of Aberdeen City. An examination of Appendix C to the *Finance and Resources Committee Report: Financial Strategy – Revenue Budget 2010/11* (Aberdeen City Council 2009) shows that each individual proposal contains a heading *Deliverability Issues and Risks*. For example, the proposal to reduce two mental health day centres to one suggests a cost saving of £150,000 and a risk that 'opposition from some service users [is] very likely [and] adverse publicity for the Council [is] likely' (Aberdeen City Council 2009: 279).

This small-scale local illustration demonstrates the care which public and government agencies have to take when implementing policy. Behind the condensed assessment that there is likelihood of adverse publicity for the Council, there is a greater counterbalancing risk that failure to manage the budget deficit will result in bankruptcy of the local government of Aberdeen and a complete loss of services for its citizens.

Taking a wider view of such matters, consider that every policy made by local and central government alike will have to contain detailed risk assessment of its potential impact. The final twist in this discussion is that such risk assessment is required even for policies which are floated to manage risk. In other words, modern government is expected to identify risks in its orbit of governance and then to propose plans to manage those risks. In order to demonstrate its effectiveness, it has then to assess the risk of harm and benefit arising out of its own policies. In some way, this situation speaks to the next step in our argument – that there is an unavoidable process in which the management of risk does nothing more than identify further risks which, in turn, themselves need to be managed. This is what we referred to above as *the unavoidable incremental growth of risk as a preoccupation of governments and services*.

The dangers in the growth of awareness of risk

The minute risk is conceived as the chance occurrence of something detrimental happening, there is a danger that a person or body will be identified as having a responsibility to prevent it from happening. Hence the above-mentioned need of policy makers to risk-assess their own policies. It can then become an exercise in apportioning blame when bad things do occur. Turn this idea out into the public domain, in close proximity to the political arena, and it will grow exponentially. We are all too familiar with the results being paraded across the media. See, for example 'Who is to Blame for Britain's Knife-Crime?' (Daily Telegraph 2008) and 'Binge Britain: Under 21s Now Face Ban on Buying Alcohol' (Hale 2008), to mention but two contemporary preoccupations of UK politics in relation to risks to health and public order. Another example of the linkage between risk and blame is found in the well publicised case of Baby Peter (or Baby P), who was killed by his mother's partner and subsequently featured in a long-running trial by media of various parties in Haringey Council.

In the following discussion, the author of this text does not wish to impute any moral significance to any failings on behalf of Haringey Council, or to deny that inquiry shows that there were such failings (Laming 2009). The focus of our discussion relates more to the consequences of *The Sun* newspaper's coverage of the tragic death of Baby Peter (Pascoe-Watson 2008), which implies that the Council in general, and social work in particular, had a responsibility to predict his death and prevent it.

In this discussion, it is not disputed that Baby Peter's death is an instance in which there were systemic failings, which arguably ought to have been addressed in order to detect the risk to the baby and to prevent the occurrence of his awful death. However, living life in this world involves constant engagement with unpredictable forces. We meet these forces by taking risks in order to address our needs. Yet it is difficult to resist the process by which it ought to become someone's responsibility to reduce the dangers we face. It is this aspect of the Baby P case that we wish to focus upon: for the purposes of policy formation, governments seem to be trapped into a situation in which there is a risk to them of not having identified and managed all potential risks. *The Sun*'s coverage of the Baby P case demonstrates very clearly what the potential dangers are for any government (in this case, Haringey Council) of failing to manage a significant risk. It seems disrespectful to reduce a small child's tragic death to this equation, but a major driving force in modern policy making must be the awareness of the power of media-amplified public outrage about failure to identify and manage a particular risk.

To illustrate this point, consider the differences between the 2009 response to the global swine flu pandemic and the response when the Black Death arrived on British shores in 1348 (Kelly 2005). In 2009, the UK government faced criticism from its opponents and critics that it ought to have done more to anticipate the risk of swine flu and that it had a responsibility to manage the risk of catching it once the spread of the illness was pandemic. On the other hand, while governments did make some responses to it in the 1340s and 1350s, there would have been no consideration that the plague, which killed at least one in three people across Europe, was anyone's responsibility to anticipate, prevent or minimise. The problem that confronts us in the change of perception from 1348 to 2009 is the growing idea that everything ought to be predictable in a basically unpredictable world and that, where it remains unpredicted, it is someone's fault. This results in a growing attempt to create policy structures which will meet every possible contingency from global financial crisis to the prediction of who is likely to commit crimes of violence, where and when. This, in turn, increasingly erodes civil liberties (for example in moves to make everyone carry identity cards or in the growth of CCTV cameras in public places) and it tends to standardise and therefore to bureaucratise the systems in which professionals like the police, social workers and doctors work.

Many of these ideas are synthesised in the thinking of Ulrich Beck (1992), whose work postulated the *risk society*, in which post-modern society is increasingly organised and motivated by its responses to the perceived dangers that it faces. Beck, amongst others, suggested that this preoccupation with risk permeates all aspects of society. For our purposes, it is evident in the world of politics, in the influence of media, in the process of government and policy making and in the design and delivery of services. Aspects of this are closely linked to the work of a sociologist of an earlier generation: Max Weber was interested in the growth of bureaucracy (1947). Characterised by regulation, standardisation and hierarchical organisation, we can see much of Weber's early nineteenth-century observation in modern civil services. The link between Weber and Beck, for our purposes, is that Weber foresaw that rational bureaucracy is a form of organisation which will multiply and grow into all corners of civil life. In the same way, Beck saw that the concept of risk will pervade all of society, from concern about the environment to regulation of sexual behaviours.

The benefits of the growth in awareness of risk

What the above argument fails to capture is that we know far more about the world than we did at the time of the Black Death. In 1348 it was not even understood that disease is caused by microbiological infections, invisible to the naked eye. It was not evident, as it is now, that we can find out how a disease like H1N1 (swine flu) comes into being, how its transmission may be minimised and how it may be treated. (At the time of writing it is now acknowledged that H1N1 is not as dangerous to the human race as was first anticipated.) Once these things are known, the world still remains unpredictable, but the growth in governmental responsibilities to its citizens means that it is reasonable to ask the state to minimise known risks (see, for example, *Swine Flu: What is the Government Doing?* at www.direct.gov.uk).

Balancing benefit and detriment in the analysis of risk policy

So far, we have ranged widely over the topic of risk, looking at the positive and negative consequences of our great and growing preoccupation with it in our lives. We have hinted at the powerful dynamic that is generated by the media and public concern and the influence this exerts upon policy making in a political democracy. Now we are going to move on to a more specific examination of policy relating to risk in Scotland. In this discussion, we wish to maintain an awareness of the duality, that there are detriments and benefits in our preoccupation with risk.

In relating this to practice, we will now look at aspects of policy which propose wide and standardising use of what are popularly called *risk assessment tools.*

Risk assessment and management practice and policy in Scotland

As the term *risk society* implies, risk is such a diverse and widespread preoccupation of the state that it would not be possible to cover all the bases of even social work's narrow corner of the field. Besides, the following, subject-specific chapters will touch on specifics relating to risk in their own areas. Therefore we will only draw on a few illustrative examples to advance our thesis:

- that harm (and benefit) is unavoidable in life;
- that preoccupation with it is ever-growing and has to be managed in itself;
- that awareness of risk is essential to practice; and
- that it has both beneficial and detrimental aspects, which if properly managed, will enhance practice outcomes for all.

From the discussion above, a fairly common process may be deduced: imagine that something harmful or undesirable happens in the public domain. Ever-growing responsibilities of government and interested professionals and watch-dog bodies require them to make inquiry into what went wrong, in order to learn lessons and to prevent the same thing happening again. The lessons learned result in the need for policy and sometimes changes in law, to shift practice away from a recurrence of what is now perceived as a fault in the system. Sometimes (as in the case of Baby Peter) the process is muddied by too much media-driven public interest, and predictably this occurs more around emotive issues, for example, where children are involved.

We do not wish to imply a cynical tone, but this process will be never-ending, simply because life is a risky business and it is entirely unpredictable. This observation would indeed be cynical if it were not counterbalanced by the fact that public services rightly have specific and common law duties to keep the public in general, and vulnerable people in particular, safe. Therefore, they should learn lessons and move on to further minimise risk.

Not all changes to policy in relation to risk arise out of a simple process as dramatic as Baby Peter, but it is worth considering two cases in Scotland to see how it happens.

> *The Borders Inquiry*: In the so-called Borders Inquiry (MWC and SWIA 2004), a vulnerable woman with learning disabilities, called '**Miss X**' by the Scottish media (Sunday Herald 2004), was discovered in March 2001 to have experienced serious physical and sexual assault over a number of weeks at the hands of three men. The victim was known both to the Scottish Borders Council social work service and to the Borders NHS and while there had been concerns noted by these authorities over many years, no action had been taken by them. Following police investigation, the Mental Welfare Commission for Scotland took up its responsibility to make inquiry into the situation (HMSO 1984). The report was made available to the Scottish Executive

> at the time when the law regarding protective guardianship of people with mental disorder was undergoing change through the implementation of the Adults with Incapacity (Scotland) Act 2000 (Scottish Executive 2000). The Mental Welfare Commission's report, in conjunction with the Social Work Inspection Agency, found:
>
> - a failure to investigate appropriately very serious allegations of abuse;
> - an acceptance of the poor conditions in which the people involved lived and the chaos of their lives;
> - a lack of comprehensive needs assessments, including carers' assessments, or assessments of very poor quality, despite clear and repeated indications of need from the earliest point of agency contact; and
> - a lack of information-sharing and co-ordination within and between key agencies (social work, health, education, housing, police)
>
> amongst its 25 critical findings.
>
> This was also a time of major change in mental health law and the inquiry identified a gap in legal and policy provision in that the victim of this case demonstrated in sharp focus that vulnerable adults required the same protections as were enjoyed by children through child protection law and procedure. The result was the Adult Support and Protection (Scotland) Act 2007 (Scottish Government 2007) and related policy.

From this, local authorities are required to implement frameworks which co-ordinate work with partners such as the police, health services and voluntary providers, to provide support and protection to adults who are at risk of abuse, neglect and exploitation. The range of people who might be at such risk is very wide indeed. It includes people who use or are addicted to alcohol or other drugs, people with mental disorder, older and infirm people, people with physical disabilities, people who have committed criminal offences themselves and are at risk in some way, and those who work within the sex industry (Scottish Government 2007). Risk assessment and management are central to the law, policy and practice in this new area, because it is the determination of risk factors which leads to intervention in the form of multidisciplinary packages of support and protection. The Borders Inquiry was therefore a major step in the chain of policy which led to Scotland having two groups of people for whom authorities have major responsibilities in assessing and managing risk: children under the age of 16 and adults over the age of 16.

Caleb Ness: Caleb Ness was a baby who lived his short life in Edinburgh City. He died, aged 11 weeks, at the hands of his father in 2001. While the tragedy of Caleb's death took place around the time that the Borders situation was uncovered, there are other similarities in the shortcoming of agencies – in communication and following procedures for identification and management of risk. The adults involved in Caleb's care had problems in relation to substance use and the key professional involvement with the parents was from criminal justice social work and brain injury specialists in health. They failed to recognise the risks to baby Caleb because they did not recognise child protection as their remit and they lacked the expertise in the area that might have alerted them to risks.

> There was a tendency among professionals in all agencies to make assumptions about the knowledge, training and actions of others. The doctors assumed that the social workers knew things which in fact they did not. Some professionals failed to acknowledge their own responsibilities for identifying and responding to child protection concerns. This was particularly evident in the gulf we discovered between Children and Families team social workers and the separately administered Criminal Justice social workers. We found that there was a complete failure by Criminal Justice workers and management to recognise that they did have some responsibility for child protection. Similarly, we saw an incomplete understanding of their role in child protection in the actions of addiction professionals and brain injury specialists, who are accustomed to working with adult patients. The police were handicapped by the paucity of information sent to them by the social work department, and did the best they could do in Caleb's case, but we discovered that they were not routinely passing on as much information as the social workers expected. (Edinburgh and the Lothians Child Protection Committee 2003: 8)

Both the inquiry into Caleb's death and the Borders inquiry were major contributory factors in the ensuing review of social work called by Peter Peacock, the then Minister for Children and Education in the Scottish Government. This resulted in a broad range of policies relating to issues from training to registration of social workers. The findings in the Caleb Ness case were contributing factors to a review of children's services (Scottish Parliament 2006a). The review resulted in a major and wide-ranging shift in policy known as *Getting it Right for Every Child,* or GIRFEC (Scottish Executive 2005). Details of GIRFEC will be discussed in Chapter 14 but in essence, it is a child-centred policy which calls for a strong degree of multi-disciplinary collaboration with the child's needs at the heart of practice.

GIRFEC is a more wide-ranging policy than one that simply focuses on risk and child protection. However, risk and child protection are elements that sit within the broader focus on welfare and well-being of the child (Hothersall, Maas-Lowit and Golightley 2008; Scottish Executive 2006a). More significantly for our discussion, the above quoted section of the report into Caleb's death strongly suggested that some specialised social worker practitioners may have lost sight of the general duties of their local authority employers in relation to child protection. Out of the mill of policy, the Scottish Institute for Excellence in Social Work Education produced *The Key Capabilities in Child Care and Protection* in consultation for the Scottish Executive. The *Key Capabilities* requires that higher education providers of social work education ensure the qualification 'properly equips [students] with the knowledge, skills and understanding they need to deal with child care and child protection issues' (Scottish Executive 2006b: 1). This ensures that graduates of the social work degree all have a basic level of awareness of the sort of risks which were manifested before the death of Caleb Ness.

The reader might note, from the above illustrations of how risk becomes a consideration in policy making, that we are now discussing two strands to dealing with risk: *risk assessment* (the quantification of risks in any given situation) and *risk management* (plans for how to deal with those risks now that they have been identified). In a sense the link between assessment and management is self-evident: there would be little point in quantifying risk if one was not going to put in place a plan to deal with it.

Risk assessment, management structures and risk assessment tools

We have repeatedly asserted that life is both risky and unpredictable. This means that there are too many variables for *risk assessment* to ever be an exact science. However, as Titterton indicates (2004), two strands combine to give it a scientific veneer: actuarial elements drawn from statistical data and approaches developed in the insurance industry on the one hand, and refined professional or clinical judgement on the other.

The insurance industry would make an interesting point of study if this chapter had the word-space. It is based on gambling with risk in an informed way. Insurers sell you insurance against risk and they base the insurance cost upon analysis of statistical likelihood of harm occurring. A very obvious example would be that health insurance will cost you more if you smoke, simply because statistics show that smokers are more likely to have health problems (Surgeon General 1964). This way of working has been imported into risk analysis in the public domain. For example, addiction to heroin would indicate a statistically significant likelihood that a person might commit certain criminal offences (Drugscope 2010).

However, statistics and the correlation of statistics can be a dangerous and misleading thing if it is not mediated by a degree of specialised professional knowledge. For example, very few people affected by mental illness commit criminal offences, but some do. It takes a highly specialised knowledge of forensic psychiatry or psychology to understand the causes and natures of various mental disorders in order to negotiate the statistical data which suggests risk in this area.

HCR20 (Webster et al. 1995) is a good example of a risk assessment tool which blends actuarial elements with clinical judgement. The 'H' stands for *historical*, the 'C' for *clinical* and the 'R' for *risk*, in a 20-item inventory which asks questions about the subject's history, such as history of violence related to substance misuse, clinical elements, such as ability to cooperate with services, and resulting risks. Tools like HCR20 are validated, which means that they hold up to empirical research which proves their effectiveness. However, this does not mean that they are anything less than means by which to attempt prediction in a complex and uncertain future of innumerable variables. The common usage of the term *tools* might suggest something more scientifically accurate. Nevertheless, they do serve to standardise the risk judgements made by professionals trained in their use. This has two potential effects: on the one hand, personal opinions about the risk that a person or situation may pose will vary widely. For example, personal attitudes to flight as a mode of transport will range from those who will not board an aircraft because it is too dangerous, to those who do not think twice before flying. While professional judgements on risk ought to be more reasoned and dispassionate than personal views on the risks of flying, the example is not as trivial as it seems. Personal experience can not help but influence professional judgements to some degree (Jeffrey 1992). This suggests that some regulatory framework is needed to help quantify the basis upon which judgements on degree of risk are made.

The growth in use of standardising risk assessment tools is not generally written into large-scale policies at a governmental level. However, it is favoured commonly at local levels of policy. For example, the Forensic Network (http://www.forensicnetwork.scot.nhs.uk/) governs professional practice in the orbit of the State Hospital for Scotland and medium- and low-security hospitals that contain criminal offenders who have some form of mental disorder. The network promotes the use of HCR20. And as one relevant Scottish Executive report states:

> The issue of security placement depends, in part, on a robust assessment of risk. There appears to be a significant gap in the provision of risk assessment training, except at the highest levels of security. The main instrument used is the *HCR20*, in full or in part. Risk assessment training is important and it is possible that the risk management authority proposed by the MacLean Committee will provide

> advice on the approval of risk assessors and their training. (Scottish Executive 2004: Section 4.5:12)

Many local authorities now favour one tool or other in their adult support and protection frameworks and the justice authorities, which are partnerships of police, local authorities and the Scottish Prison Services in local areas, all promote the use of a standardised tool – the Risk Assessment Guidance Framework or RA 1 to 4 (Scottish Executive 2002). However, tools need not be so formal and scientific. *My World* (Aldgate and Rose, 2007) is an exception to the rule that central policy does not promote the use of one specific tool. *My World* is a holistic framework for assessing the needs and risks faced by children and young persons under GIRFEC.

In its broadest sense, policy steers practitioners both into the use of specific tools of risk assessment and into structures for risk management. The Multi-Agency Public Protection Arrangements or MAPPA (Scottish Executive 2006a) is a good example of policy-led structures for *risk management*. The report of the MacLean Committee, out of which MAPPA grew, concluded:

> Decision making in relation to the management and care of high risk offenders with a mental disorder should be informed by a multi-disciplinary risk assessment and risk management process in accordance with the standards that apply for sentencing and sentence management .... (Scottish Executive 2000: Recommendation 35; Patrick, 2009)

MAPPA was originally set up as a way of insuring that risk management of seriously violent and sex offenders could be contained in a multi-disciplinary framework which ensured agreed assessment of risk and collaboration between local authorities, police and the Scottish Prison Service to protect the public. MAPPA policy requires those agencies around the table to agree a level of risk that any given offender poses to the public. There are three levels of risk: numbered 1 to 3 in order of degree. Arrangements made for the management of the offender must be according to restrictions required of the offender's liberty at that level. For example, this might mean that a person who is being discharged from prison after a custodial sentence for sex offences must be supervised at all times in the community, with the involvement of two agencies.

It is an illustration of how considerations of risk expand in an ever-complicated network of policy that MAPPA was expanded in 2007 to accommodate risk management of offenders with mental disorder (Hothersall, Maas-Lowit and Golightley 2008).

Chapter summary

This chapter has ranged widely across a number of different issues. We have considered how the issue of *protection* is intimately connected to *need, vulnerability* and *risk.* We have also considered how the issue of protection has increasingly become the business of everyone, from governments to professionals to private individuals and illustrated how this has generated a range of measures and mechanisms at the wider societal/group level and at the individual level. We have also shown how there is an increasing use of *fundamental principles* to underpin law and policy and that these are supported by increasing amounts of policy in the form of codes of practice that aim to assist practitioners in working in these difficult areas. The chapter has also highlighted that whilst protection, as commonly understood, has a focus upon protecting individuals from harm, there is another level at which such protective measures are increasingly operating and that is in the area of *public protection,* and we have looked at some of the arrangements that exist regarding this issue.

References

Aberdeen City Council (2009), Appendix C to *Finance and Resources Committee Report: Financial Strategy – Revenue Budget 2010/11* [Report No. CG/09/175] (Aberdeen: Aberdeen City Council).

Aldgate, J. and Rose, W. (2007), *Assessing and Managing Risk in Getting it Right for Every Child* (Edinburgh: Scottish Government).

Beck, U. (1992), *Risk Society: Towards a New Modernity* (London: Sage).

Bradshaw, J. (1972), 'A Taxonomy of Social Need', *New Society* (March 1972): 640–43.

Daily Telegraph (2008), 'Who is to Blame for Britain's Knife-Crime?', *Daily Telegraph,* 26 May 2008, Telegraph Media Group.

Drugscope (2010), *Criminal Justice Home* (London: Drugscope). Available at: http://www.drugscope.org.uk/resources/goodpractice/criminaljustice (accessed 28 May 2010).

Edinburgh and the Lothians Child Protection Committee (2003), *Report of the Caleb Ness Inquiry* (Edinburgh: Edinburgh City Council).

Hale, B. (2008), 'Binge Britain: Under 21s Now Face Ban on Buying Alcohol', *Daily Mail,* 14 August 2008, Associated Newspapers.

HMSO (1984), *The Mental Health (Scotland) Act 1984* (Edinburgh: HMSO).

Hothersall, S., Maas-Lowit, M. and Golightley, M. (2008), *Mental Health and Social Work in Scotland* (Exeter: Learning Matters).

Jeffrey, C. (1992), 'The Relation of Judgment, Personal Involvement, and Experience in the Audit of Bank Loans', *The Accounting Review* 67(4) (October): 802–19.

Kelly, J. (2005), *The Great Mortality: An Intimate History of the Black Death, the Most Devastating Plague of All Time* (New York, NY: HarperCollins).

Laming, H. (2009), *The Protection of Children in England: A Progress Report* (London: Stationery Office).

MWC and SWIA (2004), *Investigations into Scottish Borders Council and NHS Borders Services for People with Learning Disabilities: Joint Statement from the Mental Welfare Commission and the Social Work Services Inspectorate* (Edinburgh: Mental Welfare Commission for Scotland).

Pascoe-Watson, G. (2008), 'Baby P: *The Sun* Marches on Number 10', *The Sun*, 27 November 2008, The Sun Newsgroup.

Patrick, H. (2009), *Mental Health Incapacity and the Law in Scotland* (Wiltshire: Tottel Publishing).

Scottish Executive (2000), *Report of the Committee on Serious Violent and Sexual Offenders* (The MacLean Committee) (Edinburgh: Scottish Executive).

—— (2002), *Serious Violent and Sexual Offenders: The Use of Risk Assessment Tools in Scotland* (Edinburgh: Scottish Executive).

—— (2004), *National Mental Health Services Assessment Towards Implementation of the Mental Health (Care and Treatment) (Scotland) Act 2003: Final Report* (Edinburgh: Scottish Executive).

—— (2005), *Getting it Right for Every Child: Proposals for Action* (Edinburgh: Scottish Executive).

—— (2006a), *Implementation of the Multi Agency Public Protection Arrangements (MAPPA) in Scotland*, Circular No JD/15/2006 (Edinburgh: Scottish Executive).

—— (2006b), *The Key Capabilities in Child Care and Protection* (Edinburgh: Scottish Executive).

Scottish Government (2007), *Adult Support and Protection (Scotland) Act 2007: A Review of Literature on Effective Interventions that Prevent and Respond to Harm against Adults* (Edinburgh: Scottish Government).

Scottish Parliament (2006), *Education Committee Official Report 26 November 2006* (Edinburgh: Scottish Parliament).

Sunday Herald (2004), 'Overhaul of Social Work after Miss X', *Sunday Herald*, 7 May 2004.

Surgeon General (1964), *Report on Smoking and Health* (Bethesda, MD: National Library of Medicine).

Titterton, M. (2004), *Risk and Risk Taking in Health and Social Welfare* (London: Jessica Kingsley).

Weber, M. (1947), *The Theory of Social and Economic Organization* (London: Collier Macmillan).

Webster, C.D., Douglas, K.S. et al. (1995), *HCR-20 Assessing Risk for Violence (Version 2)* (Vancouver: Mental Health, Law and Policy Institute, Simon Fraser University).

Further reading

Patrick, H. (2006), *Mental Health, Incapacity and the Law in Scotland* (Wiltshire: Tottel Publishing). An in-depth look at many of the issues referred to above as they relate to Scotland.

Mandelstam, M. (2008), *Safeguarding Vulnerable Adults and the Law* (London: Jessica Kingsley). As above, but with the focus on England and Wales.

Pritchard, J. (ed.) (2008), *Good Practice in Safeguarding Adults: Working Effectively in Adult Protection* (London: Jessica Kingsley). A text which takes a broad look at a range of practice-based issues in the area of adult support and protection.

7 Changing patterns of care

Steve J. Hothersall, Clare Swan and Iain D. Turnbull

Introduction

In this chapter we aim to offer an account of how the manner in which care has been provided to certain groups and to individuals has changed over the years. Patterns of care provision have shifted significantly over the last 100 years and although we tend to take for granted the current arrangements and the philosophy underpinning them, they are relatively recent developments, particularly those relating to *unpaid* care and the care provided by *young carers*, and in order to fully understand the aims and ideals of current policy, we need to have some knowledge and understanding of the historical perspective (see Chapter 2).

Caring in its historical context

Historically many services for vulnerable people were provided within an *institutional context* with group care being the norm. Those with mental disorders, learning disabilities and for some older people, care provision was provided via purpose built and often very large institutions, the building of which began in earnest in the nineteenth century. Most major towns and cities will have such a place nearby, possibly nowadays having been sold to private developers and converted into luxury apartments, which is perhaps rather ironic. *Institutionalisation* was deemed at that time to be the most appropriate way to care for individuals and such practices were justified on the basis of economy of scale; it was easier and cheaper to care for 50 or 500 people in one place than to have them in different places. Such provision also *segregated* people from their local communities and society at large, reflecting prevailing societal attitudes of the time towards vulnerable and other marginalised groups (Wolfensberger 1972; 1975; and see Chapter 13).

We now know that people who lived in these large hospitals and other places often became 'institutionalised'. By this we mean that all day-to-day activities were organised to cater for the needs of the *group* rather than the individual. Daily routines were rigid and people had little or no choice about the food that they ate, the clothes they wore, the activities they took part in, or the people that they socialised with. There was a very clear hierarchy within these institutions with 'patients' or 'inmates' firmly at the bottom and the staff at the top. Doors were often locked and people's freedom was restricted, and the fact that many of these institutions were located in the countryside added to the sense of isolation and dislocation from mainstream society (Means, Richards and Smith 2008).

The effect that this type of regime had on people was that they became dependent on the routines of the hospital. They lost the ability to make everyday decisions about their own lives and became heavily dependent on the *perceived* safety and protection of the hospital or institution. Many people found it difficult to form what would be seen as healthy attachments and relationships with other people and some went on to display more extreme forms of institutionalised behaviour characterised by repetitive movements or patterns of speech and forms of what we might well now refer to as 'learned helplessness' (Seligman 1975). These factors were highlighted and brought to academic and public attention by Goffman (1961) in his seminal work *Asylums*, which took ethnographic sociology to new heights and illustrated the debilitating effects of such forms of care and fuelled the de-institutionalisation debate (Wolfensberger 1972; 1982).

The post-war welfare consensus (see Chapter 2) paved the way for developments such as the report of the Royal Commission on mental illness and mental deficiency in 1957 (HMSO 1957). This was the first official document to make mention of the term 'community care' and it argued that the time had come for a shift from hospital care to community care, although implicitly there was still recognition that smaller forms of *residential* and *group-based* care, located within communities, would continue to be required to provide an alternative to care at home where this was not feasible for some individuals, although this was still a form of *institutional care*, with all that that brought. The move away from hospital-based care for significant groups of people was continued with the introduction of the Mental Health Act of 1959 and momentum increased as a result of a number of high-profile inquiries into the care and treatment provided within state run hospitals such as the Ely Hospital in Cardiff (HMSO 1969). This inquiry identified that people living in large institutions were not only adversely affected by being institutionalised, but were also in some instances, treated badly and abused by the very people employed to care for them.

However, it is important to remember that the notion of *care in the community* (Finch and Groves 1980), as distinct from *community care* as it is referred to today, effectively began in the 1950s. A view emerged which argued that domiciliary care as opposed to institutional or custodial care would be better economically as well as being more in keeping with people's preferences (Ham 2009). Coupled with this was an increased awareness of the dangers and inhumanities inherent within institutional care, exemplified by the experiences of those individuals with learning difficulties and mental health problems (including mental illness[1]).

These developments, fuelled both by empirical research and by economics, led to a range of assumptions becoming evident in relation to the role of the family within society, particularly concerning its care functions, particularly *informal care* which is that undertaken predominantly by women and essentially 'hidden' because it tended to attract little or no professional interest, although as we shall see below, this position has now changed. Functional sociologists like Parsons (1952) and Parsons and Bales (1956) would argue that one of the major roles of the family is that of caring; other theorists, particularly those of a critical/feminist persuasion, would contend that the state uses the family to avoid its obligations to provide welfare and sees the family as a 'cheap' form of care (Oakley 2005) and within the context of social work and social care, the family is for some people a dangerous place (Todd, Hothersall and Owen 2010; Hothersall 2010; Hothersall and Maas-Lowit 2010; Hothersall, Maas-Lowit and Golightley 2008).

The development and growth of community-based care

It was not until the 1970s and early 1980s that there was significant policy development in relation to the care of *older people* (see Chapter 12). The aim was to keep older people out of large residential care facilities and to develop community and domiciliary supports such as day centres and home helps. In addition, there was a clear decision to enable people to enter

1 We have deliberately emphasised the fact that people with a whole range of mental health issues were often incarcerated, not just those who had clearly definable mental disorders like schizophrenia, for example. Those who today would be classed as having an anxiety disorder may well have been institutionalised, particularly if they lacked any appreciable form of social support.

private residential homes. Such policy decisions essentially channelled public sector funds into the private residential sector whilst leaving the domiciliary sector chronically under-resourced. Private residential homes increased in number and in the absence of the necessary community services, older people had little choice other than the decision about which institution they might enter in the residential private sector (Adams, Dominelli and Payne 2009). These developments were consistent with the ideologies of the Thatcher Government during the 1980s and subsequently (see Chapter 3). As a result, the primary source of support for older people in the community was identified as being informal and voluntary in nature, relying heavily on family, friends and neighbours. Thus, care *in* the community was seen as being care *by* the community (Tinker 1996).

There was considerable opposition to this new direction in policy development as it was seen as being motivated by economics and a desire to curb public spending. One of the main concerns was that care by the community effectively meant care by *women* (Oakley 2005; Orme 2000), and benefit payments that existed in no way compensated for the loss of earnings that were necessarily incurred when a woman took on extra caring responsibilities.

The Audit Commission Report, *Making a Reality of Community Care* (1986), was critically important as it stood as an objective and non-political discourse on the state of community care arrangements. From this report, the Government commissioned Sir Roy Griffiths to look at the organisation and funding for community care services and his report, *Community Care: Agenda for Action* (Griffiths 1988) represented an important milestone in that it heavily influenced the 1989 White Paper and identified three main objectives underpinning the new community care policy orientation. These focused on the individual user and carer in terms of *meeting need, improving choice* and *promoting self-determination.*

The White Paper *Caring for People: Community Care: Into the Next Decade and Beyond* (Department of Health 1989) accepted some of the Griffiths Report's proposals and held as centrally important the aims of increasing user choice, promoting non-institutional services and targeting services to those that needed them. In short, though local authorities were to retain responsibility for community care, they were to work far more closely with the private and voluntary sectors. It was also proposed that local authorities would be *less involved* in the direct provision of services and more involved in the assessment of peoples' needs and *managing* and *coordinating* the care that was provided. The White Paper was essentially the blueprint for what we recognise today as 'care management' (Means, Richards and Smith 2008). In essence,

> the government response to the Griffiths' Report must be read in the light of broader political objectives concerning the desirability of rolling back the

> state, of reducing welfare dependency, of promoting self-reliance and of creating individual and family responsibilities as a counterbalance to right and entitlements. These themes have informed welfare policies – whether Conservative or Labour – ever since. (Horner 2009: 78)

This led to a move away from authorities being (monopolistic) *providers* of services to them becoming *purchasers*. In some instances they did have a provider role from their own staff and resources ('in-house' services), although these had to be cost-effective and meet the standards of a 'best value' review. The White Paper generated similar developments within the health service with hospitals becoming self-governing trusts, GPs becoming fund-holders with their own devolved budgets and health authorities becoming purchasers of services. Such principles were enshrined in legislation in the form of the NHS and Community Care Act 1990 (UK) which was and remains the central legislative plank upon which current health and community care policy and practice rests (Powell 2001). Within Scotland, the 1990 Act is germane as is the National Assistance Act 1948 (UK), although there are a number of other statutes and a range of policy initiatives that relate only to Scotland (see Table 7.1). The 1990 Act sought to alter the balance of care in four main directions:

1. move from institutional care to community based care (which in this sense does *not* mean residential care in the community but care within people's own homes);
2. move from a supply-led, provider dominated system to a needs-led, purchaser dominated system;
3. move from public sector (state) provision to independent/voluntary/private sector provision;
4. move from NHS to local authority responsibility for funding.

One of the consequences of the creation of the purchaser/provider split was its effect upon the assessment task. One of the criticisms of the Griffiths Report was that the assessment of need had been focused too much upon the current availability of resources and was therefore essentially flawed, being resource led, with service users having little involvement in the process. Some of these issues were tied up with the rhetoric around increasing consumer choice and empowerment, two of the essential ingredients of a 'contract-culture' (Flynn and Williams 1997). It was suggested that by introducing the purchaser/provider split, the assessment of need would be more effective. The assessor would be unconcerned as to the current availability of resources to meet identified need because they would have greater autonomy and access to resources (cash) to buy whatever was required on the open market, or to create it if it did not exist. This, it was

Table 7.1 Relevant community care legislation

Major community care related legislation (all UK legislation applies to Scotland (S))	
Health Services Act 1946 (UK).	National Health Service (S) Act 1978
National Assistance Act 1948 (UK)	Adults with Incapacity (S) Act 2000
Chronically Sick and Disabled Persons Act 1970 (UK)	Regulation of Care (S) Act 2001
Disabled Persons (Services, Consolidation and Representation) Act 1986 (UK)	Community Care and Health (S) Act 2002
NHS and Community Care Act 1990 (UK)	Mental Health (Care and Treatment) (S) Act 2003
Carers (Recognition and Services) Act 1995 (UK)	National Health Service Reform (S) Act 2004
Community Care (Direct Payments) Act 1996 (UK)	Smoking, Health and Social Care (S) Act 2005
Disability Discrimination Act 1995 (UK)	Scottish Commission for Human Rights Act 2006
Care Standards Act 2000 (UK)	Adult Support and Protection (S) Act (2007)
Welfare Reform Act 2007 (UK)	Protection of Vulnerable Groups (S) Act 2007
Social Work (S) Act 1968	
Chronically Sick and Disabled Persons (S) Act 1972	

Note: Remember that the terms and conditions of the European Convention on Human Rights (1950) and the Human Rights Act 1998 apply to all UK/Scottish legislation.

argued, would increase customer choice and make for services that were more responsive to real need. In essence, services would be needs led rather than resource led. However, some commentators have suggested that in reality, customers (service users) only have options rather than choices (Myers and MacDonald 1996).

> Since community care policy is underpinned by a notion of efficiency and state financial restraint, it is not surprising that a binary split appears to develop when service provision is compared to service users' identified needs. What service users have, in effect, are options not choices because the contradictions inherent in policy that seek to both ration and prioritise resources, as well as encourage service user choice and participation, creates tensions that make them untenable. (Prior 2001: 111)

The role of the social worker in relation to community care clients was redefined as that of 'care manager' in the wake of the 1990 Act and was seen as being pivotal to the achievement of community care objectives in the following ways:

1. by encouraging more flexible and sensitive responses to the needs of users and carers;
2. by allowing a greater range of options (not choices?);
3. by emphasising *minimum intervention* in order to foster increased independence;
4. to prevent deterioration;
5. to concentrate on those individuals in greatest need.

Many social workers and other professionals acting as care managers have effectively been removed from the front-line of direct, face-to-face work with individuals, and are now heavily involved in the administration of referrals and the monitoring of care packages. Jordan and Jordan (2000: 37) ask whether social work is 'developing into an arm's length, office bound, report-writing, official kind of practice which leaves face-to-face work to others'. In addition, although most social workers would not necessarily disagree entirely with the *aims* of care management, there is a sense in which many professionals feel disengaged from the social work role and task, seeing themselves more and more simply as bureaucrats, a theme recently considered within *Changing Lives* (Scottish Executive 2006a) for social work as a whole.

An essential part of the process of care management is the assessment of people's needs. Law (sections 5A and 12A Social Work (S) Act 1968 as inserted by s52 of the 1990 Act) and policy clearly instructs local authorities and practitioners to focus on individual need and not on the resources available. This remains the cornerstone of good practice but it is perhaps unavoidable that knowledge of the limited availability of local resources may have some impact on the assessments carried out (McDonald 2006). The creation of the *Joint Future Agenda* in Scotland was significant in a number of respects, not the least of which was the recommendation that assessments for community care services should avoid being repetitive with several professionals (for example a social worker, an occupational therapist and a public health nurse) assessing the same individual as part of the same process. As a result of these concerns the *Single Shared Assessment* process has evolved with the aim of minimising the level of intrusion into the individuals life and minimising professional repetition and ultimately (and rightly in this regard) the cost of professional time in undertaking assessments.

The main focus for community care policy in Scotland comes from the Joint Future Agenda (Scottish Executive 2000). Joint Future is the lead policy on joint working between local authorities and the National Health Service in community care. Its main aims, as stated by the then Scottish Executive, and based upon the issues raised within *Modernising Community Care: An Action Plan* (Scottish Office 1998) were to facilitate quicker and more effective decision making through delegated decision-making and financial responsibility, provide more flexible and better quality home care services, including a shift in the balance of care towards such services, and more partnership working between agencies at the local level through better operational and strategic planning, joint budgets, joint services and joint systems.

The Joint Future Unit within the former Scottish Executive was charged with delivering policy on Joint Future. It began by developing an infrastructure, which emphasised the joint management and joint resourcing of community care services along with the development of the *Single Shared Assessment (SSA)* and an emphasis on performance management. These orientations clearly reflect the aims of the 1990 Act in relation to the utilisation of business principles within welfare systems, notably the reference to market forces and competition and, significantly, the emphasis on *managerialism*. This refers to the tendency for services to have to provide solutions to resource difficulties by reference to more effective resource *management*, rather than any thought about the need to *increase* available resources. Essentially, people have to manage what they have more effectively; get more for the same, or less (Harris 2003).

Another point is that the interface between community care services and health services is very prominent. In fact, many of the services which social workers commission and/or coordinate in their roles as care managers often include *significant* elements of health related services. Whilst social workers may coordinate and commission such services, they may not be the person or the service representative that *delivers* them. Therefore, when we speak about community care, we must remember that a large element of this is health related. Similarly, a huge amount of the care that goes on in people's own homes and within local communities is *social care* as opposed to *social work*. The social work and social care workforce in Scotland is estimated at 138,000 people, having grown by approximately 33 per cent over recent years and being predominantly female (82 per cent in 2004). Those who are employed in social services in Scotland work in the voluntary sector (25 per cent), the private sector (33 per cent) and in local authorities (42 per cent) (Scottish Executive 2005a).

Some assumptions and realities of community-based care

Underpinning the policy and legislative developments discussed above are certain aims and assumptions. Though on the surface, they are widely held and adhered to, it is useful to look at them in a little more detail and to acknowledge some of the realities of community care as experienced by service users, carers and social care and social workers.

One of these is the belief that people would rather be cared for in their own homes. On the face of it, this is a fairly uncontroversial statement. Most people, when asked, would state that should they need assistance when they are older or if they became unwell or disabled, they would far rather receive this care from people coming to their own home than have to move into residential care. Indeed social workers and care managers are often in the position of supporting families who are struggling with the reality of being no longer able to care for a relative that they promised not to 'put in a home'. What is the reality though?

Exercise 7.1

With reference to policy objectives, as a social worker/care manager what would your priorities be when assessing someone whose health had deteriorated but who wanted to remain in their own home? Consider the case study below.

Case study

Iain lives on his own in a three-bedroom council flat. His only daughter lives abroad and visits once a year. Iain had always been determined that should he need assistance as he grew older, that this should be provided in his own home. His daughter was determined to uphold Iain's wishes with regard to this and was reluctant to discuss the possibility that her father might at some point need to be cared for in a residential setting.

Iain was diagnosed with severe dementia and was disorientated to time, space and people. Carers came to his house to help him to get up in the morning and dress him, to administer his medication, to prepare his food and supervise him whilst he ate it, to do his shopping and collect his pension and to help him to wash and get into bed at the end of the day.

The reality of providing this level of support is that a number of agencies (private, voluntary and local authority) needed to be involved. This necessitated a high number of staff providing care and support. There was the occasional, perhaps inevitable, breakdown in communication if a carer was off sick or rotas had been changed. This meant that sometimes Iain could sit waiting for one of his meals, or be waiting to get in or out of bed, and no-one would turn up to assist him.

Even when services did run smoothly, Iain was often confused by the number of people, often unfamiliar due to high staff turnover, that came to his house. He became frightened and suspicious and often refused to let people in. When this happened staff spent an increasing amount time trying to negotiate their way into the flat and therefore had little time to spend with Iain. This resulted in support being provided in a very functional way with little time for social interaction.

This picture is not one normally associated with the ideal of caring for people in their own home in accordance with their and their families' wishes. This is in no way an argument against the provision of community care through domiciliary services but hopefully illustrates some of the complexities involved in caring for people in their own homes. One of the key challenges then is to ensure that domiciliary services, and indeed all services, are 'fit for purpose' and can adequately meet the needs of the most vulnerable people (Fink 2004).

Unpaid care: The position of carers

The shift towards care in (and by?) the community raised concerns that the burden of care would fall on women who were understood to constitute the largest proportion of unpaid carers in the community. The term 'carer' has had varying definitions but there are some essential elements in the current definition of 'carer'. These are that the care is *unpaid*, that it is provided to a *relative, friend* or *child*, and that the *recipient could not manage independently at home without this care*. In relation to the caring *task*, this may involve physical and intimate care (personal care) alongside the provision of other activities to meet the needs of daily living and also involve the maintenance of the safety or security of the cared-for person through appropriate and adequate supervision. All of these elements when seen together should remind us of the *intensity* of this task and its central importance to anything like a decent quality of life.

As the socio-demographic picture changed over recent years (Clark and Lynch 2010) increasing life expectancy meant that more spouses were becoming carers. Alongside this the number of women working outside the home grew as the generation of single women carers diminished. Increasingly the responsibility for looking after others, generally older people, fell on their married daughters (or daughters-in-law). Many of these women would also have caring responsibility for children and found themselves with a growing burden of care.

The roots of the carers' movement can be found in The National Council for the Single Woman and Her Dependents, established in 1965, which had campaigned for recognition of the isolation and hardship experienced by single women carers. The council became known as the National Council for Carers and their Elderly Dependents (NCCED) in 1982 in recognition of the socio-economic changes of the previous decade, which had seen a broader and more diverse body of unpaid carers emerge. Other carers' organisations soon emerged including the Association of Carers (UK) and at that time some initial policy development was visible. The National Health Service Act 1977 (UK) made provision to enable local authorities to use their powers to provide support to carers through the provision of information and by other means such as assisting carers' support groups. This is perhaps a more symbolic moment in policy development as it is not clear to what extent these powers were actually exercised by the local authorities or how many carers benefitted from these measures.

However, in 1981 the Association of Carers was launched which was to be a broader-based organisation for all carers, regardless of their age and sex and originated partly as a response to the frustrations of carers at the limited support being offered by local authorities. Whilst taking account of the changing nature of carers and the caring task, this also reflected the growing influence of self-help and mutual support groups in the UK. The establishment of the Association coincided with and was influenced by this broad movement. More than 300 carers' groups were set up across the UK in the wake of the new association. This meant not only that carers would have access to new means of information, advice and mutual support, but also that the foundations of a powerful and influential campaigning and lobbying group were being laid.

The Disabled Persons Act 1986 (UK) recognised carers in that local authorities were required to '... have regard to the ability of that other person to continue to provide such care on a regular basis' (section 8(1)(b)) when making an assessment of the cared-for person. This, however, did not amount to a separate assessment of need for the carer. The growing awareness of the needs and desires of carers as evidenced in these policy developments demonstrated the influence of carers' organisations, further consolidated by the creation of the Carers National Association formed from the Association of Carers and the NCCED. This offered a single, stronger voice with which to address government and the media on the concerns of carers.

Having achieved some recognition for carers the movement continued to lobby for change and The Carers (Recognition and Services) Act was passed in 1995 (the Carers Act 1995). This Act defined a carer for the first time and set out in law the basic rights of carers. A carer is defined as:

> an individual [who] provides or intends to provide a substantial amount of care on a regular basis (section 1(b)).

The terms *substantial* and *regular* are not defined in the Act and were open to interpretation as is often the case with legislation; this is where policy plays its part. There does remain an issue about those who provide care which is perhaps less *quantifiable* and perhaps 'visible', such as emotional support or supervising the security or safety of an individual. The definition does not specify that the carer must be related to the person cared for or living with them – recognising a broader understanding of care, the carer and the caring task. The basic rights that the Carers Act 1995 provided were those for a full assessment of the carer's needs in the context of the assessed care needs of the individual being cared for, and for the results of this assessment to be taken into account when the local authority makes decisions about services to be provided. This supports the idea that the carer is generally the principal provider of care and recognises the knowledge and experience they have of that persons needs.

The Carers Act 1995 also recognises and defines *young carers* within the same descriptors of someone providing substantial and regular care. As we shall see, the sometimes detrimental effects of caring on both adults and young people have been demonstrated and as a consequence the Children (Scotland) Act 1995 may be helpful in identifying and providing support to young carers as 'children in need', the terms of section 93(4)(a)(iv) being particularly relevant here. The utilisation of other relevant statutes is a vital component in ensuring that full explication is given to the crosscutting nature of the caring task and that all possible means of support are made available to carers.

Following the general election of 1997 and the formation of a New Labour Government, an announcement was made in June during Carers Week that a national strategy would be developed for carers. This was possibly the most important policy document in the history of the carers' movement. In 1999 Prime Minister Tony Blair in his foreword to the strategy stated

> What carers do should be properly recognised, and properly supported. Carers should be able to take pride in what they do. And in turn, we should take pride in carers. I am determined to see that they do – and that we all do. (Department of Health 1999: 4)

This recognition came in the form of almost one hundred pledges in relation to support, services and employment for carers. One of the important consequences of the strategy was the development of local carers' strategies involving new partnerships of carers with local authorities, voluntary organisations, employers and other interested parties. This in turn strengthened and located the carers' movement in local planning, commissioning and service delivery as well as providing new avenues for influencing policy and practice. The national strategy had three strands – information, support and care.

The creation of the Scottish Parliament following the passing of The Scotland Act 1998 allowed devolved power in relation to many welfare-related matters to be assumed by that Parliament (see Chapter 1). This meant that while broad-based policy would still be influenced by developments across the UK, a new emphasis was lent to the carers' movement in Scotland. Scotland-based carers' groups along with the Scottish elements of UK-wide bodies had more direct routes to legislators within a new and more accessible parliamentary process. The Community Care and Health (Scotland) Act 2002 (the 2002 Act) introduced new provisions to support carers. There is now a broad duty to inform carers of their rights to assessment, thus strengthening the identification of carers needs as being separate to those of the cared-for person. Carers defined as providing 'substantial and regular care' become entitled to an assessment independent of the assessment of the person cared for and, for the first time, carers under the age of 16 have the right to an assessment.

Carers were a central element within the recent review of Scottish social work (Scottish Executive 2006a) and one of the many working groups supporting the broad review group was a Users and Carers Panel which gave service users and carers the opportunity to influence directly the outcome of the review. Amongst quotes used throughout the report from the Users and Carers Panel is the following which policy makers must acknowledge:

> We expect services to make a positive difference to our lives. We are people first. The outcomes we want include having power and control, being able to take risks and contribute to society. This means that there needs to be a shift in power away from people who commission and provide services to service users and carers. (Scottish Executive 2006a: 33)

The shift towards putting carers at the centre of policy was further demonstrated by the creation of the process known as Care 21. In 2005 the Scottish Government commissioned widespread research and consultation across a number of work streams which included health, respite, training and young carers. This was the most comprehensive evidence base assembled in relation to unpaid care and put Scotland in the forefront of policy development for carers and young carers. Information gathered included a national survey of more than 4,000 carers supported by focus groups and individual interviews (a process known as 'The Voice of Carers') and a national household survey of the general population looking at perceptions of caring and what participants anticipated about their own future caring responsibilities.

The subsequent report (Scottish Executive 2006b) set out a vision that put the needs of carers within a human rights framework and recognised a number of rights for those who care for a relative, friend or neighbour. The report also set out 22 recommendations for moving towards this rights-based approach and included the establishment of a Carers Rights Charter in Scotland, specific representation of young carers through a national young carer's forum and the development of training, planning and delivery of services for and with carers, and outlined how it intended to focus on initial priorities while not losing sight of the wider objective. It remains to be seen how far the influence of Care 21 will go in improving outcomes for carers.

The movement towards a rights-based approach was further consolidated by proposals to ensure that the rights of carers will be protected from discrimination by inclusion in the Equality Bill which was published by the UK Parliament in April 2009. The Equality Act received Royal Assent in April 2010 and progressive implementation from October 2010. As part of wide ranging measures within the Act to reduce 'the inequalities of outcome which will result from socio-economic disadvantage' (section 1(1)), the rights of carers will be protected. The Equality Act 2010 strengthens the law, protecting people from discrimination when they are associated with someone who is themselves protected, for example as their carer (Government Equalities Office 2009).

Young carers

Whilst the carers' movement was improving the visibility and understanding of the needs and conditions of predominantly *adult* carers, the recognition of young people who provide care was lagging behind. Carers' organisations were 'discovering' hidden young carers and responding in a piecemeal way to their needs. The whole notion of young carers depended to a degree on the conceptualisation of children as carers and identifying and understanding what young carers do and how it affects them (Christie 2007). In general, young carers often provide substantial and regular care to another person and in consequence

> assume a level of responsibility which would usually be associated with an adult [and often] experience impaired psychosocial development, including poor educational attendance and performance, and restricted peer networks, friendships and opportunities ... [which] ... will have implications for their own adulthood. (Becker 2000: 378)

There are, however, debates about the extent to which any definition can be applied to young carers and whether the use of the word 'carer' is in itself helpful. There is a need to recognise that young carers are both young people *and* carers and this puts them in a different position to adult carers. Whilst there are arguments against the use of the term 'young carer', progress has been made in recognising and addressing the dual needs of these young people as both carers and children. The range of circumstances in which children can find themselves caring is quite broad: the impacts of caring for a parent with a physical disability can be quite different from those of caring for an adult with a mental illness or indeed caring for parents with problematic drug or alcohol use, whilst caring for a sibling or other family member will bring different challenges and consequences for young people.

There is a further issue in relation to defining young carers and this lies in a tension between defining caring solely in terms of quantity and regularity and in terms of thinking about the outcomes for young people in relation to their social and personal development (Christie 2007). As we saw above, the Carers (Recognition and Services) Act 1995 extended the definition of caring to include young people so that a young carer is a person who provides or intends to provide a substantial amount of care on a regular basis. This means that service providers need to be alert to children in need (however defined) and use whatever legal or policy means available to support and intervene with and on behalf of young carers. It took many years and much lobbying and campaigning by many to assist adults to come to an understanding of the term 'carer' and moreover to identify themselves explicitly as such. Similarly the process will be a long one for young carers. Many know no different or accept their circumstances as normal. For some there may be fears in relation to the possibility of being removed from the home or concerns about the stigma or illegality related to the adult's care needs. There does, however, seem to be a movement towards reconciling these two positions with policy makers recognising that young people who may not be providing 'substantial' care may still be harmed by the responsibilities they face. Perception is reality (Social Care Institute for Excellence 2005; Frank 2002).

The continuing development of carers' policy in Scotland will be progressed by a new National Carers Strategy for Scotland to be published in 2010. The revised National Strategy will build on the 1999 Strategy for Carers and take account of Care 21. In order to support the development of this strategy, a young carers steering group was established which included representation from young carers groups and groups working with children and young people. The government outlined that the strategy would be developed within the context of existing policies relating to children and young people, particularly *Getting it Right for Every Child* (GIRFEC) (Scottish

Executive 2005b), *The Road to Recovery* (Scottish Government 2009) and the *Curriculum for Excellence* (Scottish Executive 2004). This shows an intention to incorporate young carers into wider policy initiatives for young people in line with the stated intentions of the GIRFEC methodology (see Chapter 14).

Ongoing themes and issues within policy

Changing demographics

Older people (Clark and Lynch 2010; Crawford and Walker 2008; and Chapter 12) are often seen as the main users of health and welfare services in Scotland and the UK generally. The reasons for this are obvious; increasing age brings with it increasing frailty and changes to health and well-being generally, which will often require assistance. However, it is important to bear in mind that the vast majority of older people manage quite well and do not require assistance from the state. Those that do are often impeded in their capacity to cope by a range of other factors, not the least of which is an absence of family and/or social supports, which can add to the cumulative impact of increasing age. The UK, in common with most other first-world countries, has an *increasing* elderly population with a distinct gender bias evident in favour of women (Clark and Lynch 2010). A better quality of life, supported by better housing, more disposable income and better health care and so on have all contributed towards increased longevity. From a strictly humanistic perspective, this has to be applauded, and provides evidence that policy initiatives over the past century or more have been largely effective. However, from a policy-making perspective, this success brings with it a range of other challenges. One of these is how to pay for the services that are likely to be required by an increasing number of older people, many of whom are economically *inactive* within the formalised labour markets. The costs of health and community care services as well as pensions, have to be met from the public purse via taxation (see Chapter 3). Debates concerning such matters have been ongoing for some time, particularly in terms of which agency should be mainly responsible for the costs of long-term care for older people. The NHS and Community Care Act 1990 gave local authorities the lead role in this regard and legislation and policy exists to facilitate the complex partnership arrangements required to facilitate this. The Community Care and Health (S) Act 2002 is one example of this (Petch 2003). Part two of the 2002 Act (sections 13–17) refers to joint working arrangements between authorities whilst part one deals with the whole issue of free personal care which has been introduced in Scotland but not as yet in the rest of the UK (Sutherland 1999).

Funding

Alongside the aims and objectives contained in community care legislation and policy, one of the key factors in the development and delivery of services is the availability of finance. The experiences of all those in receipt of community care services and those involved in its implementation are inevitably affected by the level of funding made available. Community care is one of the highest areas for revenue spending for most local authorities (see Chapter 3). Policy and legislation state that assessments should be *needs-led* and not *resource-led* but the reality is that there are insufficient resources or finances to meet the needs of all those assessed as requiring a service. Allocation criteria have been devised and employed to distribute the resources as fairly as possible. This inevitably leads to concerns about the system being overly bureaucratic with a danger of different client groups competing against each other for their share of the pot. The challenge for each local authority is to ensure that these limited resources are targeted at the most vulnerable members of society.

The whole area of how to pay for community care is, in policy terms, highly significant. As we saw above, the NHS and Community Care Act 1990 had economic concerns firmly in its remit and legislated for ways in which resources should be used and where lead responsibility should lie (with local authorities). The issue of 'who pays?' is not new. The *Report of the Royal Commission on Long Term Care for the Elderly* (Sutherland 1999) added fuel to this debate. It recommended that, where possible, older people should remain in their own homes for as long as possible and, secondly, that where a person required personal care, either in their own home or in a residential setting, then this should be free of charge. The previous Labour Government in Westminster refused to accept this second recommendation, although the Scottish Parliament's Health and Community Care Committee *did* accept it and free personal and (in some instances) nursing care was introduced in Scotland in July 2002, brought into force by the Community Care and Health (S) Act 2002. This represents a significant divergence between the policies of the Westminster and Scottish Parliaments, although how the decision was arrived at in Holyrood is a matter of speculation, with political expediency, rather than concerns for older people perhaps being higher on the agenda (Shaw 2003). Whilst this may present as cynicism, it merely represents the realities of policy and policy making, much of which *is* pragmatic and expedient, thereby offering further proof to the maxim that intentions and outcomes may often be different things. In this context, the intention was to *reject* the recommendations of the Royal Commission, but in the event, the outcome was the opposite because of parliamentary pressure that would have split the coalition Government of Scotland.

An understanding of the use of direct payments related to the Community Care (Direct Payments) Act 1996 may be of particular help here where the person can purchase their own care package, which would not include the use of relatives as the policy precludes payments to immediate family members. The Carers (Recognition of Services) Act 1995 can, however, provide an assessment of need and support for carers with shopping, cooking, respite and a range of other services.

Personal care

Significantly, a large proportion of domiciliary care services are still provided by statutory organisations (usually the local authority). These are primarily delivered under the duties imposed upon local authorities in all countries of the UK, by the NHS and Community Care Act 1990 and other related legislation and regulations. It makes provision for a range of people in need, including older people to be cared for within their own homes. Significantly, the Community Care and Health (Scotland) Act 2002 made free personal care available to older people. This has impacted significantly on the increased uptake of domiciliary services in Scotland.

There is a specific emphasis on *personalisation* and *empowerment* (see Chapter 9) in Scotland and the UK where public services should be adapted to meet the individual needs of clients. While this creates a tension with diminishing resources and the talk of restricted funding of public services in future budgets, it addresses and moves forward the agenda of person-centred and individualised services.

Delayed discharges

One of the rationales behind the shift to community care and an emphasis on improving day and domiciliary care services was the number of older people who often remained in hospital beds for no other reason than they did not have anywhere else to go. This was often because they had no one to support them within their own homes. Because of a perceived lack of community care services and poor coordination of service delivery, concerns grew around this increasing tendency (Audit Scotland 2005). One of the other effects of this 'bed-blocking' was that hospital beds for those that required them were unavailable. As a result, the Scottish Executive and NHS (Scotland) (in line with other parts of the UK) has developed policy to address these issues along with the creation of *Community Health Partnerships* (CHPs) under the terms of the National Health Service Reform (Scotland) Act 2004. These CHPs seek to bridge the divide between primary and secondary care *and* (interestingly) between health and social care. It is also planned to devolve more budgetary and resource control to *front-line staff*, an evolving and generalised theme which has found itself evident in the *21st Century Social Work Review* (Scottish Executive 2006a).

Home (domiciliary) care

Home care services are those that provide very practical support to people within their own homes. For example, a home help may visit someone each morning to ensure that they are out of bed and may assist with some daily living tasks. Nowadays, this service is often means-tested, unlike many European countries and with the introduction of free personal care in Scotland, the definition of what is and is not regarded as 'personal' has become an issue that has affected home care services. For example, imagine that you are able to attend to your own personal needs adequately, but cannot manage to wash your clothes, clean the house or go and buy shopping. At what point do these things impinge upon your self-care and become issues around *personal* care? If you cannot afford to pay a charge for home care services, do you wait until your well-being deteriorates to such an extent that you require personal care?

Exercise 7.2

Consider the scenario referred to above regarding the provision of home (domiciliary) care. As a social worker, how would you deal with this dilemma? How would you feel if you were told that you could not provide home care services, but *could* provide free personal care once it was necessary, knowing that, in your professional judgement, this would entail an unnecessary deterioration in the person's situation?

Is this an example of managerialism versus professional autonomy? If so, does current policy appear to favour the former over the latter and what does this say about other trends that appear to favour increasing autonomy for front-line workers?

Is there evidence of a contradiction here? If so, how might the tensions and contradictions manifest themselves in practice?

Nursing and residential care services

Prior to the introduction of the NHS and Community Care Act 1990, those people whose income fell below a certain level were entitled to the payment of residential and nursing home fees through the social security system. In line with the then Conservative Government's view of the need to restrict public spending, the 1990 Act altered these priorities. Residential and nursing home care services were seen as but one arena where, through the introduction of community care policies, savings could be made, user choice and empowerment increased and a wider range of services developed. Residential and nursing home care then became the service of choice, so to speak, of the most needy and dependent. In terms of political rhetoric, such a rearrangement of service provision made sense. Those who preferred to stay at home, with appropriate support could do so, whereas those who had greatest need could use the provisions of residential and nursing home care.

In keeping with the introduction of the *purchaser/provider* split, the local authority became the 'gatekeeper' of these services, the assessment of need being used to determine who required these particular services. This therefore begs the question as to whether or not service user choice was actually increased when the local authority in fact determined whether what you wanted was in reality what you got via their assessment. Because of this shift in policy, local authorities began to invest heavily in providing domiciliary services (see above) to the most frail and elderly in their own homes. However, this did not slow down the numbers of people entering residential and nursing homes, partly because it was not always cheaper to provide care within a person's home. Furthermore, the cuts made to lower levels of domiciliary care threatened the preventative and rehabilitative aspects of such interventions with the fear that this would, ultimately, be counter-productive.

Health care

The whole issue of health care for older people in particular is one that is inherently bound up in the broader debates around the nature of health and health *inequalities* (see Chapters 10 and 12). The NHS and Community Care Act 1990 made local authorities the lead agency in relation to health and community care services. Over time, and certainly since devolution, a range of facilitative mechanisms to assist in this process have emerged including the Community Care and Health (Scotland) Act 2002 and the Community Care (Joint Working etc.) (Scotland) Regulations 2002.

From a policy perspective, the need to ensure that health and community care services are integrated is essential. As the demands placed upon services increase and become more complex, the inter-dependency of these services becomes more and more apparent. In some respects, the increasing levels of sophistication we see in terms of legislation, regulatory frameworks, funding patterns, organisational structuring and professional diversity brings with it a symbiosis which in its wake generates a momentum of its own. One of the concerns inherent in sophisticated structures used to deliver services is that as these become more complex, they begin to demand that more and more essential resources be diverted to sustain organisational and other structures, which has the possibility of diluting the impact of core services. In some respects, the advent of care management could be seen to be one example of this with increasing levels of bureaucracy taking social workers *away* from front-line service provision.

There is then a clear need for policymakers to ensure that 'joined-up' approaches are workable (McLean 2007). Health care provision for older people is intimately tied up to issues around funding, discharge policies, the availability or otherwise of domiciliary and/or residential and/or nursing home provision and cannot therefore be developed in isolation. The same can also be said for those services required by other service user groupings including those with a learning difficulty (Williams 2008; and see Chapters 9 and 13), mental health issues and mental disorders (Hothersall, Maas-Lowit and Golightley 2008; and Chapter 11) and other forms of disability (Maas-Lowit 2010; and see Chapter 13).

The development of a range of patterns for the provision of care has evolved steadily over the years and law and policy has guided and informed these. Importantly though, the experiences of service users, carers and practitioners have had a profound influence on the shape law and policy has taken. One of the distinct realities of care and caring is that imagination, creativity and compassion are necessary policy ingredients.

Chapter summary

This chapter has looked at some of the historical, ideological, political and economic factors underpinning the development and growth of community-based care policy and practice. We have considered some of the issues that face service providers and service users as well as considering some of the (sometimes difficult) realities of trying to get it just right for people. We have also referred you to a number of other important sources regarding some of the more detailed and specific issues of these forms of care for particular groups.

References

Adams, R., Dominelli, L. and Payne, M. (eds) (2009), *Social Work: Themes, Issues and Critical Debates* (3rd edn) (Basingstoke: Palgrave Macmillan).

Audit Commission (1986), *Making a Reality of Community Care* (London: HMSO).

Audit Scotland (2005), *Moving On? An Overview of Delayed Discharges in Scotland* (Edinburgh: Audit Scotland).

Becker, S. (2000), 'Young Carers', in M. Davies (ed.), *The Blackwell Encyclopaedia of Social Work* (Oxford: Blackwell): 378.

Christie, E. (2007), 'The Experience of Young Carers in the Context of a Range of Parental Conditions: Physical Disability, Mental Health Problems and Substance Misuse', unpublished PhD Thesis, The Robert Gordon University, Aberdeen.

Clark, A. and Lynch, R. (2010), 'Older People', in S.J. Hothersall and M. Maas-Lowit (eds), *Need, Risk and Protection in Social Work Practice* (Exeter: Learning Matters): Chapter 7.

Crawford, K. and Walker, J. (2008), *Social Work with Older People* (2nd edn) (Exeter: Learning Matters).

Department of Health (1989), *Caring for People: Community Care in the Next Decade and Beyond* (White Paper, Cmnd 849) (London: HMSO).

— (1999), *Caring about Carers: A National Strategy for Carers* (London: HMSO).

Finch, J. and Groves, D. (1980), 'Community Care and the Family: A Case for Equal Opportunities', *Journal of Social Policy* 9(4): 487–511.

Fink, J. (2004), *Care: Personal Lives and Social Policy* (Milton Keynes: Open University Press).

Flynn, R. and Williams, G. (eds) (1997), *Contracting for Health: Quasi-Markets and the National Health Service* (Oxford: Oxford University Press).

Frank, J. (2002), *Making it Work: Good Practice with Young Carers and their Families* (London: The Children's Society and The Princess Royal Trust for Carers).

Goffman, E. (1961), *Asylums: Essays on the Social Situation of the Mental Patient and Other Inmates* (Harmondsworth: Penguin).

Government Equalities Office (2009), *A Fairer Future: The Equality Bill and Other Action to Make Equality a Reality* (London: HMSO).

Griffiths, R. (1988), *Community Care: An Agenda for Action* (London: HMSO).

Ham, C. (2009), *Health Policy in Britain* (6th revised edn) (Basingstoke: Palgrave Macmillan).

Harris, J. (2003), *The Social Work Business* (London: Routledge).

HMSO (1957), *Report of the Royal Commission on the Law Relating to Mental Illness and Mental Deficiency* (Cmnd 169) (London: HMSO).

— (1969), *Report of the Committee of Inquiry into Allegations of Ill-Treatment of Patients and other Irregularities at the Ely Hospital, Cardiff* (Cmnd 3975). London: HMSO.

Horner, N. (2009), *What is Social Work? Context and Perspectives* (3rd edn) (Exeter: Learning Matters).

Hothersall, S.J. (2010), 'Need, Risk and Vulnerability', in S.J. Hothersall and M. Maas-Lowit (eds), *Need, Risk and Protection in Social Work Practice* (Exeter: Learning Matters): Chapter 1.

Hothersall, S.J. and Maas-Lowit, M. (eds) (2010), *Need, Risk and Protection in Social Work Practice* (Exeter: Learning Matters).

Hothersall, S.J., Maas-Lowit, M. and Golightley, M. (2008), *Social Work and Mental Health in Scotland* (Exeter: Learning Matters).

Jordan, B. and Jordan, C. (2000), *Social Work and the Third Way* (London: Sage).

Maas-Lowit, M. (2010), 'Mental Health', in S.J. Hothersall and M. Maas-Lowit (eds), *Need, Risk and Protection in Social Work Practice* (Exeter: Learning Matters): Chapter 6.

McDonald, A. (2006), *Understanding Community Care: A Guide for Social Workers* (2nd edn) (Basingstoke: Palgrave Macmillan).

McLean, T. (2007), 'Interdisciplinary Practice', in J. Lishman (ed.), *Handbook for Practice Learning in Social Work and Social Care* (2nd edn) (London: Jessica Kingsley).

Means, R., Richards, S. and Smith, R. (2008), *Community Care: Policy and Practice* (4th edn) (Basingstoke: Palgrave Macmillan).

Myers, F. and MacDonald, C. (1996), '"I Was Given Options Not Choices": Involving Older Users and Carers in Assessment and Care Planning', in R. Bland (ed.), *Developing Services for Older People and their Families* (London: Jessica Kingsley).

Oakley, A. (2005), *The Ann Oakley Reader: Gender, Women and Social Science* (Bristol: Policy Press).

Orme, J. (2000), *Gender and Community Care: Social Work and Social Care Perspectives* (Basingstoke: Palgrave Macmillan).

Parsons, T. (1952), *The Social System* (London: Tavistock).

Parsons, T. and Bales, R.F. (1956), *Family Socialization and Interaction Process* (London: Routledge and Kegan Paul).

Petch, A. (2003), 'Care in the Community', in D. Baillie, K. Cameron, L.-A. Cull, J. Roche and J. West (eds), *Social Work and the Law in Scotland* (Basingstoke: Palgrave Macmillan/Open University Press).

Powell, J.L. (2001), 'The NHS and Community Care Act (1990): A Critical Review'. Available at: http://sincronia.cucsh.udg.mx/nhs.htm (accessed 28 May 2010).

Prior, J. (2001), 'Older People', in M. Chakrabarti (ed.) (2001), *Social Welfare: Scottish Perspective* (Aldershot: Ashgate): 101–19.

Scottish Executive (2000), *Community Care: A Joint Future* (Edinburgh: Scottish Executive).

—— (2004), *Curriculum for Excellence* (Edinburgh: Scottish Government).

—— (2005a), *National Strategy for the Development of the Social Service Workforce in Scotland: A Plan for Action* (Edinburgh: Scottish Executive).

—— (2005b), *Getting it Right for Every Child: Proposals for Action* (Edinburgh: Scottish Executive).

—— (2006a), *Changing Lives: Report of the 21st Century Social Work Review* (Edinburgh: Scottish Executive). Available at: http://www.scotland.gov.uk/Publications/2006/02/02094408/0 [full report] (accessed 28 May 2010) or http://www.scotland.gov.uk/Publications/2006/02/02094718/2 [summary report] (accessed 28 May 2010).

—— (2006b), *The Future of Unpaid Care in Scotland* (Edinburgh: Scottish Executive).

Scottish Government (2009), *'The Road to Recovery': A New Approach to Tackling Scotland's Drug Problem* (Edinburgh: Scottish Government).

Scottish Office (1998), *Modernising Community Care: An Action Plan* (Edinburgh: Scottish Office).

Seligman, M. (1975), *Helplessness: On Depression, Development and Death* (San Francisco, CA: W.H. Freeman and Co.).

Shaw, E. (2003), 'Devolution and Scottish Labour: The Case of Long-Term Care for the Elderly', paper presented to the Annual Conference of the Political Studies Association, Leicester.

Social Care Institute for Excellence (SCIE) (2005), *The Health and Well Being of Young Carers*, Research Briefing 11 (London: Social Care Institute for Excellence). Available at: http://www.scie.org.uk/publications/briefings/briefing11/index.asp (accessed 28 May 2010).

Sutherland, S. (1999), *With Respect to Old Age: Long Term Care-Rights and Responsibilities*, Report of the Royal Commission on Long Term Care for the Elderly (London: Stationery Office).

Tinker, A. (1996), *Older People in Modern Society* (Essex: Longman).

Todd, M., Hothersall, S.J. and Owen, J. (2010), 'Intimacies and Relationships', in C. Yuill and A. Gibson (eds), *Sociology for Social Work: An Introduction* (London: Sage).

Williams, P. (2008), *Social Work and People with Learning Difficulties* (2nd edn) (Exeter: Learning Matters).

Wolfensberger, W. (1972), *The Principle of Normalisation in Human Services* (Toronto: NIMR).

—— (1975), *The Origin and Nature of Our Institutional Models* (New York: Human Policy Press).

—— (1982), 'Social Role Valorisation: A Proposed New Term for the Principle of Normalisation', *Mental Retardation* 21(6): 234–9.

Further reading

Hothersall, S.J. and Maas-Lowit, M. (eds), (2010), *Need, Risk and Protection in Social Work Practice* (Exeter: Learning Matters). This text offers a thorough introduction to a number of central themes relevant to vulnerable service users who are likely to be recipients of community-based care services. It looks in depth at need and vulnerability, risk and protection and locates these within specific service user and practice contexts.

Means, R., Richards, S. and Smith, R. (2008), *Community Care: Policy and Practice* (4th revised edn) (Basingstoke: Palgrave Macmillan). Offers a thorough account of the development of community care services and practice with a particular emphasis on the issues surrounding inter-disciplinary working, especially with health services.

Web-based resources

For access to a range of useful information regarding carers and caring in Scotland and the CARE 21 strategy, go to: http://www.carersscotland.org/Policyandpractice/Scotlandscarersstrategy (accessed 28 May 2010).

For information regarding the current position of the Scottish Government regarding carers and caring, including access to information relating specifically to young carers, go to: http://www.scotland.gov.uk/Topics/Health/care/Strategy (accessed 28 May 2010).

8 Welfare rights

Janine Bolger

Introduction

This chapter will begin with a look at the historical development of welfare support and the systems which deliver it. A case study will then be utilised to allow you to consider some of the key benefits available. Finally, the chapter will end by examining the current agenda for welfare support and the implications of this for funding and service delivery.

Since 1969 'Welfare Rights' has been the generic term used to explain the activity of ensuring that people are informed of and are receiving their entitlement to state benefits in the United Kingdom. Advisors are usually employed through the local authority or advice agencies and offer free and independent information, support in applying for welfare benefits and can represent appeals regarding benefits.

Such a system of welfare support has not always been readily available, however, and it is interesting to reflect on chronological developments of the provision of relief for those who are unable to provide for themselves adequately, or at all, through paid employment.

A history of the welfare rights and benefits system

In 1579 in Scotland an Act for Poor Relief established a system that would last for more than 300 years and would provide for the '... Punischment of Strang and Idle Beggars, and Reliefe of the Pure and Impotent'. Local parishes were compelled to make lists of their poor to ensure lodgings for those who could not take care of themselves, and to allow land-owners to take the offspring of beggars into unpaid work. The administration of poor relief was later (1597) undertaken by the church authorities who raised monies through donations, collections, interest from loans, land rental and fees for church services.

From the late 1500s the notion of 'settlement' in a specific parish was introduced in order to tie people to particular locations in line with feudal ideas. With this notion of settlement in place, people could be removed if they attempted to draw relief outside the area of their residence. Their parish of origin was accountable for costs incurred in their removal. To aid in identifying where poor people originated from, certificates of settlement were given in England and in Wales while in 1586 in Scotland, poor people were given their town's mark. Residence was initially defined as living in one parish for five or more years without begging or claiming relief. Resident status could be lost through non-residence in a specific parish of four years or more. Women could gain residence through marriage.

Presumably to deter the 'idle', Scotland established correction houses in 1672 in all its burghs where beggars could be detained and put to work. By 1774 'out-relief', where benefits or cash could be made available outwith the workhouse, was introduced in Glasgow. The demand for payments exceeded the supply and provision was inconsistent. With Scotland retaining its own judicial system as a result of The Act of Union in 1707, resulting in English Acts not having the force of statute in Scotland, it was 1845 before reform came about through The Scottish Poor Law Act. The implementation of this Act outlined the responsibility for administering poor relief in the form of cash, kind or in the form of poorhouses overseen by Parochial Boards in each parish. All applications for relief were assessed by an inspector appointed to each parish for this purpose. In Scotland there was no access to poor relief for the able-bodied poor (those who were fit and healthy but in low-paid work or unemployed) nor was there any legal right to appeal if it was denied.

The Local Government (Scotland) Act 1889 established county councils which assumed many of the powers previously held by parochial boards and Justices of the Peace. By the time a further Local Government (Scotland) Act was passed in 1929 many poorhouses had been transformed into Public Assistance Institutions offering care to the sick, the elderly and infirm and to unmarried pregnant women. With the functions of parish councils being passed on to larger district councils, poorhouse buildings were refurbished, sold or demolished in readiness for the National Health Service.

Although the Poor Law was not abolished until the 1948 National Assistance Act came into force, stigmatised provision through the Poor Law was replaced by the 1911 National Insurance Act (which was actually passed in 1908). National Insurance is a system of taxes and social security benefits. The Act, often regarded as the foundation of modern social welfare in the

UK, provided medical and time-limited unemployment benefits through funding by fixed payments from employers and workers. These reforms were part of a larger collection of social reforms but at this point social welfare provision only offered the right to a minimum level of income, support or service for those aged over 70 years and for some unemployed people. UK Social Security reform on a larger scale was not actually completed until 1948 (Bateman 2006). Welfare rights advocacy became evident from the 1930s through groups such as the National Unemployed Workers Movement who represented those who had been refused benefits through ruthless means testing and those who were entitled to, but not receiving, payments (Bateman 2006).

Citizen's Advice Bureaus (CABs) were created in the 1940s specifically to assist those whose situation had changed as a result of the war. In 1948 the legal aid scheme, designed to offer free or low cost legal advice to those living on low incomes, was implemented and in 1967 the UK's first law centre opened with the first local authority-employed welfare rights workers appearing in 1969 (Bateman 2006). Increasing levels of employment due to the high demand for un-skilled labour during the 1950s and 1960s resulted in a low demand for benefits. The Child Poverty Action Group (CPAG), instituted in 1965, became a leader in the welfare rights field in the UK only developing its advocacy role 'as a result of publicising the problem of poor take-up of benefit entitlement and being asked by individual claimants for help with benefit problems from about 1967 onwards' (Bull 1982 cited in Bateman 2006: 8).

Margaret Thatcher's Conservative Government in 1979 implemented free-market economic policies that impacted on inflation and unemployment and instituted policy changes on both benefits and taxation. High inflation not only lost people their jobs but brought retired people on low incomes into poverty. Along with increased numbers of lone parents the recognition of the roles and responsibilities of carers and a growing realisation of the needs of young disabled people all served to increase the need for welfare advice while throughout the 1980s aspects of the benefits system were whittled away (Bateman 2006). Opposition from a range of professional social work bodies and trade unions resulted in the investment in in-house welfare rights services by local authorities, publicity campaigns encouraging claims for additional help under schemes that were about to be cut or altered and the affirmation of local authority staff as advocates (Bateman 2006).

The election of a New Labour Government in 1997 resulted in major reforms to the benefit system through the 'welfare to work' initiatives for lone parents, young people and those with a disability, tax credit schemes, improvements to maternity benefits, gradual increases to mean-tested benefits for older people and changes to the administration of social security. However, we also saw the abolition of higher rates of benefit for

Table 8.1 Possible benefit entitlements

Circumstances	Corresponding Benefits/Tax Credits
Bereaved	Bereavement payment Widowed parent's allowance Bereavement allowance Funeral expenses payment
Carer – responsible for a child	Carer's allowance (CA) Child tax credit (CTC) Child benefit (CB) Guardian's allowance (GA) Statutory maternity pay (SMP) Statutory paternity pay (SPP) Statutory adoption pay (SAP) Maternity allowance (MA) Health benefits (HB) Cold weather payment (CWP)
Disabled	Disability living allowance (DLA) Attendance allowance (AA) Industrial injuries benefits (IJB) Cold weather payment
Incapable of work	Incapacity benefit (IB) Non-contributory incapacity benefit Statutory sick pay Severe disablement allowance (SDA) Cold weather payment Employment and support allowance (ESA)
Have a mortgage	Income support (IS) Income-based Jobseeker's Allowance (IJA) Pension credit (PC) Council tax benefit
Not enough money to meet certain needs	Community care grant Budgeting loan Crisis loan
Pensioner	State retirement pension Pension credit (PC) Winter fuel payment Cold weather payment
Pregnant	Statutory maternity pay Maternity allowance Sure start maternity grant Health benefits
Tenant	Housing benefit Council tax benefit
Unemployed and seeking work	Contribution-based Jobseeker's Allowance (CJA) Income-based Jobseeker's Allowance

lone parents, changes in incapacity benefit and in benefits for people from abroad, additional use of sanctions to modify the behaviour of claimants and the introduction of a range of benefits with no right of appeal (Bateman 2006). Under New Labour welfare rights provision improved through the increase of advice available in health settings and the funding of some advice through community regeneration projects and government initiatives such as Sure Start (aimed at giving children the best possible start in life through improvement of child care, early education, health and family support).

The benefit and tax credit system

The Department for Work and Pensions (DWP) has responsibility for the overall administration of social security benefits (other than council tax benefits and housing benefits which are administered by local authorities). Tax credits, child benefit and the guardian's allowance are dealt with through Her Majesty's Revenue and Customs. Most claims for benefits under state retirement age are administered through Jobcentre Plus, an executive agency of the DWP, while the Pension Service deals with pensions and pension credit. The Disability and Carers Service deals with carer's allowance and disability benefits. The Child Support Agency was replaced in 2008 by the Child Maintenance and Enforcement Commission, a new non-departmental public body established to take responsibility for the child maintenance system in Great Britain. The Tribunals Service, an executive agency of the Ministry of Justice, is responsible for administering appeals over benefits and tax credits.

Means-tested benefits are paid only if, on investigation, it is found that you have limited income and capital. You are not required to have made National Insurance contributions. Means-tested benefits include:

- income support/income-based Jobseeker's Allowance
- pension credit
- housing benefit and council tax benefit
- social fund payments
- child tax credit/working tax credit (Child Poverty Action Group 2008)

Certain benefits are available if specific conditions are met and do not require investigation into your finances, although earnings or occupational pensions will be taken into account for benefits designed to compensate for loss of income. These are known as *non-means-tested benefits* and include:

- attendance/carers allowance
- child benefit
- disability living allowance
- bereavement payments
- incapacity benefit
- industrial disablement benefit
- statutory maternity/paternity/adoption pay
- statutory sick pay (Child Poverty Action Group 2008)

An example of how confusing the welfare benefits system can be is evident when considering benefits such as jobseeker's (JSA) and employment and support allowances (ESA) which are both means-tested and non-means-tested; income-based Jobseeker's Allowance are means-tested and contributions-based while JSA is non-means-tested; income-related ESA is means-tested and contributory ESA is non-means-tested!

A combination of tax credits, means-tested and non-means-tested benefits may be claimed (all possible benefit entitlements are listed in Table 8.1).

It is impossible in just one chapter to consider all these tax credits and benefits in detail. Instead, we will examine some of the individuals in the following family case study and identify what benefits they might be entitled to.

This extended family lives in a four bed flat in a council housing estate. Financially they struggle, especially since the birth of Ebony and because Edna refuses to apply for any 'hand-outs' from the state.

The Taylor/Bradford family

Edna Taylor	86 years	great grand-mother
Mary Taylor	36 years	mother
Derek Bradford	42 years	co-habitee
Charlie Taylor	38 years	father and separated partner to Mary
Jennifer Taylor	17 years	daughter
Ebony Taylor	2 months	grand-daughter
Ross Taylor	15 years	son
Jane Taylor	11 years	daughter

Edna

Edna has suffered from angina for 15 years but recently the attacks have been more frequent and as a result Edna has moved in with her granddaughter Mary and her family. Edna's daughter Rose died from cancer last year. Edna can no longer bend over or lift anything without bringing on an attack. Inactivity has resulted in deterioration in Edna's mobility without a Zimmer frame and the support of a family member. She is refusing to eat and is struggling to maintain good levels of personal hygiene.

Edna has passed the pensionable age of 60 (to be changed to 65 for a woman in 2010–20). Whether she receives a Category A, B or D retirement pension depends on her marital status and whether she/her (late) husband made sufficient National Insurance contributions.

> Category A pension: individuals qualify on the basis of their own contribution record and can claim from State Pension age. There are two parts to a category A pension:
>
> - the basic State Pension (based on the number of qualifying years that have been built up during years of employment)
> - the additional State Pension (which depends on earnings during years of employment since additional State Pension was introduced in April 1978)
>
> Category B pension: based on National Insurance contributions of the spouse.
>
> Category D pension: a non-contributory State Pension for people of 80 years or older who are not in receipt of a State Pension or have one which pays less than the sum of a Category D pension. They must also meet other conditions, for example, a residence test, in order to qualify.
>
> (Thurley 2009 cited in House of Commons Library 2009)

If her husband died before 2001, and given her age, she may be able to claim Widow's pension and/or retirement pension. Other increases in pension entitlement will depend on whether she/her husband deferred on collecting pension payments. Increased payments are not made for any period whereby any other contributory benefit, carer's, maternity or severe disablement allowance was paid. Edna may be entitled to claim pension credit (guarantee or savings) depending on her 'income' while recipients of all categories of retirement pension receive an additional 25p per week and may be entitled to a Christmas bonus. She will be entitled to a winter fuel payment of £300, being over 80 years old, if there is no one else living in the house with an entitlement (that is, over 60 years old and so on). If Edna is in receipt of pension credit a period of seven consecutive days of average daily temperatures equal to or below nought degree Celsius should result in her being automatically awarded a cold weather payment from the DWP.

Edna is not eligible for disability living allowance (DLA) as the claim must be made prior to the 65th birthday of the claimant. As a UK resident over the age of 65 and requiring assistance to complete basic care tasks, she may be able to apply for attendance allowance (AA). The level at which she can claim will be tested according to a set of disability conditions. These criteria do not contain a mobility component, unlike the DLA assessment. Edna appears to have received support from Mary for more than six months and so she could be entitled to claim if she needs ongoing supervision to ensure her safety and requires attention during the day and/or the night in relation to bodily functions.

Mary

Mary Taylor has had some social work involvement in the past through the Community Mental Health Team. She has suffered intermittently from depression and spent some time in a psychiatric hospital following the birth of her daughter Jane. She was diagnosed with post-natal depression.

This was a difficult time for the family with problems in the relationship between Mary and husband Charlie surfacing. The couple eventually separated some six years ago. Charlie has maintained contact with the children although this has been erratic at times. Mary is finding the situation with Jennifer and the new baby very difficult. The house is overcrowded and trying to help Jennifer with the baby leaves her feeling exhausted. She and Derek are arguing more and she is worried he might leave.

If Mary had not been in employment as a result of the initial deterioration in her mental health (20 years ago) she may have been claiming long-term incapacity benefit (IB) (since its introduction in 1995 and invalidity benefit prior to this) on the grounds that she is incapable of work. Although Mary may not have qualified for IB on the basis of early National Insurance contributions, it would appear that she was under 19 years of age when she became incapacitated and would therefore be entitled to make a claim. If, however, since the birth of Jennifer, Mary has either been employed or has been considered fit for work and is now seeking employment then she could be claiming (contribution or income-based) Jobseeker's Allowance. She might have claimed the two (IB and jobseeker's) intermittently depending on when or whether she is or has been capable of working. If Derek is also currently out of work, and even though they are unmarried but living together as husband and wife, he and Mary may qualify as a joint-claim couple for JA. A claim for income-based JA would result in eligibility for a cold weather payment should the previously stated weather conditions occur. If recent developments in the family home result in Mary being unavailable for work due to illness/disability then a new claim would be made for employment and support allowance (ESA) which was introduced in October 2008.

If Edna's claim for AA is successful, Mary may be able to claim carer's allowance (CA) if the care (supervision and assistance) she offers is considered to be regular and substantial. Both Edna and Mary would then be entitled to a Christmas bonus.

Mary should be claiming child benefit for both Ross and Jane who are both under 16 years of age. Jennifer does not count as a 'qualifying young person' as, in order to be considered as such at the age of 17 years, she would be required to be in, or registered for, full-time education or training. If Mary's income is sufficiently low she may qualify for child tax credit (CTC) for her two dependent children. It should be remembered that carer's allowance is counted in full as income with regard to CTC but CTC does not count as income if Mary is claiming income-based Jobseeker's Allowance. No previous NI contributions are required to qualify for CTC.

If Mary is paying rent and her income is low enough she would be able to claim housing benefit and council tax benefit. If Edna and Jennifer are residing with her but are not liable for rent then Mary may be able to claim for a second adult rebate on her council tax.

Jennifer

Jennifer Taylor left school at 16 years with little in the way of qualifications. She started work in a supermarket but quickly became pregnant to the boyfriend she met at school. That relationship is now over and he has no contact with Jennifer or the baby. She is finding the care of the baby difficult and is tired all the time. She did not realise that Ebony would cry so much. She would like to move out of the family home but cannot see how she could manage on her own. Her situation is further complicated in that she has recently been arrested and charged for the possession with intent to supply cannabis and ecstasy. She is awaiting a date for her case to be heard.

It is unclear as to whether Jennifer continued working up to the baby's birth. If so it is likely that she would be entitled to either statutory maternity pay (SMP) or maternity allowance (MA) for a period of 39 weeks. Both can be claimed even if no National Insurance contributions have been made as long as she was working for her employer for a continuous period of at least 26 weeks ending with the 15th week before the 'expected week of childbirth' for SMP; that she was working for the same employer for at least 26 weeks out of the 66 week 'test period' for MA, and received average gross weekly earnings (during that period) equal to or beneath that of the lower earnings limit (for National Insurance contributions) for SMP; or are at least equal to the MA threshold of £30 per week. Payments from SMP and any arrears from work carried out will be considered as 'earnings' when calculating a claim for MA and SMP while MA is not considered to be taxable income. To qualify for SMP the claimant does not need to intend to return to work after their maternity leave and having qualified for the benefit would not be required to re-pay the money if she did not return to her job. MA cannot be paid at the same time as SMP and if Jennifer is not eligible for either then she may be able to claim statutory sick pay (SSP) or incapacity benefit.

If Jennifer continues working but her income is less than her 'applicable' amount the possibility of claiming income support should be explored. If she has terminated her employment in the supermarket but is considered to be available for, and actively seeking, employment Jennifer could apply for contribution or income-based JSA. This would necessitate making a current 'jobseeker's agreement' containing information with regard to availability for, and any restrictions placed on her, *vis-à-vis* employment.

Child benefit will be paid and, as she is now 17 years old, if her income is sufficiently low she may be entitled to claim child tax credit (CTC). If an award for income support, income-based Jobseeker's Allowance or the CTC has been made then Jennifer may be entitled to a Sure Start maternity grant from the *regulated Social Fund*. Her claim would need to be made before Ebony reaches three months of age.

The Social Fund (SF) is a scheme to help people with needs which are difficult to meet from regular income. It is made up of two distinct parts:

- a *regulated* scheme providing access to maternity, funeral, cold weather and winter fuel payments for those who satisfy specific conditions. Decisions on regulated payments are made by officers authorised to do so by the Secretary of State, although winter fuel and cold weather payments are usually paid automatically to those entitled to them.
- a *discretionary* scheme whereby people may be eligible in certain circumstances for a community care grant (CCG); a budgeting loan (BL); or a crisis loan (CL). Unsuccessful applicants may ask for a review of the decision.

The Social Fund was set up under the Social Security Act 1986 and is currently delivered by Jobcentre Plus.

(Department for Work and Pensions 2009b; National Audit Office 2005)

If Jennifer decides she is going to move out of the family home then she may be able to apply for a community care grant (CCG) to assist with some resettlement costs if it can be justified that her move was made in order 'to ease exceptional pressures' on her and the extended family given their overcrowded living conditions (Child Poverty Action Group 2008: 490).

If Jennifer (or a partner) has capital amounting to more than £500 this will reduce the amount of payment made through a CCG whereas a budgeting loan would only be affected as a result of capital held of more than £1000 (The Law Centre 2009).

It is usually recommended that a CCG rather than a crisis or budgeting loan be applied for in the first instance. A budgeting loan (interest free) is intended to assist in purchasing occasional or exceptional items that are hard to budget for after a period of dependency on IS, income-based JSA or pension credit. Unlike with budgeting loans the applicant is not required to be in receipt of benefits to qualify for a crisis loan (to help with immediate short-term needs in a crisis), which is also interest free.

The welfare rights agenda

The current welfare rights agenda highlights pressures which direct ongoing work. These include:

- increased levels of means-testing
- the anti-fraud agenda
- the welfare to work agenda
- abolishing child and pensioner poverty
- levels of migration
- poverty and inequality
- increasing numbers of older people
- health inequalities
- housing (Bateman 2006)

Increased levels of means-testing

Changes in the social security system since 1979 have resulted in greater numbers of people falling below the threshold for means-tested benefits and have necessitated the development of benefits which can be claimed by wider sections of the population (for example pension and tax credits). Means-tested benefits can, in themselves, create poverty traps discouraging claimants from undertaking paid employment and encouraging them to rely on benefits which will render them less well off in the long-term (Bateman

2006). Means-testing aims to redistribute wealth through ensuring an adequate income for all, however, they are costly to administer and prone to high levels of error. Means-testing appears to favour both the poor and the rich at the expense of the middle classes for example through targeting pension provision (Economic and Social Research Council 2009). The rich are favoured due to a reluctance to impose tax increases and a preference to make spending cuts with the more affluent people assuming that cuts will not be aimed at them (Green 2009).

Greater entitlement arises from the problem of benefits such as retirement pensions increasing only in line with prices rather than with earnings (that is, they are index linked) which results in a need for a safety net for poorer pensioners without adequate retirement provision (Bateman 2006). The current economic climate means that the income from savings will also be much reduced because of a lower interest rate.

The main drawbacks *vis-à-vis* delivering benefits through means-testing are around poor take-up levels and the complexity of making a claim which can result in delays, errors and overpayments which lead to a greater number of challenges by applicants. In his book *Inequality and the State* (2004) John Hills refers to official estimates from the Department for Work and Pensions to demonstrate that in 2000–2001 take up for Child Benefit was almost 100 per cent while means-tested benefits showed take-up shortfalls (Hills 2004 cited in TUC 2009). Hills also discovered a shortfall of between 20–30 per cent in the number of claims of those entitled to benefits such as minimum income guarantee, council tax benefit, income-based JSA and family credit (TUC 2009). The stigma and embarrassment associated with sharing, in detail, one's lack of resources along with the complexity of making a claim is thought to be largely responsible for poor take-up levels for means-tested benefits. Universal benefits such as child benefit reach more low-income families than any of the tax credits or means-tested benefits intended for them (Green 2009). This finding has fuelled concerns over recent suggestions to cut government spending through stopping universal benefits for the better off and increasing means-testing for all.

Green suggests that a more appropriate way to ensure that the better off bear more of the burden is through increased means-testing in the tax system (Green 2009). A study commissioned by the Institute of Fiscal Studies (IFS) (Brewer et al. 2008) makes several suggestions on the means-testing and tax rates on earnings: that people could be supported to enter work for low earnings if the amount that can be earned before means-tested benefits are withdrawn was increased; that the amount a second earner can earn prior to the withdrawal of family tax credits be raised; that the rate at which working and child tax credits are withdrawn be reduced; and that increases in working tax credit be targeted to other groups. The money to finance these changes, they suggest, 'could be raised through cutting child benefit and/or increasing the basic rate of income tax' rather than through raising the rate for the highest earners (Brewer et al. 2008).

The anti-fraud drive

Benefit fraud has been a political focus since the 1980s, although figures published often overestimate the scale of the problem by including figures for incidences where the DWP has, through their own error, overpaid the claimant. Figures taken from local authority 'weekly benefit savings' have been shown to grossly exaggerate the situation in comparison to the DWPs calculations. Sainsbury (1999) emphasises that:

- benefit fraud represents only a fraction of what is spent in the economy and is thought to be roughly equal to the amount of unclaimed income-related benefits;
- a large amount of monies lost through fraudulent claims and DWP error can be recovered from claimants.

Benefit fraud

The focus on fraud is thought to be responsible for preventing many people claiming benefits to which they are entitled. Bateman (2006) suggests that negative associations linked with benefit claims are perpetuated and left unchallenged. He offers an example of asylum seekers, most of whom

> have been denied access to benefits since 1996 and they receive payments at 80 per cent of the very basic benefit rates via a bureaucratic and almost discretionary alternative system. Yet public perception is that asylum seekers live a life of luxury and have more favourable treatment than the general population (Bateman 2006: 30).

In 2008 the Social Security Agency claimed that benefit fraud was costing the government approximately £12.6 million each year; the largest sum (£5.1 million) being lost through fraudulent income support claims and the lowest (£0.2 million) to cheque fraud (Social Security Agency 2009). Though it cannot be denied that this money could be put to other uses, comparison should be made to the monies involved in the tax breaks for the wealthiest which, in 2006, resulted in payments well below the current 45 per cent highest rate tax level by 54 British billionaires. Research by the Trade Union Congress (TUC) suggests that tax avoidance by the City, UK PLC and the super rich is costing the Exchequer about £25 billion every year (Labourspace 2009).

Welfare to work agenda

Prior to the economic crisis, the New Labour government had reduced joblessness and supported people back into paid work through strategies such as skills training, establishing a national minimum wage and implementing disability discrimination legislation (Bateman 2006). An evaluation of the impact of one such strategy, the New Deal for Young People, during the first two years of the programme suggests that the number of young people in jobs has risen by approximately 15,000 (Riley and Young 2001). It should be taken into consideration, however, that this programme was introduced at a time when the economy was relatively buoyant and unemployment was at its lowest for several years. Bateman (2006) states that there is evidence of jobless people disappearing from the unemployment count due to long-term illness; the growth in numbers of young men refusing to register as unemployed; and cases of self-employed people failing to legitimise their business in order to survive economically.

Abolishing pensioner and child poverty

The New Labour Government has focused its anti-poverty measures on two of the most potentially vulnerable groups in our society, children and older people (see Chapters 14 and 12). As a result, the percentage of both children and pensioners in low-income households had fallen (Palmer et al. 2004) but may still do not reach government targets to abolish child poverty by 2020 or their aim to encourage at least 70 per cent of eligible older people to receive pension credit. The Office for National Statistics suggest that the introduction of pension credit in 2003 appears to have encouraged over 800,000 extra pensioners to claim but this still equates to only 68–76 per cent of the possible take-up rate (BBC 2006). Age Concern estimated that overall £4.1 billion in money benefits is failing to reach the pockets of pensioners (BBC 2006). A number of studies including one focusing on the Glasgow economy (Hamilton and Catterall 2005) established links between benefit take-up and increased economic activity in the community through purchasing of goods and services and enhanced levels of independence and participation.

Although there are 80,000 fewer children in poverty in Scotland than ten years ago (Child Poverty Action Group 2008) approximately one in five children still reside in families living in poverty. In addition to the human cost of poverty, deprivation results in higher public spending on housing and children's social services to the cost of a half to three quarters of a billion pounds each year (Scottish Government 2008a). Longer term costs include underachievement at school with consequences reaching into early adulthood and beyond. Support costs for those young people not in education or employment (NEETs) could result in annual spending of an additional £1bn (Scottish Government 2008a). It is estimated that a reduction of child poverty in Scotland through an increase in income transfers via the benefits and tax credits system would cost roughly £4,000–£5,000 per child in the first instance (Scottish Government 2008a). Increasing measures to help parents find employment, thus improving the long-term prospects for their children, could pay for themselves. However, since nearly half of children in poverty currently live in a family supported by an adult who is in employment (albeit on low pay), a 'work first' approach is insufficient on its own to end child poverty (Harker 2006). The key may be in the lack of consideration with regard to family commitments in welfare to work programmes (other than in the New Deal for Lone Parents). Progress in the personalisation of such support 'moving beyond categorising jobseekers according to their benefit entitlement (which channels individuals into separate programmes according to the benefits they are claiming) towards viewing jobseekers in the wider context of their family and building a flexible package of support to meet their particular needs' may be the way forward (Harker 2006: 8).

Migration

Much of the research available with regard to immigrants, legal and illegal, challenge perceptions that they might be in the UK to profit from the benefits system. Research commissioned by the Joseph Rowntree Foundation discovered that all minority groups studied believed that claiming benefits was a process which created dependency on the state although it was not viewed as a barrier to gaining employment (Law et al. 1994). A study into the provision of benefits to minority ethnic communities (Law et al. 1994) found that cultural and religious factors are responsible for influencing negative perceptions of benefits leading to non-claiming, under-claiming and delayed claiming and the attachment of shame and stigma (particularly amongst Bangladeshi and Chinese households). This reluctance to claim benefits is more concerning when we consider the gap between employment rates for ethnic minorities and that for whites (Crawford et al. 2008). In examining the outcomes Crawford et al. (2008) were unable to explain all the differences between the experiences of both groups of similarly qualified and experienced jobseekers. The possibility of labour market discrimination and self-discriminatory behaviour (for example, not applying for a job for fear of being discriminated against) were proposed factors (Crawford et al. 2008).

In 2003 CPAG reported that 73 per cent of Bangladeshi children, 63 per cent of black African and 40 per cent of Caribbean children were living in poverty with links made between these levels and the low up-take of benefits (CPAG as cited in BBC 2003). (See Chapter 18.)

Poverty, inequality and the benefits system

Despite UK Government measures to reduce poverty in 2006/2007, 17 per cent of the Scottish population were living in relative low (below 60 per cent of the median) income poverty before housing costs. One quarter of individuals living in relative low income poverty are children, just over half are working age adults and the remainder are pensioners (Scottish Government 2008c). Hirsch (2008) reported the following deterioration:

- the proportion of pensioners not taking up benefits to which they are entitled covers housing benefit, council tax benefit and pension credit. All three are about a third higher than a decade ago (in 1998);
- the proportion of all low-income households paying full council tax (that is, receiving no council tax benefit) has also risen by a third. Entitlement rules are a major factor for the almost 90 per cent of low-income, working families who pay the tax in full;
- the value of out-of-work benefits for adults without dependent children, relative to earnings, has inevitably declined and is now 20 per cent below where it was a decade ago;
- the proportion of people aged 75 and over helped by social services to live at home [is down by a quarter since 1997] (Hirsch 2008:5).

Further difficulties are created within the social security system as a result of tension between government departments such as policy makers in the DWP, who wish to reduce numbers of claimants, and those who wish to address issues of poverty (the Social Exclusion Unit) (Bateman 2006). Such issues should have been resolved as a result of the policy making promised by the 'Modernising Government' white paper (1999), which is '... strategic, outcome focused, joined up (if necessary), inclusive, flexible, innovative and robust' (Strategic Policy Making Team 2009: 3). An emphasis on meaningful outcomes rather than reactions to short-term pressures has been promised.

Increasing numbers of older people

Figures released from the 2001 Census show that for the first time the UK has more people aged over 60 than under 16 years of age (BBC 2002a). Also reported was a five-fold increase on the 1951 survey of people aged over 85 years (BBC 2002a). The general improvement of living standards and health care has contributed to an increased ageing population (see Chapters 10 and 12). An ageing population alters the balance between those paying into the system (workers) and those being supported (for example pensioners). Currently for each pensioner there are four workers, however, with estimates that by 2060 the over 65s will make up nearly a quarter of the total population, this will be reduced to two employed people to every older person (The Independent 2008). Age alone is not a good indication of hardship as in general, more affluent people tend to live longer (Middleton et al. 2007). Although, generally people are remaining healthier, with the predicted levels of growth in numbers of older people it is likely that the numbers of sufferers of chronic diseases will also grow (Majeed and Aylin 2005). The costs of monitoring patients, administering drugs, diagnostic tests, surgical procedures and the development of new technology will further increase costs to the NHS (Majeed and Aylin 2005). With people living longer there will also be greater pressure on:

- Housing – the challenge will be to cater for the needs of a more diverse group of older people 'more women than men, more people living alone, more childless people, more owner occupiers and more people who have spent their life in good quality spacious housing ... poor people, lonely people and people who feel excluded from the mainstream society' (National Affordable Housing Association 2008: 1). Such diverse living situations will also have an impact on claims for housing and council tax benefits and discretionary housing payments.
- Employment – the government is already encouraging employers to consider the benefits of an 'age diverse workforce' (National Audit Office 2004: 1). It is increasingly likely that the age of retirement will be increased with estimates of it reaching 69 years by 2050 (The Independent 2008). From 2012 workers will be automatically enrolled into a work-based pension scheme. Increasing numbers of older people result in the payment of more retirement pensions and pension credits for the most needy.
- Retail services – we know that people spend smaller proportions of their income as they get older but there is no conclusive evidence with regard to what happens to the surplus income (Middleton et al. 2007). Low interest returns on savings will do little to encourage pensioners to save.
- Transport – although more older people hold a driving licence, changes in ability to drive and in their financial situation might result in a high proportion of older people coming to rely on public transport (Department of Transport 2001). Cost, accessibility, flexibility and reliability will need to be addressed. A lack of access to good transport links for the poorest will inadvertently impact on income from benefits if people are forced to shop at local independent retailers.

- The benefits system – State Pensions will be increased through restoring the earnings link and the age at which it can be claimed will be raised (see below) (Department for Work and Pensions 2008b). (See Chapter 12.)

Health inequalities

Despite a general decline in death rates, Scotland still has higher mortality rates in almost all age groups and amongst both men and women in comparison to similar groups in England, Wales and across most of Western Europe (Sridharan et al. 2007). Deaths in Scotland most commonly occur as a result of:

- ischemic heart disease – mortality rates have fallen by 64 per cent in males and 65 per cent in females between the ages of 45 and 59 but only by 36 and 31 per cent respectively for those aged 74 years and over;
- lung cancer – fell by 53 per cent in males and 23 per cent in females aged between 45 and 59 with a decrease of 19 per cent in men over 75 years and an increase of 135 per cent in women of this age;
- strokes and accidents – have seen reductions of almost 50 per cent;
- suicide – there has been a 43 per cent increase in suicide rates;
- alcohol and drug related deaths – include an increase in the behavioural and mental disorders resulting from the use of these substances (Leyland et al. 2001).

Deaths of those in routine or semi-routine occupations were found to be 3.7 times greater than those in professional/managerial occupations (Leyland et al. 2001). In comparisons made of male mortality rates in Clydeside an increase is noted from being 9 per cent above the Scottish average in the 1981 Census to 17 per cent higher by the 2001 Census (Leyland et al. 2001). Furthermore, the life expectancy of a male child born in Glasgow is 5.4 years lower than in Edinburgh (Leyland et al. 2001). Patterns of decreasing mortality rates in affluent areas and increasing ones in the more deprived areas were found. In short, standards of health can be directly related to inequalities in income and for the less well off this means to living standards determined by the benefit system. In order to improve the health of the most vulnerable in society, policies that increase income through the tax and benefits system will need to remain high on the Government's agenda. (See Chapter 10.)

Housing

At the end of September 2008 it was estimated that there were 322,900 council houses in Scotland following an 11-year programme of sales to tenants (approximately 150,000), transfers to housing associations (100,000) and about 40,000 demolitions (Scottish Government 2008b). In 2000/2001 a study by the Accounts Commission claimed a rise in rent arrears of 10 per cent resulting in local authorities being deprived of approximately 42 million pounds revenue (BBC 2002b). Properties standing empty resulted in a loss of £28.1m rental income while administrative errors and delays were thought to be responsible for the financial hardship and resulting rental arrears from vulnerable groups such as the elderly or unemployed and lone-parents (BBC 2002b). (See Chapter 19.)

The social work role in relation to benefits

The bulk of welfare rights work is carried out by welfare benefit advisers and welfare rights caseworkers working mainly in the voluntary sector and in local authorities. Advisers and caseworkers are employed to ensure that service users receive their full entitlement through advising them on employment rights and benefits, including housing benefits and tax credits. They frequently work directly with the public and are also involved in making assessments and helping make applications for benefits. Welfare rights caseworkers represent service users at appeal tribunals and other hearings. Most social workers, therefore, are not required to have detailed knowledge of welfare rights but should have an awareness of the structure of the benefit and tax credit system. They should, however, be able to identify issues that may affect entitlement and should appreciate the importance of advice and advocacy as they have frequent contact with those who are reliant on benefits or who might have financial or debt problems.

Chapter summary

In examining the future of the welfare system and taking into account the issues highlighted in this chapter with regard to funding, demographic change and the additional services which might be required to meet those changing needs, consideration must also be made of the possibility that a situation where there is a dependency on social welfare has been created. The last but one UK Prime Minister, Tony Blair, was accused of creating a nanny state that served to maintain an underclass. In 2006 an independent report *Reducing Dependency, Increasing Opportunity: Options for the Future of Welfare to Work* (Freud 2007) was commissioned by the Department for Work and Pensions. This report praised the UK Government for its progress on the welfare to work programme whilst acknowledging that efforts must be made to improve the skill level of the working age population given that 35 per cent of that group do not have the equivalent of a good school leaving qualification (Freud 2007). Freud argues that the impact of multiple disadvantages on employment rates should be considered (Freud 2007). He goes on to suggest that a single, well-designed system of working age benefits would eliminate any possibility of a poverty trap and might challenge the perception that moving from benefits to work does not pay (Freud 2007).

For new claimants, replacing incapacity benefit (IB) with employment and support allowance (ESA) in 2008 emphasised the government's focus on 'welfare to work'. With in excess of 2.6 million people dependent on incapacity benefit (Department for Work and Pensions 2008a) in the UK the government decided upon an overhaul of this key provision. Existing claimants of IB must satisfy specific criteria in order to avoid being transferred to ESA. Evidence that being in work improves people's situation financially but also in terms of self-esteem, health, well-being and future prospects is key to the personalised support and financial assistance offered through this allowance (Directgov 2009). The ESA involves a new medical assessment (Work Capability Assessment) to assess ability and to identify necessary health-related supports to allow a return to employment.

Whatever the Government's plans for encouraging people off benefits, what is clear is that the value of benefits currently in the UK is significantly below the poverty line. The index linked nature of benefits means that those households currently dependent on state assistance have seen their relative incomes fall over time. A number of pressure groups have called for alterations to the benefits system to reflect changes in earnings rather than fluctuations in cost.

References

Bateman, N. (2006), *Practising Welfare Rights* (London: Routledge).

BBC News (2002a), 'Census Paints Portrait of Ageing UK'. Available at: http://www.news.bbc.co.uk/1/hi/uk/2287650.stm (accessed 6 November 2009).

— (2002b), 'Councils Rebuked over Rent Arrears'. Available at: http://www.news.bbc.co.uk/2/hi/uk_news/scotland/1765151.stm (accessed 6 November 2009).

— (2003), 'Ethnic Minorities Hit by "Severe" Poverty'. Available at: http://www.news.bbc.co.uk/2/hi/uk_news/2682139.stm (accessed 6 November 2009).

— (2006), 'Billions in Benefits "Unclaimed"'. Available at: http://www.news.bbc.co.uk/2/hi/business/4666396.stm (accessed 6 November 2009).

Brewer, M., Saez, E. and Shephard, A. (2008), *Means-Testing and Tax Rates on Earnings* (Oxford: The Institute for Fiscal Studies; Oxford University Press).

Child Poverty Action Group (2008), *Welfare Benefits and Tax Credits Handbook* (London: Child Poverty Action Group).

Crawford, C., Dearden, L., Mesnard, A., Shaw, J. and Sianesi, B. (2008), 'Ethnic Parity in Labour Market Outcomes for Benefit Claims'. Available at: UCL, http://eprints.ucl.ac.uk/14876/ (accessed 6 November 2009).

Department for Work and Pensions (2008a), 'Employment and Support Allowance'. Available at: http://www.hackney.gov.uk/print/dwp-overview.pdf (accessed 4 November 2009).

— (2008b), 'The Challenges Presented by an Ageing Population'. Available at: http://www.dwp.gov.uk/aboutus/2008/09-10-08b.asp (accessed 6 November 2009).

— (2009a), 'Benefit Thieves: We're Closing In'. Available at: http://www.dwp.gov.uk/campaigns/benefit-thieves/ (accessed 6 November 2009).

— (2009b), 'Social Fund Guide'. Available at: http://www.dwp.gov.uk/docs/social-fund-guide.pdf (accessed 29 October 2009).

Department of Transport (2001), 'Older People: Their Transport Needs and Requirements – Summary Report'. Available at: http://www.dft.gov.uk/pgr/inclusion/older/olderpeopletheirtransportnee3261?page=2 (accessed 6 November 2009).

Directgov (2009), 'Employment and Support Allowance'. Available at: http://www.direct.gov.uk/en/DisabledPeople/financialSupport/esa/DG_171894 (accessed 4 November 2009).

Economic and Social Research Council (2009), 'Pensions, Means-Testing and Early Retirement'. Available at: http://www.esrc.ac.uk/ESRCInfoCentre/Plain_English_Summaries/econ_performance (accessed 29 October 2009).

Freud, D. (2007), *Reducing Dependency, Increasing Opportunity: Options for the Future of Welfare to Work* (Leeds: HMSO).

Green, K. (2009), 'Means-Testing Child Benefits Will Hit the Poor, Not the Rich', *The Guardian*. Available at: http://www.guardian.co.uk (accessed 29 October 2009).

Hamilton, K.L and Catterall, M. (2005), 'Towards a Better Understanding of the Low Income Consumer', *Research* 32(1): 627–32. Available at: http://strathprints.strath.ac.uk/4533/1/strathprints004533.pdf (accessed 6 November 2009).

Harker, L. (2006), 'Delivering on Child Poverty', Department for Works and Pensions. Available at: http://www.official-documents.gov.uk/document/cm69/6951/6951.pdf (accessed 6 November 2009).

Hirsch, D. (2008), 'Estimating the Cost of Child Poverty in Scotland: Approaches and Evidence', Scottish Government Social Research. Available at: http://www.jrf.org.uk/publications/estimating-costs-child-poverty (accessed 6 November 2009).

House of Commons Library (2009), 'Married Women and State Pensions'. Available at: http://www.parliament.uk/commons/lib/research/briefings/snbt-01910.pdf (accessed 6 November 2009).

Labourspace (2009), 'Minimum Tax Rates: Countering Tax Evasion by the Super Rich'. Available at: http://minimumtax.labourspace.com/view_campaign?CampaignId=143 (accessed 29 October 2009).

Law, I., Hylton, C., Karmani, A. and Deacon, A. (1994), 'The Provision of Social Security Benefits to Minority Ethnic Communities', *Social Policy Research* 59. Joseph Rowntree Foundation. Available at: http://www.jrf.org.uk (accessed 6 November 2009).

Leyland, A.H., Dundas, R., McLoone, P. and Boddy, F.A. (2001), 'Inequalities in Mortality in Scotland 1981–2001'. Available at: http://www.sphsu.mrc.ac.uk/files/File/current_research/Inequalities/Exec_summary.php (accessed 6 November 2009).

Majeed, A. and Aylin, P. (2005), 'The Ageing Population of the United Kingdom and Cardiovascular Disease', *British Medical Journal* 331: 1362.

Middleton, S., Hancock, R., Kellard, K., Beckhelling, J., Phung, V.H. and Perren, K. (2007), 'The Needs and Resources of Older People', Joseph Rowntree Foundation. Available at: http://www.jrf.org.uk (accessed 6 November 2009).

National Affordable Housing Association (2008), 'Housing for Older People'. Available at: http://www.housingcorp.gov.uk/cfg/server/show/nav.381 (accessed 3 June 2010).

National Audit Office (2004), 'Tackling the Barriers to the Employment of Older People'. Available at: http://www.nao.org.uk/whats_new/0304/03041026.aspx?alreadysearchfor=yes (accessed 6 November 2009).

— (2005), 'Helping Those in Financial Hardship: The Running of the Social Fund'. Available at: http://www.nao.org.uk/publications/0405/the_running_of_the_social_fund.aspx (accessed 29 October 2009).

Palmer, G., Carr, J. and Kenway, P. (2004), 'Monitoring Poverty and Social Exclusion in Scotland 2004, Joseph Rowntree Foundation. Available at: http://www.jrf.org.uk (accessed 6 November 2009).

Riley, R. and Young, G. (2001), *Does Welfare-to-Work Policy Increase Employment?: Evidence from the UK New Deal for Young People* (London: National Institute of Economic and Social Research).

Sainsbury, R. (1999), 'Combating Housing Benefit Fraud: Local Authorities' Discretionary Powers'. Available at: Social Policy Research Unit, University of York, http://php.york.ac.uk/inst/spru/pubs/742/ (accessed 6 November 2009).

Scottish Government (2008a), 'Estimating the Cost of Child Poverty in Scotland: Approaches and Evidence'. Available at: http://www.scotland.gov.uk/Publications/2008/01/28111819/1 (accessed 6 November 2009).

— (2008b), 'Housing Statistics'. Available at: http://www.scotland.gov.uk/Topics/Statistics/Browse/Housing-Regeneration/HSfS/H (accessed 6 November 2009).

— (2008c), 'Scottish Households below Average Income, 2006/07'. Available at: http://www.scotland.gov.uk/Publications/2008/06/09143258/0 (accessed 6 November 2009).

Social Security Agency (2009), 'The Cost of Benefit Fraud'. Available at: http://www.stopbenefitfraudni.gov.uk/cost.htm (accessed 29 October 2009).

Sridharan, S., Tunstall, H., Lawder, R. and Mitchell, R. (2007), 'Explaining Scotland's High Mortality: The Geographical Patterning of Socio-Economic Deprivation and Death', Research Findings 15. Research Unit in Health, Behaviour and Change, University of Edinburgh.

Strategic Policy Making Team (2009), 'Professional Policy Making for the Twenty First Century'. Available at: http://www.civilservant.org.uk/profpolicymaking.pdf (accessed 6 November 2009).

The Independent (2008), 'The Big Question: Why is the UK's Population Growing So Fast, and is This a Good Thing?', *The Independent*. Available at: http://www.independent.co.uk/news/uk/home-news/the-big.question-why-is-uks (accessed 6 November 2009).

The Law Centre (2009), 'Social Fund'. Available at: http://www.lawcentreni.org/EoR/social_fund.htm (accessed 29 October 2009).

TUC (2009), 'Means-Testing Benefits Reduces Take Up'. Available at: http://www.touchstoneblog.org.uk/2009/09/means-testing-benefits-reduces-take-up (accessed 29 October 2009).

Further reading

Department for Work and Pensions (2007), 'Welfare Reform'. Available at: http://www.dwp.gov.uk/welfarereform/legislation_bill.asp (accessed 6 November 2009).

Directgov (2009), 'Changes to the State Pension Age'. Available at: http://www.direct.gov.uk/en/Pensionsandretirementplanning/Statepension/DG_4017919 (accessed 9 October 2009).

Gregg, P. (2008), 'Realising Potential: A Vision for Personalised Conditionality and Support', Department for Works and Pensions. Available at: http://www.dwp.gov.uk/policy/welfare-reform/legislation-and-key-documents/realising-potential/ (accessed 6 November 2009).

NHS (2005), 'UK's Ageing Population Will Impose Huge Healthcare Burden', *British Medical Journal* 12 December.

Palmer, G., MacInnes, T. and Kenway, P. (2008), 'Monitoring Poverty and Social Exclusion 2008', Joseph Rowntree Foundation. Available at: http://www.jrf.org.uk (accessed 6 November 2009).

Population Ageing Associates (2007), 'Our Population is Ageing'. Available at: http://www.populationageing.co.uk/demographics.htm (accessed 6 November 2009).

9 Social policy perspectives on empowerment

Rob Mackay

Introduction

This chapter examines the impact that empowerment as an idea, or as a set of ideas, has had on UK and Scottish social policies over the past 20 years. It explores specific policies in relation to children and adults and considers implications for social workers and social work practice.

The chapter explores what we mean by empowerment and places this in a political context in which the notion of power and dominant discourses are crucial to understanding policy development. The question is raised as to the similarities and differences between consumerism and empowerment. The discussion of advocacy raises issues and questions about the practice of a rights-based approach and how social workers may make positive use of legislation to promote anti-oppressive practice.

Lastly by focusing on the contemporary debate about implementing a 'personalised' approach to delivering services, this chapter not only highlights what the social policy developments in this are but also speculates on the challenges in the implementation of this policy drive.

What is empowerment?

The challenge about getting to grips with empowerment is that it involves complex issues of understanding and actions, which go right to the heart of the interaction between the citizen and the state. Empowerment represents different things to different people and therefore is open to questions, debate and disagreements. In other words, it is a contested topic in which a widely accepted definition does not exist. This section explores concepts that communicate ideas of power, powerlessness and empowerment.

Power and power relationships are central to our understanding of discrimination, oppression, social exclusion, social inclusion and empowerment. So what is power, and who has it? The very word is evocative and can summon up ideas of power being exercised repressively by an individual or a group. According to Sawicki (1991) this equates to the traditional models of power (Dalrymple and Burke 2006) and this has three assumptions:

- power is possessed
- power flows from top to bottom
- power is essentially repressive

This perspective suggests that because of power relations within society, unequal relationships exist.

However an alternative perspective has been developed by the post-structuralist theorists, notably by the French philosopher Michel Foucault who rejects this view of power and argues instead that power is exercised rather than possessed and is mediated through everyday relationships (Fook 2002). It is suggested that social control is exercised through the construction of norms that impact upon perceptions of personal identity and that this is achieved through 'normalising judgements' (White 2007).

Foucault's theories have been summarised around three key ideas:

- power is exercised rather than possessed
- power is not primarily repressive but productive
- power is seen as coming from the bottom up (Dalrymple and Burke 2006; Fook and Morley 2005; Sawicki 1991; Healey 2005)

The post-structuralist position therefore questions universal truths about people's lives and privileges ideas of multiple perspectives and the relativity of knowledge. As such this can raise questions about universal concepts that have been widely used in the analysis of social policies, such as class, gender and inequality. Does a post-structuralist perspective deny the reality of inequalities based around class differences? It is argued, however, that so long as post-structuralist writers explore not a single difference like class but the meaning of a range of differences then this enriches the understanding of the lived experience within a society (Widdowson 2001).

Exercise 9.1

Can you describe yourself in terms of class, age, disability, gender and ethnic origin?

A related question is how are we to understand discrimination and oppression in the context of power relations?

Solomon (1976), in reflecting on her social work practice with oppressed black communities in the United States, argued that personal and political power are involved in the production of the sense of oppression. She identified both direct power blocks and indirect power blocks for African-American people. By direct power blocks she was referring to processes that 'are applied directly by some agent of society's major social institutions' and by indirect power blocks she was referring to internalised negative self perceptions that are 'incorporated into the developmental experiences of the individual as mediated by significant others' (Solomon 1976: 21).

The 'PCS Analysis' as expressed by Thompson (2001) provides a theoretical underpinning to an understanding of the processes of discrimination in British society. The central idea being that disempowerment occurs at three inter-connected levels. This influential model is used to analyse processes of discrimination and oppression at different levels of policy and practice – personal, cultural and structural (PCS).

Another concept related to discrimination and oppression is 'social exclusion', which came to prominence with the election of New Labour in 1997. Their view was that disadvantage had to be understood in broader terms than financial poverty and should encompass social disadvantages, such as housing, education, employment and health. The Social Exclusion Unit was established in 1997 and its working definition of social exclusion was:

> ... A shorthand term for what can happen when people or areas suffer from a combination of problems such as unemployment, discrimination, poor skills, low incomes, poor housing, high crime, and family breakdown. These problems are linked and mutually reinforcing. Social Exclusion Task Force (2009)

This definition has been criticised on the grounds that it focuses too much on personal exclusion and does not sufficiently address structural issues (Dominelli 2004).

Strands of empowerment

There are three strands of ideas that are relevant to an understanding of the factors which may influence degrees of empowerment, which have been referred to by Means and Smith (1994) and Ramcharan (1997). These three strands (which are not mutually exclusive) help to explain different perspectives on empowerment and an awareness of these can be very helpful to unpack and analyse social issues.

Exit

This strand is sometimes described as 'voting with your feet' which means each one of us can operate as a consumer and decide in which shop or in which service we are going to spend our money. This originates from the commercial realities of the United States. In the social work context this means that service users can potentially switch services – this notion is of course only possible where there are multiple providers and choice is a realistic option. This has been described as the 'power of the pound' in which choice is promoted through the mechanism of the social care market. Questions have been raised as to whether consumerism can be classed as a form of empowerment (Malin, Wilmot, and Manthorpe 2002).

Voice

'Having a say' in what is provided by an existing service and attempting to influence changes and improve services. This does exist within social work and takes many forms at both the individual and institutional levels. These include meetings with individual service users, case conferences, advisory committees, consultation meetings, customer satisfaction surveys and so on. The structures used are not ones of power sharing in relation to decisions, but rather ensuring that the organisation is well informed by a range of stakeholders. This approach depends upon the level of active listening by social workers and agencies, to ensure that the voice of the service user is genuinely incorporated into the decision-making process.

Rights

'Power to exercise rights which we all have'. This power reflects that there are entitlements to services based on legislation, which as citizens we can invoke. These entitlements are based on both legislation and service standards (Morris 1997).

Exercise 9.2

Can you reflect on your own sense of empowerment in relation to exit, voice and rights?

The use of legislative rights can be a very empowering strategy, but it does depend on people's knowledge of their rights, as well as support and resources to ensure these rights are enacted. Dalrymple and Burke (2006) suggest using the law as part of enlightened anti-oppressive practice.

Advocacy

Advocacy carries with it the threads of voice and rights, so what is it? Advocacy is one of those terms that carries with it different meanings according to the diversity of contexts and roles within which it is being expressed and discussed. It is also confusing because different writers list different types of advocacy and in Scotland the role of an 'advocate' traditionally belongs to a person with a legal training and occupation. Advocacy is one of the routes by which people may develop a sense of having more influence and control.

At its simplest, advocacy is about making sure that people are encouraged to give voice to their choices and rights through the provision of independent information and support. In other words, that individuals, groups and communities have the capacity – and the opportunity and resources – to be self-advocates. There are many definitions of advocacy, but this one explains both the processes involved and possible outcomes:

> Advocacy involves a person(s), either an individual or groups with disabilities or their representative, pressing the case with influential others, about situations which affect them directly or, and more usually, trying to prevent proposed changes, which will leave them worse off. Both the intent and the outcome of such advocacy should increase the individual's sense of power; help them to feel more confident; to become more assertive and gain increased choices. (Brandon, Brandon and Brandon 1995: 1)

The types of advocacy referred to normally include self-advocacy, citizen advocacy, collective/group advocacy, independent professional advocacy, family advocacy and peer advocacy. Use of the phrases 'independent advocate' or 'independent advocacy services' is significant because it positions independence as an essential factor in the provision of advocacy both at the level of the individual person and of an advocacy organisation. Why might this be? It is argued that whilst employed professionals can undertake advocacy tasks, the constraint on this is that they are working to multiple accountabilities and thus the issue of conflict of interest does arise (Brandon, Brandon and Brandon 1995; Gray and Jackson 2002).

The introduction of the Mental Health (Care and Treatment) (Scotland) Act 2003 (see Chapter 11) has provided the clearest statement in national social policy terms of the valuing of independent advocacy. A right of access to independent advocacy is stated for a person with a mental disorder and moreover due to the provisions of Section 259 of the Act it imposes a duty on local authorities and health boards to ensure that independent advocacy is available. This right is extended to people of all ages including children (Hothersall, Maas-Lowit and Golightley 2008). Mental disorder is defined in respect of the Act as including:

- mental illness
- learning disability
- personality disorder

The statutory position with regard to children is that whilst there is no specific provision for advocacy in the Children's (Scotland) Act 1995, one of the three underpinning principles is that the child's views should be taken into account when major decisions are being considered for his/her future (Hothersall 2008). Some local authorities have used the general welfare provisions in the Act to justify the employment of children rights workers; they work specifically with looked after children and provide information about the rights of children and support them to express their point of view and ensure participation. Who Cares? Scotland is a national advocacy organisation for looked-after children and young people, which is funded through the Scottish Government. Who Cares? Scotland has produced a Charter of Rights (Who Cares? Scotland 2009) which includes the right to have access to individual advice and advocacy; this Charter of Rights is claimed to have been adopted by most local authorities in Scotland.

A further legislative development was the passing of the Education (Additional Support for Learning) (Scotland) Act 2004 (see Chapter 15), which makes provision for additional help to be made available to those children and young people who may require it. This provides young people and their parents the right to have an independent advocate present at meetings, but local authorities do not have a duty to pay for the services of an advocacy service.

Of national significance has been the appointment since 2004 of a Scottish Commissioner for Children and Young People. This arose out of a long campaign by child care organisations in Scotland and the case for a Commissioner with responsibilities for children and young people was accepted by the Scottish Parliament when the Commissioner for Children and Young People (Scotland) Act 2003 was passed and the first Commissioner was appointed in 2004. The remit of this post is to promote and safeguard the rights of children and young people in Scotland, based around the United Nations Convention on the Rights of the Child. The Commissioner can be seen as an advocate at a national level for the rights of the child and the young person.

These social policy developments have been driven in part by an ideological commitment to a rights-based approach to participation and choice. A rights-based approach is based on the idea of entitlement and it is argued this affords more respect and dignity than discretionary benefits, which are subject to the vagaries of individual assessment systems (Morris 1997). Rights are then expressed through laws, conventions, charters and national standards which may be interpreted through guidance from Government and then implemented at a local level through adopted policies and procedures by agencies. The employed social worker is then expected in his/her role to work to these standards and policies and laws. We shall explore later in the chapter the issues around the application of the law in social work practice – is the operation of the law inevitably oppressive or can it be used as a tool to support empowerment?

Social inclusion-based policies

Comment was made earlier in the chapter as to the formulation of social exclusion by the New Labour Government of Tony Blair. This resulted in the establishment of the Social Exclusion Unit in 1997 in order to co-ordinate Government departments with the aim of combating poverty and promoting social inclusion. Initially in England and Wales the focus was targeted on problems such as school truancy, homelessness and youth unemployment (Adams 2002). Four of the first six reports by the Social Exclusion Unit addressed issues of disadvantage experienced by children and young people (Kendrick 2005).

In Scotland, following a period of consultation in 1997, the Social Inclusion Network was established and significantly the preference was for 'inclusion' as opposed to 'exclusion'. Members of this network were centrally involved in the preparation of a paper 'Social Inclusion: Opening the Door to a Better Scotland' (Scottish Office 1999). This came about just as the devolution settlement was achieved, so there is a sense that a commitment to social inclusion and social justice was a major priority for the Scottish Executive and the Scottish Parliament right from the outset in 1999. Principles adopted to underpin this social inclusion approach in Scotland include:

- integration
- prevention
- understanding
- inclusiveness
- empowerment

The Scottish Executive and then the renamed Scottish Government (from 2007) have made a number of policy initiatives over the past ten years. These include a statement of policy objectives, identified targets and the need for outcomes to be evidenced. Significantly these policies have received cross-party support. Four policy statements have particular significance in this regard:

1. 'Social Justice: A Scotland Where Everyone Matters' (Scottish Executive 1999);
2. 'A Partnership for a Better Scotland: Partnership Agreement between the Scottish Labour Party and the Scottish Liberal Democrats' (Scottish Executive 2003a);
3. 'Closing the Gap: Scottish Budget for 2003–2006' (Scottish Executive 2003b);
4. 'Achieving Our Potential' (Scottish Government 2008).

This set of policy implementations is to be understood as co-existing with the policy framework established by the New Labour UK Governments since 1997. These have included the use of targets, such as the eradication of child poverty by 2020, and the application of a raft of policies designed to move people from welfare to work. Some of these have included major initiatives such as the New Deal and Jobseeker's Allowance to support unemployed people back to work. Considerable effort and resources have been directed at children and families which include:

- the Sure Start programme
- increases in child benefit
- child benefit vouchers
- child tax credits
- changing the benefit rules for lone parents regarding employment

The Scottish Government has made contributions to reducing child poverty through measures of its own, which include:

- free school meals
- school clothing grants
- energy assistance package

A contemporary report casts doubt on the effectiveness of these policies in making a significant impact on severe child poverty (Save the Children 2010). This report claims that 1.7 million children in the UK live in severe poverty, which is 13 per cent of all children. The comparative figure for Scotland is 95,000 (10 per cent of all children). A further claim is that there has been no change in the number of children living in poverty in Scotland since 2004–2005. The report identifies a range of factors in and through which children are at particular risk from experiencing severe child poverty, and these include:

- adults who are out of work
- educational inequalities
- single parents
- disability
- ethnicity

In other words, this report implies that poverty is itself the major cause of social exclusion and recommends a much greater focus on anti-poverty policies by the UK and the Scottish Governments. However, the UK Government is claiming the measures it has taken have already lifted two million children out of poverty and is proposing a law that will underpin its commitment to end child poverty in 2020.

This debate takes place at a time when the worst recession in the UK in the post-war period has had a serious impact on job opportunities and hence resulted in large unemployment figures. It is estimated that the unemployment figure for the UK in 2009 was 2.46 million and for Scotland 202,000 people (National Statistics Online 2009). A significant trend has been the increase in the number of people who are in part-time employment, which rose by 99,000 to reach a record high of 7.7 million people. The inference is that there is now a trend of employers moving people from full-time to part-time status as a strategy for reducing costs but retaining skilled employees. This might just be an additional barrier for those at-risk groups identified in the Action for Children report (2010).

It is argued by some that anti-poverty strategies in the UK and Scotland have been focused on social exclusion and that this has not addressed equality of outcome. Evidence for this comes strongly from the recently published report by the National Equality Panel (2010); of its many findings the starkest is that the gap between rich and poor is wider than it was 40 years ago and that social background really matters. So the primary aim has been to strengthen equality of opportunity rather than equality of outcome (Scott, Mooney and Brown 2005). The Scottish dimension has been to use the language of social justice in conjunction with social inclusion policies. Whether this has resulted in actually closing the opportunity gap is open to interpretation and possibly doubt, but there has been greater willingness in Scotland to engage in a political dialogue about ways of promoting social justice in relation to specific groups that are subject to social exclusion and social injustices. This brings out the political dimension of these policy debates and notably the tensions that exist between the UK Government and the Scottish Government over devolved and reserved powers.

Exercise 9.3

Can you identify an example of a 'welfare to work' policy that has impacted on you, or a family member or a friend? Has this been positive or negative in its effects?

Human rights-based policies

> Human rights are rights inherent to all human beings, whatever our nationality, place of residence, sex, national or ethnic origin, colour, religion, language, or any other status. We are all equally entitled to our human rights without discrimination. These rights are all interrelated, interdependent and indivisible.
>
> Universal human rights are often expressed and guaranteed by law, in the forms of treaties, customary international law, general principles and other sources of international law. International human rights law lays down obligations of Governments to act in certain ways or to refrain from certain acts, in order to promote and protect human rights and fundamental freedoms of individuals or groups. (United Nations 2009)

This is an outline of the principle of universality of human rights that was enshrined in the Universal Declaration on Human Rights in 1948. This has being reiterated in many forms including the Convention on the Rights of the Child (UNCRC) and the European Convention on Human Rights (ECHR). This was a response by the world community to the horrors of the Second World War and especially to the Holocaust, in which it is estimated that 11 million people were killed, including 1.1 million children.

In philosophical terms the concept of rights has been discussed and argued for centuries; some suggest that the modern conception of human rights crystallised in the eighteenth century through the 1776 American Declaration of Independence and the French Revolution. It is suggested by some (Clapham 2007) that this relates not to all human rights but to a narrow set that place value on two principles:

1. All human beings are born equal.
2. All human beings have to be treated equally with dignity and respect.

Social work values have been influenced by these principles for decades and find expression in the British Association of Social Workers (BASW) Code of Ethics, in which two key principles are human dignity and worth, and social justice (British Association of Social Workers n.d.).

The political consensus about human rights appears to have been diluted with a sceptical view by right-wing commentators and politicians that the rights of the majority have been sacrificed to protecting the rights of the minority, for example criminals, asylum seekers (see Chapter 18). The British Conservative Party's declared policy is that should they come into power, they plan to replace the Human Rights Act with a British Bill of Rights. The point is that the very idea of human rights is open to interpretation and different perspectives.

It has been pointed out that the UN conventions have no legal status and that even where countries do sign up, improvements are slow and patchy. For example, it was only in 2009 that the UK Government agreed to withdraw its reservations to two articles of the UNCRC:

- Article 22 (refugee children)
- Article 37c (children in custody with adults)

It is argued that the UNCRC has improved the rights of children living in this country. For example, it is claimed by Marshall et al. (2002) that it was a deliberate intention of the legislators to incorporate three key principles from the UNCRC into the framing of the Children (Scotland) Act 1995:

- non-discrimination (Article 2)
- a child's welfare as the prime concern (Article 3)
- listening to children's views (Article 12)

The distinctive approach adopted in the framing of this Act was that these principles were translated into specific legal requirements that underpin the rights of children. The government decided against the use of 'overarching' principles but rather it was decided to write the principles into the Act section by section in order to secure effective application.

It does raise the question as to different kind of rights; a concept of legal rights suggests that some may be considered substantive and some procedural rights (Dalrymple and Burke 2006). Substantive rights are those that are legally enforceable, whilst procedural rights are those that relate to how legal processes are enacted and to ensure fairness.

In the case of the Children (Scotland) Act 1995, it is possible to evaluate how the principle of listening to children's views has been implemented. This relates to the 'voice' strand of empowerment referred to in an earlier section of this chapter.

Exercise 9.4

In practical terms, what could you do in the role of a social worker to promote more active and respectful listening to the views of children and young people at meetings?

There has been an increasing awareness of the need to consult with children about major decisions affecting their lives and to listen to their views. The Scottish Executive not only made public statements to this effect but also funded initiatives such as the Scottish Youth Parliament. In a mapping report (Marshall et al. 2002), the authors found that there are inconsistencies in the application of this principle of listening to children's views impacting not only on children, but also with regard to parents, social workers, service providers and legal professionals. The very complexity raises moral and practical questions such as children being given access to confidential information about their parents and the issue of a finding a consistent approach for informing children of decisions made and whether this should be affected by the legal status. For example, in the making of a child assessment order, notice is discretionary, whilst in the making of a child protection order, a notice is mandatory.

The involvement of children and young people in the system of children's hearings provides a good testing ground for this principle of listening to children's views. In an earlier part of this chapter reference was made to advocacy as an important contribution to a sense of empowerment. A report commissioned by the Scottish Executive explored the experiences of taking part in children's hearings and also evaluated the role of different types of advocates (Creegan, Henderson and King 2006). The findings suggest that certain processes encourage participation, such as being prepared, knowing what to expect and being given papers which are accessible. Also the interpersonal skills and attitudes of the adults present were a factor especially that there be evidence of listening and the creation of a comfortable environment. The advocates identified were mostly family members and key workers from residential settings. Most of the children had allocated social workers but they did not perceive these as providing advocacy support. Positive experiences of advocacy cited including somebody who knows the child well, who is able to explain things, who is able to communicate with children and who has the skills to challenge panel members at their hearings. The authors comment:

> The relationship between advocacy and participation is crucial. It is apparent in terms of Article 12 of the UNCRC that, if children and young people are to be able to participate in a meaningful way, they require information, support, sometimes encouragement to be their own advocate and at other times appropriate representation. The important issue is that children's and young people's needs in this crucial area are themselves seen as relevant and a right which others have a duty to fulfil. (Creegan, Henderson and King 2006: 55)

The issue of inconsistency was also commented upon in a report produced by HM Inspectorate of Education that noted whilst some children's panel members took the time to establish children's views, this is not always the case in other decision-making meetings. This report commented on the positive role that advocacy services can play in supporting children to express their point of view at meetings. The author suggests that advocacy services in the context of child protection services are not always available and that the purpose of independent advocacy is not always clear to staff (Donaldson 2009).

Dalrymple and Burke (2006) argue strongly that social workers need to adopt the position that the law, or at least certain Acts, can be used to promote good practice. Their position is that knowledge of the law can be used to inform anti-oppressive practice. This can be done to ensure that people's rights are not disregarded but also that people's participation in decisions can be strengthened through a rights-based approach. It has been observed that if people do have a sense of having their rights respected through a positive process, then this feeds into greater self-esteem and a sense of personal integrity. Some have suggested this is a sense of becoming a citizen and affords a positive affirmation of struggles for social justice.

Exercise 9.5

Do you agree that the Law can be used in an empowering sense? Can you identify laws that might be perceived as being oppressive?

Supported self-care

It can be argued that with regard to care in the community policies there has been a deliberate and planned shift away from institutional models of care towards more community-based models of care since the 1960s (see Chapter 7). This has resulted in the closure in the UK of many long-stay hospitals for people with mental health problems and people with learning disabilities. The prevailing view has been that community-based provisions of 'care' offers individuals greater dignity, more respect, greater opportunities for individualised choices and in general a more fulfilling life. In recent years, there has been increasing questions about the mainstream arrangements for providing 'care' and interest expressed in processes that are designed to support self-care.

The National Health Service and Community Care Act 1990 (NHSCCA) is recognised as one of the most radical and significant pieces of welfare legislation in the post-war period (Adams 2002). This followed a process of review by the Conservative Government which saw the publication of the Griffiths Report (1988) and the White Paper *Caring for People* (Department of Health 1989). This provided a definition of community care, which stated:

> Community care means providing the right level of intervention and support to enable people to achieve maximum independence and control over their own lives.

This suggests that part of the thinking of the community care reforms was a shift towards independent living with people living longer in their own homes and within their own communities. The inclusion of the word 'control' is significant given this concept features heavily in the literature on empowerment and suggests there was some idea of moving away from a service-led model of providing 'care'. It is strongly argued by some that these reforms were influenced by the then Conservative Government's ideological stance on privatisation and therefore positioning people as consumers rather than citizens (Malin, Wilmot and Manthorpe 2002). It could be argued this relates to the exit model of empowerment in which the implication appears to be that purchasing power could be wielded by consumers. This concept of consumerism is clearly evident in the official guidance on care management and assessment that declared:

> The rationale for this reorganisation is the empowerment of users and carers. Instead of users and carers being subordinate to the wishes of service providers, the roles will be progressively adjusted. In this way, users and carers will be enabled to exercise the same power as consumers of other services. This redresssing of

> the balance of power is the best guarantee of a continuing improvement in the quality of service. (Department of Health, SSI and Scottish Office 1991: 9)

The reforms instigated by the NHSCCA involved the creating and development of an internal market through what was known as the 'contract culture'. Local authorities went from being providers of services to taking an enabling role in which they used their budgets to commission services. This was done at two levels:

1. by entering into a contract with another organisation to provide a specified service to a designated group of people that was normally paid for through the means of a block grant;
2. by introducing the new role of care managers in order to provide a system of assessment of need and managing packages of care.

There was much talk in 1993 that these reforms represented a shift from a service-led model to a needs-led model. In other words, rather than users and carers having to fit in with services that were being provided, an individualised package of care would be fashioned around the assessed needs of an individual. The role of the care manager was and still is pivotal to the whole process, combined as it is with the tasks of assessing personal needs including risk factors and applying this to the complex machinery of budgets, commissioning services from providers, making contracts and then instigating a process of monitoring and review.

Primarily local authorities have delegated this to care managers who have been allocated a budget, though some have delegated it to service managers, and some to a committee, sometimes known as a resource allocation panel. In other words, the control of care management resources is held by local authorities and as such is *outwith* the control of service users and carers. It has been pointed out that this is where the concept of consumerism falls down and as such does not work especially in the context of finite resources:

> whilst the government espoused principles of consumerism, it can be seen that, in reality, practitioners and social service authorities still held the major hand. (Malin, Wilmot and Manthorpe 2002: 58)

This is presumably a sceptical view as to the amount of personal finances that service users have at their disposal and as such is challenging the assumption that people can operate as consumers of social care services. The idea that service users can operate as consumers of social care services appears to be a different proposition to the person who has a £100 to spend on new clothes and can choose between Marks & Spencer, Next or Tesco.

With the election of the new Labour Government in 1997 we entered into another period of social policy development in which public service reform was accorded a high priority. The concept of consumerism was also central to this Government's ideology position as can be seen from this speech by Prime Minister Tony Blair:

> All four principles have one goal – to put the consumer first. We are making public services user-led; not producer or bureaucracy led, allowing far greater freedom and incentives for services to develop as users want. (Prime Minister's Office 2001)

This speech – entitled 'The Key to Reform is Re-Designing the System around the User' – had echoes of the earlier NHSCCA reforms by highlighting the importance of choice and the promotion of greater choice. Some seven years later, Tony Blair's successor as Prime Minster, Gordon Brown, highlighted in 2008 'personalisation' of public services as a priority for Government action and stated:

> we must make our services respond to what users want: services that genuinely serve you and your family by meeting both personal requirements and the demand for excellence. Services which are shaped by the user. (Prime Minister's Office 2008)

Exercise 9.6

Does the introduction of 'personalisation' imply a change of approach in social policy terms? What does it mean and how might it impact on service users and carers having a sense of empowerment?

It is argued that the application of personalisation ideas could have as much impact on public services over the next decade as privatisation did in the 1980s (Leadbeater 2004). In Leadbeater's pamphlet the problems of service users and carers being placed in the role of consumers is highlighted:

> We need to find a way for users to be treated with respect and consideration when they cannot exercise the sanction of taking their business to another supplier. (Leadbeater 2004: 52)

Leadbeater argues that whilst the concept of voice is important for service users and carers to influence public service reform, authentic transformation will only come about through the enactment of personalisation through participation. A number of steps are involved with this process:

- intimate consultation
- expanded choice
- enhanced voice
- partnership provision
- advocacy
- co-production
- funding

The fundamental principles underpinning personalisation are stated:

> Users should not be utterly dependent upon the judgement of professionals; they should be able to question, challenge and deliberate with them. Nor are users merely consumers, choosing between different packages offered to them; they should be more intimately involved in shaping and even co-producing the service they want. Through participation users have greater voice in shaping the service, but this is exercised where it counts, where services are designed and delivered. (Leadbeater 2004: 60)

Exercise 9.7

This statement resonates with that of core social work beliefs – can you relate this statement to the requirements of the Social Work Code of Practice (SSSC)?

The idea of contributing to the design of a service is what is meant by co-production and can be understood as a strengths-based process of recognising and working with people. It works on the basis that people are best placed to know what would make a difference to them. This implies a sharing of power and that front-line workers would need to be delegated with the authority to co-produce unique solutions to individual situations.

Funding, it is suggested, should be placed in the control of the service or carer with advice from the professionals.

What exactly is meant by personalisation?

In social policy terms, personalisation is envisaged by both the UK and Scottish Governments as an organising principle for a whole raft of public policies. The UK Government Policy Review describes personalisation as:

> Personalisation is the process by which services are tailored to meet the needs and preferences of citizens. The overall vision is that the state should empower citizens to shape their own lives and the services they receive. (HM Government 2007a)

And then a similar statement was published in a Scottish consultation document about personalisation that stated:

> It enables the individual alone, or in groups, to find the right solutions for them and to participate in the delivery of a service. From being a recipient of services, citizens can become actively involved in selecting and shaping the services they receive. (Changing Lives Service Development Group 2009)

Whilst both these statements neatly avoid the issue of funding, they both position the user or carer as a citizen and indicate some level of influencing the public service they receive.

How has personalisation been expressed in public policy?

We have seen significant activity in England and Wales in which personalisation has been a key idea that has influenced the development of thinking in social care. So a ground-breaking concordat (HM Government 2007b) was agreed between central government, local government and the social care sector. This sets out a shared vision of key principles for an adult social care system and commits to a number of objectives including personal budgets for eligible adults. Since then the work has been taken forward in a number of ways; by individual councils, through the 2008 Carers Strategy and by the piloting of individual budgets in 13 projects. The use of individual budgets builds on the experience of Direct Payments and InControl (an independent social enterprise) that has contracts with 107 English local authorities.

In Scotland, issues of personalisation were identified in the *Report of the 21st Century Social Work Review* (Scottish Executive 2006) and five recommendations were made to increase the capacity to deliver personalised services. The Scottish Government accepted the recommendations of the report and has approved an implementation plan which includes five change programmes one of which is service development; the group taking this work forward has chosen personalisation as its major theme. It has published two papers on personalisation in order to stimulate debate and comment. Guidance has been issued on self-directed care in 2007 and 2009 that is designed to provide clarity on the use of Direct Payments in Scotland for all the partners involved including service users and carers.

What might be some examples of personalised approaches?

The development of individual or personal budgets has been greatly informed by the experience of initially the Independent Living Fund and then the use of Direct Payments. The latter were enabled by the Community Care (Direct Payments) Act 1996; this involves a cash payment by a local authority to individuals who have been assessed as needing social work services. Individuals can use this money to employ a personal assistant, to buy equipment and to purchase services, but can not purchase residential services. The personal budget is considered to be the allocation of funding from a local authority, whereas the individual budget is considered to be the total of the personal budget plus money from additional sources such as housing support. The results of the evaluation of the individual budget (IB) pilots were published in 2008 and the main findings included:

- people receiving an IB were more likely to feel in control of their daily lives;
- IB's were cost effective for care outcomes, except for older people;
- mental health service users and younger physically disabled people reported receiving higher quality care and were more satisfied;
- older people reported lower psychological well-being with IB's (Glendinning and Challis 2008).

It is suggested that the use of online self-assessments, being able to access independent advocacy and participating in mutual support groups are all examples of higher levels of participation in the process of assessment. This relates to the concept of the co-production of services.

InControl started in 2003 to develop a new system, which they called Self-Directed Support, as they considered the old social care system did not put people in control of their lives. Their mission is to help people to be in full control of their lives. They have developed a practical seven-step approach to help people have a personal budget and to purchase the supports they require.

What might be the challenges involved with the embedding of personalisation in social care provision?

The Scottish Development Group's paper on a personalised commissioning approach (2009) identified a number of barriers which included some of the following:

- lack of information
- lack of independent advocacy
- dominance of vested interests
- lack of flexibility in procedures and financial systems
- staff lacking in skills related to personalisation
- discriminatory attitudes towards service users and carers

The Association of Directors of Social Work in Scotland in their report on personalisation (Harrington 2009) identified a number of challenges to a personalised approach that included the issues of:

- *Funding.* The report suggests that whilst there might be lower costs in the longer-term, there could be higher costs in the short-term associated with changes to the infra structure of organisations. In addition, some of the findings from the Individual Budget Evaluation Network's report (2008) indicate that Local Authorities found it difficult to integrate additional funding streams into Individual Budgets because of differences in eligibility criteria across different schemes. This will require action by central government.
- *Risk.* ADSW highlight the balancing act between more choice and control on the one hand whilst at the same time being vigilant towards those who may be vulnerable and in need of protection (Hothersall and Maas-Lowit 2010). Indeed the report states:

  > Local authorities have a 'duty of care' and should not agree a support plan if serious concerns exist that the individual may be at risk, or that their needs will not be met. (Harrington 2009: 9)

The principles of personalisation are congruent with the values of social work including affording dignity and respect to the individual alongside a commitment to social justice, empowerment and social inclusion. The inclusion of personalisation approaches needs to be understood as a long-term project that has implications and challenges for all partners, but also holds significant opportunities not only for service users and carers but also for social workers.

Chapter summary and conclusion

This chapter has explored the meaning of empowerment in a twenty-first-century post-industrialised society. It has recognised that the concept of power is complex and attention has been drawn to the Foucauldian concepts of discourse and normalising judgements (Fook 2002). There has been a mapping of the influence of empowerment-related ideas onto a range of social care policies that have emerged over the past 20 years. These have related to the whole population of the UK, including adults and children. For example, the policy on community care has had a far-reaching effect on our services: the structures of organisations, resources, staff posts including contract officers and the language used. This has been paralleled by a growth in human rights that have been embodied through legislation. There has arguably been a cultural shift towards people being more prepared to use their 'voice' to express their point of view, their concerns and on occasions to complain. For some people they use existing skills to advocate for themselves and for others they draw upon the support of independent advocates. Much of this policy talk has been situated around shifting power to individuals and away from professionals and organisations; in other words, the individual is able to exercise more control and choice over the directions over his or her life. And yet this is taking place against the backdrop of major structural disadvantages and social inequalities including poverty, social exclusion and discrimination. These pose serious risks and challenges for some groups in society and major questions need to be asked as to whether an equality of opportunity approach is sufficient to encourage social equality and social justice

One of the questions is that if empowerment is about people assuming control over their own lives, how true can that be when a policy or a set of regulations determines that the approach will be empowerment? This sounds contradictory as whilst professionals and agencies may provide opportunities for change, the initiative for empowerment comes from the individual person. Where this has not happened, then it is claimed that in fact agencies and professionals are colonising empowerment and taking control away from the very people who are supposed to be empowered (Parker, Fook and Pease 1999). So there is a paradox of empowerment which some describe as the 'dilemma of difference' (Parker, Fook and Pease 1999: 151). The argument goes that if a rationalist problem-solving approach is pursued via policies that target certain groups in society, this will have a stigmatising effect. The social difference is viewed negatively rather than as a starting point for celebrating difference and embracing rich dialogue.

I suggest that an understanding of policies influenced by contested ideas of empowerment is strengthened through an analysis of the multiple

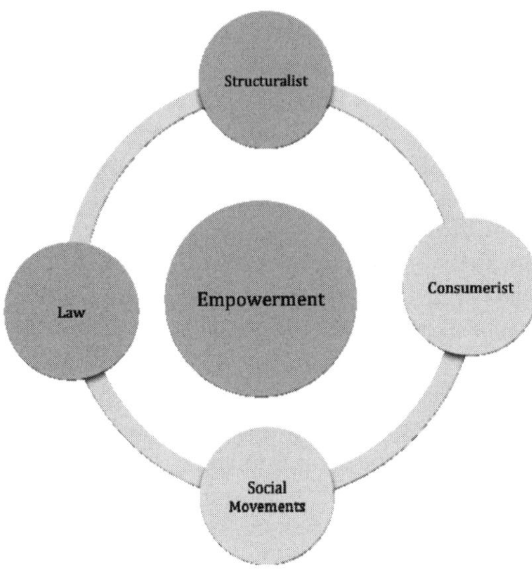

Figure 9.1 Discourses relating to empowerment

discourses that are at play and that compete with each other. These are illustrated in Figure 9.1.

The structuralist discourse is concerned with the major structural disadvantages and inequalities that are present within Scottish and British society. Issues of severe poverty experienced by children have been highlighted in the recent Measuring Severe Child Poverty in the UK report (Save the Children 2010). Campaign groups have made recommendations for changes in tax and benefit rules and regulations that would benefit all people, such as the raising of the level of the child benefit; in other words, a universal strategy. To some extent it could be said the policies on social inclusion are working to the same goal, but the criticism is that these policies are targeting specific groups in society, which could be seen as stigmatising, and that obtaining the benefits (for example child benefit vouchers) is a time consuming bureaucratic exercise. Furthermore, campaigners advocate for social equality-based policies whilst the Scottish and UK Governments have distanced themselves from this agenda.

The consumerist discourse focuses on policies whose purpose is to support the individual in having more control and choice over the public services they need through the use of budgets. A number of different models are in operation, including the 'traditional' Care Management one in which the local authority is the budget holder, whilst with Direct Payments the service user becomes the budget holder.

The personalisation agenda undoubtedly sits within the consumerist discourse and is being given political and professional backing at this stage, albeit with some reservations. The challenges will be managing the tension between individually-driven processes, and for public authorities to be accountable for legal duties and responsibilities, especially in relation to the duty of care towards children and adults that are assessed as needing protection.

The social movements discourse positions service users and carers as groups or networks of people with similar lived experience who come together to campaign around issues of social equality and press for improved rights, for example the Independent Living movement and self-advocacy organisations such as People First. There is often much emphasis on campaigning for participatory policies and practices, which recognises multiple social roles that a person may hold: a service user, a person with rights, a stakeholder, a partner.

The law discourse has been described as one of the dominant discourses in society (Healy 2005). This discourse is a core area for empowerment-related policies with the foundation being laid by the UN Convention on Human Rights and the use of legislation to state the rights and responsibilities of individuals in society. The discourse suggests the law is authoritative whilst this chapter has recorded observations that the implementation of rights-based law is highly complex and subject to inconsistencies. The proponents of this discourse suggest that through the empowering use of certain laws, vulnerable people can be protected from harm and are able to access services and benefits from the state.

It can be recognised that these four discourses interact with each other and stimulate the political and policy-making scene. These feed into the policy-making process and in time result in the formulation of policy statements from a Government or the passing of an Act of Parliament. Just as interesting is the enactment of a policy or a law in which public bodies and professionals have the responsibility and the task of translating laws and policies into actions and outcomes.

For social work practice this requires the social worker to commit fundamentally to the processes of empowerment and to draw upon knowledge of the multiple discourses that feed social policy debates. It is also important for social workers to align themselves to issues of social justice as partners in this long process of change and to contribute to the development of social policy debate in this area.

References

Action for Children (2010), *Ending Poverty, Exclusion and Inequality*. Available at: http://www.actionforchildren.org.uk/content/422/Ending-poverty (accessed 2 June 2010).

Adams, R. (2002), *Social Policy for Social Work* (1st edn) (Basingstoke: Palgrave).

Brandon, D., Brandon, D. and Brandon, T. (1995), *Advocacy: Power to People with Disabilities* (Birmingham: Venture Press).

British Association of Social Workers (n.d.), 'The BASW Code of Ethics for Social Workers'. Available at: http://www.basw.co.uk/Default.aspx?tabid=64 (accessed 30 November 2009).

Changing Lives Service Development Group (2009-last update), 'Commissioning for Personalisation: More of the Same Won't Do' [Homepage of Scottish Government]. Available at: http://www.scotland.gov.uk/Publications/2009/04/07112629/0 (accessed 7 November 2009).

Clapham, A. (2007), *Human Rights* (1st edn) (Oxford: Oxford University Press).

Creegan, C., Henderson, G. and King, C. (2006), *Big Words and Big Tables* (Edinburgh: Scottish Executive).

Dalrymple, J. and Burke, B. (2006), *Anti-Oppressive Practice: Social Care and the Law* (2nd edn) (Maidenhead: Open University Press).

Department of Health (1989), *Caring for People* (White Paper).

Department of Health, SSI and Scottish Office (1991), *Care Management and Assessment: A Practitioners' Guide* (London: Department of Health).

Dominelli, L. (2004), *Social Work: Theory and Practice for a Changing Profession* (Cambridge: Polity Press).

Donaldson, G. (2009), *How Well Do We Protect Scotland's Children?* (Edinburgh: HMIE).

Fook, J. (2002), *Social Work: Critical Theory and Practice* (London: Sage).

Fook, J. and Morley, C. (2005), 'Empowerment: A Contextual Perspective', in S. Hick, R. Pozzuto and J. Fook (eds), *Social Work: The Critical Turn* (Toronto: Thompson Educational Publishers).

Glendinning, C. and Challis, D. (2008), *Evaluation of the Individual Pilots Programme* (York: University of York).

Gray, B. and Jackson, R. (eds) (2002), *Advocacy and Learning Disability* (London: Jessica Kingsley).

Griffiths, R. (1988), *Community Care: Agenda for Action* (London: HMSO).

Harrington, W. (2009-last update), 'Personalisation: Principles, Challenges and a New Approach' [Homepage of Association of Directors of Social Work]. Available at: http://www.adsw.org.uk/Our-Work/Publications/ (accessed 15 December 2009).

Healey, K. (2005), *Social Work Theories in Context* (Basingstoke: Palgrave Macmillan).

HM Government (2007a), *Building on Progress* [Homepage of HM Government]. Available at: http://archive.cabinetoffice.gov.uk/policy_review/documents/building_on_progress.pdf (accessed 27 November 2009).

— (2007b), *Putting People First* [Homepage of HM Government]. Available at: http://www.dh.gov.uk/en/Publicationsandstatistics/Publications/PublicationsPolicyAndguidance/DH_081118 (accessed 27 November 2009).

Hothersall, S.J. (2008), *Social Work with Children, Young People and their Families in Scotland* (2nd edn) (Exeter: Learning Matters).

Hothersall, S.J. and Maas-Lowit, M. (eds) (2010), *Need, Risk and Protection in Social Work Practice* (Exeter: Learning Matters).

Hothersall, S., Maas-Lowit, M. and Golightley, M. (2008), *Social Work and Mental Health in Scotland* (Exeter: Learning Matters).

Kendrick, A. (2005), 'Social Exclusion and Social Inclusion: Themes and Issues in Residential Child Care', in D. Crimmens and I. Milligan (eds), *Facing Forward: Residential Childcare in the 21st Century* (Lyme Regis: Russell House).

Leadbeater, C. (2004-last update), 'Personalisation through Participation'. Available at: http://www.demos.co.uk/publications/personalisation (accessed 5 September 2009).

Malin, N., Wilmot, S. and Manthorpe, J. (2002), *Key Concepts and Debates in Health and Social Policy* (Maidenhead: Open University Press).

Marshall, K., Tisdall, E.K.M. and Cleland, A. (2002-last update), '"Voice of the Child": Under the Children (Scotland) Act 1995'. Available at: http://www.scotland.gov.uk/Publications/2002/09/14905/6733 (accessed 30 November 2009).

Means, R. and Smith, R. (1994), *Community Care: Policy and Practice* (London: Macmillan).

Morris, J. (1997), *Community Care: Working in Partnership with Service Users* (Birmingham: Venture Press).

National Equality Panel (2010), *An Anatomy of Economic Inequality in the UK*, CASE Report 60 Summary (London: Government Equalities Office).

National Statistics Online (2009), 'Employment'. Available at: http://www.statistics.gov.uk/cci/nugget.asp?ID=12 (accessed 25 January 2010).

Parker, S., Fook, J. and Pease, B. (1999), 'Empowerment: The Modern Social Work Concept Par Excellence', in B. Pease and J. Fook (eds), *Transforming Social Work Practice* (London: Routledge).

Prime Minister's Office (2001-last update), 'Speech on Public Service Reform'. Available at: http://www.number10.gov.uk/Page1632 (accessed 12 November 2009).

—— (2008-last update), 'Lasting Prosperity and Fairness for All'. Available at: http://www.number10.gov.uk/Page15535 (accessed 10 November 2009).

Ramcharan, P. (ed.) (1997), *Empowerment in Everyday Life: Learning Disability* (London: Jessica Kingsley).

Save the Children (2010), 'Measuring Severe Child Poverty in the UK'. Available at: http://www.savethechildren.org.uk/en/docs/Measuring_child_poverty_in_the_UK.pdf (accessed 27 January 2010).

Sawicki, J. (1991), *Disciplining Foucault: Feminism, Power and the Body* (New York: Routledge).

Scott, G., Mooney, G. and Brown, U. (2005), 'Managing Poverty in the Devolved Scotland', in G. Mooney and G. Scott (eds), *Exploring Social Policy in the 'New' Scotland* (1st edn) (Bristol: Policy Press).

Scottish Development Group (2009), *Commissioning for Personalisation: More of the Same Won't Do*. Available at: http://www.scotland.gov.uk/Publications/2009/04/07112629/6 (accessed 2 June 2010).

Scottish Executive (1999-last update), 'Social Justice: A Scotland Where Everyone Matters'. Available at: http://www.scotland.gov.uk/Publications/1999/11/4174/File-1 (accessed 18 November 2009).

—— (2003a-last update), 'A Partnership for a Better Scotland'. Available at: http://www.scotland.gov.uk/Publications/2003 May 2017150/21952 (accessed 2 December 2009).

—— (2003b-last update), 'Closing the Gap'. Available at: http://www.scotland.gov.uk/Publications/2002/10/15579/11898 (accessed 15 December 2009).

—— (2006-last update), 'Changing Lives: Report of the 21st Century Social Work Review Group'. Available at: http://www.scotland.gov.uk/Resource/Doc/91931/0021949.pdf (accessed 21 September 2009).

Scottish Government (2008-last update), 'Achieving Our Potential'. Available at: http://www.scotland.gov.uk/Publications/2008/11/20103815/0 (accessed 16 January 2010).

Scottish Office (1999), 'Social Inclusion: Opening the Door to a Better Scotland'. Available at: http://www.scotland.gov.uk/library/documents-w7/sist-00.htm (accessed 11 June 2009).

Social Exclusion Task Force (2009). Available at: http://www.cabinetoffice.gov.uk/social_exclusion_task_force.aspx (accessed 6 November 2009).

Solomon, B. (1976), Black Empowerment: Social Work in Oppressed Communities (New York, NY: Columbia University Press).

Thompson, N. (2001), *Anti-Discriminatory Practice* (3rd edn) (Basingstoke: Palgrave).

United Nations (2009), *Convention on the Rights of the Child*. Available at: http://www.unicef.org/crc/ (accessed 4 December 2009).

White, M. (2007), *Maps of Narrative Practice* (London: Norton).

Who Cares? Scotland (2009), *Charter of Rights*. Available at: http://www.whocaresscotland.org/charter_of_rights.htm (accessed 11 December 2009).

Widdowson, B. (2001), 'Cultural Turns, Post-Structuralism, and Social Policy', in M.P. Lavalette, (ed.), *Social Policy: Theories, Concepts and Issues* (3rd edn) (London: Sage).

Further reading

Council of Europe (1953), *European Convention on Human Rights*. Available at: http://conventions.coe.int/Treaty/Commun/QueVoulezVous.asp?NT=005&CL=ENG (accessed 27 January 2010).

Scottish Government (2009-last update), 'Personalisation: A Shared Understanding'. Available at: http://www.scotland.gov.uk/Publications/2009/04/07112629/5 (accessed 14 November 2009).

United Nations (1989), *UN Convention on the Rights of the Child*. Available at: http://www.dcsf.gov.uk/everychildmatters/strategy/strategyandgovernance/uncrc/unitednationsconventionontherightsofthechild/ (accessed 11 January 2010).

— (1996), 'What are Human Rights?'. Available at: http://www.ohchr.org/EN/Issues/Pages/WhatareHumanRights.aspx (accessed 30 November 2009).

Part III

Policy for practice

10 Health and health inequalities

Pedro Morago

Introduction

This chapter does not intend to provide a comprehensive analysis of health policy as a key area within the broad subject of social policy, nor does it provide a discussion of different health care systems. Rather, the main focus is on the phenomenon of socio-economic inequalities, which negatively affects a considerable proportion of social work service users. Thus, the chapter begins by presenting a brief introduction to the concept of health and other associated notions like health care and health care policy, which is followed by an overview of health care provision in the UK as well as of the organisation of the National Health Service (NHS) in Scotland. The chapter then examines the phenomenon of socio-economic health inequalities in the UK and the policies developed in order to tackle it, to end considering some of the implications of such inequalities for social work practice.

Health, health care and health care policy

The World Health Organisation (WHO) defines health as 'a state of complete physical, mental and social well-being and not merely the absence of disease or infirmity' (World Health Organisation 1992). Such a wide definition of health has been criticised as idealistic and impractical (Doll 1992) as well as for describing a state which seems to correspond more to happiness than to health (Saracci 1997). Furthermore, different commentators have urged the WHO, over the last years, to provide a more realistic definition of health that allows us to measure and compare states of health and disease as well as to evaluate objectively the effectiveness of health programmes wherever these are implemented (Bok 2004; Saracci 1997; Üstün and Jakob 2005). However, the definition provided by the WHO has also the merit of presenting an integral view of health which takes into consideration the different dimensions of the human being. Largely as a result of such a holistic approach, health care is now widely regarded as the delivery of services aimed at (i) preventing and treating illness, (ii) promoting, preserving and restoring mental and physical health, and (iii) tackling socio-economic factors that may have a negative impact upon the individual's health. Health care policy, therefore, refers to the set of governmental strategies and initiatives related to the financing and provision of services the scope of which falls within any of those three broad areas. The following sections will provide an overview of how health care is organised in the UK as well as of the structure of the National Health Service in Scotland.

Health care provision in the UK

In the UK, the health care market is dominated by the public sector, with the National Health Service (NHS) providing around 74 per cent of all health care services. The private sector provides almost 20 per cent of health care services while the rest of the market is served by the voluntary sector. However, since some private and voluntary services are funded with public money, it is estimated that more than 81 per cent of the total health care provided in the UK is publicly funded (Ham 2004; Laing and Buisson 2003). The vast majority of public expenditure on health is paid for by general taxation, while the rest of the money is financed through sources such as National Insurance contributions, charges, land and property sales and tobacco duty.

From a comparative point of view, levels of health care expenditure in the UK are below those of France, Germany and the Scandinavian countries. However, publicly-funded health care spending is higher in Scotland than in England. For example, in 2003 Scotland had a total NHS expenditure of £1,262 per capita compared to £1,085 spent by England in the same period (Alvarez-Rosete et al. 2005). Whether it results in Scotland having better health outcomes and services than England still remains uncertain (Irvine and Ginsberg 2004).

Finally, it is necessary to highlight that a considerable amount of health work is carried out every day by the informal sector, namely, carers who are not formally integrated into the healthcare market, for example women caring for and giving support to relatives who are ill or frail (Allsop 2003). The contribution of this unpaid labour in the community to the functioning of the whole health care system is so important that the Scottish Parliament has formally acknowledged the needs of unpaid carers and promoted strategies for their support (Scottish Parliament 2002).

The National Health Service

Despite the importance of the private and the voluntary sector (formally integrated in the health care market) as well as the informal sector, the vast majority of health care in the UK is provided, as stated above, by the NHS. Before 1948, health care was provided through different sources such as private services, insurance schemes, and charities and voluntary hospitals. However, these services did not cover the health needs of large sectors of the population like those who were not insured workers and chronic patients who could not afford to pay for their health care, the care of whom was often left to overcrowded and poorly-resourced infirmaries. In addition, hospital care was not included within insurance-based schemes, so that only primary care was provided to insured workers in return for their contributions.

The above situation was addressed in 1948 with the creation of the NHS, which was founded upon the following principles:

- *comprehensiveness* of the services provided, covering all health needs of the population;
- *universality and equity*, which means that all members of the UK population have the right to equitable access to NHS services regardless of income, socio-demographic background and health status;
- *free health care* at the point of delivery, financed from general taxation.

While the NHS has remained a cornerstone of British society since 1948, the above principles have been somehow eroded over the last decades with the introduction of charges for some services – for example prescriptions, some dental treatment and spectacles – and the prioritising and rationing of resources. On the other hand, the growing importance – over the last decades – of service user's right to receive high quality, a transparent and accountable service has resulted in a relative decline of medical dominance within the NHS. Another major change to the NHS was the process of decentralisation in the organisation and provision of health care services introduced by the 1990 NHS and Community Care Act (Department of Health 1990). The 1990 Act also established the *purchaser/provider system* – which applies market principles to the provision of health care services – and the NHS Trusts, independent organisations which provide hospital services as well as care in the community in the areas of mental health, learning disabilities and older people.

The National Health Service in Scotland

In 1999 responsibility for health was devolved to the Scottish political institutions. Thus, the Scottish Parliament has now the legislative power to pass laws in the area of health and the Minister for Health and Community Care within the Scottish Executive is the responsible for the overall running of the health and community care services in Scotland. The Scottish Executive Health Department is the government department designed to set health care policies as well as to manage the NHS.

In Scotland, the NHS provides the following services or levels of care:

- Primary care, which includes general practice, dentistry, optics, pharmacy and community nursing. These services are mostly delivered by *community health partnerships* which, although formally integrated within NHS boards, manage their own budget and have relatively high decision-making levels.
- Secondary or hospital care, provided by the NHS Boards – which own hospitals and are managed by their own board of governors – and several Special Health Boards.
- Tertiary care, which consists of highly specialised services for unusual or complex clinical problems.
- Community care for older people, individuals with mental health problems and individuals with a learning disability is also provided by NHS Boards in partnership with local authorities.
- Public Health, which involves major initiatives aimed at disease prevention as well as health promotion among the general population of Scotland. These areas are the responsibility of Public Health Departments integrated into each NHS Board.

Health inequalities in the United Kingdom

Despite the NHS principles of comprehensiveness of care and equitable access to NHS services for all sections of the UK population, some groups appear to be significantly healthier than others. This phenomenon is not new: health inequalities in Britain have been reported since the nineteenth century (Davey Smith, Dorling and Shaw 2001; Farr 1864), nor is it exclusive to the UK, with health inequalities being consistently found within other countries (Blane 2001; Braveman and Tarimo 2002; Dobson 2006; Fox 1989; Kunst et al. 1998; Marmot 2005; Pearce and Dorling 2006). What is worrying is that, since the 1970s, the health gap in the UK has increased faster than in previous decades and seems to have considerably widened compared to other developed countries (Benzeval et al. 1995; Davey Smith et al. 2002; Donkin et al. 2002; Shaw et al. 1999).

While health inequalities can be somehow associated to factors such as geography, age, gender, ethnicity, mental health status and disability, a considerable body of evidence – which will be examined below – suggests that socio-economic inequalities are the main contributor to the health divide. The first major study addressed to investigate health differentials between social classes in the UK was commissioned by the Labour Government in 1976. The study – known as the *Black Report* (Black et al. 1980) – showed an overall poorer health experience amongst lower occupational groups: for example, mortality levels for unskilled manual workers were 2.5 times higher than for professional workers. The findings of the *Black Report* were confirmed and expanded by *The Health Divide* (Whitehead 1987) and the *Independent Inquiry into Inequalities in Health* (Acheson et al. 1998). This inquiry, also known as the *Acheson Report*, found that the health gap in the UK was still widening since the 1970s. Thus, by the early 1990s mortality amongst unskilled workers was three times higher than for those in professional occupations. Another example is the increase in life expectancy between the late 1970s and the late 1980s, which was bigger for individuals in the highest occupational groups – two years for men and women – than for those in the lowest classes – 1.4 years for men and one year for women (Hattersly 1997).

The problem of health disparities is particularly serious in Scotland. First of all, comparative studies show that health and life expectancy in Scotland are poor compared to the rest of the UK and most Northern and Western European countries (Hanlon et al. 2001; Leon et al. 2003; Palmer et al. 2008). For example, life expectancy for both women and men in Scotland is between three and five years lower than in countries such as Denmark, Norway, Iceland, Finland and Ireland. In addition, health inequalities between socio-economic groups in Scotland have increased over the last decades (Shaw et al. 1999). A major study commissioned by the Health Promotion Policy Unit in partnership with the Public Health Institute of Scotland (Blamey et al. 2002) has reviewed the evidence in this area providing, amongst others, the following examples of health differentials within Scotland:

- The differential in premature death rates between the 'best health' and the 'worst health' areas of Scotland increased over the 1990s (Rahman et al. 2000).

- Individuals living in the most deprived areas of Scotland are between two and three times more likely to experience lung cancer than those living in the least deprived areas (Scottish Executive 2001; Sharp and Brewster 1999).
- The risk of dying from coronary heart disease is 2.5 times greater amongst individuals living in the most deprived areas of Scotland compared to those living in the least deprived areas (Scottish Executive 2001).
- Since 1995, consumption of fresh fruit increased more in the least deprived areas of Scotland than in the most deprived ones (Shaw et al. 2000).

A more recent study produced by the New Policy Institute for the Joseph Rowntree Foundation shows similar findings. For example, individuals aged 35 to 59 living in social housing are three times more likely to have a limiting longstanding illness than owner-occupiers within the same age range, and the proportion of babies born with a low birth weight is two times higher in the most deprived areas compared to areas with below-average deprivation rates (Palmer et al. 2005). The above and other examples demonstrate that, despite certain progress in Scotland's overall health profile, substantial health inequalities still remain between different socio-economic groups. Why does it occur? This question will be explored in the following section.

Explanations for socio-economic inequalities in health

When examining the literature we can find a wide range of theories that try to account for the phenomenon of socio-economic health inequalities. Some of the commonest categories of explanation will now be examined.

The artefact explanation

It has been suggested that the differentials in health between socio-economic groups are simply the *artefactual* result of deeply flawed research studies (Gravelle 1998; Rodgers 1979). Certainly, defining and measuring such broad variables as health and socio-economic status presents considerable methodological challenges to researches (Braveman et al. 2005). However, a consistent body of evidence from a large number of studies using different methodologies and timescales allows us to say that socio-economic inequalities are real rather than artificial.

The 'health selection' hypothesis

Some authors maintain that health affects social class and social mobility to the extent that individuals with good health move up into higher social classes while those who have poor health tend to move down (Illsley 1986; Stern 1983; West 1991). Therefore, health would be the cause, rather than the effect, of social status. Although it is commonly acknowledged that health-related mobility occurs (Blane et al. 1993; Power et al. 1996), the importance of the *Health Selection Hypothesis* is not clear, with some authors arguing that health selection has a major effect on socio-economic health inequalities (West 1991) and others suggesting that the contribution of such an explanation is limited (Blane et al. 1993).

The role of health services

This explanation associates significant inequalities in the access to and use of health services across different social classes with socio-economic variations in health status. In the UK, early studies found that middle and affluent socio-economic groups had access to more and better health care services (Blaxter 1984; Le Grand 1978). However, later evidence suggests that, at least in relation to primary care, lower socio-economic groups have been favoured in terms of service provision (Evandrou et al. 1992; Haynes 1991; O'Donnell and Propper 1991). Although other studies report that some population groups experiencing different dimensions of social disadvantage have poorer access to immunisation services (Bennett and Smith 1992), specialist diagnostic and inpatient services (Majeed et al. 1994; Payne and Saul 1997), it still seems insufficient in order to explain the overall phenomenon of socio-economic inequalities in health (Wilkinson 1996). As MacIntyre (2000) points out, the evidence suggests that, although health care systems have important responsibilities in reducing inequalities in health, many of the factors contributing to such inequalities lie outside the health care sector.

Health-related behaviours (cultural/behavioural explanation)

The hypothesis that health-related behaviours – in particular diet, smoking, exercise and alcohol consumption – can explain inequalities in health has traditionally attracted considerable interest, to the extent that such behaviours have been the focus of major policies to improve public health in the UK. For example, in the 1980s and early 1990s strategies in this area primarily tended to encourage individuals to take personal responsibility for their own health. Also more recent initiatives, like those intended to promote fresh fruit and vegetable consumption, emphasise the need for healthier lifestyles among the general population. Certainly, research studies provide some evidence of the impact of health-related behaviours across different socio-economic groups. For example:

- Vitamin levels appear to be higher in the diets of those individuals in middle and affluent social classes (Braddon et al. 1988; Cade et al. 1988; Dowler and Calvert 1995; Morgan et al. 1989).
- Individuals in lower social classes are more than twice as likely to smoke cigarettes as those in more affluent social groups (Bunting 1997).
- Leisure time exercise – which is protective against some major diseases – is more frequent among middle and higher social classes, while exercise at work – not particularly protective – is more common among members of the working class (Shaw et al. 1999).
- The risk of having alcohol-related problems is twice as great amongst individuals from deprived socio-economic groups compared to those in more affluent groups (Colhoun and Prescott-Clarke 1996). In addition, unemployed people and those who are experiencing homelessness show significantly high levels of alcohol consumption (Catalano 1991; Forcier 1988; Gill et al. 1996; Hall and Farrell 1997; Hammarstroem 1994).

Despite such evidence, it has been suggested that health-related behaviours can only account for between 10 and 30 per cent of the total gradient between socio-economic status and health. Furthermore, a number of studies show that lifestyles are often influenced by people's social and economic circumstances, so that unhealthy behaviours such as poor dietary patterns, smoking, lack of exercise and alcohol abuse might not be simply the result of personal choice or lack of knowledge but outcomes closely related to adverse socio-economic factors (Graham 1995; 1996; Lobstein 1995; Shaw et al. 1999; Sooman et al. 1993; Wrigley 1998).

The psychosocial explanation

Wilkinson (1996; 1997; 1998) argues that, in developed societies, psychosocial factors associated with social status are a major contributor to inequalities in health. In particular – the author claims – the stress caused by a sense of relative deprivation with respect to other members of society operates as a serious determinant of socio-economic inequalities in health. This hypothesis would account for lower life expectancy in Britain – a society with relatively high income inequalities – compared to more egalitarian countries. Another environmental stressor such as low levels of control over work has also been found to have a negative impact on the health status of individuals in lower status jobs (Karasek et al. 1988; Marmot et al. 1997).

Materialist explanations

A large amount of evidence from research studies shows a strong association between material circumstances in which people live and work and health. In particular, the following factors – largely determined by socio-economic status – are increasingly recognised to have a direct impact on individuals' health and well-being:

- *Low income and poverty*: several studies show a relationship between low income and poor health (Benzeval and Webb 1995; Blaxter 1990; Davey Smith et al. 1996; Ecob and Davey Smith 1999; Wilkinson 1989; 1990; 1992).
- *Deprivation in childhood*: adverse material circumstances during the early years of life may cause a higher incidence of cardiovascular and respiratory diseases in adulthood (Barker and Osmond 1986; Davey Smith et al. 1998; Forsdahl 1977; 1978; Kaplan and Salonen 1990). In addition, poverty-related factors like low birthweight and poor maternal nutrition are also associated to increased morbidity and mortality in adult life (Barker 1992; Koupilova et al. 1997).
- *Educational attainment*: this is related to self-reported health in later life, through the socio-economic circumstances derived from occupational status and also – although to a slightly lesser extent – through a higher propensity to follow advice in relation to health-related behaviours (Shaw et al. 1999; White et al. 1999).
- *Unemployment*: this is regarded as having a negative impact on physical and mental health as well as on social participation (Bartley 1993; 1994; Bartley et al. 1999; Laurance 1986; Wadsworth et al. 1999; Warr 1987).
- *Lone parenthood*: this has been linked to significant health disadvantages, often caused by a combination of insufficient income and the stress of being the sole carer (Dorsett and Marsh 1998; Shouls et al. 1999). In addition, infant mortality rates are higher among babies of lone mothers compared to those born to couple parents (Whitehead and Drever 1999).
- *Work environment*: poor working conditions – like those still experienced by many individuals in the lower occupational groups – are associated to worse health outcomes (Blane et al. 1998; Lynch and Kaplan 2000; Marmot and Wilkinson 1999; Moncada 1999).
- *Housing*: there is strong evidence of the relationship between homelessness and inadequate housing conditions – like dampness

– and a higher prevalence of respiratory diseases (Lowry 1989; Martin et al. 1987; McCarthy et al. 1985; Platt et al. 1989) and mental health problems (Randall and Brown 1999a; 1999b; Scott 1993). Also the influence of different types of tenure have been studied and the results show that renters have, in general, lower socio-economic status and poorer health than owners (MacIntyre et al. 2000).

- *Area influence*: deprived areas are more exposed to material hazards such as pollution and heavy road traffic (MacIntyre 1997). Besides, people living in those areas have poorer access to shops, recreation and sport facilities, public transport and healthcare services compared to those living in more affluent areas (Lupton and Power 2002; MacIntyre 1986; 1997), which might partly explain differential life chances based on socio-economic status.

Although the above factors play an important role in determining the health status of individuals from different socio-economic groups, their impact – some authors claim – does not occur overnight but, rather, over the lifetime of individuals, an argument which underlies the following explanation.

The life course perspective

For this approach, mutually reinforcing dimensions of deprivation and social exclusion which operate throughout the lifetime of individuals in lower socio-economic groups (for example poverty and low income, unemployment, poor skills, unfair discrimination, poor housing or homelessness, a dirty and dangerous environment, poor access to services and so on) have a significant influence on their health status through both material and psychosocial processes (Barker 1998; Davey Smith 2003; Davey Smith, Gunnell and Ben-Shlomo 2001; Kuh and Ben Shlomo 1997). Therefore, health inequalities would be the 'outcome of cumulative differential exposure', throughout the life course, to such adverse factors (Graham 2000: 15).

Policy developments and strategies

As noted above, initiatives in this area during the 1980s and early 1990s put considerable emphasis on the role of health-related behaviours (Fulop et al. 1998). However, the evidence presented in the *Independent Inquiry into Inequalities in Health* (Acheson et al. 1998) showed the major impact of socio-economic factors on health inequalities. Shortly after the publication of the *Independent Inquiry* the British government published the public health White Paper *Saving Lives: Our Healthier Nation* (Department of Health 1999a).

Besides broad priority areas and new targets for health improvement, the White Paper expressed the Government's commitment to reducing health inequalities. This area was expanded in the report *Reducing Health Inequalities: An Action Report* (Department of Health 1999b), in which the government explained its policies in relation to each of the 39 recommendations contained in the *Acheson Report* (Acheson et al. 1998). The role of the National Health Service within the Government's broad plan was heralded by *The NHS Plan* (Department of Health 2000), which establishes a stronger role for the NHS in reducing health inequalities through prevention strategies and work in partnership with local authorities and other agencies.

In 2001, the Government announced the creation of national health inequalities targets and launched a public consultation on the action needed to meet such targets (Department of Health 2001). Such an initiative opened a process which resulted in *Tackling Health Inequalities: A Programme for Action* (Department of Health 2003). The programme sets out the national strategy to tackle health inequalities in England over the following three years and is underpinned by the following core themes:

- adequate support to families, mothers and children;
- engaging communities and individuals;
- illness prevention as well as provision of effective treatment and care, with a major role to be played in this area by the NHS;
- the need for addressing the underlying determinants of poor health and health inequalities.

The programme also highlights the national target for 2010 to reduce the gap in infant mortality and life expectancy at birth between socio-economic groups, for which purposes the following key interventions among socially disadvantaged groups are identified:

- improved antenatal care and early years support;
- prevention of teenage pregnancy and adequate support for teenage parents;
- smoking prevention;
- improved nutrition in pregnancy and early years;
- adequate housing conditions;
- prevention and control of poor diet, obesity and hypertension as well as promotion of physical exercise, with especial attention to people over 50 years old;
- prevention of accidents at home and on the road.

A new White Paper was released in 2004: in *Choosing Health: Making Healthy Choices Easier* (Department of Health 2004), the Government focuses on reducing and preventing unhealthy lifestyles and also outlines the increasingly important role of primary care trusts – particularly those serving deprived areas – in tackling health inequalities. In addition, the White Paper reiterates the targets and commitments contained in *Tackling Health Inequalities: A Programme for Action*. Progress regarding those targets has been reviewed in *Tackling Health Inequalities: Status Report on the Programme for Action* (Department of Health 2005). The report notes significant developments in child poverty reduction since 1997 as well as improvements in housing quality among lower socio-economic groups. Death rates from circulatory disease and cancer are other areas in which the health gap seems to be narrowing. However, although the indicators reported are promising in the long-term, it is not clear whether they will be sufficient in order to meet the targets set for 2010.

Tackling health inequalities is also a major goal of the Scottish Executive's health policies. The White Paper *Towards a Healthier Scotland* (Scottish Office Department of Health 1999) set targets in relation to coronary heart disease, cancer, smoking, alcohol abuse, unwanted teenage pregnancy and dental health to reduce health inequalities between socio-economic groups by 2010. Narrowing the health gap also appears as one of the main themes of the papers *Improving Health in Scotland: The Challenge* (Scottish Executive 2003), *Building a Better Scotland* (Scottish Executive 2004) and, especially, *Better Health, Better Care Action Plan* (Scottish Government 2007), a major programme intended to accelerate progress in several health related areas, among them health inequalities. In addition, the Scottish Government created in 2007 a Ministerial Task Force on Health Inequalities with the objective of identifying and prioritising action to reduce the health divide in Scotland. The Ministerial Task Force's work led to the publication of the report *Equally Well* (Scottish Government 2008) which, although acknowledging some improvement in Scotland's overall health status, also stresses that health inequalities remains a major challenge to the country's well-being. In particular, the report identifies four areas in which urgent action is required: (i) children's early years, (ii) mental health, (iii) the 'big killer' diseases: cardiovascular disease and cancer, and (iv) drug and alcohol problems and their links with violent behaviour.

Conclusions and implications for social work and social care

Despite the principles of free and equitable access to NHS services for all the members of the population and comprehensiveness of the services provided, health inequalities remain a major public health problem in the UK. In past decades, the debate around such a challenging phenomenon has often been characterised by the advocacy of simple hypotheses (West 1998). However, a large body of evidence from research studies suggests that a combination of mutually reinforcing socio-economic factors is the driving force behind the health divide. Consequently, reducing health inequalities requires a strategic, multidimensional response which addresses the underlying determinants of such inequalities, such as poverty and social exclusion, unequal distribution of wealth and life chances, and adverse living and working conditions. Although recent policies in the UK seem to adopt a holistic approach to tackling health inequalities, it is not clear whether such initiatives, still largely focused on behaviour change, will be sufficient to achieve higher levels of social justice and a better distribution of wealth, resources and opportunities (Bywaters 1999). In addition, policies in this area are unlikely to have short-term effects: there is increasing evidence that the socio-economic determinants of health inequalities operate throughout the life course, so that even if current initiatives helped improve the circumstances of the most deprived social groups, it might take years or decades for such policies to produce a significant reduction of the health gap (Leon et al. 2001).

The implications of the phenomenon of socio-economic health inequalities for social work are broad since a high proportion of social work service users experience poor health. As shown by the evidence examined in this chapter, health inequalities and unhealthy lifestyles are not simply the result of choice or lack of knowledge among lower social groups but outcomes derived from the interaction of a range of adverse socio-economic factors. Therefore, it is essential for social work agencies to promote non-judgemental attitudes towards service users as well as to lessen a culture of blame in relation to this phenomenon. Besides, social work can actively collaborate in the process of tackling health inequalities by:

- promoting the social inclusion of service users;
- ensuring that anti-discrimination practice is fully developed;
- empowering service users to gain control over their lives;
- providing appropriate material, emotional and social support to families – especially single-parent families – living in deprivation;
- making sure that service users are getting all the benefits they may be entitled to;
- helping service users to access appropriate health care services, particularly those – like cancer screening services – that are less available in deprived areas;
- providing appropriate support to individuals who are particularly vulnerable to poor health such as looked-after children, individuals

with a learning disability, older people, individuals with substance misuse problems, and individuals with HIV/AIDS.

Finally, and given that tackling health inequalities requires holistic, multi-factorial – and, consequently, multi-agency – strategies, it is crucial that social services engage and work in partnership with health services, housing services and any other agency with an active role in reducing deprivation and inequality.

Chapter summary

This chapter has looked at the phenomenon of health inequalities and considered some of the theories and explanations advanced to account for this. We have also looked at some of the effects of such inequalities and considered what the implications might be for social work and social care practice.

References

Acheson, D., Barker, D., Chambers, J., Marmot, H. and Whitehead, M. (1998), *Independent Inquiry into Inequalities in Health: Report to the Secretary of State for Health* (London: Stationary Office).

Allsop, J. (2003), 'Health Care', in P. Alcock, A. Erskine and M. May (eds), *The Student's Companion to Social Policy* (2nd edn) (Oxford: Blackwell Publishing).

Alvarez-Rosete, A., Bevan, G., Mays, N. and Dixon, J. (2005), 'Effect of Diverging Policy across the NHS', *British Medical Journal* 331: 946–50.

Barker, D.J.P. (1992), *Fetal and Infant Origins of Adult Disease* (London: British Medical Journal Publishing).

—— (1998), *Mothers, Babies, and Health in Later Life* (2nd edn) (Edinburgh: Churchill Livingston).

Barker, D.J.P. and Osmond, C. (1986), 'Childhood Respiratory Infection and Adult Chronic Bronchitis in England and Wales', *British Medical Journal* 293: 1271–5.

Bartley, M. (1993), 'Health and Labour Force Participation: "Stress", Selection and the Reproduction Costs of Labour Power', *Journal of Social Policy* 20: 327–64.

—— (1994), 'Unemployment and Ill Health: Understanding the Relationship', *Journal of Epidemiology and Community Health* 48: 333–7.

Bartley, M., Ferrie, J. and Montgomery, S.M. (1999), 'Living in a High Unemployment Economy: Understanding the Health Consequences', in M. Marmot and R.G. Wilkinson (eds), *Social Determinants of Health* (Oxford: Oxford University Press).

Bennett, P. and Smith, C. (1992), *Beliefs and Attitudes towards Vaccination: Good Health Wales Briefing Report no. 6* (Cardiff: Health Promotion Authority for Wales).

Benzeval, M., Judge, K. and Whitehead, M. (1995), *Tackling Inequalities in Health: An Agenda for Action* (London: King's Fund).

Benzeval, M. and Webb, D. (1995), 'Family Poverty and Poor Health', in M. Benzeval, K. Judge and M. Whitehead (eds), *Tackling Inequalities in Health: An Agenda for Action* (London: King's Fund).

Black, D., Morris, J., Smith, C. and Townsend, P. (1980), *Inequalities in Health: Report of a Research Working* Group (London: Department of Health and Social Security).

Blamey, A., Hanlon, P., Judge, K. and Muirie, J. (eds) (2002), *Health Inequalities in the New Scotland* (Glasgow: Public Health Institute of Scotland).

Blane, D. (2001), 'Commentary: Socioeconomic Health Differentials', *International Journal of Epidemiology* 30: 292–3.

Blane, D., Davey Smith, G. and Bartley, M. (1993), 'Social Selection: What Does it Contribute to Social Class Differences in Health?', *Sociology of Health and Illness* 15: 1–15.

Blane, D., Montgomery, S.M. and Berney, D.R. (1998), 'Research Note: Social Class Differences in Lifetime Exposure to Environmental Hazards', *Sociology of Health and Illness* 20: 532–6.

Blaxter, M. (1984), 'Equity and Consultation Rates in General Practice', *British Medical Journal* 288: 1963–7.

— (1990), *Health and Lifestyles* (London: Routledge).

Bok, S. (2004), *Rethinking the WHO Definition of Health*, Working Paper Series 14(7) (Cambridge, MA: Harvard Center for Population and Development Studies).

Braddon, F.E.M., Wadsworth, M.E.J., Davies, J.M.C. and Cripps, H.A. (1988), 'Social and Regional Differences in Food and Alcohol Consumption and their Measurement in a National Birth Cohort', *Journal of Epidemiology and Community Health* 42: 341–9.

Braveman, P.A., Cubbin, C., Egerter, S., Chideya, S., Marchi, K.S., Metzler, M. and Posner, S. (2005), 'Socioeconomic Status in Health Research: One Size Does Not Fit All', *Journal of the American Medical Association* 294: 2879–88.

Braveman, P. and Tarimo, E. (2002), 'Social Inequalities in Health within Countries: Not Only an Issue for Affluent Nations', *Social Science and Medicine* 54(11): 1621–35.

Bunting, J. (1997), 'Morbidity and Health-Related Behaviours of Adults: A Review', in F. Drever and M. Whitehead (eds), *Health Inequalities* (London: Stationery Office).

Bywaters, P. (1999), 'Social Work and Health Inequalities', *British Journal of Social Work* 29: 811–16.

Cade, J.E., Barker, D.J.P., Margetts, B.M. and Morris, J.A. (1988), 'Diet and Inequalities in Health in Three English Towns', *British Medical Journal* 296: 1359–62.

Catalano, R. (1991), 'The Health Effects of Economic Insecurity', *American Journal of Public Health* 81: 1148–52.

Colhoun, H. and Prescott-Clarke, P. (1996), *Health Survey for England 1994* (London: Her Majesty's Stationery Office).

Davey Smith, G. (2003), *Health Inequalities: Lifecourse Approaches* (Bristol: Policy Press).

Davey Smith, G., Dorling, D., Mitchell, R. and Shaw, M. (2002), 'Health Inequalities in Britain: Continuing Increases up to the End of the 20th Century', *Journal of Epidemiology and Community Health* 56: 434–5.

Davey Smith, G., Dorling, D. and Shaw, M. (2001), *Poverty, Inequality and Health in Britain: 1800–2000 – A Reader* (Bristol: Policy Press).

Davey Smith, G., Gunnell, D. and Ben-Shlomo, Y. (2001), 'Life-Course Approaches to Socio-Economic Differentials in Cause-Specific Adult Mortality', in D. Leon and G. Walt (eds), *Poverty, Inequality, and Health: An International Perspective* (Oxford: Oxford University Press).

Davey Smith, G, Hart, C., Blane, D. and Hole, D. (1998), 'Adverse Socioeconomic Conditions in Childhood and Cause-Specific Adult Mortality: Prospective Observational Study', *British Medical Journal* 316: 1631–5.

Davey Smith, G., Neaton, J.D., Wentworth, D., Stamler, R. and Stamler, J. (1996), 'Socioeconomic Differentials in Mortality Risk among Men Screened for the Multiple Risk Factor Intervention Trial', *American Journal of Public Health* 86: 486–504.

Department of Health (1990), *The NHS and Community Care Act* (London: HMSO).

—— (1999a), *Saving Lives: Our Healthier Nation* (Cmnd 4386) (London: Stationery Office).

—— (1999b), *Reducing Health Inequalities: An Action Report* (London: Department of Health).

—— (2000), *The NHS Plan: A Plan for Investment, A Plan for Reform* (London: Stationery Office).

—— (2001), *Tackling Health Inequalities: Consultation on a Plan for Delivery* (London: Department of Health).

—— (2003), *Tackling Health Inequalities: A Programme for Action* (London: Department of Health).

— (2004), *Choosing Health: Making Healthier Choices Easier* (London: Department of Health).
— (2005), *Tackling Health Inequalities: Status Report on the Programme for Action* (London: Department of Health).
Dobson, R. (2006), 'Health Gap between Educated and Less Educated Russians Widens', *British Medical Journal* 332: 1350.
Doll, R. (1992), 'Health and the Environment in the 1990s', *American Journal of Public Health* 82: 933–41.
Donkin, A., Goldblatt, P. and Lynch, K. (2002), 'Inequalities in Life Expectancy by Social Class, 1972–1999', *Health Statistics Quarterly* 15: 5–15.
Dorsett, R. and Marsh, A. (1998), *The Health Trap: Poverty, Smoking and Lone Parenthood* (London: Policy Studies Institute).
Dowler, E. and Calvert, C. (1995), *Nutrition and Diet in Lone-Parent Households in London* (London: Family Policy Studies Centre).
Ecob, R. and Davey Smith, G. (1999), 'Income and Health: What is the Nature of the Relationship?', *Social Science and Medicine* 48: 693–705.
Evandrou, M., Falkingham, J., Le Grand, J. and Winter, D. (1992), 'Equity in Health and Social Care', *Journal of Social Policy* 21: 489–523.
Farr, W. (1864), *Letter to the Registrar General on the Years 1851–1860: Supplement to the 25th Report of the Registrar General* (London: General Register Office).
Forcier, M. (1988), 'Unemployment and Alcohol Abuse: A Review', *Journal of Occupational Medicine* 30: 246–51.
Forsdahl, A. (1977), 'Are Poor Living Conditions in Childhood and Adolescence and Important Risk Factor for Arteriosclerotic Heart Disease?', *British Journal of Preventive and Social Medicine* 31: 91–5.
— (1978), 'Living Conditions in Childhood and Subsequent Development of Risk Factors for Arteriosclerotic Heart Disease: The Cardiovascular Survey in Finnmark 1974–7', *Journal of Epidemiology and Community Health* 32: 34–7.
Fox, J. (1989), *Health Inequalities in European Countries* (Aldershot: Gower).
Fulop, N., Elston, J., Hensher, M., McKee, M. and Walters, R. (1998), 'Evaluation of the Implementation of the Health of the Nation', in Department of Health (ed.), *The Health of the Nation: A Policy Assessed* (London: Stationery Office).
Gill, B., Meltzer, H., Hinds, K. and Petticrew, M. (1996), *Psychiatric Morbidity among Homeless People* (London: Stationery Office).
Graham, H. (1995), 'Cigarette Smoking: A Light on Gender and Class Inequality in Britain?', *Journal of Social Policy* 24(4): 509–27.
— (1996), 'The Health Experiences of Mothers and Young Children on Income Support', *Benefits* September/October: 10–13.
— (2000), 'The Challenge of Health Inequalities', in H. Graham (ed.), *Understanding Health Inequalities* (Buckingham: Open University Press).

Gravelle, H. (1998), 'How Much of the Relation between Population Mortality and Unequal Distribution of Income is a Statistical Artefact?', *British Medical Journal* 316: 382–5.

Hall, W. and Farrell, M. (1997), 'Co-morbidity of Mental Disorders with Substance Misuse', *British Journal of Psychiatry* 171: 4–5.

Ham, C. (2004), *Health Policy in Britain* (5th edn) (Basingstoke: Palgrave Macmillan).

Hammarstroem, A. (1994), 'Health Consequences of Youth Unemployment: Review from a Gender Perspective', *Social Science and Medicine* 38: 699–709.

Hanlon, P., Walsh, D., Buchanan, D., Redpath, A., Bain, M., Brewster, D., Chalmers, J., Muir, R., Smalls, M., Willis, J. and Wood, R. (2001), *Chasing the Scottish Effect: Why Scotland Needs a Step-Change in Health if It Is to Catch Up with the Rest of Europe* (Glasgow: Public Health Institute of Scotland).

Hattersly, L. (1997), 'Expectation of Life by Social Class', in F. Drever, M. Whitehead (eds), *Health Inequalities: Decennial Supplement* (London: Stationery Office).

Haynes, R. (1991), 'Inequalities in Health and Health Service Use: Evidence from the General Household Survey', *Social Science and Medicine* 33: 361–8.

Illsley, R. (1986), 'Occupational Class, Selection and the Production of Inequalities in Health', *Quarterly Journal of Social Affairs* 2(2): 151–65.

Irvine, B. and Ginsberg, I. (2004), *England versus Scotland: Does More Money Mean Better Health?* (London: Civitas).

Kaplan, G.A. and Salonen, J.T. (1990), 'Socioeconomic Conditions in Childhood and Ischaemic Heart Disease during Middle Age', *British Medical Journal* 301: 1121–3.

Karasek, R.A., Theorell, T., Schwartz, J., Schnall, P., Pieper, C. and Michela, J. (1988), 'Job Characteristics in Relation to the Prevalence of Myocardial Infarction in the US HES and HANES', *American Journal of Public Health* 78: 910–18.

Koupilova, I., Leon, D.A. and Vâgerö, D. (1997), 'Can Confounding by Sociodemographic and Behavioural Factors Explain the Association between Size at Birth and Blood Pressure at Age 50 in Sweden?', *Journal of Epidemiology and Community Health* 51: 14–18.

Kuh, D. and Ben Shlomo, Y. (eds) (1997), *A Lifecourse Approach to Chronic Disease Epidemiology* (Oxford: Oxford University Press).

Kunst, A., Groenhof, F., Mackenbach, J. and the EU Working Group on Socioeconomic Inequalities in Health (1998), 'Occupational Class and Cause Specific Mortality in Middle Aged Men in 11 European Countries: Comparison of Population Based Studies', *British Medical Journal* 316: 1636–41.

Laing, W. and Buisson, E. (2003), *Laing's Healthcare Market Review 2003–2004* (Suffolk: William Clowes).

Laurance, J. (1986), 'Unemployment Health Hazards', *New Society* 21 March: 492–3.

Le Grand, J. (1978), 'The Distribution of Public Expenditure: The Case of Health Care', *Economica* 45: 125–42.

Leon, D., Morton, S., Cannegieter, S. and McKee, M. (2003), *Understanding the Health of Scotland's Population in an International Context* (Glasgow: Public Health Institute of Scotland).

Leon, D.A., Walt, G. and Gilson, L. (2001), 'International Perspectives on Health Inequalities and Policy', *British Medical Journal* 322(7286): 591–4.

Lobstein, T. (1995), 'The Increasing Cost of a Healthy Diet', *Food Magazine* 31: 17.

Lowry, S. (1989), 'Housing and Health: Temperature and Humidity', *British Medical Journal* 299: 1326–8.

Lupton, R. and Power, A. (2002), 'Social Exclusion and Neighbourhoods', in J. Hills, J. Le Grand and D. Piachaud (eds), *Understanding Social Exclusion* (Oxford: Oxford University Press).

Lynch, J. and Kaplan, G.A. (2000), 'Socioeconomic Position', in L. Berkman and I. Kawachi (eds), *Social Epidemiology* (New York, NY: Oxford University Press).

MacIntyre, S. (1986), 'The Patterning of Health by Social Position in Contemporary Britain: Directions for Sociological Research', *Social Science and Medicine* 23(4): 393–415.

— (1997), 'What are Spatial Effects and How Can We Measure Them?', in A. Dale (ed.), *Exploiting National Survey Data: The Role of Locality and Spatial Effects* (Manchester: Faculty of Economic and Social Studies, University of Manchester).

— (2000), 'Modernising the NHS: Prevention and the Reduction of Health Inequalities', *British Medical Journal* 320: 1399–400.

MacIntyre, S., Hiscock, R., Kearns, A. and Ellaway, A. (2000), 'Housing Tenure and Health Inequalities: A Three Dimensional Perspective on People, Homes and Neighbourhoods', in H. Graham (ed.), *Understanding Health Inequalities* (Buckingham: Open University Press).

Majeed, A., Chaturvedi, N., Reading, R. and Ben-Shlomo, Y. (1994), 'Monitoring and Promoting Equity in Primary and Secondary Care', *British Medical Journal* 308: 1426–9.

Marmot, M. (2005), 'Social Determinants of Health Inequalities', *Lancet* 365: 1099–104.

Marmot, M.G., Bosma, H., Hemingway, H., Brunner, E. and Stansfeld, S. (1997), 'Contribution of Job Control and Other Risk Factors to Social Variations in Coronary Heart Disease Incidence', *Lancet* 350: 235–9.

Marmot, M. and Wilkinson, R.G. (eds) (1999), *Social Determinants of Health* (New York, NY: Oxford University Press).

Martin, C.J., Platt, S.D. and Hunt, S. (1987), 'Housing Conditions and Health', *British Medical Journal* 294: 1125–7.

McCarthy, P., Byrne, D., Harrison, S. and Keighley, J. (1985), 'Respiratory Conditions: Effect of Housing and Other Factors', *Journal of Epidemiology and Community Health* 39: 15–19.

Moncada, S. (1999), 'Working Conditions and Social Inequalities in Health', *Journal of Epidemiology and Community Health* 53: 390–91.

Morgan, M., Heller, R.F. and Swerdlow, A. (1989), 'Changes in Diet and Coronary Heart Disease Mortality among Social Classes in Great Britain', *Journal of Epidemiology and Community Health* 43: 162–7.

O'Donnell, O. and Propper, C. (1991), 'Equity and the Distribution of UK NHS Resources', *Journal of Health Economics* 10: 1–19.

Palmer, G., Carr, J. and Kenway, P. (2005), *Monitoring Poverty and Social Exclusion in Scotland 2005* (York: New Policy Institute/Joseph Rowntree Foundation).

Palmer, G., MacInnes, T. and Kenway, P. (2008), *Monitoring Poverty and Social Exclusion 2008* (York: Joseph Rowntree Foundation).

Payne, N. and Saul, C. (1997), 'Variations in Use of Cardiology Services in a Health Authority: Comparison of Coronary Artery Revascularation Rates with Prevalence of Angina and Coronary Mortality', *British Medical Journal* 314: 257–61.

Pearce, J. and Dorling, D. (2006), 'Increasing Geographical Inequalities in Health in New Zealand, 1980–2001', *International Journal of Epidemiology* 35: 597–603.

Platt, S.D., Martin, C.J., Hunt, S. and Lewis, C.W. (1989), 'Damp Housing, Mould Growth and Symptomatic Health State', *British Medical Journal* 298: 1673–8.

Power, C., Matthews, S. and Manor, O. (1996), 'Inequalities in Self Rated Health in the 1958 Birth Cohort: Lifetime Social Circumstances or Social Mobility?', *British Medical Journal* 313: 449–53.

Rahman, M., Palmer, G., Kenway, P. and Howarth, C. (2000), *Monitoring Poverty and Social Exclusion* (London: New Policy Institute).

Randall, G. and Brown, S. (1999a), *Homes for Street Homeless People: An Evaluation of the Rough Sleepers Initiative* (London: Department of the Environment, Transport and the Regions).

—— (1999b), *Prevention is Better than Cure: New Solutions to Street Homelessness from Crisis* (London: Crisis).

Rodgers, G.B. (1979), 'Income and Inequality as Determinants of Mortality: An International Cross-Section Analysis', *Population Studies* 39: 343–51.

Saracci, R. (1997), 'The World Health Organisation Needs to Reconsider its Definition of Health', *British Medical Journal* 314: 1409.

Scott, J. (1993), 'Homelessness and Mental Illness', *British Journal of Psychiatry* 162: 314–24.

Scottish Executive (2001), *Health in Scotland 2000: Report of the Chief Medical Officer for Scotland* (Edinburgh: Stationery Office).

— (2003), *Improving Health in Scotland: The Challenge* (Edinburgh: Stationery Office).

— (2004), *Building a Better Scotland: Spending Proposals 2005–2008: Enterprise, Opportunity, Fairness: Technical Notes* (Edinburgh: Scottish Executive).

Scottish Government (2007), *Better Health, Better Care: Action Plan* (Edinburgh: Scottish Government).

— (2008), *Equally Well: Report of the Ministerial Task Force on Health Inequalities* (Edinburgh: Scottish Government).

Scottish Office Department of Health (1999), *Towards a Healthier Scotland: A White Paper on Health* (Edinburgh: Stationery Office).

Scottish Parliament (2002), *The Community Care and Health (Scotland) Act 2002* (Edinburgh: Stationery Office).

Sharp, L. and Brewster, D. (1999), 'The Epidemiology of Lung Cancer in Scotland: A Review of Trends in Incidence, Survival and Mortality and Prospects for Prevention', *Health Bulletin* 57(5): 318–31.

Shaw, A., McMunn, A. and Field, J. (eds) (2000), *The Scottish Health Survey 1998: A Survey Carried Out on behalf of the Scottish Executive Health Department* (Edinburgh: Scottish Executive).

Shaw, M., Dorling, D., Gordon, D. and Davey Smith, G. (1999), *The Widening Gap: Health Inequalities and Policy in Britain* (Bristol: Policy Press).

Shouls, S., Whitehead, M., Burström, B. and Diderichsen, F. (1999), 'Trends in the Health and Socio-Economic Circumstances of British Lone Mothers over the Last Two Decades', *Population Trends* 95: 5–10.

Sooman, A., MacIntyre, S. and Anderson, A. (1993), 'Scotland's Health: A More Difficult Challenge for Some?', *Health Bulletin* 51: 276–84.

Stern, I. (1983), 'Social Mobility and the Interpretation of Social Class Mortality Differentials', *Journal of Social Policy* 12: 27–49.

Üstün, B. and Jakob, R. (2005), 'Calling a Spade a Spade: Meaningful Definitions of Health Conditions', *Bulletin of the World Health Organisation* 83: 802.

Wadsworth, M.E.J., Montgomery, S.M. and Bartley, M.J. (1999), 'The Persisting Effect of Unemployment on Health and Social Well-Being in Men in Early Working Life', *Social Science and Medicine* 48: 1491–9.

Warr, P. (1987), *Work, Unemployment and Mental Health* (Oxford: Clarendon Press).

West, P. (1991), 'Rethinking the Health Selection Explanation for Health Inequalities', *Social Science and Medicine* 32(4): 373–84.

—— (1998), *Perspectives on Health Inequalities: The Need for a Lifecourse Approach* (Glasgow: Medical Research Council Social and Public Health Sciences Unit, University of Glasgow).

White, I., Blane, D., Morris, J.N. and Mourouga, P. (1999), 'Educational Attainment, Deprivation-Affluence and Self-Reported Health: A Cross-Sectional Study', *Journal of Epidemiology and Community Health* 53: 535–41.

Whitehead, M. (1987), 'The Health Divide', in P. Townsend, M. Whitehead and N. Davidson (eds), *Inequalities in Health: The Black Report and the Health Divide* (London: Penguin).

Whitehead, M. and Drever, F. (1999), 'Narrowing Social Inequalities in Health? Analysis of Trends in Mortality among Babies of Lone Mothers', *British Medical Journal* 318: 908–12.

Wilkinson, R.G. (1989), 'Class Mortality Differentials, Income and Distribution and Trends in Poverty 1921–81', *Journal of Social Policy* 18: 307–35.

—— (1990), 'Income Distribution and Mortality: A "Natural" Experiment', *Sociology of Health and Illness* 12: 391–412.

—— (1992), 'Income Distribution and Life Expectancy', *British Medical Journal* 304: 65–8.

—— (1996), *Unhealthy Societies: The Afflictions of Inequality* (London: Routledge).

—— (1997), 'Socioeconomic Determinants of Health: Health Inequalities: Relative or Absolute Material Standards?', *British Medical Journal* 314: 591.

—— (1998), 'Low Relative Income Affects Mortality', *British Medical Journal* 316: 1611.

World Health Organisation (1992), *Basic Documents* (39th edn) (Geneva: WHO).

Wrigley, N. (1998), 'How British Retailers Have Shaped Food Choice', in A. Murcott (ed.), *The Nation's Diet: The Social Science of Food Choice* (London: Longman).

Further reading

Scottish Executive (2004), *Closing the Opportunity Gap* (Edinburgh: Scottish Executive).

Scottish Executive (2004), *Fair to All, Personal to Each: The Next Step for the NHS Scotland* (Edinburgh: Scottish Executive).

Scottish Executive (2005), *Delivering for Health 2005* (Edinburgh: Scottish Executive).

11 Mental health

Jackie Loxton, Mike Maas-Lowit and Rob Mackay

Introduction

Any discussion of policy in the arena of mental health requires some explanation of terms. Even this chapter heading speaks to the misnomer that conflates the two distinct concepts of mental illness and mental health. Mercifully, the central Scottish policy document of the moment, *Towards a Mentally Flourishing Scotland,* begins by attempting to separate them out (Scottish Government 2007), while tentatively recognising that the debate around them is complex and unresolved. For this reason, we suggest that the reader approaches the concepts of mental health and mental illness as fluid ideas, rather than tangible entities.

The document chooses the phrase mental well-being as the term of preference to describe the positive attributes of mental health. It defines mental well-being as a state of 'emotional, social and psychological well being' (Scottish Government 2007: 3). It goes on to locate mental well-being in 'our ability to cope with life's problems and make the most of life's opportunities, to cope in the face of adversity and to flourish in all our environments; to feel good and function well, both individually and collectively' (Scottish Government 2007: 2).

Mental health and mental illness

Mental illness is described as 'clinically identifiable illness or conditions that affect our cognitive functioning' (Scottish Government 2007: 3). The Scottish Government have opted for the tradition set in law, in generations of mental health acts, of saying the minimum by way of definition of mental illness and thereby implying that, if a medically qualified doctor can diagnose it in you, then you have it (Scottish Office 1960; Scottish Office 1984; Scottish Executive 2003a). A text on social policy is not the place to have a lengthy discussion on the complexities of medical evidence in favour of the existence of a thing called mental illness, and so we will accept the Scottish Government's definition at face value – that it is 'clinically identifiable'. In other words, that

- its features or symptoms correspond to pre-set diagnostic criteria generally accepted as being drawn from the ICD 10 (WHO 2007);
- that it is 'illness or conditions', meaning that it is a more or less temporary or permanent malfunctioning of the otherwise normal processes of the body and mind; and
- that this malfunctioning 'affect(s) our cognitive functioning' (WHO 2007). In other words, that which has gone wrong in the bio-chemistry, neurological-circuitry or tissue mass of the brain has a detrimental result upon how the person thinks and therefore functions.

The 2007 policy referred to above also speaks about 'mental health problems'. Traditionally there has been a tendency in common language to confuse all these concepts by thinking of health – or good health – as being the opposite of illness. In the recent history of psychiatry, with its anti-psychiatry movement in the middle of the last century, ownership of terms became an issue, which was casually resolved by equating poor mental health with mental illness. For this reason, the sequential Mental Health Acts (1960, 1984, 1999 and 2003) all carry the euphemistic term mental health, when everyone knows that they are actually about mental illness.

It is therefore very helpful that the 2007 policy speaks about a dual continua approach, in which we conceive of mental health as a spectrum, ranging from good (or 'flourishing') to poor (or 'languishing'), and a separate continuum ranging from absence of illness to presence of severe mental illness. This, in turn, opens the door for discussion of the concept of mental health problems as 'generally refer(ing) to having difficulties with our mental health which affect how we go about our everyday lives' (Scottish Government 2007: 3). By implication, one does not have to be mentally ill to be languishing with poor mental health. However, it is also worth reflection that the difficulties of living with mental illness in our society mean that it poses particular challenges of stigma, exclusion and discrimination, such that it is arguably more difficult to maintain a state of mental well-being compared to a person who has no mental illness.

These, then are the terms of reference of this chapter. It is divided, as is the policy, into

- that which addresses mental well-being and mental health (in its true sense) and
- that which has a greater orientation to health and to the legal duties of local authorities in providing care and treatment for people affected by mental illness.

Historical perspective

Before looking in detail at aspects of current policy, let us briefly consider the historical context of law and policy relating to mental health.

Mental illness has never enjoyed good press and has been characterised by fear and stigma with the resulting social exclusion. It is important that the reader has some understanding of the legal and policy journey surrounding mental illness over centuries to reach the current more enlightened position.

Prior to 1745, provision for the mentally ill was provided by the local parish within workhouses or in private 'madhouses'. The Victorian response may be viewed as a humanitarian one in terms of undertaking the building of asylums between 1745 and 1790.

The Lunacy (Scotland) Act 1857 represented the first comprehensive piece of legislation in Scotland dealing with the detention and treatment of the mentally disordered. Here we see mirrored some of the current issues which will be discussed in this chapter in terms of the tension between care and protection whether that be the protection of the individual or protection of others.

In policy terms, from this point until the 1960s containment was the prevailing objective. Over the next two decades a number of factors signified the beginning of what has been a slow process in changing attitudes and policy towards those diagnosed with a mental illness and in recognising the importance of mental well-being for all. Firstly, the development of a group of anti-psychotic drugs called phenothiazines meant that the grosser symptoms of illness could be better controlled and secondly, a developing understanding of the debilitating effects of institutionalisation led to a greater commitment to preventing hospital admission. As our understanding of the nature of mental disorders has grown, and very significant here is the influence of the service user movement, individuals have begun to demand that they have a say in their treatment and in the kinds of services provided (Campbell 1996).

The enactment of the National Health and Community Care Act 1990 provided the legal basis for the move to community care with the resulting closures of asylums and other long-stay institutions and the move to resources in the community. While Scotland was more cautious than England in the rate of its adoption of community care policies, there has been a noticeable and growing commitment to the importance of population-based approaches to mental well-being and to the enactment of law and policies which offer care and treatment for those with 'enduring mental illness'. To this end the Mental Health (Care and Treatment) (Scotland) Act 2003 and the *National Programme for Improving Mental Health and Wellbeing* (Scottish Executive 2003a) were immensely significant in terms of pushing this neglected area into a higher priority status (Hothersall, Maas-Lowit and Golightley 2008).

Before considering in more detail aspects of current policy Table 11.1 provides a summary of the main policy initiatives since 2000.

Table 11.1 Scottish mental health related policy from 2000 onwards

The National Programme for Improving Mental Health and Well-Being: An Action Plan 2003–2006 (Scottish Executive 2003a)
This initiative had four key aims relating to the promotion of mental well-being; the elimination of stigma and discrimination; the prevention of suicide and the promotion of recovery.
Delivering for Mental Health (Scottish Government 2006)
Building on the work started through the National Programme, this policy consisted of a number of targets and commitments across a broad range of areas in mental health. The emphasis here was on the NHS, local authorities, the voluntary sector and service users and carers working together to reach targets across a given timescale. These commitments and targets related to both the care of people with a diagnosed mental illness and population based approaches.
Towards a Mentally Flourishing Scotland: The Future of Mental Health Improvement in Scotland 2008–2011 (Scottish Government 2007)
The emphasis in this policy initiative is rooted firmly in mental health improvement and population approaches. The intention of such a policy is best understood in words taken from the policy itself: 'We wish to see a Scotland where we all understand that there is no health without good mental health, where we know how to support and improve our own and others' mental health and well-being and act on that knowledge …' (Scottish Government 2007: 1).

Current policy that addresses mental illness

Writing about the very different situation regarding mental health policy in Northern Ireland, Daley and Wilson suggest

> that dominant trends in mental health care ... have tended to prioritise the more coercive aspects of the social work role and reinforce existing power inequalities with service users. It is argued that such developments underline the need for a 're-focusing' debate in mental health social work to consider how a more appropriate balance can be achieved between its participatory/empowering and regulatory/coercive functions. (Wilson and Daly 2007: 423)

The reason we draw on this quote is because it clearly identifies the tension that lies within any modern service which targets itself upon the needs of people with mental illness: it is not just in Northern Ireland (where the process of review of mental health law is focusing the debate) that these tensions exist. Examination of coercion versus empowerment in any country's mental health policy will reveal the close proximity of mental health law. This in itself is problematic, because there is a danger that the student of policy will confuse the subject with the separate study of law. Therefore, let us take a moment to separate out these issues, for the very reason that this area of policy brings them so close as to be difficult to differentiate.

For our immediate purpose, policy can be described as the broad plan for the shaping and development of services in accordance with the ruling party's grand design. Law is a (generally) more lasting set of rules which is ultimately interpreted by the courts and may be brought to be binding upon the public or professional workers or any organisation.

There is a problem for both law and policy if they come too far adrift from one another. In this case, the over-arching piece of statute which dominates the legal field is the Mental Health (Care and Treatment) (Scotland) Act 2003 (Scottish Executive 2003b), which we will refer to as the 2003 Act.

The 2003 Act was the first major piece of legislation attempted by the Scottish Parliament after its inception in 1999. It arose out of a lengthy consultation and it was based upon a detailed review document, popularly known as the Milan Report (Scottish Executive 2001). The creation and implementation of the 2003 Act dominated mental health policy in Scotland for several years. Amongst the many things it does, it attempts to place in a more proportional balance the elements of coercion and empowerment than did the previous Mental Health (Scotland) Act 1984 (Scottish Office 1984).

It would therefore be very important to say a little about these seemingly opposing elements at this stage.

What we said, above, about the assumption of a medically oriented entity called mental illness is most crucial in this regard. Medicine contains a body of scientific knowledge, which is applied to the patient by an expert practitioner in order to identify and treat the illness or condition. To revert to the definition in *Towards a Mentally Flourishing Scotland* (Scottish Government 2007: 3), that illness is manifested in the way it 'affect(s) our cognitive functioning', there is a supposition on behalf of the state that, in extreme cases, some of these effects may result in loss of the ability to make competent and safe judgements about one's best interests. In this case, it is the responsibility of the state to apply coercive measures to secure the necessary care and treatment for the so-called patient. The crux of this matter is three-fold:

1. It objectifies the 'patient',[1] making him or her a passive recipient of the controlling forces of medical and social care.
2. The removal of the choices available to most of us as patients of health care (whether to accept or refuse medical advice, care and treatment) is disempowering. As such it may not be conducive to the mental health of the subject, in the sense that anything which removes personal power also undermines self-esteem and other attributes which support mental health.
3. The process of so restricting a person's freedom has complicated implications, which flow through the legislation and case law relating to our human rights.

This is the complicated balancing act that both law and its surrounding policy has to attempt: on the one hand, the state has duties, no less relating to our human rights, to uphold our right to life (Council of Europe 1950: Article 2) and our safety and security, when our judgement is impaired by mental illness. On the other, it has duties to make sure our broader human rights to liberty (Article 5), family life (Article 8) and freedom of expression (Article 7) are not injured by the coercive powers of imposed care and treatment.

Largely speaking, the law provides broad-brush instruction on how this will be done through the 2003 Act. Related Codes of Practice (Scottish Executive 2005) fine tune the practice of those specialist doctors and social workers (Mental Health Officers) charged with formal functions under the

1 The term 'the patient' is used in the 2003 Act to describe any person who is subject to the various powers of the Act.

Act. Policy sets the direction in which services shall go, in keeping with the dictates of the law.

To illustrate this from a multitude of policies surrounding the operation of the 2003 Act we will briefly look at the planned reduction of the number of readmissions to hospital per patient (Scottish Executive 2006) and the development of medium- and low-security provision for mentally disordered offenders (NHS 2009).

Against the broad back-drop of shrinking hospital bed provision and the move away from the old model of mental health care, with its preoccupation with large and long-term asylum type institutions, community care needs to support people adequately in their ordinary living environments. This happens successfully to the extent that there are resources in the community to facilitate the change. The Scottish Government identified that there was an identifiable failing in the system, insofar as there was a high rate of readmissions to hospital of people who had been discharged into the community. The policy to fix the problem is contained in the last generation of policy, coined by the Scottish Labour-led administration of 2003 to 2007, with a commitment to 'reduce the number of readmissions (within one year) for those that have had a hospital admission of over 7 days by 10 per cent by the end of December 2009' (Scottish Executive 2006: Part 9, Target 3).

The broad policy intentions relating to mentally disordered offenders could be conceived as sitting at the most coercive end of the range of policy complexion. Mentally disordered offenders (we will abbreviate the term to MDO) are those people who have committed serious offences in situations where some form of mental illness has been a significant factor in their actions. The law relating to this group states that, where the criminal court is persuaded that mental disorder (the technical term for mental illness, personality disorder or learning disability) was a significant factor in the commission of an offence, the person should be forced to receive care and treatment for that mental disorder in lieu of the routine range of disposals used by the court (from probation to prison) (Scottish Executive 2003b). Because of issues of public safety, the provision for MDOs is surrounded by a wealth of policy and guidance relating to containment in facilities ranging from high-security hospital (the State Hospital near Carstairs in South Lanarkshire) to local low-security hospitals and provision in the community.

In this specialised provision, the tension between coercion versus empowerment takes on a special significance. The existence of the European Convention on Human Rights (ECHR) (OPSI 1998; Council of European 1950) and the Human Rights Act 1998, which contains the ECHR within UK law, implies that every MDO has a right to be detained only at the level of restriction of liberty appropriate to the risk that the person poses to self and others. In other words, it must be proportionate. Take the example of a man who experienced paranoid schizophrenia, which caused him to murder his wife and child 20 years ago. Let us assume the medical assessment is that his illness continues, but that he is compliant with treatment and therefore at lesser risk of reoffending, provided the treatment is monitored. In this case it would be a breach of his liberty under the Articles of the ECHR for him to remain in the maximum restriction of high-security compulsion in the State Hospital. He is entitled to rehabilitation as far down the secure provision system as he can get without posing undue threat to other people. This may result in absolute discharge at some point.

Until the implementation of the 2003 Act there was a problem in this regard, in that there were few appropriate services in Scotland outside the major security of the State Hospital. There was also such a gulf between the State Hospital and low security of local hospital provision that it was difficult to move from one to the other. Therefore, a number of patients in the State Hospital were needlessly detained there, potentially in breach of their human rights. The term 'patient flow' has been coined to give shape to the complex policy which has resulted in the construction of three medium-secure, regional hospitals which should provide steps towards local resources for those MDOs at lesser risk to the public. It has also directed funding to voluntary organisations like the Scottish Association for the Care and Rehabilitation of Offenders (SACRO), to provide community-based support for those MDOs who are able to leave secure hospital provision altogether.

Suicide and Scottish policy

At a global level, suicide ranks among the top ten causes of death and the second most common cause of non-illness-related deaths. The need for national strategies to prevent suicide is therefore clearly identified by the World Health Organisation (WHO 2009). The WHO National Strategy Guidelines comprises a multi-sectorial approach (that is, includes both health and non-health sectors), the implementation of which should be tailored to meet specific national requirements in terms of cultural, economic, demographic, political and social needs (UN/WHO Guidelines for the Development of National Strategies for the Prevention of Suicidal Behaviours 1993). This international focus on the problem of suicide has led to a range of countries developing national suicide prevention strategies, including Scotland. Launched in December 2002, as a key part of the National Programme for Improving Mental Health and Wellbeing (NPIMHW), the Choose Life strategy is a ten-year action plan aimed at reducing suicides in

Scotland by 20 per cent by 2013. Phase I ran from 2003 to 2006, and Phase II ran from 2006 to 2008.

Based on work undertaken by the Canadian Centre for Suicide Prevention, the Choose Life strategy takes both a population- and community-development approach to reducing the suicide rate in Scotland. It seeks to provide leadership and direction, as well as linkage among relevant organisations and groups, and it is a key source of support and information related to research, education and practice in suicide prevention and postvention. Training forms a central plank in the influencing of practice and the raising of standards. Commitment 7 of 'Delivering for Mental Health' (Scottish Government 2006: Part 8) states:

> ... a commitment has been made for frontline mental health services, primary care, and accident and emergency staff to be educated and trained in using suicide assessment tools/suicide prevention training programmes. (Scottish Government, 2006)

There are four national training programmes that have been funded to meet Commitment 7:

- Applied suicide intervention skills training (Asist) is a two-day workshop. There is also a 5 day course that prepares participants to become ASIST trainers.
- SuicideTalk is a one to three hour exploration and awareness-raising session.
- SafeTALK is a half day session.
- STORM is a suicide training package for frontline staff.

Suicide prevention commitments and targets feature in 'Delivering for Mental Health' (Scottish Government 2006).[2] Outcomes related to this area of activity also feature as Health Efficiency Access and Treatment (HEAT) targets,[3] and there is some evidence that some local outcomes in the Single Outcome Agreements (SOAs) specify suicide prevention activities (Collins 2008).

HEAT targets are those that tie the NHS and local health boards into meeting specific items as agreed with the Scottish Government. They are a strong means of Government control over health delivery on specific

2 A document which sets out targets and commitments for the development of mental health services in Scotland.

3 HEAT comprises a core set of ministerial objectives, targets and measures for the NHS. The targets are set for a three-year period, the progress for which is measured through the Local Delivery Plan process.

issues at local levels. In short, it is a strong way of securing health outcomes which are the political objectives of the Scottish ministers. Please note this discussion because there is reference to another HEAT target: to 'reduce the annual rate of increase of defined daily dose per capita of anti-depressants to zero by 2009/10, and put in place the required support framework to achieve a 10 per cent reduction in future years' (Scottish Government 2010).

A recent review of the NPIMHW (NHS Health Scotland 2008) also offered a brief evaluation of Choose Life, which highlighted the role of the National Implementation Support Team (NIST) and the amount of flexibility afforded to local areas given the range of priority groups. The Scottish Government issued a consultation document in 2007 entitled *Towards a Mentally Flourishing Scotland: The Future of Mental Health Improvement in Scotland 2008–2011*, the content of which is intended to build on the NPIMHW and now forms the national strategic framework for the period 2008–11. The issue of suicide prevention is also addressed within that document (Scottish Government 2007: Sections 8.4 and 9.3).

Both of these reports also highlight the extent to which health inequalities in Scotland contribute to the prevalence of mental illness in society. Future mental health strategies, including those pertaining to suicide, are aimed at addressing the needs and concerns of individuals as well as promoting effective change at organisational, community and societal levels. Of particular interest is the extent to which the Choose Life strategy has reached groups in society that experience social exclusion and, as such, may be at a high risk of suicide.

Recovery-focused mental health services

There has been an increasing interest in developed nations over the past 20 years not only in reshaping mental health services to have a more community orientation but also to re-frame the understanding of 'recovery'.

Traditionally, this has been understood as occurring when the symptoms of mental illness have been clinically treated and this intervention is judged to have been successful by the professionals not by the person (Slade 2009). This position has been questioned and the promotion of a personal recovery approach has been promoted through national policies, most notably in New Zealand and the United States.

In New Zealand the Government established in 1996 the Mental Health Commission (www.mhc.govt.nz) and this statutory body has been very active in commissioning research in the area of recovery and furthermore in producing guidelines on personal recovery. There has been a clear policy goal to create change in mental health services in order that these be responsive to individual needs and to incorporate personal recovery throughout the whole mental health system.

In the United States, the President's New Freedom Commission on Mental Health concluded in 2003 that there was a need for system transformation to focus not only on treating and managing symptoms, but also on promoting recovery and resilience. Individual states that are adopting progressive recovery policies include California, Philadelphia, New York, Georgia and Massachusetts (Slade 2009).

What is personal recovery?

There are various definitions of personal recovery, all of which incorporate a number of the following elements:

- recovery is a process like a journey
- each person's recovery journey is different and unique
- it is about moving from illness to wellness
- hope of a preferred life is a central idea
- recovery is not the same as cure
- recovery is about the person taking back control over their own life

These can be witnessed in the definition of recovery produced by the Scottish Recovery Network (www.scottishrecovery.net):

> Recovery is being able to lead a meaningful and satisfying life, as defined by each person, in the presence or absence of symptoms. It is about having control over and input into your own life. Each individual's recovery, like his or her experience of the mental health problems or illness, is a unique and deeply personal process. (Scottish Recovery Network 2010)

The Scottish policy context for recovery

The *Framework for Mental Health Services in Scotland* (Scottish Office 1997) provided for co-ordinated action at both the local and national levels in Scotland. This in part focused on the needs of people with long-term mental health problems to have an improved quality of life in their own communities.

The introduction by the Scottish Executive of the *National Programme for Improving Health and Wellbeing* took policies relating to mental illness and mental health to another level (Scottish Executive 2003a). This included a statement of four core objectives for the National Programme, one of which was to promote and support recovery. The means of doing this was to create a new organisation funded by the Scottish Executive and so in 2004 the Scottish Recovery Network (SRN) was launched.

The significance of personal recovery within the plans for transforming mental health services in Scotland was evidenced with the publication of 'Delivering for Mental Health' in 2006. This document is effectively a national policy plan for mental health services in which commitments are made and targets are identified. This stated:

> We must ensure we deliver on our commitments in respect of equality, social inclusion, recovery and rights. Doing this is central to the vision and to the success of the plan. (Scottish Executive 2006: 6).

This document made one commitment specific to recovery and that was the development of a tool to be called the Scottish Recovery Indicator and the responsibility for developing this was passed to the Scottish Recovery Network.

What is the Scottish Recovery Network and what does it do?

By indicating it is a network, SRN signifies it does not provide direct services to individuals, but rather it uses its resources to connect individuals, groups, organisations and communities together all in the cause of promoting personal recovery. SRN has a small staff group with a base in Glasgow but a network consisting of many organisations, groups and individuals. The staff group promotes awareness of recovery through a variety of information strategies: cards, leaflets, reports, web-based materials and conferences. Specific initiatives undertaken by SRN include the following:

> *Local recovery networks*: SRN provides information and support to enable the setting up of recovery networks that bring together partners at a local level.
>
> *Narrative Research Project*: This involved a major piece of research that ran for two years and involved interviewing 64 people who defined themselves as either being recovered or in a process of recovery. The research reported on common elements that contribute positively to the process of recovery.
>
> *The Scottish Recovery Indicator*: The Scottish Recovery Indicator (SRI) is a tool that mental health organisations may use to monitor their orientation to recovery-based approaches and to implement changes.

Wellness Recovery Action Planning (WRAP): SRN have facilitated the running of several WRAP courses that aim to help people develop skills about moving towards wellness whilst being able to anticipate future crisis points.

Realising Recovery training materials: These six modules were developed jointly with the NHS Education for Scotland and are designed to support all mental health workers to have the knowledge and skills to adopt a recovery orientated approach.

Peer support: SRN has been promoting the development of peer support workers in conjunction with NHS Scotland. This has been done through conferences and training courses that have borrowed on expertise initially from the United States. This has resulted in the employment of a number of peer support workers within the NHS in Scotland.

Exercise 11.1 Case study

At 43 years of age, Mona Laster lives alone. She is unemployed and draws incapacity benefit, an income awarded her because of her severe depression and anxiety.

She is currently being assessed by the Benefits Agency as part of their policy-shift towards getting people away from dependency on incapacity benefit and back into employment. This has the effect of increasing her levels of anxiety. For example, on the day of her most recent assessment interview, she was awake from three o'clock in the morning, worrying about the fact that, if she was forced into employment, she might not cope and she might lose the hard-earned place she has achieved in her road to recovery. For Mona, her worst fears are three-fold: she might have to go back into a psychiatric hospital, a place in which she has spent periods of time in the past; she might not be able to offer her 70-year-old father the care and support she currently gives him; and she might let her friends down in the Spainnie Road Centre.

Mona's father has had a long-standing diagnosis of schizophrenia. He lives a slightly chaotic but reasonably well-managed existence in his own tenancy. Despite the difficulties in their relationship, stemming from back into her childhood, Mona has always been protective of her father and offers him such care as he will allow. As he gets older, she fears that he would not cope without her occasionally cleaning out of his flat, her shopping for him and her cooking him a meal every Sunday. Other than a regular depot injection from his GP surgery, he receives no other supports since his home-care service was withdrawn when Tayforthshire Council redefined its criteria for assessing the needs of those demanding community care services (see Chapters 1 and 7).

Spainnie Road is a small, independently run voluntary organisation, which offers a place for people with *mental health problems* (their term of preference) a place to go for mutual and informal support. Mona has been using the Centre for several years now and is a member of the Board of Directors, which manages the service. It was through her involvement in the Centre that Mona developed an interest in recovery and the Scottish Recovery Network.

Recently, Mona has been finding it rather difficult to manage the anxiety generated by her involvement on the Board of Directors. She is particularly worried by two strands of discussion: firstly, because she is well informed by discussion of policy around the board table, she is worried that her anti-depressant medication will be reduced, in furtherance of the HEAT target. Secondly, she is greatly worried by the threat to the funding of the Centre by proposed local government spending cuts: two years ago, the Centre lost lottery funding. Some say that this was in part due to the strain that the 2012 Olympics is placing on the Big Lottery, making it increasingly difficult for small organisations to be successful in their applications. Since then, the Centre has been almost 100 per cent dependent on the local government for funding. Now that Tayforthshire Council is beginning to receive less money from central government, in line with reductions in public spending, it looks as though global recession is threatening Mona's main support.

Discussion

From a reading of the above case, are you able to recognise several points at which policy impinges upon Mona's life? Not all the points fall within the scope of this chapter, but we have inserted them into this fictitious case study in order to let you see the interface between politics, economics, policy and the service delivery which impinges upon the lives of people (see Chapter 1). For example, it is beyond our scope to say much about the theme in the case study, in which, at the time of writing, local authorities are anticipating reductions in their spending power and are therefore aligning their budgets towards reduction in the services they purchase. Therefore, we can do no more than hint at the two ends of this strand: at the time of writing, it only exists as hints and budget projections amongst the major political parties. However, it is closely related to the massive deficit in the economy, resulting from the global financial crisis. At the other end of the proposals to cut public spending, local governments – like the fictitious Tayforthshire Council – will have to limit the scope of services they purchase. We suggest two ways that this will impact upon Mona: a number of councils have already redefined the level of need at which a person (in this case, Mona's father) will merit certain community care services. Some councils are also reducing their funding of those services which they have a duty to fund under the NHS and Community Care Act 1990 and, in this case, under section 26 of the Mental Health (Care and Treatment) (Scotland) Act 2003. This may impact on the scope of delivery or survival of the Centre which Mona identifies with.

We do not throw these aspects of policy and politics in at the end of this chapter to confuse you with additional complexity. We do so to illustrate how a range of factors interact to impact upon basic policy tenets such as the improving of the mental well-being of those with mental disorder and the right of the individual to experience recovery.

In respect of these aspects of the case study more rooted in the substance of this chapter, are you able to identify an interaction between Mona's mental health (precarious though it may be) and her mental illness (assuming that her chronically entrenched depression and anxiety are illnesses)? From this, did you pick up that the sense of purpose she derives from both caring for her father and from her role on the Board of the Spainnie Centre are core attributes in maintaining her well-being? It is also a focus for realising the policy of recovery.

Were you able to identify the complexities of the HEAT target on reduction of anti-depressants, as embodied in the policy, Delivering for Mental Health (Scottish Executive 2006)? It requires skilled clinical judgement to apply this policy by identifying who ought to receive such treatment and who can do without it. Antidepressant medication can be an expensive and unnecessary crutch, but in Mona's current predicament, it would appear to be a necessary support without which her delicate mental health might collapse. Furthermore, if it was withdrawn, it would have to be replaced by something by way of talking therapy.

Conclusion

Mental health and well-being and mental illness are central concepts in the policy in this area. They relate to the twin strands of population-based development of a mentally flourishing Scotland and a critical regard for the care and treatment of those affected by mental illness. In this, Scotland has launched an attack on its poor record of public mental health and it has sought to redress much that was impoverished in its care and treatment of people with mental disorder. Since devolution in 1999, we have enjoyed a spotlight on mental health and a huge amount of policy, legislation and service delivery. However, before this time of rapid change, policy planning was moving in this direction anyway, with awareness that the old Mental Health Act (Scottish Office 1984) was no longer fit for purpose at a time of established care in the community, decarceration of populations from large-scale institutions and expansion in the endeavour of human rights. Were we to subject the period from 1999 to 2007 to a critical gaze, it might be suggested that it was too ambitious a time, with too rapid a change. Certainly, anecdotally, professionals in the field seemed to be struggling to assimilate all the layers of policy and legislative change imposed upon them: the operation of kick-starting the Mental Health (Care and Treatment) (Scotland) Act 2003 was huge. It involved establishing a completely new Mental Health Tribunal for Scotland, to hear applications and review orders. This act was sandwiched between two other major and influential pieces of law in related fields: the Adults with Incapacity (Scotland) Act 2000, which dealt with making decisions for people who have lost capacity to do so themselves (Scottish Executive 2000) and the Adult Support and Protection (Scotland) Act 2007, which dealt with broader support and protection for a range of adults susceptible to harm (Scottish Government 2007). While we would certainly not wish to convey that any of this was unnecessary, the large volume of policy, some of which is discussed above – the Delivery Plan, Recovery and so on – imposed a challenge on a small nation with limited resources. Indeed, it seems to be greatly to Scotland's credit that it rose so energetically to that challenge.

Moving on, as we seem to be, from this period, we can give you no substantiation for our suggestion that economic crisis will impact upon the newly developed and ambitious mental health policy. The emergence of this sting of recession is too new for there to be many books or journal articles about it as yet. It may be that, by the time you read this, there will be a growing academic body of knowledge about it. But, as yet, it only lies in newspaper conjecture and political rhetoric. The questions we pose are: How will this anticipated reduction in service affect the fairly expensive and ambitious policies which both the New Labour and SNP Governments have passed on to those who provide services? How will the resulting melee affect people more real than our fictitious Mona Laster and her father?

Chapter summary

This chapter has looked at the range of law and policy currently informing mental health, mental illness and recovery within Scotland. We have explained how these differing terms are used and have provided an overview of the differing strands of practice that are currently developing and have emphasised the central importance of involving service users and carers in creative dialogue with policy makers.

References

Campbell, P. (1996), 'The History of the Service User Movement in the United Kingdom', in T. Heller, J. Reynolds, R. Gomm, R. Muston and S. Pattison (eds), *Mental Health Matters: A Reader* (Basingstoke: Macmillan).

Canadian Centre for Suicide Prevention (2004), *National Suicide Prevention Strategies*. Available at: http://www.suicideinfo.ca (accessed 21 September 2009).

Collins, A. (2008), *SAMH Briefing on Single Outcome Agreements* (Glasgow: SAMH Centre for Research, Influence and Change).

Council of Europe (1950), *The European Convention on Human Rights* (Rome: Council of Europe).

Hothersall, S.J., Maas-Lowit, M. and Golightley, M. (2008), *Social Work and Mental Health in Scotland* (Exeter: Learning Matters).

NHS (2009), *Current Awareness Bulletin: Forensic Mental Health Services 7*, February 2009, Forensic Mental Health Services Managed Care Network, NHS Scotland.

NHS Health Scotland (2008), *A Review of Scotland's National Programme for Improving Mental Health and Wellbeing*. Available at: http://www.healthscotland.com/documents/2388.aspx (accessed 15 January 2010).

OPSI (1998), *Human Rights Act 1998 (Ch 42)* (London: OPSI).

Scottish Executive (2000), *Adults with Incapacity (Scotland) Act 2000 (asp 4)* (Edinburgh: Scottish Executive).

—— (2001), *New Directions: Report on the Review of the Mental Health (Scotland) Act 1984* (Edinburgh: Scottish Executive).

—— (2003a), *National Programme for Improving Mental Health and Wellbeing: An Action Plan 2003–2006* (Edinburgh: Scottish Executive). Available at:

http://www.scotland.gov.uk/Publications/2003/09/18193/26508 (accessed 28 May 2010).

—— (2003b), *Mental Health (Care and Treatment) (Scotland) Act 2003 (asp 13)* (Edinburgh: Scottish Executive).

—— (2005), *Mental Health (Care and Treatment) (Scotland) Act 2003: Code of Practice* (3 vols) (Edinburgh: Scottish Executive).

—— (2006), *Delivering for Mental Health: the Mental Health Delivery Plan for Scotland, 2006 to 2009* (Edinburgh: Scottish Executive).

Scottish Government (2006) 'Delivering for Mental Health'. Available at: http://www.scotland.gov.uk/Topics/Health/NHS-Scotland (accessed 25 January 2010).

—— (2007), *Towards a Mentally Flourishing Scotland: The Future of Mental Health Improvement in Scotland 2008–2011* (Edinburgh: Scottish Government).

—— (2010), *NHS Performance Targets* (Edinburgh: Scottish Executive). Available at: http://www.scotland.gov.uk/Topics/Health/NHS-Scotland/17273/targets (accessed 1 June 2010).

Scottish Office (1960), *Mental Health (Scotland) Act 1960 (Ch 61)* (Edinburgh: Scottish Office).

—— (1984), *Mental Health (Scotland) Act 1984 (Ch 36)* (Edinburgh: Scottish Office).

—— (1997), *A Framework for Mental Health Services in Scotland* (Edinburgh: Scottish Office).

Scottish Recovery Network (2010), 'What is Recovery' [Scottish Recovery Network: Recovery homepage]. Available at: http://www.scottishrecovery.net/What-is-Recovery/what-is-recovery.html (accessed 25 February 2010).

Slade, M. (2009), *Personal Recovery and Mental Illness* (Cambridge: Cambridge University Press).

UN/WHO Guidelines for the Development of National Strategies for the Prevention of Suicidal Behaviours (1993), World Health Organisation, National Strategy Guidelines. Available at: http://www.who.int/mental_health/prevention/suicide/suicideprevent/en/index.html (accessed 25 January 2010).

World Health Organisation (2007), 'Mental and Behavioral Disorders' (F00-F99), *International Classification of Diseases and Related Health Problems* (10th revision) (London and New York, NY: WHO).

—— (2009), 'Suicide Prevention (SUPRE)'. Available at: http://www.who.int/mental_health/prevention/suicide/suicideprevent/en/index.html (accessed 28 May 2010).

Wilson, G. and Daly, M. (2007), 'Shaping the Future of Mental Health Legislation in Northern Ireland: The Impact of Service User and Professional Social Work Discourses', *British Journal of Social Work* 37: 423–39.

Further reading

Andreasen, N.C. (2004), *Brave New Brain: Conquering Mental Illness in the Era of the Genome* (New York, NY: Oxford University Press). Offers a detailed explanation of modern medical understandings of the causation of mental illness.

Heller, T., Reynolds, J., Gomm, R., Muston, R. and Pattison, S. (eds) (2000), *Mental Health Matters* (Basingstoke: Palgrave Macmillan).

Tew, J. (ed.) (2005), *Social Perspectives in Mental Health: Developing Social Models to Understand and Work with Mental Distress* (London: Jessica Kingsley).

These texts offer a social discourse on mental health and mental illness.

12 Older people

Rory Lynch

Introduction: Definition of terms

This chapter considers social policy for social work with older people. The focus here will be on relevant policy and the impact this has on social work practice. A starting point for all social work with older people has to be the definition, as far as we can, of older age. This is particularly the case in relation to the terms 'old age' and the 'elderly'. Old age is largely a social construction where there are culturally held beliefs (Thompson 2005) as to the abilities and role of older people. This is further reinforced if older people are perceived purely in the context of their declining health and the wider structural context of their perceived 'non-contributory' status. This one dimensional, medicalised focus denies older people an inclusive and meaningful role in society and this is frequently reinforced by the often negative media stereotypes that focus on the vulnerability of older people (Hockey and James 2003). These overarching negative themes stigmatise older people into that generic and discriminatory focus of the 'elderly' where all older people are perceived in this light and where structural oppression becomes the focus of the lives and lived experience of all older people. Sadly the term 'elderly' is still in common usage even within agencies and journals dedicated to the alleviation of discrimination against older people in general.

Ageism is related to the way in which older people may be treated less equitably within society, which is at the heart of discrimination and disadvantage (Bytheway 1995). Old age therefore needs to be seen and experienced in the context of an accumulation of years rather than a specific, defined set of absolutes based on misunderstanding and an unwillingness to engage with the specific and individual life events of all older people.

Our core beliefs come from our childhood and our relatives, culture, education and media influence us. Ageism is the systematic mistreatment of individuals in relation to the role they are accorded within society. This discrimination can be at the personal, cultural and structural levels (PCS). The personal may refer to the way that older age is viewed by individuals, particularly the young, where there is a lack of awareness of the individuality of older people and their positive role within society. At a cultural level society may view older people as a generic, homogenised group with similar characteristics and who may be perceived in the context of their vulnerability as opposed to their potential for contributing to society. At a structural level older people may live in poverty and lack basic support services related to benefits, pensions and access to community-based services. This structural reinforcement is characterised by a lack of awareness of the needs of older people irrespective of their age or abilities (Thompson 2005).

Exercise 12.1

How do you perceive older people and ageing and where do your beliefs and values regarding older people come from?

What is the one thing you would do to change ageist practices in your profession?

Workers therefore need to be sensitive to and aware of the various dilemmas experienced by the 'young' old and the 'old' old with a wider consideration of the language we use in relation to older people and old age generally. In a more philosophical sense negative attitudes may also make the wider population, particularly the young, fearful of old age with a concurrent and abiding fear of the ageing process that may impact negatively on their own capacity for a meaningful future journey through the life course (Bond et al. 2007).

Exercise 12.2

Do you think that there should be more specific legislation in relation to older people generally and what may be the implications for this? How might this define older people as a separate group as opposed to individuals who are included and considered within the wider community? How might older people be considered in the context of their 'ills' rather than their 'skills'?

Poverty and pensions in old age

Older people are more likely to be poor than the general population. While older men may have an occupational pension supported by the state pension this may not be the same for women. They may have foregone the capacity for economic independence and the ability to accrue disposable capital while undertaking child care and the care of other dependents. The fact that women have a higher life expectancy may mean that women not only experience poverty in old age but also over a longer period due to their increased life expectancy. The findings of the *Poverty and Social Exclusion Survey* suggested that between 32 per cent and 62 per cent of pensioner households are in poverty (Patsios 2006). According to the White Paper on Pension Reform 2006, however, pensioners living on state benefits have seen an improvement in their standards of living since 1997. Age UK (2010a) challenge this claim. They suggest that in the fourth richest country in the world there are 1.8 million older people of pensionable age living below the poverty line. More importantly they suggest that this poverty has a direct impact on disability, health and lower life expectancy. This is not a new phenomenon and as far back as the 1950s John Kenneth Galbraith postulated on the nature of relative and absolute poverty in its wider societal context. Galbraith speculated that if older people do not have those assets and resources that any 'decent' person would expect as a right then in a real sense older people may come to see themselves as 'indecent' in respect of the rest of society (Galbraith 1999).

Older people and perceptions of coping

In addition, older people may have a greater pre-disposition to 'making do' and in the process deny themselves adequate food, heating and clothing. In the Joseph Rowntree Foundation research on 'The Material Resources and Well-Being of Older People' (Burholt and Windle 2006) this premise was further exemplified where the evidence shows that respondents over the age of 75 appeared satisfied with their limited material resources even though their income did not meet their financial needs. The reality is that those pensioners who experience poverty will experience a commensurate diminution of their general health and well-being. As they struggle to cope financially at the expense of those more holistic needs of engagement and inclusion with the wider community this may have a significant impact on both their physical and psychological health and well-being.

Older women and poverty

Generally women have been too reliant on men for financial support in old age, which can contribute to their poverty and vulnerability. In the Scottish Government findings in People and Society only 10 per cent of women were in receipt of a full basic state pension based on their own National Insurance contributions. This is because women in the past have had less opportunity to gain employment and contribute to an occupational or personal private pension. This is primarily due to women taking on caring roles and child care until they are able to return to the labour market where they have often been forced to take on unskilled and low-paid work with a commensurate impact on their future pension entitlement. These women are more at risk of economic deprivation and social exclusion in the longer term and this situation can be further exacerbated by widowhood and divorce in older age.

Men's occupational careers are less likely to be disrupted compared to women who may be responsible for taking on particular family roles as referred to above. Older people, practitioners, social service planners and politicians need an energetic study of the challenges of an increasing ageing population. This is particularly the case when we consider the demographics of ageing and the reshaping of services for older people in the future. The Scottish Government through its document on Reshaping Services has identified the key areas of policy that need to be addressed to meet this demographic challenge. The next 20 years are critical in addressing the future needs of older people in a way that optimises health, independence and well-being. This programme will be taken forward in collaboration with the Scottish Government, the NHS and the Convention of Scottish Local Authorities (COSLA) to ensure that future policy and services for older people are developed in a way that is sustainable in the longer term. The lead body in this development is the Ministerial Strategic Group on Health and Community Care which will address the following strategic areas of development: Vision and Engagement; Future Planning of Long-Term Care: Demographic Pressures; Care at Home; Future Role of the Care Home Sector; Wider Planning for an Ageing Population – Housing and Communities; Healthy Life Expectancy – Healthy/Independent Ageing; Workforce Issues; Pathways.

Retirement

A capitalist approach may view older people as inherently 'problematic' because of their perceived drain on resources and lack of engagement with the active creation of wealth. While aspects of ageing may occur over a period of time and may not be obvious to the person or his/her acquaintances, the same cannot be said for retirement. This is a constructed, arbitrary event where a person may feel themselves making an unhappy transition from being a person who feels included and productive to a person who may feel excluded overnight (Giddens 2006; Wilson et al. 2008). A rationalisation of the retirement age to 65 for men and women may refer more to Governmental wishes to pay less in pensions – particularly given the increased life expectancy of older people – than to any wider awareness of the inequitable nature of society dominated by both paternalistic and patriarchal systems. We therefore need to consider old age in the wider political context and particularly in relation to the medicalisation of old age and its 'treatment', the mandatory retirement age and the role of the welfare state (Phillipson 1998). This is particularly important when we consider that old age has been structured into particular categories by social policy itself and particularly pension policy. Ironically, it was never intended that the arbitrary ages of 65 for men and 60 for women should define when people retire but act more as a benchmark to which people could add extra credit by working for a longer period. The new coalition government, as part of its initial legislation, has speculated that it will raise the pension age to 67 to meet current economic needs. These arbitrary ages have now become the benchmark for perceptions of appropriate retirement ages irrespective of the changing demographics of the older person's world. When diminishing pension rights are taken into account then there are clear links between the construction of old age and its political progenitor. While the answer to old age poverty related to pension rights is relatively easy to conceptualise, the rationale for failing to meet this most basic of needs is less so. Since 1979 the basic state pension has been index-linked to prices as opposed to the gross national wage and consequently there has been a decline in the value of this pension in relation to overall earnings. Two million people of pensionable age will be unable to afford heat and food on current payments (Age UK 2010b). While there are plans to reinstate this link to the national wage this is not predicted to happen until 2012 and is less certain in a climate of economic decline where vulnerable groups may be at further and longer-term risk, although the new coalition government has made a commitment to reinstate this link which should benefit pensioners in the shorter term at least.

Exercise 12.3

Is old age socially constructed? What role might politics play in this?

Older people can experience distress and unhappiness through poverty, social exclusion and isolation. What might be the detrimental effects?

Write down a list of why and how older people may experience poverty.

Demographics of old age

Overall lower life expectancy in the early 1900s was largely due to a higher rate of childhood mortality. Advances in medical science means that many childhood illnesses such as smallpox, polio, diphtheria, tuberculosis and measles have been brought under control or eradicated. Women in the UK can now expect to live to approximately 80 years of age and men to 76 years. The difference in longevity is attributed to men being more likely to experience acute life threatening illness resulting in death whereas women are more likely to experience long-term disabling conditions (Victor 2005). This then tends to exacerbate the sense that mortality is the direct result of old age and as such services directed at positive health for older people may be wasted (see the section 'Domiciliary Support and Personalisation of Care' below). This structural approach to the wider health of an older population lacks a needs-led focus and will inevitably result in policies with an increasingly ageist and medicalised approach.

There are also areas of major social deprivation throughout Britain and if you live in certain locations in Glasgow or Manchester life expectancy is lower – 76 years for women and 69 years for men (Leyland 2004).

The population in 2006 in the UK was 60,587,600 of whom 16 per cent were 65 or over. The number of people aged 65 and over is expected to rise by nearly 60 per cent from 9.6 million in 2005 to over 15 million in 2031. Of that 15 million it is projected that 3.8 per cent will be 85 and over. The number of people over 85 in the UK is predicted to double in the next 20 years and treble in the next 30 (National Statistics 2008). There are more women than men among the very old, and it is likely that this trend will continue. From the point of view of the demographics we can define younger-old in the range 55–75 years of age as opposed to the older-old adults who fall into the 75–89 years age range.

Women's tendency to live longer than men means that there is the potential for a protracted period of widowhood in old age. This has major implications for the widowed in terms of the lost relationship with the spouse, for their family and friends as well as how the widowed person may perceive their sense of identity and worth (Payne, Horn and Relf 2000). There are also more serious implications for mental ill health and poverty related to personal and societal isolation. Older people may lack that resilience and sense of autonomy throughout life that leaves them vulnerable to feelings of worthlessness and hopelessness. These feelings can be exacerbated by the lack of resources (both financial and community-based) as well as a deeper sense of that social opprobrium that can exist as part of a wider structural oppression (Victor 2005). This may be further reinforced where there are significant differences in expectation between gender groups. In a more general sense, less than 5 per cent of the population had an opportunity to access further education in the 1960s compared to approximately 50 per cent in 2009. This will have a significant impact on the individual's capacity to gain economically and to provide for an extended older age. More tellingly, in the current political and financial climate this may be exacerbated by a reduction in returns on investments, particularly with low interest rates for savers and increased charges for basic support services.

'Make do and mend'

There is a certain irony in the longer-term promotion of thrift and fiscal prudence that may ultimately result in the impoverishment of greater numbers of older people. While older people may have been brought up to 'make do and mend', they may also have seen thrift as a future means of supporting their needs and independence. Given the large numbers of people who will have worked in low-paid and unskilled work it is likely that these savings will be modest. In the current climate of 'boom and bust', with very significant decreases in the interest rates paid on savings, this will have a very direct financial impact on older people who may already be struggling on a basic state pension. If capitalism has at its heart the promotion of profit, then older people may be perceived as a commodity that is a net user and recipient of services as opposed to a producer and contributor. It is unlikely within this paradigm that perceptions of worth based on experience and wider social contribution will be seen as a negotiable asset.

A short history of social policy for older people: Social policy and old age in context

The basic provision for welfare provision in Britain stems from the 1942 Beveridge Report on social insurance. Interestingly Beveridge suggested that old age, disability, widowhood and unemployment were seen as the 'causes' of poverty as opposed to those more structured forms of stigma and discrimination that we recognise today. How else could old age itself be viewed as a cause of poverty when a person may already have worked for 50 years in occupations which left little if any disposable income for the future (Victor 2005)?

Beveridge identified the 'five giant ills' of society that he viewed as the most threatening for the welfare of the wider population in the post-war period. These were want (an insufficient income); idleness (unemployment through insufficient job opportunities); squalor (poor housing conditions); ignorance (insufficient or poor quality education); disease (ill-health exacerbated by insufficient medical assistance) (Hudson, Kuhner and Lowe, 2008). Scotland has had an historical reputation as a 'welfarist' and more socially democratic country and evidence for this exists within the free personal care for older people in Scotland (McEwen and Parry 2005; and see Chapter 2). (Table 12.1 provides a list of social policy and legislation since 1990 in Scotland relevant to older people.)

State pensions

The modern equivalent of the policy agencies that work in these areas are social security, employment, housing, education and health. The Beveridge Report of 1942 adopted the idea of a contributory social security system that would protect the most vulnerable at times of illness and unemployment. This had the additional impact of reinforcing gender stereotypes of the role of women within the home while the focus of the policy was on protecting the breadwinner within the family. The creation of the National Health Service in 1948 guaranteed universal health care at the point of contact where formerly access to health services was largely dependent on personal wealth. The post-war period from the 1950s through to the early 1970s was a time of sustained economic growth that culminated in the inflation and unemployment leading up to the election of 1979 when the Conservatives came to power and remained there until 1997. The Government focus on wage restraint and privatisation focused on the curbing of public services with a greater emphasis on the private sector in the provision of housing and pension benefits. A significant aspect of this was where discretionary single payments for those on supplementary benefits to meet specific needs was replaced by the social fund where vulnerable people were more likely to be given loans. This focus on benefits was compounded by the generally poor state pension that was increasingly related to the retail price index and rate of inflation as opposed to the gross national wage which has left older people increasingly dependent on state benefits that are below a liveable standard although the new coalition government has indicated that it will renew this link to ensure that pensions for older people keep pace with current costs.

Community care

The inception of the National Health Service and Community Care Act 1990 provided for a focus of community-based support for older vulnerable people taking account of the wider support systems that existed within those local communities. While these support systems were acknowledged this did not take account of those wider structural changes within society and that policy makers could not legislate for those more psychological aspects such as the feelings of loneliness and potential abandonment that older people experience within the community. At the time of writing the government has agreed to an increase in the state pension of 2.5 per cent but only on the basic level of pension which is made of several component parts which will remain static and will result in a minimal net pension gain.

The acknowledgement that widening demographic changes in an increasingly ageing population raised the wider issue of how payments for personal care could be managed, and in Scotland the Community Care and Health (Scotland) Act 2002 proposed that everyone over the age of 65 should be entitled to 'free personal care'. This is an issue that is still being debated for England and Wales and the current coalition Government has not made a firm commitment to support and fund this in the longer term.

Housing

Housing has presented a significant challenge for policy makers and older vulnerable people since the 1920s. The needs of adequate housing had to be balanced with wider issues of welfare provision which came to a head in 1980 when the Conservative Government enacted legislation to ensure tenants had a right to buy. Considerable numbers of older people used this opportunity to buy their properties which further reduced the public housing stock. These new owner-occupiers now had the responsibility of maintaining these properties which added a considerable financial burden on older people who may already have been struggling to manage on state benefits.

Table 12.1 Social policy and legislation in Scotland relevant to older people

1990 NHS and Community Care Act

1995 Carers (Recognition and Services) Act

1996 Community Care (Direct Payments) Act

1997 White Paper – Designed to Care: Renewing the NHS in Scotland

1997 The Framework for Mental Health Services in Scotland

1998 Modernising Community Care: An Action Plan

1998 Royal Commission on Long Term Care – Report to UK Parliament in March

1999 'With Respect to Old Age: Long Term Care – Rights and Responsibilities'

1999 White Paper – Aiming for Excellence: Modernising Social Work Services in Scotland

1999 Making the Right Moves – Rights and protection for adults with incapacity

1999 Strategy for Carers in Scotland

2000 The Same as You? Review of services for people with learning disabilities

2000 Adults with Incapacity (Scotland) Act

2000 Our National Health: A Plan for Action, a Plan for Change

2000 Report of the Joint Future Group (RJFG)

2001 NHS Plan

2001 Scottish Executive's response to the RJFG

2001 Report of the Chief Nursing Officer for Scotland Group on Free Nursing Care

2001 Regulation of Care (Scotland) Act

2001 Care Development Group – Fair Care for Older People

2001 New Directions – Millan Committee Report – Review of mental health legislation

2001/2002 Introduction of National Care Standards – revised in 2005

2002 Adding Life to Years – Expert group on the healthcare of older people

2002 Choose Life: A National Strategy and Action Plan to Prevent Suicide in Scotland

2002 Community Care and Health (Scotland) Act

2002 Implementation of Free Personal and Nursing Care

2003 Supporting People programme

2003 White Paper – Partnership for Care: Scotland's Health

2003 Mental Health (Care and Treatment) (Scotland) Act

2004 NHS Reform (Scotland) Act

Table 12.1 (continued)

2004 Range and Capacity Review of Community Care Services for Older People (second report produced in 2006)
2004 Vulnerable Witnesses (Scotland) Act
2005 Better Outcomes for Older People
2005 Delivering for Health
2005 Smoking, Health and Social Care (Scotland) Act
2005 Care 21: The Future of Unpaid Care in Scotland (Executive response published in 2006)
2006 Delivering for Mental Health
2007 Adult Support and Protection (Scotland) Act
2007 Protection of Vulnerable Groups (Scotland) Act
2007 Towards a Mentally Flourishing Scotland: Policy and Action Plan (second report published in 2009)
2007 All Our Futures: Planning for a Scotland with an Ageing Population
2007 National Guidance on Self-Directed Support
2007 Better Health, Better Care: Discussion Document/ Action Plan
2008 Public Health etc. (Scotland) Act
2008 Independent Review of Free Personal and Nursing Care in Scotland – A Report by Lord Sutherland
2008 Personalisation: A Shared Understanding
2009 Commissioning for Personalisation
2009 A Personalised Commissioning Approach to Support and Care Services

Note: These can be accessed through the www.opsi.gov.uk and the www.scottish.gov.uk websites.

Future policy and impact on older people

The ratio of retired people to those of working age is projected to rise over the next two decades. Fewer wage earners (because of sustained low birth rates) mean that there will be less people contributing to the older generations' basic state pensions and this will have widespread consequences for fiscal policy (although recent research (Hills 1993) speculates that the funding of pensions for older people will still be sustainable at 5 per cent of the Gross Domestic Product until 2050). It is now likely that the coalition Government of 2010 will raise the official state pension age to 67. This might be seen as a straightforward solution to the shortfall in the level of pension contributions.

Unfortunately this will not benefit people from lower socio-economic groups. Variations in the average life expectancy suggests that there is a probability of older people from a more socio-economically poorer group dying before reaching the age of 70 and this is supported by figures from the Joseph Rowntree Foundation in 1997 on mortality throughout the UK. This suggests that in areas of Scotland and particularly Glasgow, 'people were 66 per cent more likely to die prematurely than people living in rural Dorset – and 31 per cent more likely than people living in Bristol' (Dorling 1997).

The UK Government plans to equalise retirement ages between men and women from 2010, which perhaps addresses wider issues of age discrimination with a more equitable approach to issues of rights in this area. Whether this makes for a more equitable distribution of resources, related to future policy for older people, remains to be seen.

Successive Governments have tried to encourage people to save for their own retirement because of this shortfall and low level of basic state pension. Confidence in this plan received a setback in the early 1990s when people were miss-sold private pensions. Recently the Government has encouraged people to postpone collecting their state pension in return for a lump sum payment.

Exercise 12.4 Social policy and legislation

Can you make links between policy and legislation and why older people may be seen as complicit in their own poverty?

Can you give examples of this across your wider understanding of policy in relation to older people?

Social Policy and Legislation Case Study

Nora Milne is 78 years of age. She lives in a council flat in the north of the city with poor access to local amenities such as shops, community services and transport links. Nora's husband Jim, a former employee of the City Council, died two years ago. Nora and Jim had one son, Frank, who currently works in the oil industry and is based in North Africa. Nora and Jim's relationship was characterised by stress and occasional violence due to Jim's heavy drinking, directed at both Nora and Frank. Frank left home at an early age and has only kept up very sporadic contact with his parents.

He is now settled in North Africa and only visits once a year on holidays. Nora lives on a pension of £115 pounds per week to cover all her expenses and is not in receipt of any other benefits. Since the death of Jim and the re-location of her son abroad Nora has become increasingly depressed and isolated within her home. She rarely goes out and no longer accompanies her friends into town for shopping and bingo. They are concerned about Nora's appearance which has become dishevelled in recent months whereas before she was a person who took great pride in her appearance. Nora is embarrassed by her poor appearance and how she presents but states that she 'hasn't got the energy to do anything about it'. Nora has stated to the friends that visit her that she is finding it increasingly difficult to cope on her own and that she is fearful of what will happen to her in the future. She is also very concerned about the level of crime in the area and is worried about her personal safety.

Exercise 12.5

You are a social worker asked to visit Nora to assess her care needs and whether she may need to access care and support agencies. Underpinning this you need to take due note of issues of social policy in relation to older people as well as significant legislation and how it may potentially impact on Nora. You also need to consider the sociology of ageing in the context of ageism, the significance of the body in the construction of ageing and its impact on potential care. You can also consider the negative and positive aspects of ageing as well as aspects of structured dependency, social constructs of ageing, the invisibility of old age and potential double standards in relation to the care of older men and women. Finally you need to consider the personal skills that you may potentially bring to bear on this intervention as well as some sense of your use of self.

1. How would you assess Nora's immediate care needs and what agencies might you need to contact as part of a multi-agency approach?
2. What potential care needs and support might Nora need for the future and how would these be negotiated in the context of recent social policy?
3. What processes would you need to put in place to assess, plan for and finance Nora's potential access into a care home if this was required?

Family dynamics and kinship care

Many people over retirement age continue to work through choice or if jobs are available or engage in unpaid voluntary work and live contented and fulfilled lives. Increasingly, older people are called on to provide kinship care for grandchildren where the biological parents may struggle with issues of mental health and substance misuse (Hothersall 2008), thereby perhaps contributing to a change in the stereotypical image of grandparents over the years to meet this new need. This may also be associated with that more psychological and philosophical dimension of generativity, that is, the capacity for recognising individual coping strengths and negotiating change through the life course, in meeting the challenges of substance misuse, mental illness and unplanned pregnancy within the family (Bond et al. 2007).

In the past families were the main source of help for domestic tasks and tending to the needs of vulnerable members within that family. Conversely, where resources are limited within the family, women are more likely to have an inequitable share of meeting these resources in the context of their socially acquired and perceived gender function (Roberts 1996; Dominelli 1997; Victor 2005).

Future care for older people within the family is likely to continue if in the past an older person has provided family and friends with support and reciprocity is a major factor regarding continuing informal care. This reciprocity may be based on that continuum and dynamism of modern relationships, which may not be based on the more traditional feelings of love but where affectional bonds within families predominate (Bond et al. 2007). In essence, modern relationships where love has died may not be sustained either in marriage or the care of parents, and a more reciprocal relationship based on affection may prevail for the long-term support of older people.

Intimacy and the potential for isolation

Consideration also needs to be given to a family member carrying out personal care. The informal carer may feel embarrassed performing these tasks for a relative and prefer a formal carer to carry out these more personal and intimate roles. An older person might also feel that a relative providing personal care changes the nature their relationship from one of reciprocity to one of dependence with all that this may entail in relation to needs, independence and the right to choose. An understanding of direct payments related to the Community Care (Direct Payments) Act 1996 may be of particular help here where the client can purchase their own care package and where the policy precludes payments to immediate family members.

Family structures

Changes in family structure have meant that older people may now be more physically and psychologically distant from their families which can lead to vulnerability, isolation and less family support. This may also be underpinned by a lack of awareness of those wider aspects of legislation and policy that exist to support older people and vulnerable people generally. In Scotland there is a raft of legislation including the Adults with Incapacity (Scotland) Act 2000, The Mental Health (Care and Treatment) (Scotland) Act 2003 and the Adult Support and Protection (Scotland) Act 2007 that seek to engage with issues of care and a more general awareness of how abuse of older people is as likely to exist within the family as within institutional care and the wider community (see Chapters 7, 11 and 13).

Domiciliary support and personalisation of care

Older people generally want to remain in their own home and 95 per cent do so with varying levels of personal care support (Scottish Executive 2002). Services for older people should help them to remain in their own home as long as possible if this is their choice and this has to be considered in the nature of the personalisation of care and what this means in reality for older people. Ideally older people will be actively involved in the design and development of services as opposed to passive recipients of services based on limited resource allocation.

Domiciliary care services are generally agreed to be the most effective way to meet the needs of older people where this is their choice. This has to take consideration of those more holistic needs of older people in the context of inclusion, role, independence and the ability to make informed choices about their future care needs. Domiciliary care can be provided by a range of statutory, voluntary and private agencies to meet the range of complex and competing needs for an older population (Rothwell-Murray 2000).

Significantly a large proportion of domiciliary care services are still provided by statutory organisations (usually the local authority) and these are primarily delivered within the NHS and Community Care Act 1990 which provided for the fundamental right of older people to be cared for within their own homes. Research in Scotland in 1998 indicates that 76 per cent of all domiciliary care is still provided by local authority social work services with the rest made up of a combination of the independent sector and NHS trusts.

Significantly the Community Care and Health (Scotland) Act 2002 identified free personal care as a critical feature and this has impacted significantly on the increased uptake of domiciliary services in Scotland. In England the Department of Health, within their strategic policy on Putting People First, has identified that supporting and extending greater control and choice to the clients they support should be the main focus of social work intervention. There is a specific emphasis on 'personalisation' where the public services can be adapted to meet the needs of clients that addresses and moves forward the agenda of person-centred and individualised services. This builds nationally on existing legislation within the Community Care (Direct Payments) Act 1996 that supports independent living by direct payments to clients with identified needs but with the additional legal responsibilities of employment legislation in relation to any services contracted to provide this care. While it is commendable that vulnerable clients can now take control over their own care needs by effectively purchasing services, there is also an onus on the purchaser to address issues of employment legislation as that purchaser. This could result in considerable additional pressure on any recipient of this care in terms of paperwork at a time when he/she may be more vulnerable because of presenting care needs and a lack of experience in negotiating the often complex world of finance and human resources.

Personal care and what this means

At the same time there has been a consistent debate on the more specific details of what 'personal care' entails, particularly in the area of food preparation and nutrition generally in the older population. At a time where there is increased pressure on the finances of older people to meet these basic human needs (if not rights), this is an area that needs addressing with some urgency given the large numbers of older people who have recently been identified as malnourished within care and hospital settings throughout the UK. This is particularly the case when we consider the implications of free personal care in the longer term. In *Scotland on Sunday* on 2 March 2008, in an article on free care for the elderly, the writer speculated that there would be a shortfall of £60m in the coming fiscal year to support this policy (Barnes 2008). What inspires even less confidence is that the Confederation of Scottish Local Authorities (COSLA) have already published a paper where they have suggested that local authorities should have something of a pre-emptive strike in apportioning blame to the Scottish Government in expectation of the public backlash to come. This is specifically in relation to the under-provision of resources to meet this need in the longer term and how it will be resourced effectively in the shorter term. As recently as November 2009 the Scottish government minister, Shona Robison, has committed to the retention of free personal care for the 'elderly' population in the face of speculation by the Association of Directors of Social Workers that this may have to be means tested in light of recent spending cuts (Dunning 2009).

Who cares and who pays?

Within the more psychological aspects of human development this personal care could be considered as an absolute right and necessity in relation to how older people may feel able to cope when their most basic needs are not being met. Maslow (1968) identified that it was highly unlikely that an individual would achieve that sense of self-actualisation or homeostasis of ego when they had to use all their psychic energy to meet basic survival needs (see the section 'Definition of Terms' above).

In a systematic review and meta-analysis related to 15 studies of home visits carried out by Elkan et al. (2001) clear evidence was presented to suggest that effective domiciliary services contributed to a reduction in both mortality and admission to longer-term institutional care. These findings seem to suggest that where poor health and vulnerability were in evidence, if services were focused on those specific areas of vulnerability, positive outcomes were more likely.

In Scotland the Scottish Executive Care Development Group in 2001 explored the wider philosophical issues over whether it is ethical to have a wider debate on the differing services and who should pay for these, given that it is the user's needs and perspectives that should be at the heart of service delivery. Incorporated within this should be the conceptual overview of *capacity* as opposed to *incapacity* (Hothersall, Maas-Lowit and Golightley 2008). The basic premise of this is that the state will not seek to interfere in the choices and freedoms of individuals as long as these subscribe to what is deemed legal. At the same time, if the state (through local authorities) supports the ideology of free personal care then it has a duty to support and develop this free personal care as part of the wider forum of addressing need and vulnerability. At the inception of free personal care within the Scottish Parliament in 2001 the First Minister declared that in this context there would be 'no ifs or buts or maybes'.

Care settings

Under the National Assistance Act 1948, Section 21, a duty was laid on local authorities to make accommodation available for all persons who by reason of age or infirmity (amended to illness and disability in the National Health

Service and Community Care Act 1990, Section 42) were in need of care support to meet their needs.

Admission to a care home can be a traumatic experience for older people. The majority of residents in care homes are women aged over 80, often with multiple disabilities. There is a clear correlation here between the wider focus on community-based care and ensuring that older people retain the capacity for independent living for as long as possible. Fries (2000) suggests through the 'compression of morbidity' theory that while the range of diseases or conditions people can die from has been reduced or brought under control that this means people are living longer. This may mean that older people 'buy' longer life but live with disability for a longer period of time.

Process of admission to care settings

During admission the practitioner is required to achieve high quality practice. The worker needs to understand the past and present experience of the older person, their emotional intelligence as well as attending to the physical task. The Scottish 21st Century Social Work Review (Scottish Executive 2006) is an overview of actual and aspirational facets of professional social work practice, now and in the future, and suggests that a fundamental role of social work is the development of a therapeutic relationship between the client and the professional to ensure actual defined need is met through an engaged, collaborative and empathic relationship. This relationship should be genuine, warm and respectful, with a mutual understanding of the purpose of the referral. It is important that the older person agrees with a referral to social services and that they are given an explanation of the processes and procedures involved in the admission and, very importantly, that they can retain some sense of control during the processes involved here. We need to ensure that older people are involved in decisions about their future as, too often, they are marginalised and excluded where decision-making is concerned (personalisation).

The worker has to justify taking decisions where individuals may not have the capacity to make decisions for themselves due to the severity of their mental illness, learning disability or a physical disability, which makes communication of decisions impossible (Adults with Incapacity (Scotland) Act 2000). Whatever the circumstances there needs to be an implicit understanding that a person has capacity unless there is clear evidence to the contrary. This may take the form of prior statements and wishes about future care and these should be actively sought out as opposed to assumptions about incapacity being made.

Exercise 12.6

What is the potential impact on older people when admission procedures are neglected?

How might older people benefit from being included within all aspects of their transition between their own accommodation and a care setting?

What are the social work practice and ethical considerations during this process?

Resilience in older age

Misca (in Adams, Dominelli and Payne 2009) refers to resilience as the capacity that individuals, groups and families have to resist the negative aspects of harm and experience and still develop a positive and generative aspect. In the context of older people, practitioners need to be aware of the accumulation of inequalities that may have impacted on an older person throughout the life course (Davey Smith 2003). This may be more pronounced where cultural and structural oppression may impact on older people at a time when they are experiencing a real loss of place, role and a hopeful expectation for the future. Resilience in old age may be challenged at the same time when an older person is experiencing the loss of a spouse or where their physical and emotional resources may be diminished (Phillipson 1998). While there is good evidence to support resilience being built up over the life course in relation to attachments (Bowlby 1969), our emotional attachment and engagement with others needs to be sustained and nurtured in the longer term. One way to support resilience in older age is both to acknowledge and focus on the previous coping strategies of the older person and to support and encourage these in the present through inclusive practice. If an older person feels that they are being listened to and included in any decision-making that impacts on their future care and provision, then they are much more likely to feel engaged with this process. The former can relate to life events and the coping with stress and traumatic events and the latter could relate to life history working (Atkinson 2002) and wider considerations of growth, maintenance and recovery and a full consideration of the impact of loss on the older person (Baltes, Lindenberger and Staudinger 1998).

Resilience may also be compounded across the life course because of the wider aspects of socio-economic deprivation and leave an older person more vulnerable to the vagaries of public opinion and market forces at a vulnerable time. Older people may be further disadvantaged at a time of economic depression where their 'non-contributory' role can easily be interpreted as a participatory causal effect of this economic downturn. This socio-economic difference may have very direct implications for older people as there is some evidence to suggest that people from a higher socio-economic group with more disposable assets tend to enjoy a greater life expectancy (Siegrist and Marmot 2006). In effect, it is possible to buy good health in terms of access to proper nutrition, living conditions and better access to support and medical services. At a time of current economic and potentially long-term recession, and with a significant downturn in the return on investments that older people may have made over the course of a lifetime, this may have not just personal implications, but wider implications for the society we want to live in and how it supports and maintains the vulnerable citizens within that society (see Chapter 10).

Exercise 12.7

How can we maintain/develop resilience in older people?

What role has personalisation and inclusion to play in the development of resilience across the life course?

Chapter summary

Social work with older people is at a challenging time with increasing demands on resources and an increasing awareness and engagement with the wider needs of older people. This work has to be addressed in the context of inclusion, empowerment and the personalisation of services now and in the future. For these services and interventions to be effective there needs to be a full engagement in meeting the care needs of older people and these need to be underpinned by a more holistic consideration of those aspects of loss, resilience and the lived experience and inner worlds of all older people. All of these facets of care and support have to be underpinned by a broadly-focused, inclusive policy range to ensure that a third age does not become invisible.

References

Adams, R., Dominelli, L. and Payne, M. (2009), *Social Work: Themes, Issues and Critical Debates* (Basingstoke: Palgrave Macmillan).

Age UK (2010a), *Our Response to the Latest Poverty Figures* (London: Age UK). Available at: http://www.ageuk.org.uk/latest-press/archive/poverty-figures-response/?paging=false (accessed 11 June 2010).

— (2010b), *Poverty in Retirement* (London: Age UK). Available at: http://www.ageuk.org.uk/get-involved/campaign/poverty-in-retirement/ (accessed 14 June 2010).

Atkinson, R. (2002), 'The Life Story Interview', in J. Gubrium and J.A. Holstein (eds), *Handbook of Interview Research: Context and Method* (London: Sage): Chapter 6, 121–40.

Baltes, P.B., Lindenberger, U. and Staudinger, U.M. (1998), *Life Span Theory in Developmental Psychology* (New York, NY: Wiley).

Barnes, E. (2008), 'Free Care for Elderly on Brink of Collapse', *Scotland on Sunday*, 2 March.

Bond, J., Peace, S., Dittman-Kohli, F. and Westerhof, G. (2007), *Ageing in Society* (3rd edn) (London: Sage).

Bowlby, J. (1969), *Attachment and Loss* (vol. 1) (London: Hogarth).

Burholt, V. and Windle, G. (2006), 'The Material Resources and Well-Being of Older People'. Joseph Rowntree Foundation. Available at: http://www.jrf.org.uk/publications/material-resources-and-well-being-older-people (accessed 3 June 2010).

Bytheway, B. (1995), *Ageism* (Buckingham: Open University Press).

Davey Smith, G. (ed.) (2003), *Health Inequalities: Lifecourse Approaches* (Bristol: Policy Press).

Dominelli, L. (1997), *Sociology for Social Work* (Basingstoke: Macmillan).

Dorling, D. (1997), 'Changing Mortality Ratios in Local Areas of Britain 1950's–1990's'. Joseph Rowntree Foundation. Available at: http://www.jrf.org.uk/publications/changing-mortality-ratios-local-areas-britain-1950s-1990s (accessed 19 February 2010).

Dunning, J. (2009), *ADSW Head Harriet Dempster Raises Possibility of Means Testing – Shona Robison Pledges to Continue Free Care* (Surrey: Community Care). Available at: http://www.communitycare.co.uk/Articles/2009/11/27/113291/scots-reiterate-commitment-to-free-personal-care.htm (accessed 11 June 2010).

Elkan, R., Kendrick, D., Dewey, M., Hewitt, M., Robinson, J., Blair, M., Williams, D. and Brummell, K. (2001), 'Effectiveness of Home Based Support for Older People: Systematic Review and Meta-Analysis', *British Medical Journal* 323: 719.

Fries, J.F. (2000), 'Compression of Morbidity in the Elderly', *Vaccine* 18: 1584–9.

Galbraith, J.K. (1999), *The Affluent Society* (London: Penguin).

Giddens, A. (ed.) (2006), *Sociology: Introductory Readings* (Cambridge: Polity Press).

Hills, J. (1993), *The Future of Welfare: A Guide to the Debate* (York: Joseph Rowntree Foundation).

Hockey, J. and James, A. (2003), *Social Identities across the Life Course* (Basingstoke: Palgrave Macmillan).

Hothersall, S. (2008), *Social Work with Children, Young People and their Families in Scotland* (2nd edn) (Exeter: Learning Matters).

Hothersall, S., Maas-Lowit, M. and Golightley, M. (2008), *Social Work and Mental Health in Scotland* (Exeter: Learning Matters).

Hudson, J., Kuhner, S. and Lowe, S. (2008), *The Short Guide to Social Policy* (Bristol: Policy Press).

Leyland, A.H. (2004), 'Increasing Inequalities in Premature Mortality in Great Britain', *Journal of Epidemol Community Health* 58: 296–302.

Maslow, A. (1968), *Towards a Psychology of Being* (New York, NY: Wiley).

McEwen, N. and Parry, R. (2005), 'Devolution and the Preservation of the United Kingdom Welfare State', in N. McEwen and L. Moreno (eds), *The Territorial Policies of Welfare* (London and New York, NY: Routledge): 41–61.

National Statistics (2008), 'Population Estimates for UK, England and Wales, Scotland and Northern Ireland'. Available at: http://www.statistics.gov.uk (accessed 1 June 2010).

Patsios, D. (2006), 'Pensioners, Poverty and Social Exclusion', in D. Gordon, R. Levitas and C. Pantazis (eds), *Poverty and Social Exclusion in Britain: The Millennium Survey* (Cambridge: Polity Press): 431–58.

Payne, S., Horn, S. and Relf, M. (2000), *Loss and Bereavement* (Buckingham: Open University Press).

Phillipson, C. (1998), *Reconstructing Old Age: New Agendas in Social Theory and Practice* (London: Sage).

Roberts, E. (1996), *Women and Families, An Oral History, 1940–1970* (Oxford: Blackwell).

Rothwell-Murray, C. (2000), *Commissioning Domiciliary Care: A Practical Guide to Purchasing Services* (Oxford: Radcliffe Medical Press).

Scottish Executive (2002), *Adding Life to Years Report of the Expert Group on Healthcare of Older People* (Edinburgh: Scottish Executive).

—— (2006), *Changing Lives: Report of the 21st Century Social Work Review* (Edinburgh: HMSO).

Siegrist, J. and Marmot, M. (eds) (2006), *Social Inequalities in Health: New Evidence and Policy Implications* (Oxford: Oxford University Press).

Thompson, N. (2005), *Anti-Discriminatory Practice* (4th edn) (Basingstoke: Palgrave).
Victor, C. (2005), *The Social Context of Ageing: A Textbook of Gerontology* (London: Routledge).
Wilson, K., Ruch, G., Lymbery, M., Cooper, A., with Becker, S., Brammer, A., Clawson, R., Littlechild, B., Paylor, I. and Smith, R. (2008), *Social Work: An Introduction to Contemporary Practice* (London: Pearson Longman).

Further reading

Arber, S., and Ginn, J. (eds) (1997), *Connecting Gender and Ageing: A Sociological Approach* (Buckingham: Open University Press).
Mo, R., Bernard, M. and Phillips, J. (2009), *Critical Issues in Social Work with Older People* (Basingstoke: Palgrave Macmillan).
Phillips, J., Ray, M. and Marshall, M. (2006), *Social Work with Older People* (Basingstoke: Palgrave Macmillan).
Ray, M., Bernard, M. and Phillips, J. (2009), *Critical Issues in Social Work with Older People* (Basingstoke: Palgrave Macmillan).

13 Disability: A question of perception

Jeremy Millar

Introduction: Impairment, disability and its social construction

Valuing difference is now embedded within the various codes of practice regulating those working in the field of social care (Scottish Social Services Council 2003). In addition the workforce has a mandate to promote well-being for those who use services and this includes addressing aspects of personal growth and realising each individual's potential (Scottish Executive 2006). These are aspirational and noble endeavours but to what extent are they achievable?

This chapter will explore how attitudes to people with a range of impairments including learning difficulties have changed over time influenced by factors encompassing religious belief, scientific advancement, changing demographics, political ideology, disability rights, poverty and key legislative and social policy developments.

Terminology, language and oppression

The reader will note that in the above paragraph I used the word impairment. The manner in which language has been utilised to identify, demean and often oppress those that are different is central to many of the themes in this chapter and I will return to the use and power of linguistic terminology as the chapter progresses. The term impairment can be taken to mean the loss or abnormality from birth or subsequently of any psychological and/or physical functioning within the context of environmental factors (WHO 2001). Disability is the restrictions placed on the individual with the impairment, in their ability to perform activities and complete tasks that would be considered appropriate for other individuals of their age. Put simply, the impairment is a fact and the disability is experienced in relation to the social and environmental barriers placed in the path of the person with impairment that serve to exclude and discriminate against them.

The reality of life is that we will all be affected by physical and psychological impairments over our lifespan. Some will be of a transitory nature such as a broken limb that restricts our movement for a period of time, an experience of reactive depression as a consequence of profound loss; others may be experienced from birth as in genetic conditions such as Down's Syndrome and as we get older the number and complexity of our impairments tend to increase.

The value judgements that we personally make in respect of people's differing impairments coupled with broader societal views have a part to play in how disabling the impairments are perceived by the individual. The views or prejudices expressed toward individuals and groups with physical and psychological impairments can also be communicated through more structurally oppressive barriers to individuals' full participation in society such as access to social space and the absence in the general population of communication skills such as British sign language. The struggle for social inclusion and access to the full panoply of citizens' rights by people with impairments will be discussed with reference to the disability rights movement and its role in achieving progressive legislative changes (Oliver and Barnes 1998).

Prevalence of the medical model

Central to this analysis of the development of social policy in relation to people with impairments will be the dominance of the medical model in determining/diagnosing who is to be deemed disabled. In respect of the medical model we are looking at a deficit-based interpretation of the human condition, one that presupposes an 'ideal' human specimen and measures the presenting patient's symptoms/deficits against it.

The medical establishment have, over time, through scientific research drawn up the parameters for normal growth and development. These normative benchmarks fulfil the role of assigning people to the deficit-based sub-groups according to the presenting impairment. The language of disability can be oppressive in that it takes the normal range of diversity one would expect in a population and pathologises individuals for being different from the narrow band of those in the population defined as normal (Foucault 1973).

Stigma and discrimination

I make no apology for the critical nature of the preceding paragraph. The historical discourse around disability has left a legacy of predominantly negative images of people with impairments. More recently a range of social policy initiatives and legislative reforms have endeavoured to promote social inclusion through innovative approaches such as employment opportunities in social firms and improved access to further and higher education. Having said this, people with impairments, especially women, children, people from ethnic minorities and older people, continue to be amongst the poorest members of society and we need to look critically at the reality of the net gains achieved by people labelled as being disabled (The Poverty Site 2010).

Historical context: Children of a lesser God

In an attempt to make sense of personal attitudes towards people with impairments and how current legislative and policy responses have been framed it is essential to understand the lived experience of people with impairments over time.

Early history

In going back to early historical records from the ancient world we are presented with a picture of children with impairments being subject to infanticide; the actions of the Spartans weeding out weak babies through exposure over night on the mountain side would be an example. The Spartans may not have had a clearly articulated policy but there were strong cultural factors influencing this warrior society in which strength and warlike attributes were most valued. The survival of the tribe in terms of being able travel quickly in times of danger and live through periods of famine meant that it could be seen as expedient not to be burdened by members unable to fend for themselves (Sinason 1992).

Spawn of the devil or blessed innocent?

In the Christian era we see moral and theological oscillations between the care and healing of people with impairments and their outright persecution, often leading to their being characterised as the spawn of the devil. In this category we may place the persecution of so-called witches who may have been ostracised from the community by merit of physical deformity or mental illness (Goodare 2002).

In medieval Scotland, leprosy was still a common disease and churches refused admittance to lepers who were expected to receive communion through a specially constructed hole in the wall. However, the care of those with acquired impairments through warfare, such as blindness from arrows, prompted the earliest forms of institutional care at the hands of religious orders and it was the monasteries that provided hospital care for the infirm in the middle ages (Gerber 2000).

Exercise 13.1

Reflect on your own awareness of the historical treatment of people with impairments as related through literature and films. What sort of images come to mind?

Additional reading: see Chapter 3 in Sinason (1992) and for a wide-ranging review of writings on impairment through the ages see Kudlick (2003) in the online *American Historical Review*

(http://www.historycooperative.org/journals/ahr/108.3/kudlick.html).

Enlightenment and superstition

Before the emergence of Enlightenment thought in the eighteenth century, the Western Christian view of impairment was intricately linked to the will of God, as was all of human life. There was, in addition to the influence of religious belief, a large measure of magical and superstitious thinking attached to the understanding of people having impairments. These stigmatising perceptions linger on into our current era maintaining barriers to the fullest inclusion in society of those with impairments (Sinason 1992; Stiker 1999).

Exercise 13.2

Consider for a moment the language used within our lifetimes to describe people with a range of impairments. Many of the charitable disability organisations have only recently rebranded. What did Capability Scotland used to be called?

For this research, *Mapping Scotland's Disability Organisations* offers a review of the extent of provision (Johnston 2009) (http://www.scotland.gov.uk/Resource/Doc/294586/0091088.pdf).

Into the modern era

The visibility of learning difficulties in pre-industrial Scotland was less apparent than in the modern era due to low levels of literacy in the general population and the mainly agrarian nature of society that made few demands of people's skills beyond that of manual labour.

The modern age also saw the development of the natural and subsequently the social sciences. The notion of divine control and pre-ordained fate gave way to the belief in rationality and human intervention through scientific study and controlled experimentation. Medical science commenced a systematic study and categorising of individuals according to their type of impairment or perceived deficit. Taxonomy of physical and mental deficits started to be developed, one example being the DSM IV (American Psychiatric Association 2000), which informs psychiatric assessment and intervention. This type of diagnostic tool is constantly updated as scientists indentify new mental health conditions (Longmore and Umansky 2001).

Exercise 13.3

The medical model described above looks to the deficit in the individual and seeks to cure or compensate through medical intervention. Reflect on your own experience of the medical establishment and the health service. Identify any feelings related to the patient/professional contact.

Hopefully you have an awareness of the history of negative labelling and persecution applied to people with impairments and the echoes that continue into our era.

Condemned to poverty

Industrialisation in the late eighteenth and into the nineteenth century drastically changed the demographics of Scotland with many from the rural population moving to employment in the emerging industries in the cities of Glasgow, Edinburgh, Aberdeen and Dundee.

The care of those people unable to work and provide for themselves, often through ill health and impairment, became the responsibility of the parish. Their needs were assessed very much in terms of deserving and undeserving categories of the poor. Parish records from this time offer insights into the moral judgements of the parish elders in respect of how alms (charity) should be distributed. In a publication drawing on records from the time entitled *The Kirk's Care of the Poor* (McPherson 1941) we find the term portable poor who were

> Objects carried from door to door. Cripples and other disabled beggars were carried round the country upon what were called barrows, but which in most cases, were really wooden frames or stretchers upon which these disabled creatures were laid. They were thus transported from house to house, from farm to farm, by the persons at whose door they were last deposited. (McPherson 1941: 198)

An early example of the post code lottery of care!

The rise of institutional care

The Poor Law Act of 1845 identified able and disabled categories of the poor but this differentiation would be more related to the ability to perform some kind of work rather than being specific to some form of impairment. The identification of disability in the sense that we understand it was not as clearly defined in nineteenth-century Scotland (Hutchison 2007).

The harsh working conditions, endemic poor health and increased likelihood of industrial injury led to many of the population living with impairments and adjusting their labours accordingly in order to eke out a living. Some groups such as blind people were offered specific forms of institutional care that came with obligations to engage in productive activity. The large Victorian institutions or asylums housed a small minority of the general population. The majority of people with impairment relied on family and local charitable aid to get by (Barnes et al. 1999).

Society's understanding of, and response to, people with impairments was radically different in the era prior to the introduction of the welfare state in 1948. Without a safety net and a real fear of the stigma associated with entry into the poorhouse, people looked to informal networks of support from within their own communities.

Exercise 13.4

Many of the charitable voluntary social care organisations have their roots in the philanthropic movement of the Victorian era. Reflect on how this legacy still influences public perception of services for people with impairments.

By way of engaging with the oppression of the 'other' read the article by Pemina Yellow Bird (n.d.) entitled *Wild Indians* (http://dsmc.info/pdf/canton.pdf).

The appliance of science

Eugenics

The ruling elites of the Victorian age quickly assimilated the emerging scientific theories to increase industrial productivity and also to address the visible conditions of poverty which they characterised in terms of the moral and physical degeneracy of the working classes. One scientific view which gathered respectability and had a direct impact on people with impairments was that of the eugenics movement. Francis Galton drew on the work of his cousin Charles Darwin to propose that selective breeding should be applied to humans in order to eradicate from society inferior types of the human species. These views were closely linked to notions of racial purity which found their most extreme expression in the genocide committed by the Nazis. The movement gained substantial support in developing Western societies with many adopting programmes of enforced sterilisation of people deemed to be intellectually deficient, affected by hereditary disease and mental illness (Longmore and Umansky 2001).

The science that informed this movement was largely discredited following the exposure of the Nazi extermination programmes, but countries such as Sweden continued with eugenic policies into the 1970s and there continues to be a debate fuelled by advances in genetics offering new ways of controlling and influencing reproduction. Campaigners within the disability rights movement work to raise awareness of the continuing, albeit minority, voice within the scientific community which supports what could be termed eugenicist approaches (Shakespeare 1995).

Exercise 13.5

Consider your personal views on selective reproduction and medical intervention to eliminate congenital conditions.

This whole area of debate is emotive and polarised. To get a flavour of the debate go to the BBC site *Ouch!* (http://www.bbc.co.uk/ouch/). Tom Shakespeare has written on eugenics.

We can rebuild you!

The other element of medical and technological advance that relates to people with impairments manifests itself in the form of corrective surgery and the use of prosthetics to replace missing limbs. Here we can see the focus being one in which the patient has deficits corrected or minimised in order to bring them closer to 'normality'. Many of these medical interventions are intrusive, invasive and undertaken without the informed consent of the person themselves.

One 'survivor' of this treatment is the artist Alison Lapper who as a result of the medical condition phocomelia was born without arms and with shortened legs. She powerfully documents the story of her life in residential institutions during which time she experienced corrective surgery and a succession of prosthetic limbs all of which the doctors photographed and recorded in minute detail. Through her art she defined her identity as a beautiful person with impairments and now campaigns for disability rights and challenges public perceptions of the disabled body (Lapper 2005). The majority of Alison's childhood was spent in institutions during the 1960s and '70s, which tended to be the lived reality for many people with severe congenital impairments.

Exercise 13.6

How do you respond on an emotional level to the greater visibility in the community of people with impairments similar to those of Alison?

The increase in numbers of soldiers with impairments in society will have an interesting influence on public opinion. For further information on war and medicine visit the 'War and Medicine page at the website of the Wellcome Collection (http://www.wellcomecollection.org/whats-on/exhibitions/war-and-medicine/image-galleries.aspx).

Embedding structural oppression

Safety net or universal entitlement?

The following section will look at the legislative reforms, social policy and the influence of the disability rights movement. Welfare reforms at the beginning of the twentieth century evolved from the differing Liberal/ Conservative and Socialist ideological positions that can be illustrated by the concepts of residual welfare and institutional welfare. Residual welfare was favoured by the capitalist classes. They viewed welfare as a safety net given only in extreme circumstance to those deemed as deserving poor. They saw a danger in offering welfare to all as it would interfere in the 'natural' operation of the capitalist free market which requires that the market dictates the value of a worker's labour. From this ideological position we can identify the potential for the exclusion of people with impairments who could not be considered economically active or productive. Opposing the capitalist position we find the Fabian/socialist belief that welfare provision should be institutional and available to all according to need. Within this ideological perspective there would be guaranteed welfare provision for people with impairments regardless of their level of economic productivity (Smout 1997).

Towards the welfare state

Two key pieces of research that informed this debate were undertaken by Seebohm Rowntree in York and Charles Booth in the slums of East London at the end of the nineteenth century. It was their exposure of the dire living circumstances of the poor that stimulated debate regarding society's response to the effects of poverty and deprivation. Should they be addressed through structural changes to society, that is, improving housing, access to health care, employment and social activities?

These ideas were progressed by bodies such as the Fabian Society. A critical watershed came in the shape of the 1905–1909 Royal Commission on the Poor Laws. This Commission produced two reports, one representing the majority and the second the minority views of the committee members. The majority report backed by the Charity Organisation Society (the first social work body) advocated reform of the Poor Laws to tighten them up in terms of targeting the residual poor whilst the minority report favoured state intervention to improve housing, health and employment security. Had this minority option been pursued the country could have embraced the concept of the welfare state nearly 40 years ahead of its actual implementation in 1948.

The position of people with impairments remained subject to means testing and charitable giving continuing a paternalistic tradition which saw little recognition of individual citizenship and influence in relation to decision making, either by people with impairments themselves or their family members (Oliver and Barnes 1998).

Exercise 13.7

Whose role is it to provide for the most vulnerable in society? What is your position on the provision of services to people with impairments through charitable giving? (See Chapters 1–4.)

The welfare state

The formation of the welfare state in 1948 instigated a new social contract, one built on the findings of the Beveridge report, which aspired to eliminate the five social evils of want, disease, ignorance, squalor and idleness. Services for those identified as disabled people were brought under either state control or regulation. The position of people with impairments was arguably enhanced in terms of opportunity of access to institutional provision rather than the residual model of welfare. The reality was somewhat different with marginalisation still prevalent due in part to the economic expectations placed on citizens in terms of employability (see Chapter 2).

Economic rationality

Borsay (2004) talks of economic rationality in relation to the employment of people with impairments. By this she means that employers look for the most productive and cheapest people to employ from the pool of labour. People with impairments tend not to fulfil these criteria and are discriminated against when it comes to gaining employment.

Institutionalised welfare provision and support through a benefits system for certain groups within society such as children, women, older people and those with impairments were perpetuated and normalised negative perceptions of these citizens' value to society. The inequalities that had always existed for individuals with little or no economic power became entrenched in a system that whilst purporting to provide a safety net in reality offered a life at the margins of society. Poverty remained and remains the most significant structural barrier to full participation in civil society.

Voices of dissent

Fighting back

The new order of the welfare state came under attack on two fronts as the disability rights movement of the 1960s and '70s demanded greater recognition and inclusion for people with impairments coupled with the advent of Thatcher's neo-liberal agenda for rolling back state intervention in people's lives.

Initially, I will look at the role of the disability activist groups in challenging the mainstream view of people with impairments as the 'other', unfortunates requiring charity and professional support, rather than citizens with a voice and the expertise in terms of the solutions to their personal challenges.

DIG

One of the early disability activist groups, the Disablement Incomes Group (DIG) formed in 1965, had the agenda of improving both the accessibility to and amount of the benefits available to those classed as disabled. Here we have a direct response to the lived experience of poverty and social exclusion. DIG's membership was drawn from people with impairments directly suffering the inequalities inherent in the welfare system. The group engaged in lobbying activities and significantly raised the profile of people deemed to be disabled across the policy making spectrum of national and local government decision making.

The evolution of activist groups face the inherent risk of becoming professionalised and subsumed into a wider consultative framework, one that increasingly includes professional helpers/carers without experience of having an impairment. The power of the original message becomes diluted and to a degree neutralised. To an extent this process had overtaken DIG by the early 1970s.

Radical activism

The critique of this professionalised approach was articulated by the splinter group which emerged out of the disillusionment with the direction DIG was taking. The Union of the Physically Impaired Against Segregation (UPIAS) set about asserting the structurally oppressive nature of society's response to those with impairments through economic, educational, health, environmental and social barriers being maintained. They particularly took issue with the dominance in professional practice of the medical model and a language of caring for people with impairments that disempowered and oppressed those labelled as disabled (UPIAS 1976; Fleischer and Zames 2001).

The focus of this development in the activist agenda was to clearly prioritise a social model analysis of the barriers encountered by people with impairments. To this end UPIAS proposed an anti-discriminatory agenda centred on achieving disability rights legislation. The central premise of this call to action was that those people with impairments and experiencing a disabling society should be consulted on every level in relation to all policy making rather than offered a tokenistic input into areas deemed of relevance to those labelled as disabled by professional policy makers and politicians.

Exercise 13.8

Here we are facing the very political nature of the debate around policy and legislation as it affects people with impairments. Reflect on your political views regarding achieving rights, the nature of citizenship and challenging the *status quo*.

Once again the BBC *Ouch!* web page offers the opportunity to explore current issues impacting on people with impairments from their perspective (http://www.bbc.co.uk/ouch/).

The Disability Discrimination Act 1995

An example of how slowly this agenda was progressed is evidenced by the campaign for equality legislation that would outlaw discrimination on the basis of an individual's impairment. This eventually became law in the form of the Disability Discrimination Act 1995 (DDA 1995) after 13 years of campaigning. Successive Conservative Governments stood in the way of the Bill, refusing to acknowledge the institutional discrimination experienced by people with impairments (Barnes 2007).

Paradoxically it was the ideology behind those same Conservative Governments intent on rolling back the welfare state and introducing neo-liberal free market competition to the social care sector that offered disability rights activists and individuals fresh opportunities to influence service development and assume greater purchasing power in terms of the direct provision of services.

Brave new world or false dawn?

Community care

This section will highlight the reforms in terms of social policy and legislative changes that have taken place in Scotland over the last 25 years. Arguably the two most significant pieces of legislation are the aforementioned DDA 1995 and the National Health Service and Community Care Act 1990 which came in on the back of Sir Roy Griffiths' report *Caring for People* (Griffiths 1989). The Community Care Act amalgamated two strands of ideologically-based thinking: the neo-liberal move to reduce costs in the residential sector and promote community-based supports and informal networks of care which in reality placed the burden predominantly on female family members and carers, and response to the disability activist lobby that had been calling for a more individualised focus on support through the promotion of 'independent living' integrated within the community for all people with impairments (see Chapter 7).

What is normal?

Living in the community

The decanting of people with a range of impairments from the long stay institutions into community provision drew on the theories of normalisation developed initially in Scandinavia in the late 1960s then taken up by Wolfensberger (1983) in the United States under the new title of Social Role Valorisation (SVR). This theory held that society ascribed negative roles to people excluded from mainstream social participation and labelled them as deviant, socially useless and potentially a burden. To dispel this discriminatory view it would be desirable for marginalised people to occupy valued social roles in the community and take part in community life on an equal footing to everyone else. The appeal of this approach to those advocating for care in the community was that the presence of people with impairments undertaking social roles in the community such as eating out or going to see a film validated a view that institutional life was bad and community provision enhanced the individual's life.

Exercise 13.9

Supporting people with impairments to access community resources has been central to social care practice over the last two decades. What is your impression of the degree to which individuals have been truly integrated within the community?

The Scottish Government website provides access to the *Same as You* report (Scottish Executive 2000). Section 4 'A Full Life: Where You Live' provides detail regarding challenges and opportunities for people with learning disabilities living in the community (http://www.scotland.gov.uk/ldsr/docs/tsay-06.asp).

The critique of SVR centred on the fact that the valued roles deemed suitable for people with impairments remained firmly located in the bio-medical world-view of impairment as a deficit requiring professional input and the socio-economic reality of poverty, environmental barriers to participation and daily exposure to discrimination. This experience of discrimination is heightened by membership of other stigmatised groups, for example, being a member of an ethnic minority or of a different sexual orientation.

Joined up working

A joint future?

The right of people with impairments to organise and determine their own roles in society was seldom on the agenda in the late 1980s. Things were largely being done to people rather than in partnership with them. However as the 1990s progressed and the Disability Discrimination legislation took effect, policy makers, social service providers and staff working in the disability field increasingly integrated a more empowering model of practice which actively involved the person within the decision-making process. *Modernising Community Care: An Action Plan* (Scottish Office 1998) initiated a move towards multi-disciplinary working and coordinated area-based provision of services. Described as a 'tartan of services' (Petch 2008) the steering group for Joint Futures reported to the new Scottish Government in 2000 and recommended improvements in sharing resources, disseminating information and good practice along with better coordination supported by local partnership agreements. The practice element being single shared assessments aimed at ensuring the service user's needs are fully assessed and matched to services with provision made for individualised packages of care. There was a clear emphasis on the full involvement of all stakeholders.

Same as you?

In 2000 the Scottish Executive published the *Same as You* report which addressed reform of services for people with learning disabilities and took forward the more empowering aspects of the social model in terms of looking to support people in the community and enhance individual's opportunities to live what it terms 'a full life' (Scottish Executive 2000). This frenetic and complex re-evaluation of the social care and health provision in Scotland was formalised into legislation with the passing of the Community Care and Health (Scotland) Act 2002. Ironically the stated aim of involving all stakeholders overlooked the role of the voluntary sector, forcing them to produce their own response to the joint futures initiative.

Back to work

New Labour nationally and in the Scottish context envisaged social inclusion being achieved predominantly through assisting marginalised people into employment. A range of social inclusion policies were rolled out offering a focus on educational and training opportunities. The Beattie Committee, *Implementing Inclusiveness, Realising Potential* (Scottish Government 1999) identified the supports required for young people with learning disabilities and other behavioural difficulties during the transition from school to further and higher education. This led to changes within Careers Scotland.

More recently there has been the UK-wide policy *A New Deal for Welfare: Empowering People to Work* (Department for Work and Pensions 2006) that aims to reform the benefits system and reduce the numbers of claimants on long-term incapacity benefits. The link between employability, citizenship and social status is reinforced by policies such as these. Where does this leave people with impairments if social inclusion is predicated on employment as the route out of poverty and social disadvantage? The sociologist Ruth Levitas (2005) describes the New Labour model as social integrationist with citizens finding a socially valued role and economic independence through employment. This approach creates and accentuates the prejudiced view of non-productive members of society and perpetuates the exploitative and oppressive relationships placed on both the carers and the cared for. As an alternative model Levitas (2005) suggests the redistributive route out of social exclusion in which societal wealth would be shared through progressive taxation. Here we hark back to the Fabians and universal provision and also models of social welfare predominant in some of the northern European states.

The act of caring

Interdependence

The emphasis of these social inclusion policies on citizenship through perceived productivity creates a tension between those deemed productive and those that are viewed as dependent. Within the social care workforce there are decisions to be made as to whether this is the most relevant analysis and it may be useful to consider the feminist critique of the independent/dependent paradigm and look to the concept of interdependence within the context of the lifespan. Joan Tronto (1994) sets out an ethics of care in which interdependence is key and caring is a moral activity and offers reciprocity within the relationship. Within this model people with impairments are instrumental in decision making and their humanity is honoured and defined in the act of caring as opposed to being protected by a more procedurally defined rights agenda (see Chapter 7).

Exercise 13.10

What does social inclusion mean to you? Has the preceding discussion caused you to question any assumptions regarding the relationship between the care giver and the cared for?

The Inclusion Scotland website contains a Manifesto stating the goals for people with impairments in relation the social inclusion (http://www.inclusionscotland.org/SUMMARY%20Manifesto%20for%20Inclusion%202007.pdf).

Getting it wrong

The professional social work role has evolved through the implementation of successive community care legislation. It has become progressively overwhelmed by the new managerial procedural approaches (Harris 2002) and the demands of responding to ongoing policy reforms and reorganisation of local authority and partnership relationships. The distance between worker and service user has arguably become compromised, leading to poor decision making and individuals being failed and exposed to harm as in the case of Miss X in the Scottish Borders (Scottish Executive 2004) (see Chapter 6).

A comprehensive review of social work was delivered in the form of the report *Changing Lives: Report of the 21st Century Social Work Review* (Scottish Executive 2006) which reasserted the key role of the social worker to utilise the relationship to assist service users in accessing services and in addition recognising the move to the personalisation of social services that will focus on the service user as the budget holder (Scottish Government 2009a).

In control?

Nothing about us without us

The personalisation agenda has developed from initiatives such as direct payments and self-directed care which aim to place control for decision making and budgetary control in the hands of the individual with impairment. This approach is particularly relevant to people with a learning disability. The challenge for the social worker and social care worker is to practice in a person-centred manner and promote and enable maximum choice for the service user. In a mixed economy of care with a range of professional disciplines involved with service provision there are challenges in terms of achieving clarity over the core value base. As we have discussed previously, there are structural barriers and societal prejudice to overcome and the advocacy role for the worker in the face of limited resources and discriminatory attitudes is ever present. Co-ordination at a local level aims to provide a scale of service in which all service users would be known to the coordinator, thereby ensuring a individualised support and a 'can do' attitude (see Chapter 9).

Ghosts of the past

Recent research by Stalker et al. (2007) noted that service users valued the personal relationship and felt that their quality of life had improved. The journey travelled by people with impairments has been long and tortuous. The degree of control and opportunity enjoyed by people labelled as disabled is now backed by anti-discriminatory legislation, inclusive policies across health, education, employment and education. The degree to which inclusion is truly enjoyed is still compromised by echoes from the past in the form of narratives around 'deserving poor', victimhood, charitable cases, residual welfare, the medical model and full citizenship contingent on productive employment. It remains a fact that within Scottish society individuals and families affected both directly and indirectly by physical and intellectual impairments will experience poverty and social inclusion disproportionally; with women, children and people from ethnic minority groups being the most disadvantaged.

The next steps?

Current legislation and policy

The Equality Bill currently progressing through the UK Parliament offers a proposal that a duty to tackle socio-economic factors become part of statute. At the time of writing this clause is out for consultation in Scotland (Scottish Government 2009b). Will this be the point at which the key socio-economic barriers to full citizenship and inclusion are addressed? In contrast, the Welfare Reform Act 2009 asks for people to work for benefits and offers little hope in the way of real jobs for people with impairments (Inclusion Scotland 2010). Following the election in May 2010 of the Conservative/ Liberal coalition government we enter an age of new uncertainties. Savage cuts are being imposed across public services and the lessons of history indicate that people with impairments will suffer disproportionally.

Chapter summary

I will now present two case studies which illustrate many of the themes and dilemmas discussed in the chapter. There are significant challenges for workers not to repeat the mistakes of history and to look for a deeper understanding of the disabling society in order to promote better outcomes for people with impairments who are labelled as being disabled.

Case Study 1

John is a 19-year-old man diagnosed as being on the autistic spectrum with a range of attendant challenging behaviours linked to issues of sexual identity and mental health problems leading to self harming behaviours.

Despite being both looked after and accommodated and his transition needs being obvious from his early teens John fell into the grey area of provision between children and adult services. His legal right to be supported through the transition using the Pathways planning process was never implemented with the local authority instead moving him over to adult services aged 18 and straight into his own tenancy. He was receiving around two hours of support per week in his own tenancy within months of leaving a residential care setting. To compound the isolation John encountered in the tenancy his support worker moved posts and Care Management struggled to find a new worker. Inevitably John's situation deteriorated and within months debts had accrued, his self care skills had diminished and his mental health had reached breaking point. An incident of self harm led to admission to psychiatric care in hospital, the giving up of the tenancy and the breaking of the few positive social networks that John had. His position within the adult system led to discharge from the hospital into a private nursing home rather than provision with people of his own age. Despite the age range in the nursing home being predominantly over 50 the Care Commission allowed for the placement to continue. Finally a residential place was found in the community. Once again in a resource for people considerably older than John. As a consequence of the difficulties encountered by John as a result of his poorly supported transition from child to adult services, John's confidence and self esteem has suffered and he has lost some useful networks of age appropriate support.

Case Study 2

The Camphill Communities in Scotland offer a holistic continuum of care for all ages of people with a range of physical and intellectual impairments. The philosophy of the community aims to promote personal and social growth through a person-centred therapeutic community approach in which all aspects of life from diet through to spiritual needs are met with the goal of nurturing the inner potential. The majority of the co-workers live in group homes with the residents. There has been, historically speaking, a tendency to view the work of the Camphill Communities as somewhat isolated from mainstream provision. The Organisation has worked hard with bodies such as the Care Commission to engender a better understanding of the distinct nature of their particular ethos whilst meeting many of the new managerial demands of the procedural era.

The Camphill Community are offering a therapeutic approach that displays a concern for the both the human condition and respects and promotes ethical concerns regarding living in harmony with nature.

They offer a distinct training in a social pedagogic degree that equips graduates to work across the social care sector. In terms of offering an insight into other possible worlds when it comes to the care of people with impairments, Camphill is one of Scotland's quietly understated achievements (Jackson 2006) (Camphill Scotland website is at http://www.camphillscotland.org.uk/).

References

American Psychiatric Association (2000), *DSM-IV-IR Diagnostic and Statistical Manual of Mental Disorders* (Arlington, VA: American Psychiatric Association). Available at: http://www.psychiatryonline.com/resourceTOC.aspx?resourceID=1 (accessed 12 January 2010).

Barnes, C. (2007), 'Disability Activism and the Struggle for Change: Disability, Policy and Politics in the UK', *Education, Citizenship and Social Justice* (November 1) 2(3): 203–21.

Barnes, C., Mercer, G. and Shakespeare, T. (1999), *Exploring Disability: A Sociological Introduction* (Cambridge: Polity Press).

Borsay, A. (2004), *Disability and Social Policy in Britain since 1750: A History of Exclusion* (Basingstoke: Palgrave).

Camphill Scotland (n.d.). Available at: http://www.camphillscotland.org.uk/ (accessed 15 February 2010).

Department for Work and Pensions (2006), *A New Deal for Welfare: Empowering People to Work* (Norwich: Stationery Office).

Fleischer, D.Z. and Zames, F. (2001), *The Disability Rights Movement: From Charity to Conformity* (Philadelphia, PA: Temple University Press).

Foucault, M. (1973), *The Birth of the Clinic: An Archaeology of Medical Perception* (London: Routledge).

Gerber, D.A. (ed.) (2000), *Disabled Veterans in History* (Ann Arbor, MI: University of Michigan Press).

Goodare, J. (ed.) (2002), *The Scottish Witch-Hunt in Context* (Manchester: Manchester University Press).

Griffiths, R. (1989), *Caring for People: Community Care in the next Decade and Beyond* (London: HMSO).

Harris, J. (2002), *The Social Work Business* (London: Routledge).

Hutchison, I. (2007), *A History of Disability in Nineteenth-Century Scotland* (Lampeter, Lewiston, NY, and Queenston, ON: Edwin Mellen Press).

Inclusion Scotland (2010), 'Welfare Reform Act 2009: Inclusion Scotland Briefing'. Available at: http://www.inclusionscotland.org/documents/WelfareReform.doc (accessed 16 February 2010).

—— (n.d.). 'Manifesto'. Available at: http://www.inclusionscotland.org/SUMMARY%20Manifesto%20for%20Inclusion%202007.pdf (accessed 16 February 2010).

Jackson, R. (2006), *Holistic Special Education: Camphill Principles and Practice* (Edinburgh: Floris Books).

Johnston, L. (2009), *Mapping Scotland's Disability Organisations* (Edinburgh: Scottish Government). Available at: http://www.scotland.gov.uk/Resource/Doc/294586/0091088.pdf (accessed 15 February 2010).

Kudlick, C. (2003), 'Disability History: Why We Need Another "Other"', *American Historical Review* 108(3): 763–93. Available at: http://www.historycooperative.org/journals/ahr/108.3/kudlick.html (accessed 15 February 2010).

Lapper, A. (2005), *My Life in My Hands* (London: Simon and Schuster).

Levitas, R. (2005), *The Inclusive Society? Social Exclusion and New Labour* (2nd edn) (Basingstoke: Palgrave Macmillan).

Longmore, P. and Umansky, L. (2001), *The New Disability History: American Perspectives* (New York, NY: New York University Press).

McPherson, J.M. (1941), *The Kirk's Care of the Poor* (Aberdeen: John Avery and Co.).

Oliver, M. and Barnes, C. (1998), *Social Policy and Disabled People: From Exclusion to Inclusion* (London: Longman).

Ouch! (n.d.). Available at: http://www.bbc.co.uk/ouch/ (accessed 15 February 2010).

Petch, A. (2008), *Health and Social Care: Establishing a Joint Future?* (Edinburgh: Dunedin Academic Press).

Scottish Executive (2000), *The Same as You? A Review of Services for People with Learning Disabilities* (Edinburgh: Scottish Executive).

—— (2004), *Investigations into Scottish Borders Council and NHS Borders Services for People with Learning Disabilities: Joint Statement from the Mental Welfare Commission and the Social Work Services Inspectorate* (Edinburgh: Scottish Executive). Available at: http://www.scotland.gov.uk/Publications/2004 May 2019333/36718 (accessed 29 January 2010).

—— (2006), *Changing Lives: Report of the 21st Century Social Work Review* (Edinburgh: Scottish Executive).

Scottish Government (1999), *Implementing Inclusiveness, Realising Potential.* Beattie Committee report. Available at: http://www.scotland.gov.uk/Publications/1999/09/ImplementingInclusivenes/Q/Page/2 (accessed 25 January 2010).

—— (2009a), *Changing Lives: Personalisation: A Shared Understanding* (Edinburgh: Scottish Government).

—— (2009b), 'UK Equality Bill Socio-Economic Duty Analysis of Consultation Responses'. Available at: http://www.scotland.gov.uk/Resource/Doc/297563/0092564.pdf (accessed 29 January 2010).

Scottish Office (1998), *Modernising Community Care: An Action Plan* (Edinburgh: HMSO).

Scottish Social Services Council (2003), *Codes of Practice for Social Service Workers and Employers* (Dundee: Scottish Social Services Council).

Shakespeare, T. (1995), 'Back to the Future? Disabled People and the New Genetics', *Critical Social Policy* 44(5): 22–35.

Sinason, V. (1992), *Mental Handicap and the Human Condition* (London: Free Association Books).

Smout, T.C. (1997), *A Century of the Scottish People, 1830–1950* (Fontana Press: London).

Stalker, K., Malloch, M., Barry, M. and Watson. J. (2007), *An Evaluation of the Implementation of Local Area Co-ordination in Scotland* (Edinburgh: Stationery Office).

Stiker, H. (1999), *A History of Disability* (Ann Arbor, MI: University of Michigan Press).

The Poverty Site (2010), 'Work and Disability'. Available at: http://www.poverty.org.uk/s45/index.shtml (accessed 15 February 2010).

Tronto, J. (1994), *Moral Boundaries: A Political Argument for an Ethic of Care* (New York, NY: Routledge, Chapman and Hall).

UPIAS (1976), *Fundamental Principles of Disability* (London: Union of the Physically Impaired Against Segregation).

Wellcome Collection (n.d.), 'War and Medicine'. Available at: http://www.wellcomecollection.org/whats-on/exhibitions/war-and-medicine/image-galleries.aspx (accessed 15 February 2010).

Wolfensberger, W. (1983), 'Social Role Valorization: A Proposed New Term for the Principle of Normalization', *Mental Retardation* 21(6): 234–9.

World Health Organisation (2001), *International Classification of Functioning, Disability and Health (ICF)* (Geneva: WHO).

Yellow Bird, P. (n.d.), *Wild Indians*. Available at: http://dsmc.info/pdf/canton.pdf (accessed 15 February 2010).

Further reading

MacIntyre, G. (2008), *Learning Disability and Social Inclusion* (Edinburgh: Dunedin Academic Press).

14 Children and their families

Steve J. Hothersall and Patrick Walker

Introduction

In this chapter we shall look at policy as it relates to children, young people and their families within Scotland. Our coverage will be illustrative of the current policy landscape in Scotland in relation to these groupings and will consider those policies that have both a direct and an *indirect* effect.

It is important to remember that particular policies emerge as a result of a number of factors that earlier chapters have considered, and that policy generally reflects *current perceptions* of those phenomena to which it addresses itself, in this case children and their families, so we shall consider this from a broad socio-historical perspective in order to provide a working context for the discussions that follow.

The socio-historical context of law and policy for children and families

Historically, we can locate the Children Act (UK) of 1908 as being the first 'modern' attempt by society to formalise the nature of the relationship between the state, children and their families. The 1908 Act was generally regarded as the first 'Children's Charter' because of its wide-ranging impact and its explicit, if limited, recognition of the rights of children. Essentially, the 1908 Act laid the foundations for what we might today refer to as 'child protection' with a new emphasis on the role of public (local) authorities in relation to the prevention of cruelty and neglect.

The inter-war years saw the creation of a number of special committees that were established to consider and report upon a whole range of issues relating to the treatment and protection of children. These activities reflected an increasing awareness of the vulnerabilities of children and some of the shortcomings of previous governmental and state involvement and it was the Children and Young Persons (Scotland) Act 1937 that signalled a clear shift in thinking when it introduced a new and *separate* system for dealing with children who had committed offences that was no longer attached (in theory) to the adult systems of criminal justice then in place. These separate *Panels of Justices* were the forerunner of the *Children's Panels* we have today, although it was the later *Kilbrandon Committee* that articulated these arrangements in much more detail.

Of particular significance was section 49 (S49) of the 1937 (S) Act. This made the first statutory reference to the need for courts to have regard to the *welfare of the child* in all their deliberations and the '*welfare principle*' was born. All of these measures represented a significant development in the recognition that the state and its individual members had responsibilities towards and in respect of children, although the sanctity and privacy of the (patriarchal) family was still in the ascendant.

In the immediate post-war years the disruptions and dislocations brought about by the effects of the Second World War began to highlight, amongst other things, the effects that poverty and city living had been having on children, with high rates of malnourishment and illiteracy very noticeable. Concern was also growing over the public care of children, and the case of Denis O'Neill (Home Office 1945), who died whilst in 'foster care' in England led to the establishment of the Curtis Committee (E & W) (1946: Cmnd 6922) and the Clyde Committee on Child Care in Scotland (1946; Cmnd 6911) which added to the impetus for a major review of public child care provision. These and the range of other post-war reforms, including those of Beveridge (see Chapter 2), paved the way for the Children Act 1948 (UK) which created *Children's Departments* with new responsibilities for developing and implementing services to children, including 'Boarding Out' schemes, the forerunner of foster care today.

Within the broader context, the effects of nascent research at that time by John Bowlby (1951a; 1951b; 1956; 1958) and David Winnicott (1958) brought to the public's attention the importance of significant and stable relationships for a child's well-being.

Child abuse and neglect as a social issue

The 1948 Act, with its focus upon the public care of children, was soon felt to be addressing only part of the problem in relation to child abuse and neglect. Such phenomena have not always been recognised or responded to in the way that we today perhaps take for granted and it was not until the mid 1960s for example that the issue of child physical abuse was taken seriously and seen as being a significant cause for concern, with the seminal work of Kempe et al. (1962) reorienting the official approach to this issue. More emphasis on considering children in their wider environments began to emerge, foreshadowing perhaps the work of Bronfenbrenner (1979) and the importance of an *ecological approach* to policy and practice. The practice of *social casework* (Biestek 1961) was seen at this time to be the most effective way to deliver services and involved workers undertaking assessments and providing direct assistance designed to help people resolve their difficulties. Central to this approach was the *relationship* that developed between the worker and the family, a theme that seems to be enjoying a long-overdue renaissance at the moment. There was also an increasing awareness of the need for authorities and professionals to share information and to cooperate in terms of delivering services, again a theme that has re-emerged recently within the policy arena, often in the wake of child abuse tragedies and other inquiries. Interestingly, all of these themes appear in the range of recent reviews of social work across the UK, *Changing Lives* in Scotland (Scottish Executive 2006b) and *Social Work at its Best* in England and Wales (General Social Care Council 2008) giving something of the flavour of 'back to the future'.

Juvenile delinquency

Scotland, as other parts of the UK, has had its concerns over juvenile delinquency. Although not a new phenomenon *per se*, during the 1950s and 1960s the courts had been flooded with referrals and in response to these perceived trends, the Kilbrandon Committee was formed in 1961 (reporting in 1964; Cmnd 2306) with its remit to consider the provisions of the law in Scotland in relation to juvenile delinquents and those in need of care and protection. Kilbrandon, in contrast to the Ingleby Committee in England and Wales, who were considering similar issues, took a somewhat radical approach to the issue and had as its focus the *needs* rather than the *deeds* of the child or young person. This established what was and remains a distinctively Scottish *welfare-based* approach to the issue of youth crime, one of its main recommendations being the development and implementation of the children's hearing system (CHS) (Hothersall 2008).

The recommendations of Kilbrandon had to wait until the introduction of the Social Work (S) Act 1968 before they were initiated along with a number of other significant changes to Scottish social work including the integration of all existing services within one organisational framework. The Act also introduced a specific duty upon local authorities to 'promote social welfare by making available advice, guidance and assistance on such a scale as may be appropriate for their area' (section 12(1)). Section 12 of the 1968 Act (still in force and amended by the NHS and Community Care Act 1990 (UK)) meant that local authorities now had to do more than respond to need; they had to identify, categorise and respond to it before it became a problem. This new duty also extended beyond individuals so that working with *groups of people and communities* was now regarded as a legitimate and necessary activity.

The 1968 Act resulted in a clear divergence from the rest of the UK. The Scottish child care system clearly had a strong welfare basis for the delivery of its services, whilst in England and Wales there remained a strong justice-based approach. There were tensions across the UK, regarding the nature of the relationship between the state and the family and how best to manage this, which were perhaps exemplified by the passing of the Children Act 1975 (UK), which many saw as representing the pinnacle of state intervention into family life. Whilst the 1975 Act made it clear that the welfare of the child was to be paramount, there was a clear shift towards the adoption of what today might be referred to as the 'precautionary principle' (Sterling Burnett 2009; Hood and Jones 1996) in terms of the threshold for intervention which was effectively 'lowered'. This led to the view that there was a focus on child *protection* at the expense of services to those children who were *in need.*

In subsequent years, a number of developments across the UK have all added their influence to the evolution of Scottish child care law and policy. The death of Jasmine Beckford in 1984 in England resonated across the country and one of the main criticisms of the subsequent report into her death (Blom-Cooper 1985) was that social workers had been overly focused on the family as a whole and had therefore 'overlooked' Jasmine's dangerous situation because professionals were applying what was referred to as a 'rule of optimism' in their dealings with her family. In 1987 a further series of events in England again sent shock-waves through the country when social workers were severely criticised for removing children from their families in the wake of allegations of sexual abuse and the opinions of doctors in this regard. The Cleveland Report (Butler-Sloss 1988) made several recommendations which were subsequently incorporated into national guidance around child protection (Department of Health and Social Security 1988; Scottish Office 1998; Scottish Executive 2002a) and in some respects reflected an about-turn in relation to policy direction from the recommendations emanating from earlier inquiries. Events within Scotland on the Orkney islands in the early 1990s (HMSO 1992) signalled a major shift in the role the courts had in relation to decisions regarding the removal of children from their parents on formally stated grounds, and since then other events across Scotland and other parts of the UK involving the significant harm and deaths of (too many) children who were receiving social work and other supports has generated a climate where individual social workers and other professionals are often blamed for these tragedies and have their professional practice scrutinised from all quarters (Laming 2009; 2003; Hammond 2001; O'Brien, Hammond and McKinnon 2003). Inevitably, common organisational, but not necessarily *professional*, responses to such tragedies involve increased routinisation and bureaucratisation of procedures in an attempt to 'squeeze out' risk and uncertainty, with professional judgement and discretion often reduced to a (technical) 'procedure' (see Frost and Parton 2009; Hothersall 2008; Hothersall and Maas-Lowit 2010; Parton 2006).

The current landscape of law, policy and practice guidance in relation to children, young people and their families in Scotland, underpinned by the Children (S) Act 1995 and now the Adoption and Children (S) Act 2007, has developed as a result of the influence of many things and the policy 'output', so to speak, as a pointer to 'getting it right for every child' is at times far from clear. As you can see from the above commentary, there has been much concern and *confusion* over how best to support families whilst ensuring that children are safe and best provided for when living at home is no longer feasible. We now wish to consider some of this in more detail, focusing upon some important themes and issues within current policy initiatives.

Issues and debates

The Scottish Government and indeed the Westminster Government have long been active in considering the protection of children and how best to support their upbringing (Henricson and Bainham 2005). Whilst much social policy regarding children and their families has been as a result of ideological stances regarding universality, selectivism, social justice and citizenship, and influenced by the range of political perspectives such as the neo-liberal perspective, a considerable driver has arisen as a result of inquiries into child abuse and failings in social welfare institutions (O'Brien, Hammond and McKinnon 2003; Social Work Inspection Agency 2005). On the one hand the state has historically indicated and promoted family autonomy as referred to above, but on the other has positioned itself (necessarily) as 'protector' and 'guardian', most especially at points of 'significant harm'. This presents an essential dichotomy: how to reconcile and balance family autonomy, citizenship and the promotion of children's rights for all children (Archard 2004) with the requirement for the state to intervene through a protective stance as and when required? This complex social policy arena has also incorporated direct, universal approaches, such as is evident in the child benefit system, as well as targeted and selective approaches as evident within aspects of the GIRFEC policy agenda. In addition, a raft of social policy is apparent within guidance documents, framework documents, legislation and bills.

However, and as noted in Part I of this book, if the aim of social policy in relation to children and their families is to provide a coherent and consistent response to particular phenomena, how can we make sense of the messages within this ever-expanding list of policies and, indeed, translate them into practice? As Henricson and Bainham suggest (2005: 47–8):

> the challenge is whether, amongst this plethora of policies, we can detect a significant, consistent thread indicating the Government's position in reconciling child protection and family support.

Social work operates at the confluence of this dichotomy, imbued with complex narratives, discourses, and evolving social constructions regarding the family, childhood and the role of the state (Smith 2010; Ashenden 2004). Social work, along with childhood, children and the family, has been a contested area of practice but is one which is now firmly positioned, in children and families policy, as integral in achieving purported governmental aims (Frost and Parton 2009).

The need to make visible the 'consistent thread' referred to by Henricson and Bainham above is becoming increasingly apparent. Central to this is the aim of improving the life chances of every child. The 'life chances' approach, outlined by the Fabian Society (2006), indicates that by providing the means through which all children can reach their potential, be that through health services, education provision, economic support and the reinforcement of parental responsibilities, and if necessary by providing more targeted services for those most in need, for example as outlined in *Looked After Children and Young People: We Can and Must Do Better* (Scottish Government 2007c), then all children might become uniformly more able to exploit all of the opportunities that society might offer. As R.H. Tawney pointed out in 1964, using Shakespeare's Portia as inspiration (1983: 235): 'action which causes such opportunities to be more widely shared is, therefore, twice blessed. It not only subtracts from inequality, but adds to freedom.'

Hallett and Prout (2003) alert readers of children and families social policy to an issue of some contention when indicating that, when social policy is orientated towards the domestic family sphere, it often asserts that the upbringing of children is the crucible of social problems. If, however, we reflect on Tawney's quote above, then there can be recognition that families experience access to all that our society might offer in different and often unequal ways. Not every person has the same level of opportunity, or ability, to exploit that opportunity. Many commentators, including Tawney (1983), would argue that this inequality has less to do with parenting skill and capacity *per se*, but much more to do with economic and social disadvantage originating at a structural level (Mullaly 2007), so that the view that the family is the genesis of social problems becomes a more complex issue encompassing an holistic perspective reflexive of Bronfenbrenner's 'ecological' perspective referred to above.

Such arguments have proved to be not only vigorous and ill-resolved, but intractable over the years and the New Labour project, echoed in the Scottish Government's early years and not entirely dismissed by the current SNP administration, has sought out a 'third way' of managing the very real issues of disadvantage and social exclusion through key strategic approaches incorporating health, education and economic development whilst at the same time reinforcing the significance of parental responsibility and attempting to blend these target areas into a coherent, 'total' approach.

This approach, framed in terms of 'social justice' is now the 'key framework of reference for European, UK and Scottish policy' (Juleff et al. 2005: 5). Key to this social justice approach is 'system change' across public services, moving away from atomised, fragmented departmental accountability, to a position where integration, both conceptually and structurally, is central. Such a step-change became very clear in 2001 with the introduction of the *Changing Children's Services Fund* (Scottish Executive 2001a), broad access to which appears to depend upon degrees of cooperation, illustrating further perhaps some of the themes of conditionality referred to in part one of this book.

Within the broad area of children and families policy, this developing climate is intimately connected to the goal of eradicating child poverty. Whilst Scotland has a devolved parliament, significant component parts of the child poverty strategy remain with the UK Westminster Parliament, for example social security, taxation and fiscal policy (Hothersall 2008), and this somewhat dichotomous position whereby essential elements of an overarching strategy are controlled by different administrations unnecessarily complicates the process, but nonetheless, the integration of services concerning children, directly and indirectly, and joint planning across services (for example education, social work and health) is pivotal in the Scottish social policy arena.

Of significance in this area of policy relating to children and families in Scotland is the agenda represented within the *Getting It Right for Every Child* (GIRFEC) framework (Scottish Executive 2005). One of the overall aims of the GIRFEC approach is to provide an over-arching methodology that will deliver on the range of substantive policies concerning children both directly and indirectly, ranging from health initiatives, early years (Scottish Government 2008a) and the *Curriculum for Excellence* (Scottish Government 2004a). Implicit within such an approach are a number of challenges, not the least of which is effective joint working across local authority agencies, voluntary organisations and professionals (Hothersall 2008; McLean 2007).

Further key areas are identified in terms of effective technological support systems, administration and effective workforce planning. Early intervention is similarly identified, rather than waiting until crisis points are reached in children's lives. Prevention and early intervention, most particularly in the early years of children's lives, is strongly indicated. The GIRFEC approach, therefore, can be viewed as a methodology, a mechanical approach, through which to deliver the aspirations of Scottish government policy.

In order to put the foregoing in context, it is helpful to remember that it is the economy, and economic growth that is seen to sit at the apex of the policy triangle in Scotland and is seen as the pivotal mechanism through which, overall, a socially just society is achievable. As the Scottish Government state, its purpose is to

> ... focus government and public services on creating a more successful country with opportunities for all of Scotland to flourish, through increasing economic sustainable growth. (Scottish Government 2007a: v)

In order to achieve this, then, key strategic priorities are set out, consisting of:

- learning, skills and well-being
- supportive business environment
- infrastructure development and place
- effective government; and
- equity

Throughout the *Government Economic Strategy* document (Scottish Government 2007a), children and their families are positioned as fundamental not least because 'in a smarter and healthier Scotland, improving the life chances for children, young people and families at risk and sustaining and improving the health of people in disadvantaged communities will allow them to realise their economic potential' (Scottish Government 2007a: 36).

Families are, therefore, not only the target of policy initiatives, for example in the form of widened supports and early intervention in their own right, but are positioned as 'mechanisms of inclusion' (Gillies 2005: 82). This suggests a position in which families become harnessed explicitly by the state in order to further promote social inclusion, or access to social justice. By supporting families to parent, for example through parenting classes, early intervention approaches, or indeed through reforming tax and benefits, a view is proposed that parents and their children will become 'included', active citizens not only in the economic arena of employment and economic consumption, but in the area of 'moral inclusion' (Gillies 2005: 83).

Levitas (cited in Gillies 2005: 82) describes such an approach, specifically in respect of the Blair government, as a 'social integrationist discourse'.

Social policy in relation to children and families has, over time, respected the independence of the family, although arguably encroaching on autonomy and privacy particularly where this is seen as being justifiable on the basis of the need for care and protection. However, and as pointed out by Foley and Rixon (2008: 51), since the advent of the recent New Labour project 'the state has been more willing to intervene with a range of specific social and economic policy objectives', and to move beyond its approach of intervening in family life only when children's safety and wellbeing are compromised. Whilst not mutually exclusive, in essence, with 'delivering' welfare, children and families social policy has refocused towards effecting significant change in the way that the state/citizen relationship is conducted, not least in terms of establishing the 'obligated freedom' that Gillies (2005: 86) describes. The welfare consensus of the 1940s, whilst historic and profound, can be seen to have inadvertently allowed conditions of dependency, passivity and exclusion to develop and not all individuals in society have been able to 'grow to their full stature' (Tawney 1983: 235) and consequentially, reciprocity between the state and the individual has been highlighted and enhanced as a two pronged approach in tackling this state of affairs.

As noted, current social policy in relation to children and their families seeks to promote 'life chances':

> what the life chances approach encapsulates … is our vision of the good society as one that provides the necessary resources for all its members to live a full and flourishing life and to fulfil their roles, including as parents, siblings, friends, employees and employers, and citizens. (Fabian Society 2006: 22)

Sitting within this approach is not citizen passivity, or indeed inadvertent systemic barriers, but concepts of reciprocity, active engagement and social justice. Indeed, the Fabian Society indicates that the welfare system had failed 'to both recognise and require socially useful contributions on the part of citizens' (Horton and Gregory 2009: 178). Jones and Bell (2000: 60) underscore this point, when they suggest that 'conditionality' emerges in children and families social policy on a regular basis. They suggest that the contract between the state and the individual becomes contingent on reciprocal contributions, whether in kind or in behaviour and others would similarly support the view that the 'third way' of New Labour encapsulated the vision of the 'active society' much in line with many modern welfare democracies (Rodger 2000).

Exercise 14.1 Emerging themes?

Can you identify any influences of key policy themes in your own workplace? For example, what has been the influence of early intervention approaches in your profession?

Challenges in and for practice

How does all of this relate to and translate into the lived reality not only of service users but of social workers, the profession as a whole and the institutions and structures which provide the framework of service delivery?

The Scottish Executive indicated in *Transforming Public Services* (Scottish Executive 2006a: 22) that:

> we need to do away with organisational, professional and governance barriers ... this may involve structural change ... to tackle complex, multi-dimensional problems, services need to be flexible, involve local communities and users, and work together across common boundaries to meet agreed priority goals. That needs cultural change within agencies and it needs government to remove barriers to joint working.

This is a viewpoint closely echoed in the Executive Summary of the *Changing Lives* report (Scottish Executive 2006b: 8) when it suggests that joined up inter-agency working is required, with a clear focus of building capacity 'in individuals, families and communities and focusing on preventing problems before they damage people's life chances irreparably'.

Taylor and Vatcher (2005: 167) point out that social workers are well suited to adopting a 'social perspective that seeks to take into account how different aspects of a person's life work together to help them flourish or oppress or overwhelm them'. By avoiding a singular focus of an individualistic, deficit model of practice, and with a reflective, forensic, social model of understanding, social workers can bring helpful perspectives and skills to play in the implementation of the social policy agenda of social justice and life chances. Whilst this is a considerable challenge it can also be one that offers social work as a profession the opportunity to inform and influence social policy development. It has been noted elsewhere (Hothersall 2008: 40) that social work skills are as much about 'direct work with other professionals, their agencies and organisations as they are about direct work with children'. Social work, therefore, is intimately connected not only to change in the individual but change in society, its organisations and structures (Mullaly 2007).

The recent National Residential Child Care Initiative report *Higher Aspirations, Brighter Futures* (Milligan 2009) brings many of these points into focus. It reiterates the centrality of the integration agenda, arising from the *For Scotland's Children* (Scottish Executive 2001b) report and clearly states the policy thrust as being towards developing a 'coherent and sustained approach to child care and protection by interagency children's services' (Milligan 2009: 23). The Local Government in Scotland Act of 2003 introduced the requirement that local authorities develop Community Plans, bringing together local service delivery, and in 2004 *Integrated Children's Service Planning Guidance* (Scottish Government 2004b) took this forward by indicating to health, local authorities and wider partner agencies that separate planning should be joined together into integrated Children's Services plans by April 2005.

Whilst the drive towards integrated service delivery continues, not least in the introduction of the draft Children's Services (Scotland) Bill (2009), it is widely noted that the evidence base behind an inter-agency, interdisciplinary and integrated service delivery approach is very far from being favourably conclusive. Does integration and the policy of multi-agency working actually achieve the aims that current social policy regarding children and families sets out? Stone and Rixon (in Foley and Rixon 2008) suggest that conclusive evidence is elusive. Arguably much research is orientated towards the process of joining up and integrating services and in workforce development and strategic commissioning, rather than indicating that the policy *per se* produces better outcomes and achieves the vision of Scotland's children being successful learners, confident individuals, effective contributors and responsible citizens. At the same time, the various partner agencies and professions face the challenge, if engaging with the social policy agenda, of moving their practice traditions from compartmentalised disciplinarity towards what Higham (2005) describes as commonality and complementary roles.

Whilst the social policy approach appears appealing, and may be taken to be an attempt to address failings so graphically present in child death inquiries, generally poor outcomes of children affected by poverty, looked after and accommodated children and so on, outcome evidence is lacking. Indeed, Stone and Foley (in Foley and Rixon 2008) suggest that many reviews and research studies continue to reveal little evidence of improved outcomes. This, then, constitutes a fundamental conceptual challenge to current social policy agendas and strategies and arguably to the fundamental principles set out within them. Certainly child poverty has reduced in Scotland but it remains arguable as to whether GIRFEC, the 'mechanism that delivers', along with the myriad other policy frameworks, has evidentially boosted the life chances of children.

The context of children and families policy in Scotland is centred around giving every child the best possible start in life which, in turn, feeds in to the overarching Scottish agenda defined by the current SNP administration's economic aspirations as referred to above (Scottish Government 2007a: v). The aim of such an approach, couched in terms of success, opportunity, and a flourishing Scotland, sits within philosophical and ethical constructions of individual worth and what constitutes a just society and the mechanisms construed as valid by which to create this. It also reflects the belief, often stated by the Scottish Government (Scottish Executive 2001a), that disadvantage in a child's life, particularly the early years, will influence the whole of the child's life span deleteriously, reaching across subsequent generations, negatively, in the form of intergenerational social exclusion (Stafford and Vincent 2008).

Any reading of social policy in this area would benefit from keeping in mind that the significant raft of recent policy initiatives, frameworks, guidance and enabling legislation is predicated, therefore, on bringing together the previously atomised components of life that affect children, for example health, education, criminal justice, substance problems and domestic violence, and that constitute the construction of 'childhood' (James and Prout 2003; Smith 2010) into a more relational, coherent dialogue.

To this end, the then Scottish Office published the report *Social Justice: A Scotland Where Everyone Matters* (Scottish Executive 1999a), following this in the same year with its *Child Strategy Statement: Working Together for Scotland's Children* (Scottish Executive 1999b). This states that

> ... all Departments of the Scottish Executive consider the impact of all policies on children before they are implemented. (para. 5)

Such an integrated approach heralded the repositioning of children as 'the future' – oft stated by the then Scottish Executive – and therefore that significant efforts were required to be made in order that they should be afforded universal and targeted *provision*, *protection* and that their *participation* in society and in the decisions made for and on behalf of them should be ensured.

There has been a consequential rise in the volume of policy relating to children and families in the past ten years, evidencing the Scottish Executive's and, latterly, Government's efforts in achieving these aims. Whilst this can be experienced as bewildering, the boxed text, whilst not exhaustive, illustrates some of the current terrain, scope and direction of policy in Scotland, specifically by looking at *It's Everyone's Job to Make Sure I'm Alright: Report of the Child Protection Audit and Review* (2002) and *Getting it Right For Every Child* (GIRFEC).

It's Everyone's Job to Make Sure I'm Alright: Report of the Child Protection Audit and Review (2002)

This audit and review remains heavily influential, in that not only has it led to significant developments in joining up services and reviewing practice and legislation, but clearly it articulates that children and families, particularly those most vulnerable or at risk, have not always received 'the help they need when they need it' (Scottish Executive 2002a: 9). Importantly the Children's Hearing System (Scottish Children's Reporter Administration (SCRA)) was found to require review.

This report occasioned a three-year reform programme both of children's services but also of organisational structures, resulting in key developments. Central to this reform programme were the aims of providing improved early-years support and intervention, improved direct help to those children in need of protection, and improvements in continuing support to prevent the reoccurrence of protection concerns (Stafford and Vincent 2008: 58; Daniel, Vincent and Ogilvie-Whyte 2007). The Scottish Government identified key outputs involving:

- a children's charter
- a framework for standards
- multi-agency inspections

along with a refocusing and clarification of child protection with respect to Child Protection Committees, inter-agency training and the introduction of Significant Incident Review Guidance. A significant area of the review programme has been the review of the Children's Hearing System

Getting it Right For Every Child (GIRFEC)

The Scottish Government (2008b) indicates that this policy stream is:

'... the foundation for work with *all* children and young people and will also affect practitioners in adult services who work with parents or carers. It builds on universal health and education services and drives the developments that will improve outcomes for children and young people by changing the way adults think and act to help all children and young people grow, develop and reach their full potential' (Scottish Government 2008b: 6).

The Getting It Right for Every Child policy stream suggests a change in culture at both organisational and civic levels, along with an overhaul of systems and practice in direct and associated professional arenas. Importantly, the Scottish Government positions the GIRFEC approach as assisting in feeding in to the core strategy of growing the Scottish economy. In working with children and young people to become successful learners, confident individuals, effective contributors and responsible citizens (Scottish Government 2008b) individuals become more equipped to take up and contribute to economic (and moral) activity, not least in employment, which has a corresponding impact on 'develop(ing) full opportunities for all' (Scottish Government 2008b: 7).

A foundation stone of the GIRFEC approach is that policy, across boundaries and within more closely defined children and families policies, address the dimensions of a child's life represented in the SHANARRI approach. This framework indicates that children require to be *Safe, Healthy, Achieving, Nurtured, Active, have Responsibility, be Respected, and be Included.*

In order to trial, refine and develop the GIRFEC policy and practice approach, 'pathfinder' initiatives were established. For example, Inverness became a 'pathfinder' location, with representatives from the Highland Council, NHS Highland, SCRA and Northern Constabulary joining together to explore training and to practice developments along the GIRFEC integrated agenda (Scottish Government 2009).

Associated with the GIRFEC policy approach has been a flotilla of connected social policy developments concerning children and families, as can be seen in the introduction of the *Integrated Assessment, Planning and Recording Framework*, now more commonly understood as the My World Framework, to *The Mental Health of Children and Young People: A Framework for Promotion, Prevention and Care* (Scottish Government 2005; and see Hothersall, Maas-Lowit and Golightley 2008), whilst not forgetting *Getting it Right for Every Child in Foster Care and Kinship Care* (Scottish Government 2007b).

The integrationist and cross-cutting nature of much policy regarding children and families can be illustrated by the *National Domestic Abuse Delivery Plan for Children and Young People* (Scottish Government 2008c). It recognises the correlation of domestic abuse and the impact on children's optimum development, and seeks to address this. It also suggests that in order to achieve the aims set out in the GIRFEC approach, links need to be made and sustained with other policy agendas such as are evident in the policy areas of justice, health and education. Interestingly, the Delivery Plan referred to reiterates the arguably instrumental moralistic approach of much current policy when it notes that a crucial aspect of the policy is the development of '*community capacity*', as well as *family capacity*, in the provision of skills, knowledge and understanding (Scottish Government 2008c) orientated around values of equality and respect.

In late 2002, the Scottish Executive rolled out its consultation document *Integrated Strategy for the Early Years* (Scottish Executive 2002b). The document explored services to young children, identified as those in the pre-birth to five-years-old range, and set out key objectives, such as ensuring that the most vulnerable children should have integrated packages of health, care and education support, and also outlined outcomes and indicators of progress. This theme of early intervention and support to parents in the discharging of their parental responsibilities has firmly established itself in the children and families policy arena and can be seen within associated policies regarding, for example, pre-school education and the promotion of the Sure Start (Scotland) initiatives. In more recent years, the approach has been consolidated, as reflected within the *Early Years and Early Intervention: A Joint Scottish Government and COSLA Policy Statement* document published in March 2008 (Scottish Government 2008d). It articulated a move away from dealing with what it described as 'symptoms of inequality' (Scottish Government 2008d: 1) such as poor physical and mental health, towards the identification of the risk areas which, the Scottish Government argue, perpetuate inequality in the first place. The Minister for Children and Early Years, Adam Ingram, indicated at the time (Scottish Government 2008d: v) that the 'early intervention' approach provided the 'hallmark' of the Government's approach to improving lives and noted starkly that early intervention would connect to and resonate with the diversity of social policy areas.

The approach was consolidated in December 2008 through the publication of *Early Years Framework* (Scottish Government 2008a). The framework consists of key themes: building parenting and family capacity; creating communities through which to support children and families; the development of integrated services which fully meet the needs of children and families; and finally workforce development to support the framework. The framework, with an intended ten-year timeline, re-emphasises partnership working across agencies, voluntary organisations and with individual citizens.

The overarching reform programme in the children and families arena throughout the past decade has, as suggested, been one typified by cross-cutting policy agendas. Substance misuse was highlighted through the Home Office report *Hidden Harm* (Home Office 2003) leading to significant practice developments in Scotland (and see Chapter 16). Youth justice similarly has been highlighted, apparent within the Anti-Social Behaviour etc. (Scotland) Act 2004.

Exercise 14.2 Joining the dots?

In children and families social policy in Scotland, a key element is effective joint working. Reflect on your own practice environment and consider what initiatives there are to support joint working/inter-agency communication/joint decision-making processes.

The contemporary socio-political context

It appears that both the form, and to a large extent the *function*, of the family has changed in recent years, particularly since the beginning of the 1970s when a number of global factors occurred which subsequently compounded and heralded the rise of globalisation (George and Wilding 2002): electronic and other forms of mass-media, individualisation, ontological (personal) insecurity (Kraemer and Roberts 1996; Bauman 2007), social anxiety and a shift in the *governmental* function of the family. The family has always been seen as having a governance function, usually in the form of *patriarchy*, and although there have been perceived shifts in the ideologies underpinning the relationship between the state and the family, the neo-liberal policies of the 1980s and 1990s, espoused by the Thatcher Governments, increased the focus upon *individualism* which led to assumptions being made about those families who experienced difficulties with parenting, or who did not conform to stereotypical notions of 'benign functionalism' (Todd, Hothersall and Owen 2010). The perceived difficulties were assumed to arise largely from the families themselves, particularly the parents, who were often *pathologised* as being in some way inadequate and, some would say, necessarily subjected to increased surveillance by the government and its agents (Parton 2006). In those situations where there are legitimate concerns for the well being of children, these are often conceptualised as arising from within the family itself, rather than being seen as (in part at least) a response to the broader socio-economic and cultural forces impacting on society in these times of late modernity (Beck 1992; Mullaly 2007).

More recently, some of the core functions of the family (Maccoby 2000) are increasingly undertaken within the broad context of 'social parenting' whereby increasing numbers of children are often cared for by adults who are not their biological parents. Many recent policy initiatives have promoted out-of-home care for many children, often wrapped around broader employment-related policies.

The essentially neo-liberal focus on the family over recent years and its somewhat nascent position as one of the perceived moral anchor-points of late modernity has been paralleled by a raft of governmental and other initiatives designed to support it in its (sic) claim as the foundation-stone of, amongst other things, social order, morality and primary socialisation (often couched in terms of 'effective parenting'). Inevitably, these essentially stereotypical generalisations bring with them increased and perhaps unrealistic expectations which tend to reflect the norms of the ruling class, in this instance the middle classes and their behaviours, which are 'normalised' and then extrapolated for others to emulate. Walkerdine and Lucey's study (1989) illustrates one example of this in the area of parenting whilst Gillies's (2003; 2008) position could support the claim that working-class parents effectively become the target of (stigmatising?) *selective* welfare policies masquerading as 'universal beneficence'. Similarly, earlier comments regarding the governance of the family by the state should afford us a clear sense that available interpretations of child and family law, policy and practice *are* open to interpretation and in that respect should be available for negotiation; in the current climate surrounding the safeguarding of children there is a clear tendency towards *prescription, regulation* and *monitoring* on the part of government agencies which appears to compromise the capacity of professionals to use their professional knowledge and judgement in the way it was designed to be used, with the result that defensible decisions are now seen as being those which are largely made on *economic* rather than *professional* and *welfare* grounds.

An obvious example of the interface between the family and the state is that of social work with children and their families. Children are variously regarded as 'innocent', a manifestation of our futures and simultaneously demonised; witness the current demonisation of 'hoodies' and other young people who engage in what is described as 'anti-social behaviour'. This is not a new phenomenon; on the contrary, such divergent, confused, yet often parallel views have existed for millennia and represent the constructivist and relativistic nature of 'childhood' as a phenomenon (Berger and Luckman 1979; James and Prout 2003; Cunningham 2006; Smith 2010).

The family is seen as having a pivotal role to play in relation not only to the *care* of children but also in relation to their *control*. These differing dimensions are usually seen as two sides of the same coin, relative to the age and perceived level of ability and, *ergo*, of *responsibility* of the child or young person concerned. However, much social work practice is focused on the *protection* of children and young people, usually from harm occasioned upon them by others and sometimes from the harm they may do to themselves, unwittingly or otherwise, as well as the (re-?)education of parents in relation to, amongst other things, 'effective' parenting (Ghate 2002; Howe 2005).

Where a child is seen as being in need of protection, it is usually the case that such harm is likely to befall them at the hands of parents or other significant persons who have care or control of them on a regular basis. In most situations, the family is usually the core unit from within which the harm arises. The notion that the abuse of children is something generally perpetrated by strangers is something of an 'urban legend' and whilst an awareness of 'stranger danger' is a useful, culturally sanctioned self-protective strategy for children and young people, the real dangers tend to lie much closer to home (Crittenden 2008).

Child abuse and neglect in its many forms and facets (Corby 2006; Ferguson 2004) is a culturally relative phenomenon and one that 'rarely presents with unambiguous evidence' (Munro 2005: 381). The same can be said in relation to the abuse and neglect of vulnerable adults (Hothersall and Maas-Lowit 2010).

Chapter summary

This chapter has considered the development and growth of policy in relation to children and families from an historical perspective and has indicated that such developments have been representative of changes in society. We have also considered how policy responses have at times presented as being somewhat confusing with dichotomous positions being adopted at one and the same time. We have also seen how different themes and issues have developed and how ideological issues influence the shape and form of policy.

References

Archard, D. (2004), *Children's Rights and Childhood* (2nd edn) (London: Routledge).

Ashenden, S. (2004), *Governing Child Sexual Abuse: Negotiating the Boundaries of Public and Private, Law and Science* (London: Routledge).

Bauman, Z. (2007), *Liquid Times: Living in an Age of Uncertainty* (Cambridge: Polity Press).
Beck, U. (1992), *Risk Society: Towards a New Modernity* (London: Sage Publications).
Berger, P. and Luckman, T. (1979), *The Social Construction of Reality* (London: Peregrine Press/Penguin).
Biestek, F.P. (1961), *The Casework Relationship* (London: Unwin).
Blom-Cooper, L. (1985), *A Child in Trust: The Report of the Panel of Inquiry into the Circumstances Surrounding the Death of Jasmine Beckford* (London: Brent Council).
Bowlby, J. (1951a), *Maternal Care and Mental Health* (Geneva: WHO; London: HMSO; New York: Columbia University Press).
— (1951b), *Child Care and the Growth of Love* (Harmondsworth: Penguin).
— (1956), 'The Growth of Independence in the Young Child', *Royal Society of Health Journal* 76: 587–91.
— (1958), 'The Nature of the Child's Tie to his Mother', *International Journal of Psycho-Analysis* 39: 350–73.
Bronfenbrenner, U. (1979), *The Ecology of Human Behaviour* (Cambridge, MA: Harvard University Press).
Butler-Sloss, Lord Justice E. (1988), *Report of the Inquiry into Child Abuse in Cleveland 1987* (Cmnd 412) (London: HMSO).
Corby, B. (2006), *Child Abuse: Towards a Knowledge Base* (3rd edn) (Maidenhead: Open University Press).
Crittenden, P. (2008), *Raising Parents: Attachment, Parenting and Child Safety* (Devon: Willan Publishing).
Cunningham, H. (2006), *The Invention of Childhood* (London: BBC Books).
Daniel, B., Vincent, S. and Ogilvie-Whyte, S. (2007), *A Process Review of the Child Protection Reform Programme* (Edinburgh: Scottish Executive).
Department of Health and Social Security (1988), *Working Together: A Guide to Interagency Cooperation for the protection of Children from Abuse* (London: HMSO).
Fabian Society (2006), *Narrowing the Gap: Final Report of the Fabian Commission on Life Chances and Child Poverty* (London: Fabian Society).
Ferguson, H. (2004), *Protecting Children in Time: Child Abuse, Child Protection and the Consequences of Modernity* (Basingstoke: Palgrave Macmillan).
Foley, P. and Rixon, A. (2008), *Changing Children's Services: Working and Learning Together* (Milton Keynes: Open University Press).
Frost, N. and Parton, N. (2009), *Understanding Children's Social Care: Policy, Politics and Practice* (London: Sage).
General Social Care Council (GSCC) (2008), *Social Work at its Best: A Statement of Social Work Roles and Tasks for the 21st Century* (London: GSCC).
George, V. and Wilding, P. (2002), *Globalization and Human Welfare* (Basingstoke: Palgrave Macmillan).

Ghate, D. (2002), *Parenting in Poor Environments* (London: Jessica Kingsley).

Gillies, V. (2003), 'Family and Intimate Relationships: A Review of the Sociological Research', *Families and Social Capital Research Group Paper* 2 (London: South Bank University).

—— (2005), 'Meeting Parent's Needs? Discourses of "Support" and "Inclusion" in Family Policy', *Critical Social Policy* 25(1): 70–90.

—— (2008), 'Childrearing, Class and the New Politics of Parenting', *Sociology Compass* 2(3): 1079–95.

Hallett, C. and Prout, A. (2003), *Hearing the Voices of Children: Social Policy for a New Century* (Abingdon: Routledge Falmer).

Hammond, H. (2001), *Child Protection Inquiry into the Circumstances Surrounding the Death of Kennedy McFarlane, d.o.b. 17 April 1997* (Dumfries and Galloway Child Protection Committee).

Henricson, C. and Bainham, A. (2005), *The Child and Family Policy Divide: Tension, Convergence and Rights* (York: Joseph Rowntree Foundation).

Higham, P. (2005), *Multi-Professional Practice and the Art of Social Work.* Available at: http://www.ssrg.org.uk/assembly/index.asp (accessed 28 May 2010).

HMSO (1992), *The Report of the Inquiry into the Removal of Children from Orkney in February 1991* (The Clyde Report) (Edinburgh: HMSO).

Home Office (2003), *Hidden Harm* (London: Home Office).

Hood, C. and Jones, D.K.C. (eds) (1996), *Accident and Design: Contemporary Debates on Risk Management* (London: Routledge).

Horton, T. and Gregory, J. (2009), *The Solidarity Society: Why We Can Afford to End Poverty, and How to Do it with Public Support* (London: Fabian Society).

Hothersall, S.J. (2008), *Social Work with Children, Young People and their Families in Scotland* (2nd edn) (Exeter: Learning Matters).

Hothersall, S.J. and Maas-Lowit, M. (eds) (2010), *Need, Risk and Protection in Social Work Practice* (Exeter: Learning Matters).

Hothersall, S.J., Maas-Lowit, M. and Golightley, M. (2008), *Social Work and Mental Health in Scotland* (Exeter: Learning Matters).

Howe, D. (2005), *Child Abuse and Neglect: Attachment, Development and Intervention* (Basingstoke: Palgrave Macmillan).

James, A. and Prout, A. (eds) (2003), *Constructing and Reconstructing Childhood* (2nd edn) (London: Routledge Falmer).

Jones, G. and Bell, R. (2000), *Balancing Acts: Youth, Parenting and Public Policy* (York: Joseph Rowntree Foundation).

Juleff, L., Kelly, L., Adams, J. and McQuaid, R.W. (2005), *The European Influence on Social Policy in Scotland: Changing Terminology or Changing Practice?* (Edinburgh: Napier University).

Kempe, H., Silverman, F., Steele, B., Droegemueller, W. and Silver, H. (1962), 'The Battered Child Syndrome', *Journal of the American Medical Association* 181(1): 17–24.

Kraemer, S. and Roberts, J. (eds) (1996), *The Politics of Attachment: Towards a Secure Society* (London: Free Association Books).

Laming, H. (2009), *The Protection of Children in England: A Progress Report* (London: Stationery Office).

— (2003), *The Victoria Climbie Inquiry* (London: Stationery Office).

Maccoby, E.E. (2000), 'Parenting and Its Effects on Children: On Reading and Misreading Behaviour Genetics', *Annual Review of Psychology* 51: 1–27.

McLean, T. (2007), 'Interdisciplinary Practice', in J. Lishman (ed.), *Handbook for Practice Learning in Social Work and Social Care* (2nd edn) (London: Jessica Kingsley).

Milligan, I. (2009), *Higher Aspirations, Brighter Futures*. NRCCI Commissioning Report (Glasgow: Scottish Institute for Residential Child Care).

Mullaly, B. (2007), *The New Structural Social Work* (3rd edn) (Toronto: Oxford University Press).

Munro, E. (2005), 'What Tools Do We Need to Improve Identification of Child Abuse?', *Child Abuse Review* 14: 374–88.

O'Brien, S., Hammond, H. and McKinnon, M. (2003), *Report of the Caleb Ness Inquiry* (Edinburgh: Edinburgh and Lothians Child Protection Committee).

Parton, N. (2006), *Safeguarding Childhood: Early Intervention and Surveillance in a Late Modern Society* (Basingstoke: Palgrave Macmillan).

Rodger, J.J. (2000), *From a Welfare State to a Welfare Society: The Changing Context of Social Policy in a Postmodern Era* (Basingstoke: Palgrave Macmillan).

Scottish Executive (1999a), *Social Justice: A Scotland Where Everyone Matters* (Edinburgh: Scottish Executive).

— (1999b), *Child Strategy Statement: Working Together for Scotland's Children* (Edinburgh: Scottish Executive).

— (2001a), *Changing Children's Services Fund* (Edinburgh: Scottish Executive).

— (2001b), *For Scotland's Children: Better Integrated Children's Services* (Edinburgh: Scottish Executive).

— (2002a), *It's Everyone's Job to Make Sure I'm Alright: Report of the Child Protection Audit and Review* (Edinburgh: Scottish Executive).

— (2002b), *Integrated Strategy for the Early Years* (Edinburgh: Scottish Executive).

— (2004a), *Curriculum for Excellence* (Edinburgh: Scottish Government).

— (2004b), *Integrated Children's Services Planning Guidance* (Edinburgh: Scottish Government).

— (2005), *Getting it Right for Every Child: Proposals for Action* (Edinburgh: Scottish Executive).

—— (2006a), *Transforming Public Services* (Edinburgh: Scottish Executive).
—— (2006b), *Changing Lives* (Edinburgh: Scottish Executive).
Scottish Government (2005), *The Mental Health of Children and Young People: A Framework for Promotion, Prevention and Care* (Edinburgh: Scottish Government).
—— (2007a), *The Government Economic Strategy* (Edinburgh: Scottish Government).
—— (2007b), *Getting it Right for Every Child in Foster Care and Kinship Care* (Edinburgh: Scottish Government).
—— (2007c), *Looked After Children and Young People: We Can and Must Do Better* (Edinburgh: Scottish Government).
—— (2008a), *Early Years Framework* (Edinburgh: Scottish Government).
—— (2008b), *A Guide to Getting it Right for Every Child* (Edinburgh: Scottish Government).
—— (2008c), *National Domestic Abuse Delivery Plan for Children and Young People* (Edinburgh: Scottish Government).
—— (2008d), *Early Years and Early Intervention: A Joint Scottish Government and COSLA Policy Statement* (Edinburgh: Scottish Government).
—— (2009), *Changing Professional Practice and Culture to Get it Right for Every Child* (Edinburgh: Scottish Government).
Scottish Office (1998), *Protecting Children: A Shared Responsibility. Guidance on Interagency Cooperation* (Edinburgh: Scottish Office).
Smith, R. (2010), *A Universal Child?* (Basingstoke: Palgrave Macmillan).
Social Work Inspection Agency (SWIA) (2005), *An Inspection into the Care and Protection of Children in Eilean Siar* (Edinburgh: Scottish Executive).
Stafford, A. and Vincent, S. (2008), *Safeguarding and Protecting Children and Young People* (Edinburgh: Dunedin Academic Press).
Sterling Burnett, H. (2009), 'Understanding the Precautionary Principle and its Threat to Human Welfare', *Social Philosophy and Policy* 26: 378–410.
Tawney, R.H. (1983), *Equality* (London: Allen & Unwin).
Taylor, P. and Vatcher, A. (2005), 'Social Work', in G. Barrett, D. Sellman and J. Thomas (eds), *Interprofessional Working in Health and Social Care: Professional Perspectives* (Basingstoke: Palgrave Macmillan).
Todd, M., Hothersall, S.J and Owen, J. (2010), 'Intimacies and Relationships', in C. Yuill and A. Gibson (eds), *Sociology for Social Work Practice: An Introduction* (London: Sage).
Walkerdine, V. and Lucey, H. (1989), *Democracy in the Kitchen* (London: Virago Press).
Winnicott, D.W (1958), *Through Paediatrics to Psychoanalysis* (London: Hogarth Press).

Further reading

Hendrick, H. (ed.) (2005), *Child Welfare and Social Policy: An Essential Reader* (Bristol: Policy Press). This text offers a thorough exploration of a wide range of contemporary issues regarding children, families and policy.

McK Norrie, K. (1998), *The Children (Scotland) Act 1995*. Greens Annotated Acts (2nd edn) (Edinburgh: W. Green & Son).

Munro, E. (2008), *Effective Child Protection* (2nd edn) (London: Sage). A valuable text that takes a critical view of child protection.

Parton, N. (2006), *Safeguarding Childhood: Early Intervention and Surveillance in a Late Modern Society* (Basingstoke: Palgrave Macmillan). This text offers a valuable commentary on how changes in society are affecting how we perceive and respond to childhood and children.

Reder, P. and Duncan, S. (2004), 'Making the Most of the Victoria Climbié Inquiry Report', *Child Abuse Review* 13: 95–115.

— (2003), 'Understanding Communication in Child Protection Networks', *Child Abuse Review* 12: 82–100.

These two papers offer useful, pragmatic insights into different but related elements of child care and protection work.

Smith, M. (2009), *Rethinking Residential Child Care: Positive Perspectives* (Bristol: The Policy Press).

Web-based resources

The following website offers valuable information regarding the latest policy developments in relation to children and families in Scotland (and the rest of the UK).

http://childpolicyinfo.childreninscotland.org.uk/ (accessed 28 May 2010).

15 Education and training in Scotland

Janine Bolger

Introduction

This chapter will provide a summary of key developments in education since the creation of the Scottish Education Department in 1885. It will look at the state's role in the provision of education and the partnership between central and local government. The concept of life-long learning and training opportunities for 16–24 year olds will be explored. The chapter ends with the consideration of disadvantage within the education system with reference to social class, gender, disability and ethnicity.

Following devolution, new legislation dealing with education is now a matter for the Scottish Parliament. With the exception of a few sections which make reference to Scotland, Education Acts for England and Wales do not apply. The Education (Scotland) Acts are supplemented by regulations which have the force of law. They assume, unless the contrary is stated, that the provision of existing Acts are still in force.

There is a long and distinguished history of educational provision in Scotland. By the end of the fifteenth century there were already three universities in Scotland. St Andrews opened in 1411, Glasgow in 1451 and Aberdeen University in 1495. However, only the most privileged were able to attend. In the middle ages (1216–1347) schools were run by the Church and usually only the wealthiest, or those wishing to become priests, attended school at all. By the sixteenth century the burghs (towns) were involved in funding schools. In 1560 John Knox (1510–72), a renowned Protestant reformer, campaigned for elementary schools to be established in every parish (British Council, Scotland 2004).

Over the course of the seventeenth century the Scottish Parliament passed several Acts to encourage the establishing of schools. The final Act of the series (believed to be the first national Education Act) provided for a school in every parish, a fixed salary for the teacher and financial arrangements to cover the running costs. As a result of the many schools established in Scotland by the Church, societies, individuals or larger towns, by the mid nineteenth century a large proportion of the population was literate. The Factory Act 1802 and the Labour of Children in Factories Act 1833 ensured that children under the age of nine years could not work and, instead, were compelled to enrol in schools run by the factory owners. At this time children between the ages of nine and 13 years could work a maximum of eight hours each day while 14 to 18 year olds could be employed for up to 12 hours.

In 1840 the first Inspector of Schools for Scotland was appointed and major Government intervention in the education system began. Children living in the workhouse system (see Chapter 2), which operated from 1845 until 1931, were given up to three hours education each day. The focus of teaching in these institutions was on reading, writing, arithmetic and the principles of Christian religion. In 1864 a commission was set up to examine the state of education in Scotland which led to the most important event in education in Scotland in the nineteenth century: The Education (Scotland) Act 1872.

This act created a Board of Education for Scotland, established the responsibility of parents to ensure that five to 13 year olds received education and provided funding for education from a local property tax. It also established the principle that all head teachers required a certificate of competency to teach and that all teachers should be trained. It took education out of the hands of the Church and made it the responsibility of local elected bodies (school boards) through the local authorities. Initially fees were charged for school attendance unless you were lucky enough to live in an industrial area such as Edinburgh or Aberdeen where there was a charity or 'ragged school' which provided free education, food and sometimes clothing and lodging for those who were too poor to pay. The 1878 Factory Act increased the age at which children could work to ten years and reduced the number of hours that ten to 14 year olds could work to half days.

In 1885 The Scotch (later Scottish) Education Department was created. It was initially located in London but moved to Edinburgh in 1922. Following this a single external exam system was established in 1888 and 1890 saw the introduction of free primary education for all. The age for compulsory education was extended to 14 years in 1901 although this was relaxed for those over the age of ten who had reached the approved standard in reading, writing and arithmetic.

There were further striking developments up to 1945. Two hundred new secondary schools were founded between the years 1900 and 1914. From 1918 until 1936 local education authorities were created to replace school boards. Schools owned and run by the Roman Catholic Church came into the state education system in 1918. The Education (S) Act 1936 defined Scottish primary education as covering five to 12 years and separated it clearly from secondary education.

Post Second World War

After the Second World War we saw the publication of major reports reviewing primary and secondary education. 'The Primary Memorandum' (1965) set out the curriculum for primary schools and was designed to catch the interests of children with a wide range of abilities together with the development of teaching methods suitable for mixed ability classes (children proceeding at different rates in the same class). In secondary education the aim of equal educational opportunity was met via the change from selective (through the 11 plus exam) to comprehensive schools. General changes to the public examination system increased accessibility to larger numbers creating the need for bigger schools. The 1960s also saw a rapid extension of vocational further education provision through evening classes, full-time and day-release courses taught in almost 50 new F.E. colleges.

The Munn Report (Scottish Education Department 1977b) established the Curriculum in third and fourth years of Scottish secondary schools. The 1978 HMI Report (quoted in Scottish Parliament 2000) picked up on this and suggested that it necessitated an ending of remedial education in mainstream schools. *The Dunning Report* (Scottish Education Department 1977a) informed the exam system as we know it in Scotland by introducing assessment for all at the age of 16 years. Its aim was to provide for the whole school population at leaving age.

The Warnock Report of 1978 put an end to labelling and introduced the term 'special needs', stating that children with such needs should be educated in mainstream schools wherever possible. These recommendations were finally embedded in The 1981 Education Amendment (Scotland) Act. It also embodied the notion of partnership, encouraging parents to participate in decisions about their child's perceived 'special needs' (Northampton University 2002). The 1980 Education (Scotland) Act which was also based on partnership with parents gave the power to provide pre-school education and stated the ages of compulsory education. Through the 1980s the Government introduced measures to involve parents more fully through representation on school boards and resulted in the publication of a Parent's

Charter in 1991 (revised in 1995) (Bridges and Jonathan 2002). Continuing on this theme, The 1981 Education Amendment (Scotland) Act gave parents rights to choose the most appropriate school for their child (Highlight 1995). However, this Act is incompatible with the Children (Scotland) Act 1995 in that there is no independent right of action for a child under 16 years. It is also in breach of Article 12 of the United Nations Convention on the Rights of the Child in that it appears that the child does not have the right to express their view on this matter. The 1981 Act supported the concept of special needs identified in the publication of the Warnock Report (1978) and established the Record of Needs.

Case Study

Jane Gray is 15 years old. Following the separation of her parents and a subsequent house move she has developed a pattern of non-school attendance. Mrs Gray claims that her daughter is being bullied. When Jane was spoken to by the guidance teacher she disclosed that her mother's mental health has deteriorated and that she (Jane) is staying at home to help look after her baby brother. Mrs Gray would like Jane to be enrolled in the local Catholic school which is closer to the family home.

The Education (Scotland) Act 1980 and the 1981 Education Amendment (Scotland) Act can be used to help this family.

The 1981 Act amends section 28 of the 1980 Act and states that pupils should be 'educated in accordance with the wishes of their parents. Where the parent makes a written request to an education authority to place his child in a specified school, being a school under their management, it shall be their duty to place the child accordingly' unless such a move would incur additional costs or resources or would be detrimental to the child or to the discipline of others.

Mrs Gray could make a written request to the education authority asking for Jane to be moved to the Catholic school. There would be no additional costs or resources incurred as the school is closer and there is no suggestion that Jane requires any additional support.

In the meantime, Mrs Gray has a duty to secure her daughter's attendance at school.

Section 35(1) of the 1980 Act states that, unless the education authority have consented to the withdrawal of the child from school, failure to ensure regular school attendance of a child will result in the parent being guilty of an offence (against this section). Any person found guilty of such an offence 'shall be liable, on conviction by a court ... to a fine ... or to imprisonment for a term not exceeding one month or to both such a fine and such imprisonment.'

Section 14 (Part 1) of the 1980 Act may assist the family in avoiding the above situation:

'S14(1) If an education authority are satisfied that by reason of

(a) any extraordinary circumstances

(ii) it would be unreasonable to expect the pupil to attend such an establishment shall make special arrangements for the pupil to receive education elsewhere.'

It could be argued, therefore, that the current family circumstances combined with a request for a change of schools to help ensure regular attendance would constitute 'extraordinary circumstances' and that any legal action towards the parent would only serve to exacerbate existing difficulties.

The 1980s saw a debate around *new vocationalism*. It introduced new qualifications with an emphasis on work related knowledge and skills to assist effective performance in the workplace. Education became more widely available in both further and higher education throughout the 1990s. As a result there was an increase in the number of universities and the establishment of Scottish Education funding. The Education (Scotland) Act 1996 set up a new exam authority in the form of the Scottish Qualifications Authority (SQA) which took on responsibility for the development, accreditation, assessment and certification of qualifications other than degrees. It also granted powers to the Scottish Minister for Education to introduce regular testing and assessment at S1 and S2 stages.

In 1997 the Scottish Office launched *A Curriculum Framework for Children in their Pre-School Year* (H.M. Inspector of Schools 1997) which they extended with additional guidelines in 1999. It recognised the value of a range of experiences that children in the three to five age range could have both within day care and home settings. It also recognised the central importance of relationships in learning for children during the early years. Development and learning was promoted in the following areas:

- emotional, personal and social development
- communication and language
- knowledge and understanding
- expressive and aesthetic development
- physical development and movement (Scottish Consultative Council 1999: 5).

The inter-relationship between assessment, planning, staff interaction, reporting, recording, reflection and evaluating was also emphasised.

Guidance on the planning of pre-school education and childcare and the establishment of Childcare Partnerships (1998) was key to the introduction of the Green Paper *Meeting the Childcare Challenge: A Childcare Strategy for Scotland* in May 1998 (Scottish Executive 1998). Three key medium-term goals were outlined around the securing of good quality, part-time pre-school education for every child where the parent wishes to have one (by 1998/1999) and (by 2002) for every three-year-old where the parent wants a place; the increase of quality childcare, for children aged from birth to 14 years, that is accessible and affordable; an integration of early-years service provision. This document clearly linked early education and the work agenda through childcare and family tax credits. Powers were given to education authorities to provide pre-school education in centres other than its own schools, for example private day nurseries, playgroups and so on can be commissioned to offer services on behalf of the council. Such provision became known as 'partner providers'. Furthermore, the notion of planning provision would be supported and overseen by the creation of Childcare Partnerships from the network of local child care providers (Scottish Executive 1998).

The guidance and the subsequent Green Paper also led to the establishment of Childcare Information Services in each local authority. The idea behind the partnerships is to provide information for parents with regard to the availability of local child care and to assist, through funding and offering advice, the introduction of more child care and out of school care. In order to meet SSSC requirements this has necessitated training for all early years and out of school care workers.

The Beattie Committee (Scottish Government 1999) reported on post school education and training for young people with special needs.

1998 also saw the introduction of the National Grid for Learning (NGFL), which intended to support, sustain and renew IT development in schools for teachers and pupils. Over £130 million has been designated to this project since 1999. However, information communication technology (ICT) in early years education did not receive a great deal of attention until five years later, when the report *Early Learning Forward Thinking: The Policy Framework for ICT in Early Years* (2003) was published. For this age group ICT includes the use of computers, digital cameras and printers, digital toys and electronic equipment. Despite the delay, it is thought that Scotland is the first country in the world to have an ICT strategy for under fives (Scottish Executive 2003c).

1999 introduced Phase one of pilot projects on Integrated Community Schools. Thirty-seven projects were developed as part of the Scottish Executive's Social Inclusion strategy. Projects vary from single primary/ secondary schools to cluster schemes. Projects are designed locally to meet local needs around:

1. needs of individual pupils
2. engagement with families
3. engagement with the wider community
4. integrated provision of education, social work and health education and promotion services (Scottish Executive 2002a).

In 2000 Sam Galbraith, the Minister for Children and Education at that time, launched a new self-evaluation guide *The Child at the Centre*. The new guide was intended as a practical support for use by all centres providing care and education for three to five year olds (Scottish Executive 2000).

The Standards in Scotland's Schools (Scotland) Act 2000 reiterated the notion that education should be tailored to age, ability and aptitude and should aim to develop the personality, talents and mental and physical abilities of children and young persons to their fullest potential. A greater differentiation of classroom work to match the range of abilities present and the increased attention to young people with special educational needs, whether in mainstream schools or special units, was called for.

The publishing of the *McCrone Report* in 2000 (agreed in 2001) offered a clearer career structure, better conditions of service, better pay and strategies for developing and supporting the teaching profession (McCrone 2000).

In 2002 the National Care Standards for Early Education and Childcare up to the Age of 16 were introduced. They are regulated under The Regulation of Care (Scotland) Act 2001 through the Care Commission. The standards reflect the rights of children and young people as set out in the United Nations Convention on the Rights of the Child (signed up for in 1991). The emphasis is on the resource to interpret the standards and provide evidence of this to the Commission. The most specific standards are around staffing ratio, space and policies (National Care Standards Committee 2002). During this same period *Meeting the Needs of Children from Birth to Three* was published (2002) using findings from research to guide professionals in the care of very young children. Based on this document, local authorities are expected to provide training for the sector and resources are inspected using this as a guide to good practice (Scottish Executive 2003d).

The Education (Ministerial Powers of Direction) Bill (2003) strengthened ministers' powers to work with the local authority to raise standards in Scotland's schools. In cases where established steps of inspection and/or professional support and development do not secure improvements, powers are extended to intervene as a last resort. It also enables ministers to ensure that education authorities carry out actions identified by the Inspectorate (Scottish Executive 2003b).

In 2003 the criteria for free school meals was extended to include families on child tax credit and families where parents are students. New nutrient standards for school meals were also introduced along with the provision of larger portions of nutritious food at no extra cost (Scottish Executive 2003a). *Nutritional Guidance for Early Years* (Scottish Executive 2006b) followed in 2006 and is an important feature of all integrated and Care Commission-only inspections of pre-school and child care settings. The focus on guidance around the provision of meals for early years, primary and secondary levels has been keenly debated at national and local levels while the media have reported on the more extreme reactions from disapproving parents (Scottish Executive 2006c).

In 2003 the project *Building Our Future: Scotland's School Estate* resulted in the significant refurbishment or the rebuilding of 300 schools and 75 other schools were 'improved' (Scottish Executive 2003e).

Under the Education (Additional Support for Learning) (Scotland) Act 2004 the term Special Educational Needs is replaced by Additional Support Needs and the Record of Needs document is replaced by a Coordinated Support Plan. In addition, new duties are specified under this Act so that an integrated service is provided through joined-up working, co-ordinated support plans are reviewed annually and will focus on the individual's educational outcomes, and the rights for children and parents are strengthened with a duty placed on schools to provide new mediation services for those with additional support needs (Scottish Executive 2004).

Case Study

Jamie McDonald is five years old and about to begin school. He has been diagnosed with an autistic spectrum disorder and has not yet developed verbal skills. His parent would like him to be supported so that he can be educated in the local mainstream primary school.

Under the Education (Additional Support for Learning) (Scotland) Act 2004 we can determine whether Jamie has additional support needs:

Under section 1 of the Act Jamie would be considered as having 'additional support needs' if for 'whatever reason, the child or young person is likely to be unable, without the provision of additional support, to benefit from school education provided for them'. Under the same section 'additional support' describes any 'provision which is additional to, or otherwise different from, the educational provision made generally for children'.

We currently have insufficient information to inform us as to whether Jamie is likely to require additional or different provision in order to develop verbal skills. However, even if he already utilises an alternative communication system the school may require specially trained staff to assist them in communicating with Jamie.

A 'Co-ordinated support plan' (CSP) will be required if the situation satisfies one or more of the following conditions:

Under S.2(1)

'(a) if an education authority are responsible for the school education of the child or young person

(b) and [they have] needs arising from–

(i) one or more complex factors, or

(ii) multiple factors

(c) those needs are likely to continue for more than a year

(d) those needs require significant additional support to be provided'

then the child will be considered as requiring a CSP.

Under section 3 of the Act this child might be considered as 'lacking capacity' if he satisfies the following criteria:

S.3(1) if they lack capacity to do something 'if they are incapable of doing it by reason of mental illness, developmental disorder or learning disability or of inability to communicate because of a physical disability'

(2) but not by reason of a deficiency that 'can be made good by human or mechanical aid.'

If Jamie is able to communicate using alternatives to speech then he would not be considered as lacking in capacity.

If it is unclear what supports will be necessary then an assessment or examination could be requested:

S.8(1)(a)(i) 'to establish whether the child has additional support needs or requires ... a co-ordinated support plan'

The education authority must comply with the above unless it is believed to be an unreasonable request.

The education authority has a duty to prepare a CSP under S.9(1) if it established that one is required. The CSP must contain:

S.9(2)(a) 'a statement of the education authority's conclusions as to–

(i) the factor(s) from which the additional support needs arise

(ii) the educational objectives to be achieved taking into account that factor

(iii) the additional support required to achieve those objectives

(iv) the persons by whom the support should be provided'

Under section 10 of the Act the CSP will be reviewed:

S.10(2)(a) after 12 months beginning with the date the plan was prepared and

(b) every 12 months thereafter.

(3) or before that time if (a) requested or (b) deemed necessary by the authority because of a significant change in circumstances.

November 2004 saw the introduction of 12 key actions to improve Scotland's schools which emphasised achievement with rewards given for the best schools and a greater amount of inspections to be carried out.

The Scottish Schools (Parental Involvement) Act 2006 modernises the notion of partnership with parents with an expectation that education authorities will actively promote such involvement in their child's learning, the daily life of the school and in considering general educational issues. The idea behind such a partnership is that the achievement and behaviour of a child can be improved through parental involvement and emphasises the notion of shared responsibility. Specific mention is made of parental involvement in early years education and in transitional arrangements. The Act makes provision for representation by parents on the School Council through either the Parent Forum or through Parent Councils (if the forum wishes to create one) (Scottish Executive 2006d).

In 2006 ministers began to stimulate discussion and debate about aspirations for children and young people through A Curriculum for Excellence (Scottish Executive 2006a). The future shape of the curriculum and the most appropriate approaches to teaching and learning in order to achieve such aspirations have been the focus of the consultation through conferences and professional development events. A network of education authority contacts will lead change within their own authority. Related programmes, for example 'Assessment is for Learning' and 'Determined to Succeed' have been considered in order to promote coherence across policy areas. Key features for early years education are around the transition from pre-school to Primary 1 and the involvement of parents and the transfer of individual assessments of children between relevant staff. In order to assist in the transition, the P1 curriculum is to place a greater emphasis on learning through play (Scottish Executive 2006a). Furthering the political emphasis on early years education, three authorities in Scotland launched two-year pilots in April 2006 to encourage educational provision for vulnerable two year olds. Although many parents appear to be unhappy about it not being offered as a universal service, it should result in additional funding for family centres and nursery schools who agree to take on two year olds.

Additionally, in February 2006 HMIE launched its report Improving Scottish Education 2002–2005, giving an overview of the Scottish education system. Strengths and weaknesses were identified and an agenda for improvement was set and has been implemented through both local and national policy. A follow-up report, covering the period 2005–2008, examines an even more comprehensive range of services and functions including the educational psychology services, prison learning, skills and employability and local authority child protection services (HM Inspectorate of Education 2009).

As part of the key project in the National Plan for Gaelic (2007–2012), a study of existing provision, factors that facilitate and inhibit the development of Gaelic medium provision and of the support necessary to develop sustainable, high quality Gaelic medium pre-school education and child care began in January 2009 (Scottish Executive 2009).

Training

Cutting youth unemployment was one of the five pre-election pledges for the last Westminster Government. The programme was considered so important that a special windfall tax was levied upon utility companies to raise money for the New Deal for Young People (NYFDP), launched in April 1998 (BBC News Online 2002a). The NYFDP is managed and delivered by the Scottish and Highland and Island Enterprise for 18–24 year olds who have been unemployed for six months or more. It involves helping young people find employment for the first four months and if successful giving four programme options involving a combination of training and work experience (EIROnline 2002). One might question, however, what is new about it as there were Youth Training Schemes (YTS) in the 1970s and 1980s. Such schemes were unpopular because poor training allowances were given; there was evidence of poor progression to full-time employment; the poorest outcomes were attained by those who had been disadvantaged from the start, for example, those with the lowest qualifications were allocated the least desirable schemes; and these schemes operated in a restricted labour market and so success in recruitment of training was linked with a lack of jobs. So, let us consider how the NDFYP matches up. In March 2004 statistics showed that since its implementation, 56,600 young people have gained employment through the New Deal. However, it should be noted that the NDFYP came on stream when unemployment was falling anyway and we cannot be sure that many of these young people would not have gained employment without the assistance of NDFYP (BBC News Online 2002b).

In addition, over 50,000 young people had been awarded vocational qualifications through Skill-seekers, set up to assist 16–24 year olds in employment and offering guaranteed funding for 16- and 17-year-old school and college leavers, either in or out of employment. Skill-seekers is the Scottish brand for youth, work-based training run by local enterprise companies (LECs) to provide financial support to employers to allow young people to train towards a recognised workplace qualification. All skill-seekers must follow a Vocational Qualification (VQ) at level 1 or 2.

Higher levels of VQ can be gained under the Modern Apprenticeships which provide paid employment combined with the opportunity to train towards jobs at craft, technician and management levels. They are targeted at the 16–24 year old age group providing work based training to SVQ level 3 or above (with a core skills element). It is based on employer-led frameworks through the enterprise networks. Also we have seen the introduction of Modern Apprenticeships. These have employed status but seem to be allocated to the most promising young people and are offered by the most committed employers (Scottish Executive 1997).

Despite the schemes outlined above, 40 per cent of school leavers in Scotland are not in education, employment or training (NEETs), a figure similar to that of a decade ago. The Government outlined their strategy for dealing with this issue in 2006 in the form of the report *More Choices, More Chances* (Scottish Government 2006).

Disadvantage and disaffection

Class

More middle-class and upper-class children are likely to attend state schools in prosperous areas and to be among the 7 per cent who attend private schools (The Guardian 2002). Working-class children are still more likely to attend run-down schools in poorer areas (Hagell and Shaw 1996). We see that the patterns begin early. Middle-class/upper-class children are more likely to have access to facilities for carrying out homework and will possess the language skills liked and encouraged by schools. Cardak and Ryan (2006) found that teenagers with ability but from poorer backgrounds were under-represented at university. Approximately 16 out of 20 teenagers from high income families attend university. Only three from lower-income families do. However, when studying at university it was found that students from working-class backgrounds achieve as highly as those from the middle or upper classes. For those children who are looked-after the situation looks even more bleak. Only one child in every hundred gets the opportunity to attend university (Who Cares? Scotland 2004). The educational issues for looked-after and accommodated children and young people have been more recently highlighted in reports such as *We Can and Must Do Better* (Scottish Government 2007); *Count Us In: Improving the Education of our Looked After Children* (H.M. Inspectorate of Education 2008); and *Getting it Right for Every Child* (Scottish Government 2004).

Current strategies in place to help children from more disadvantaged backgrounds include alternatives to exclusions such as the Integrated Community Schools network. There is a growing recognition that under-achievement begins early in the school career and is often linked to poor arrangements for learning support. In excess of £20 million has been allocated to promote integration of children who have additional support needs and, in addition, more than £8m from the Standards Fund to promote inclusion.

Gender

Issues of gender can be seen to merge with those of class but gender is also an area of concern in its own right. Generally it appears that girls do better in education up to age 16 (BBC News Online 2001). It seems that girls continue to make stereotypical choices with regard to areas of study and with respect to choices of career. Women continue to be over-represented in low-paid jobs which include part-time employment. With regard to attainment, in public schools, boys obtain better 'A' level/higher results whilst girls obtain better GCSE/standard grade results. Girls in single-sex comprehensive schools, however, achieve higher results than their peers in co-ed schools or single-sex male comprehensives. Later on in their educational career, at university level more women obtain upper seconds while more men receive firsts, thirds and passes. We see that women tend to choose arty, creative 'soft' subjects whilst men choose science-based subjects (though not biology). Women now constitute the majority of applications to higher education. The Qualifications and Curriculum Authority (1998) concluded that the obstacle to achievement for boys is a 'laddish' culture that deters hard work and enthusiasm (Kendall et al. 2008).

Ethnicity

Underachievement in primary school can be related to levels of fluency in English and insufficient access to extra support. By the end of secondary education the results appear to be more class-specific regardless of ethnic origin. In 1994 Ofsted, the Office for Standards in Education (England), reported that the educational achievement of ethnic minority pupils was improving. However, they found that:

- Children from travelling families are most at risk educationally.
- Pakistani pupils' performance is below that of indigenous peers, however, once they become proficient in English their performance matches or surpasses that of native English speakers (Gillborn and Mirza 2000).
- Black Caribbean pupils tend to begin well at primary school but the performance deteriorates in secondary education (Department for Education and Skills 2002, as cited in Mamon 2003).
- Generally girls from ethnic minority groups attain most highly.

Even among groups born in the UK, Blackburn, Dale and Jarman (1997) show that Chinese, Other-Asian and Black-African groups were highly qualified while Black-Caribbean, Pakistani and Bangladeshi groups were far behind. Cheng (1996) suggests that for some ethnic groups there could be a cultural and traditional emphasis placed on education.

Impairment/disability

Studies on the progression of children and young people with impairments tend to be small-scale, often single cases with poor evidence. The 2001 school census showed that children with disabilities make up approximately 6 per cent of the school population in Scotland (45,701 with special education needs). About 2 per cent (16,000) of Scottish school children have a Record of Needs (RONs) under the old Act. Approx 57 per cent of children with special needs are taught in mainstream school but only 29 per cent of those with RON spend all their time in mainstream classes.

Disabled people, it appears, are three times as likely to have no qualifications as non-disabled while 19 per cent of 16–24 year olds with disabilities have no qualifications (compared to 6 per cent of non-disabled in same age group). In 2001 only 4 per cent (6,912) of higher education students declare that they are disabled (Disability Rights Commission 2003).

Little has been implemented by successive governments following the 1978 Warnock Report which stated that wherever possible children with disabilities should be educated in mainstream schools. This has been reinforced in the Great British Special Educational Needs and Disability Act 2001.

The Disability Discrimination Act 1995 ignores education other than to recommend that there is a duty to provide access. However, the Education (Disability Strategies and Pupils' Educational Records) (Scotland) Act 2002 has supported the requirements of the 1995 Act and covers such issues as accessibility strategies with regard to the building and curriculum (Scottish Executive 2002b).

Conclusion

In conclusion, then, in order to combat disadvantage in education and training more successful strategies should be employed throughout schooling rather than looking at problems of those aged 16 and over. Plans for the Education and Skills Bill (England and Wales) will require all 16 to 18 year olds to remain in education or training by 2015, however, by this stage in their schooling many youth have already become disaffected. After-school clubs during the earlier years of education can offer additional time for young people to acquire the knowledge, and practice the skills, that they require. Youth programmes can be utilised to help young people engage in diverse groups which encourage and acknowledge the contribution of participants (Miller 2004).

Educational issues which relate to the community, family and environment should be considered. Engaging with those who did not have successful experiences within the education system can also be carried out within the community. Projects through Sure Start, Skills for Life and Neighbourhood Renewal are already beginning to tackle this (National Literacy Trust 2005b). Addressing problems across all aspects of the young person's life was at the core of the Integrated (New) Community Schools projects in Scotland. Although there was little hard evidence of their success in the short term, it was suggested that three years was too short a period to judge the effectiveness of the projects (National Literacy Trust 2005a).

Long-term funding should be sought as financial interventions tend to be short-term and do not guarantee consistency or improved services in the long term.

To avoid conflict we should aim for a greater integration of policy across all agencies. Even where this exists it would appear that the enactment of such is problematic. For example, when examining the success of the Integrated (New) Community Schools in Scotland, it was found that a range of barriers resulted in problems with joint working. These included 'practical issues of different working hours, holiday arrangements and accommodation, and professional issues of confidentiality, procedures and levels of formality' (National Literacy Trust 2005a: 1).

Perhaps we should also look at what value we place on academic subjects. For example, society appears to pay little heed to the emotional IQ of children and young people. We value the 'hard' outcomes rather than 'soft' ones within the educational system as a whole and tend to neglect the importance of self-esteem and relationship building. Goleman (1996) argues that emotions play a greater role in thought and decision making than is usually acknowledged and is a key contributing factor to individual success.

Chapter summary

We have looked at the growth and development of educational provision across Scotland and the developments around training and further education opportunities. Our discussion has also considered some of the broader issues that may act as barriers to inclusion and some of the strategies in place to minimise these. We have also considered some of the issues for social work and professional practice.

References

BBC News Online (2001), 'Girls Top Exam League Again'. Available at: http://www.news.bbc.co.uk/1/low/scotland/1467053.stm (accessed 21 December 2009).

— (2002a), 'U.K. Politics. New Deal Claims "Exaggerated"'. Available at: http://www.news.bbc.co.uk/1/low/uk_politics/829839.stm (accessed 21 December 2009).

— (2002b), 'Business. Does the New Deal Work?'. Available at: http://www.newsbbc.co.uk/1/low/business/830251.stm (accessed 21 December 2009).

Blackburn, R.M., Dale, A. and Jarman, J. (1997), 'Ethnic Differences in Attainment in Education, Occupation and Lifestyle', in V. Karn (ed.), *Employment, Education and Housing among Ethnic Minorities in Britain* (London: HMSO).

Bridges, D. and Jonathan, R. (2002), 'Education and the Market'. Durham University. Available at: http://www.dur.ac.uk/r.d.smith/market.html (accessed 21 December 2009).

British Council, Scotland (2004), 'History of Scotland's Education System'. Available at: http://www.educationuk.org (accessed 21 December 2009).

Cardak, B. and Ryan, C. (2006), *Why Are High Ability Individuals from Poor Backgrounds Under-represented at University?* Available at: http://www.accessecon.com/pubs/PET07/PET07-07-00284S.pdf (accessed 10 June 2010).

Cheng, Y.C. (1996), *The Pursuit of School Effectiveness: Theory, Policy and Research*. The Hong Kong Institute of Educational Research (Hong Kong: The Chinese University of Hong Kong).

Disability Rights Commission (2003), 'Response from the Disability Rights Commission to the Consultation Regarding Principles for Reform of 1419 Learning Programmes and Qualifications'. Available at: http://www.drc.org.uk/library/consultation/education/response_from_the_disability_r1.aspx (accessed 21 December 2009).

EIROnline (2002), 'How is the New Deal for Young People Working?'. Available at: http://www.eiro.eurofound.eu.int/2000/02/feature/UK00025155F.html (accessed 21 December 2009).

Gillborn, D. and Mirza, H.S. (2000), *Educational Inequality: Mapping Race, Class and Gender* (London: Ofsted).

Goleman, D. (1996), *Emotional Intelligence* (London: Bloomsbury).

Hagell, A. and Shaw, C. (1996), *Opportunity and Disadvantage at Age 16* (London: Central Books).

Highlight (1995), *Summary of the Education Act 1981* (London: National Children's Bureau).

H.M. Inspector of Schools (1997), *A Curriculum Framework for Children in their Pre-school Year* (Edinburgh: The Scottish Office Industry and Education Department).

H.M. Inspectorate of Education (2008), *Count Us In: Improving the Education of Our Looked After Children*. Available at: http://www.hmie.gov.uk/documents/publication/cuiielac.pdf (accessed 21 December 2009).

— (2009), *Improving Scottish Education 2005–2008* (Edinburgh: HMIE).

Kendall, S., Straw, S., Jones, M., Springate, I. and Grayson, H. (2008), *A Review of the Research Evidence (Narrowing the Gap in Outcomes for Vulnerable Groups)* (Slough: NFER).

Mamon, S. (2003), 'Black Caribbean Pupils at the Bottom in GCSE League', *Independent Race and Refugee News Network*. Available at: http://www.irr.org.uk/2003/march/ak000005.html (accessed 2 June 2010).

McCrone (2000), 'A Teaching Profession for the 21st Century'. Available at: http://www.scotland.gov.uk/library3/education/tp21a-00.asp (accessed 21 December 2009).

Miller, B. (2004), 'Critical Hours: After-School Education and Success'. National Institute for Out of School Time. Available at: http://www.niost.org.uk (accessed 21 December 2009).

National Care Standards Committee (2002), *National Care Standards: Early Education and Childcare up to the Age of 16* (Edinburgh: Stationery Office).

National Literacy Trust (2005a), 'Integrated (New) Community Schools – Scotland'. Available at: http://www.literacytrust.org.uk/Database/community.html (accessed 21 December 2009).

— (2005b), 'Working with Communities'. Available at: http://www.literacytrust.org.uk/socialinclusion/communitiesresearch.html (accessed 21 December 2009).

Northampton University (2002), 'Inclusive Education'. Available at: www.northapton.ac.uk/ass/edu/specialneedsinfopages/inclusiveeducation.htm (accessed 21 December 2009).

Scottish Consultative Council (1999), *A Curriculum Framework for Children 3–5* (Edinburgh: Scottish Executive).

Scottish Education Department (1977a), *Assessment for All: Report of the Committee to Review Assessment in the Third and Fourth Years of Secondary Education in Scotland* (Edinburgh: HMSO).

— (1977b), *The Structure of the Curriculum in the Third and Fourth Years of the Scottish Secondary School* (Edinburgh: HMSO).

Scottish Executive (1997), 'Scottish School Leavers Survey'. Available at: http://www.scotland.gov.uk (accessed 21 December 2009).

— (1998), *Meeting the Childcare Challenge: A Childcare Strategy for Scotland*. Available at: http://www.scotland.gov.uk/library/documents-w4/ccp-oo.htm (accessed 21 December 2009).

—— (2000), *The Child at the Centre*. Available at: http://www.scotland.gov.uk/library2/doc11/cac.pdf (accessed 21 December 2009).

—— (2002a), *New Community Schools*. Available at: http://www.scotland.gov.uk/education/newcommunictyschools/about.htm (accessed 21 December 2009).

—— (2002b), *Planning to Improve Access to Education for Pupils with Disabilities Guidance on Preparing Accessibility Strategies*. Available at: http://www.scotland.gov.uk/library5/education/gpas-01.asp (accessed 21 December 2009).

—— (2003a), *Changes to Free School Meal Entitlement*. Available at: http://www.scotland.gov.uk/pages/news/2003/05/SEd234.aspx (accessed 21 December 2009).

—— (2003b), *Education (Ministerial Powers of Direction) Bill*. Available at: http://www.scotland.gov.uk/pages/news/2003/05/SENW531.aspx (accessed 21 December 2009).

—— (2003c), *Early Learning Forward Thinking: The Policy Framework for ICT in Early Years*. Available at: http://www.LTScotland.org.uk/earlyyears/images/ict_framework_tcm4-122121.pdf (accessed 21 December 2009).

—— (2003d), *Meeting the Needs of Children from Birth to Three*. Available at: http://www.scotland.gov.uk/Publications/2003/06/17458/22696 (accessed 21 December 2009).

—— (2003e), *Building Our Future: Scotland's School Estate*. Available at: http://www.scotland.gov.uk/Resource/Doc/47032/0023966.pdf (accessed 2 June 2010).

—— (2004), *Education (Additional Support for Learning) (Scotland) Act 2004: A Guide for Parents/Carers*. Available at: http://www.scotland.gov.uk/Publications/2007/06/20105158/8 (accessed 21 December 2009).

—— (2006a), *A Curriculum for Excellence*. Available at: http://www.scotland.gov.uk/Resource/Doc/98764/0023924.pdf (accessed 21 December 2009).

—— (2006b), *Nutritional Guidance for Early Years*. Available at: http://www.scotland.gov.uk/Resource/Doc/89729/0021563.pdf (accessed 21 December 2009).

—— (2006c), *School Meals in Scotland*. Available at: https://www.scotland.gov.uk/News/Releases/2006/06/06094851/Q/Zoom/125 (accessed 21 December 2009).

—— (2006d), *Scottish Schools (Parental Involvement) Act 2006*. Available at: http://www.scotland.gov.uk/publications/2006/08084112/0 (accessed 21 December 2009).

—— (2009), *The National Plan for Gaelic, 2007–2012*. Available at: http://www.bord-na-gaidhlig.org.uk/National-Plan/National%20Plan%20for%20Gaelic.pdf (accessed 2 June 2010).

Scottish Government (1999), *Implementing Inclusiveness, Realising Potential*. Beattie Committee report. Available at: http://www.scotland.gov.uk/

Publications/1999/09/ImplementingInclusivenes/Q/Page/2 (accessed 21 December 2009).

—— (2004), *Getting it Right for Every Child: An Overview*. Available at: http://www.scotland.gov.uk/Topics/People/Young-People/childrensservices/girfec/programme-overview (accessed 21 December 2009).

—— (2006), *More Choices, More Chances: A Strategy to Reduce the Proportion of Young People not in Education, Employment or Training in Scotland*. Available at: http://www.scotland.gov.uk/Publications/2006/06/13100205/16 (accessed 21 December 2009).

—— (2007), *We Can and Must Do Better*. Available at: http://www.scotland.gov.uk/Resource/Doc/162790/0044282.pdf (accessed 21 December 2009).

Scottish Parliament (2000), *Special Educational Needs*. Available at: http://www.scottish.parliament.uk/business/research/pdf_subj_maps/smda00-04.pdf (accessed 23 December 2009).

The Guardian (2002), 'State of Despair as Public Schools Get the Cream', *The Guardian*. Available at: http://www.education.guardian.co.uk (accessed 21 December 2009).

The Standards in Scotland's Schools (Scotland) Act 2000 (Edinburgh: Stationery Office).

Warnock Report (1978), *Report of the Committee of Enquiry into the Education of Handicapped Children and Young People* (London: HMSO).

Who Cares? Scotland (2004), *A Different Class? Educational Attainment: The Views and Experiences of Looked-After Young People* (Norwich: HMSO).

Further reading

Scottish Executive (2002), *Evaluation of New Deal for Young People in Scotland: Phase 2*. Available at: http://www.scotland.gov.uk/cru/kd01/orange/endy-02.asp (accessed 21 December 2009).

16 Substance use and social policy in Scotland: The struggle to make sense of things

George Allan

> The rise and fall of epidemics and ecologies tipped out of balance, dangers exaggerated or blithe incaution the order of the day, control responses abjectly failing or producing at least some benefits: there is no shortage of drug and drug policy experience to serve the cause of enlightenment. (Edwards 2005: xxxviii)

Introduction

From a practice perspective, the development of services and interventions for people with substance problems and their dependents might seem to be the aspect of social policy which will be of most interest to nurses, social workers or other front-line practitioners. Such a view, however, ignores the ways in which wider social contexts shape our understanding of what acceptable and unacceptable use is, what we perceive problematic use to be and how we should respond to this. A range of forces, both contemporary and historical, influence how individuals and social groupings use and view substances. Where use is deemed to be problematic, the state implements formal and informal initiatives, including treatment services, aimed at minimising or eradicating the harm. Such initiatives, in their turn, help to mould cultural attitudes and the behaviour of individuals and groups. Without an understanding of this fluid, symbiotic relationship, a front-line worker would find it impossible to make sense of what constitutes problematic behaviour and what are considered to be the best ways of helping people within a given culture. Despite a number of controversies, we understand how people use alcohol, tobacco and drugs in Scotland and have defined problematic use within our current culture and time. Our services for people with problems are based broadly on Western notions of individual, confidential counselling and our interpretations of human rights. It would be difficult for the most skilled Scottish substance problems worker to go to China or Thailand and effectively engage with a person with a drug or alcohol problem. The nuances regarding patterns of use and their meanings and what are considered to be the best ways of helping people in those cultures would be a blank map for our Scottish practitioner. Interventions, and how to apply them, are an inseparable part of the wider cultural ambience.

This chapter will attempt to explore how this wider, ever-shifting frame of reference impacts on practice by addressing the following questions:

- What are the elements which shape how a culture uses substances?
- How are problems defined? How does the state exercise control and what does it hope to achieve through doing this?
- In recent history, how have the Scots used substances and how have successive governments responded to these trends?
- What are the policies and legislation which are currently in place in Scotland and what are the debates and controversies surrounding these?

In this chapter, 'substances' are defined in their widest generic sense. They include tobacco, alcohol, volatile substances and other drugs, whether these are subject to legal restriction or not. They are mainly used because, in Griffith Edwards' succinct phrase, they are 'mind acting' (Edwards 2005: xvii). It is also important to bear in mind that legislation may be different north and south of the border. Scotland has always had separate alcohol licensing law; however the Scotland Act 1998 did not devolve drug legislation, which remains the responsibility of Westminster. To complicate matters, some drug related criminal justice legislation is the responsibility of Holyrood and Westminster is accountable for aspects of the law related to alcohol in Scotland. Examples of the latter are the Road Traffic Act 1988, which makes it an offence to be in charge of a vehicle under the influence of alcohol or drugs, and taxation of alcohol.

The shaping elements

A series of forces shape how any culture uses substances (see Figure 16.1) and, as has been noted, these shift with time. Most societies have long-term allegiances to particular drugs. Such allegiances often began pre-history when humans discovered that what grew around them had intoxicating properties. The coca bush grows in the rarefied air of the Andes foothills.

The leaf, which acts as a stimulant and can be chewed or infused as a tea, has a long history in countries such as Bolivia, Colombia and Peru where it continues to be used for medicinal and religious purposes. The growing of barley spread from the early, Middle Eastern civilisations to northern Europe and so facilitated the brewing of beer and, at a later time, distillation and the production of whisky and other spirits. Such historical traditions, based on accidents of geography, mean that people are less fearful of the harms associated with use of substances with which they have a lengthy association. They also protect production because it brings economic benefits. Many farmers in Bolivia depended for their livelihoods on coca and their current president is a coca farmer. There is, therefore, resistance to international efforts to eliminate a crop which, as cocaine and crack, causes serious problems on the streets of Aberdeen and Washington. Whilst processed coca is used in Bolivia (United Nations Office on Drugs and Crime 2008), it is not in that form that Bolivians have used the drug throughout history. Similarly, Scotland has a unique commodity in Scotch Whisky, a product the Scots feel comfortable with and which brings wealth and jobs.

Conversely, a fear of drugs which are considered to be alien can lead to the risks associated with use triggering moral panics and exaggeration of the harms involved. Ecstasy, an hallucinogenic stimulant, provides an example of this. A staple of the 1980s and 1990s dance scene, ecstasy was associated with an exclusive pocket of youth culture and with a small but persistent number of deaths. This led to a series of lurid tabloid headlines (Newcombe n.d.) and high-profile campaigns about its dangers. Ecstasy use continues at a significant level (Advisory Council on the Misuse of Drugs 2009) but press concerns have moved on.

The history of ecstasy demonstrates two other factors which mould patterns of use, namely fashion and sub-cultural acceptance. Ecstasy was developed in 1912 but it took 70 years before there was real interest in its intoxicating properties and, when that occurred, use was confined to particular groups of young people (Shapiro 2007: 94–5).

Fashion can also influence how a particular drug is consumed. The demise of snuff taking corresponded with the rise of the cigarette as the main way of ingesting nicotine from the mid nineteenth century onwards (Snuff Tobacco n.d.). In respect of sub-cultural use, there are numerous examples of how certain drugs remain the preserve of specific groups within a society. Somali communities in the south of England import khat (Edwards 2005), a leaf with stimulant properties, but its use has not spread to the majority population (Shapiro 2007: 109).

Religion can play a major role in moulding attitudes and behaviour. Some religions proscribe the use of certain drugs entirely and others make comment on how substances should and should not be used. Drugs are central to many religious ceremonies, whether it is alcohol employed as a symbol in the Christian Communion or the peyote cactus (mescaline) used by some Native American peoples for its hallucinogenic properties during their devotions (Gossop 2007: 36).

Gender is an issue. Twice as many men than women were recorded as new attendances at treatment services for drug problems in Scotland in 2007/8 (NHS National Services Scotland Information Services Division 2008). In Scotland, 15-year-old girls are more likely to smoke than their male counterparts (ISD Scotland /Ipsos MORI 2009).

It has already been noted that ecstasy use is primarily confined to younger people, an example of how age can be a consideration, one which may go hand in hand with rebellion. Drugs can become, for some young people, a

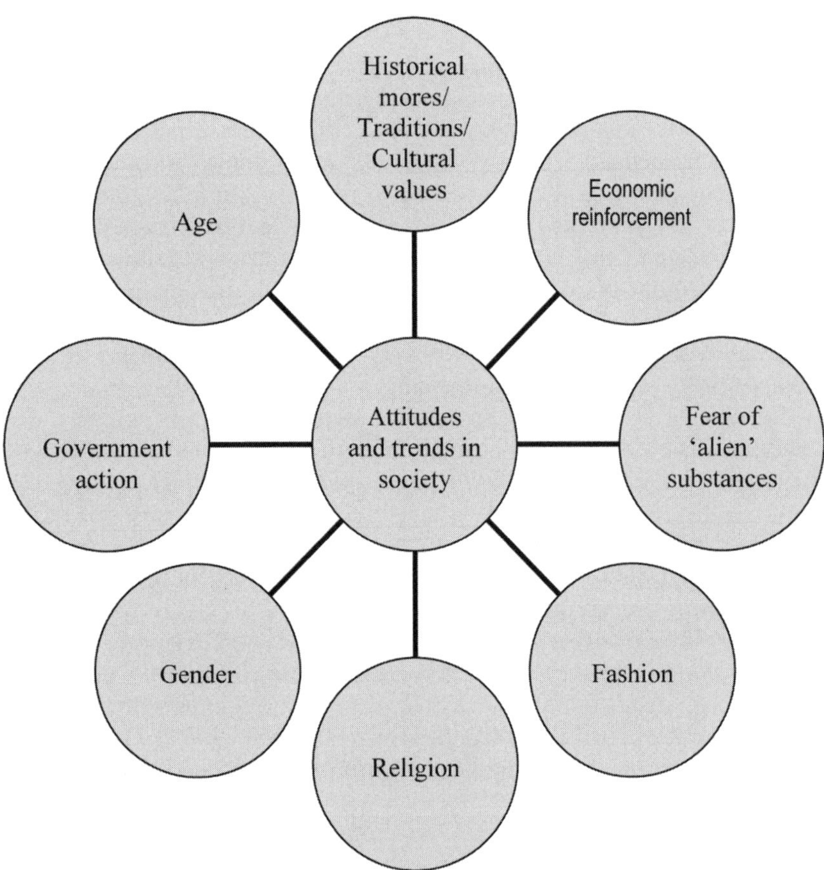

Figure 16.1 The elements which shape attitudes and trends in society

potent symbol of the rejection of the ways of their elders or the constraints of the *status quo*. The links which can occur between such rebellion and political subversion can cause consternation in the establishment. These connections were evident in the 1960s and it is interesting to note that Charles II briefly banned coffee houses in 1675 because it was thought that they were frequented by agitators, an unpopular move which forced a hurried U-turn (Edwards 2005: 56). With regard to sub-cultural use, fear of alien substances and economic reinforcement may feature less and rebellion may become a factor.

A further element which can shape attitudes and control prevalence of use is government action. The gel in temazepam capsules can, if injected, lead to the blockage of veins. Action to withdraw its availability in capsule form was almost certainly the reason for the decline in reported use by new individuals seeking treatment between 1998/9 and 2002/3 (NHS National Services Scotland Information Services Division 2003).

Figure 16.1 lays out these various elements which shape attitudes and trends in society. This fluid mix of influences such as tradition, economic benefit, religion and government activity fashions a society's attitudes and use of substances. It is responsible for the extent of problems within a community and, to a certain degree, the type of problems which a community will experience. It explains why we treat some substances very differently from others, even where logic suggests that we should not, and it is the starting point of any government's efforts to address the harms. As Roberts (2009b) says: 'without reference to cultural values and structures, the meaning goes missing'.

The nature of the beast and how we try to tame it

Illogicality can also characterise our approach to the source of the harms. The accepted view is that tobacco is a dangerous, addictive substance; we rarely give thought to the personality of the smoker. In respect of alcohol, however, we may view the 'alcoholic' as having a particular syndrome which is the cause of the problems he experiences. It is this syndrome, and not alcohol, the drug, which becomes the focus of our attention. Such inconsistencies, with their roots in the mix of cultural factors described above, are reflected in the ways by which we try to control the harms. We try to curtail the availability of heroin except for medical purposes but we allow adults ready access to alcohol, then try to persuade them to drink in harm-free ways.

Very few substances are wholly benign. Even caffeine, available without restriction in numerous products, can cause problems of over-stimulation. It is very difficult to come to clear conclusions regarding the 'dangerousness' of individual substances as the risks they pose are intertwined with the way humans take them. Continuous ingestion of nicotine leads to physical dependence but it is absorbing it via tobacco smoke which leads to an array of serious health risks, risks from which chewing nicotine gum are free. The ways in which drugs are used are as responsible for the harms caused as their chemical properties. Nor are problems confined to longer-term, heavy use. Thorley (1980) explores the wide range of problems which can follow three different modes of drinking ('intoxification'; 'excessive consumption'; 'dependence'). Such a paradigm is equally applicable to other drugs. Drinking a bottle of spirits every day can bring one set of problems; a single evening bingeing on cocaine can bring another.

Faced with this bewildering array of difficulties, how does society try to curtail them? In broad terms, the following three approaches can be adopted:

- *Supply reduction.* Supply reduction reflects concerns that a substance is inherently 'dangerous' and therefore its' availability should be controlled. The main purpose of the Misuse of Drugs Act 1971 is to proscribe certain drugs and control access to others. Another example of supply reduction is the sections of the Licensing (Scotland) Act 2005 which place age restrictions on the sale and purchase of alcohol.
- *Demand reduction.* With demand reduction, the focus shifts from the substance to the user. Its' aim is to convince people of the benefits of altering attitudes and behaviour rather than limiting the availability of substances. The recent effort in Scotland to promote a change in cultural attitudes towards binge drinking is an example of this.
- *Harm reduction.* Harm reduction accepts that substances will be used and specifically targets certain behaviours which are seen as problematic. The provision of clean injecting equipment and the banning of smoking in enclosed public places to protect the health of workers fall into this category.

(Royal College of Psychiatrists and Royal College of Physicians 2000)

These categories are not rigid or exclusive and government strategies usually reflect a mixture of such measures.

Policy makers also have to decide on whom they intend to focus their efforts. Is it intended that preventative measures will:

- discourage people from starting to use?
- curtail problems associated with recreational use, including reducing the likelihood of progression towards more excessive consumption?

- prevent those who already use heavily from developing further problems for themselves or other people?

These can be categorised as primary, secondary and tertiary prevention (Royal College of Psychiatrists and Royal College of Physicians 2000: 119; Barton 2003: 52–4).

A further set of criteria overlaps with these. Should initiatives be targeted at the whole community (universal), communities considered to be at particular risk (selective) or those already involved in use (indicated)? (Royal College of Psychiatrists and Royal College of Physicians 2000: 119.)

The Misuse of Drugs Act 1971 is a universally targeted, primary prevention measure. The provision of injecting equipment is an example of tertiary prevention aimed at an indicated community.

Social policy initiatives can fall foul of the law of unintended consequences. The objectives of imposing high levels of tax on tobacco are to raise revenue and discourage use (demand reduction). This may, however, encourage the smuggling of cigarettes and hand-rolling tobacco into Scotland (Murray 2008). Ashton (1999) describes research undertaken by De Haes and Schuurman in the 1970s in the Netherlands into various models of drug education for mid-teenagers. These included two programmes utilising single sessions – an 'information only' input to one cohort and a 'warning' input to another. The follow-up data showed that these two approaches actually increased the numbers going on to try drugs compared to a control group receiving no input at all.

The historical perspective

The history of shifting attitudes towards substances and efforts to reduce the social and personal damage with which they can be associated is a fascinating one.

Apart from alcohol licensing, there was no restriction on drugs in the first half of the nineteenth century in Britain where opium was freely available. Britain fought and won two wars against China to force that country to abandon its trade barriers and allow the importation of opium, the profits from which were needed to fund the Empire in India. The British victory was to the detriment of the Chinese people (Edwards 2005). Fifty years later the temperance movement was a significant force in Scottish politics. The First World War saw the introduction of draconian controls implemented in 1916, under the Defence of the Realm Act, in response to fears that alcohol and cocaine were undermining the war effort in both the trenches and the munitions factories (Edwards 2005; Gossop 2007). The inter-war years were characterised by low levels of consumption of drugs and alcohol and declining political interest in both, a state of affairs which shifted markedly from the 1960s onwards.

During the First World War, the approach to concerns was to apply the law, in the inter-war years problems were left to the medical profession. The history of control can be interpreted as a tension between the view that substance concerns should be a law and order matter and the belief that they should be seen as a health issue. This pendulum continues to swing to this day.

Exercise 16.1

Contrast the ramifications, both positive and negative, of substances issues being addressed primarily from a penal perspective with the benefits and problems associated with their being viewed principally as a health matter.

A more detailed consideration of recent history is indicated but, in a chapter such as this, the following is inevitably somewhat partial and simplistic, reflecting what the author sees as significant events. It is presented from the perspective of social work but the developments and shifts in direction described have shaped the wider context in which all disciplines practise.

1975 to 1989: Hopes for a relaxed drinking culture and fears of a plague

Alighting from a time machine in the mid 1970s, a social worker would enter a world very different from today. She would find herself being a Jill of all trades, holding a caseload which included older people, child care and protection cases, people with learning disabilities and the odd probation or parole case. Alcohol would play a part in the difficulties which some of her clients would experience but she would be unlikely to have had any specialist training as to how to approach this. Some of her younger clients might smoke cannabis but its use would not be considered of particular concern. If one of her probationers was involved with heroin, it would be so uncommon as to spark considerable interest in the office. Addressing the issue would be seen as the preserve of the medical profession, with services being primarily hospital based. Non-medical, community based drug agencies did not exist at the time. Alcohol and drugs, therefore, were not seen as central to the social work task. In the wider community, however, a major debate was taking place as to how best to license alcohol.

Scots have long had a reputation for drinking prowess. This has been based on an enthusiasm for drinking prodigious quantities in short periods rather than for overall per capita consumption. This reputation was much less deserved in the middle of the twentieth century (Duffy 1992). However, concerns that the restrictive licensing laws in force encouraged bingeing and the belief that a more relaxed regime would help normalise responsible, social consumption led to the Licensing (Scotland) Act 1976. This Act, based on some of the recommendations of the Clayson Committee report of 1972, allowed pubs and hotels to stay open until 11pm and to open on Sundays. The Act also allowed for applications for further regular extensions. It was not envisaged that such extensions would become commonplace, however, afternoon opening soon became the norm. Did the Act achieve its objectives of turning the Scots into devotees of low intake, relaxed consumption? We will consider the evidence further on.

If our social worker were to re-enter the time machine and fast forward to the latter part of the 1980s she would find an utterly changed landscape. Far from drugs being of peripheral concern, she would find growing numbers of people on her caseload, particularly amongst offenders, who were addicted to heroin. She would also find AIDS casting a dark shadow over health and social policy. What changes had occurred in the intervening decade to create an epidemic of heroin use? Edwards (2005: 119) suggests that this development was 'supply-led', although this is only part of the reason. Heroin did, indeed, become very easily available in Britain following the Iranian revolution of 1979 for a variety of reasons (Karan 2004: 390; Release n.d.). Unsurprisingly, the price dropped (Berridge 1998: 87). Drug epidemics cannot emerge without a ready supply but they also need a seed bed in which to grow and that seed bed is often poverty. Edwards (2005: 101) notes: 'Where there is a large population which is poor and powerless, drug epidemics often seem to take root rather easily'.

The recession of the early 1980s led to high unemployment, particularly in enclaves which had been dependent on the old heavy industries. A generation of young people, 'poor and powerless', grew up without much hope of personal advancement. In certain areas of Scotland, the prerequisites for the development of heavy substance-using communities emerged. From a sociological perspective, this scenario fits Merton's theory of retreatism, one of the responses to anomie, a state in which individuals or groups experience conditions which inhibit the achievement of normal social aspirations (Merton 1968).

Interestingly, the method of ingestion varied in different parts of the country. In Glasgow, initially, heroin tended to be 'chased' (heated and the vapour inhaled), whilst in Edinburgh a culture of injection emerged. Efforts by the authorities to prevent this by restricting access to needles, along with the closure of a major medical supplier, led to the rapid spread of HIV amongst intravenous users in the capital (Gossop 2007: 139–40; Greenwood 1992: 138), another example of the law of unintended consequences.

Fears regarding HIV signalled a shift in policy. Preventing the spread of the disease into the non-drug-using, heterosexual community became the overriding objective. Despite initial concerns that initiatives such as the introduction of needle exchanges and an increase in methadone prescribing condoned drug use, harm minimisation took centre stage. Services re-orientated towards prioritising injecting users. Fear of an AIDS epidemic in Britain has receded but its legacy is a particular model of service provision which is only now beginning to be challenged. These measures provide an example of tertiary prevention focusing on an indicated community. In contrast, government sponsored adverts on television warning of the dangers of AIDS serve as an illustration of universally targeted, primary prevention.

1989 to 1993: Social work comes in from the cold

From the 1970s onwards, how services for people with drug or alcohol problems were provided changed. Hospital based, inpatient care augmented, in the case of alcohol, by Alcoholics Anonymous, began to give way to a broader, mixed economy of care. By the end of the 1980s community-orientated, outreach medical services found themselves rubbing shoulders with private sector residential projects and a rapidly developing range of voluntary sector organisations providing both counselling and residential rehabilitation. This diversity of provision, actively encouraged by the liberal economic policies of the Conservative Government, ensured a range of treatment options. Abstinence, harm minimisation and controlled drinking existed uneasily together, with, in some cases, the ideologies of vested interest groups shaping the nature of services as much as scientifically based evidence regarding best practice. Statutory funding drove this expansion of the voluntary agencies and, in turn, transformed the sector into an agent of Government-directed social policy. It was against this background that social work finally accepted that engagement with people with substance problems should be one of its core tasks and it was two pieces of legislation which precipitated this recognition.

Whilst local authorities might have funded non-medical services for people with drug or alcohol problems by means of a block grant prior to the National Health Service and Community Care Act 1990, this Act specifically categorised alcohol or drug dependent adults as 'persons in need'. From then on, people with drug or alcohol problems were to be assessed and provided for in the same way as other vulnerable groups within the new, needs led, purchaser/provider culture. Where a person required residential rehab in particular, and could not afford this, individualised funding was now required. The specialist substance problems care manager, usually a qualified social worker or nurse, emerged and a better understanding of the nature of substance problems and what constitutes effective interventions began to permeate the profession.

The concept of the generic social worker had, for some time, been questioned as it was felt that the range and complexity of tasks facing practitioners demanded specialist skills and training. The Law Reform (Miscellaneous Provisions) (Scotland) Act 1990 further accelerated the move towards the development of separate sections within social work departments. This Act formalised the direct funding by the Scottish Office of the core criminal justice services provided by local authorities and, with this, the logic of developing discrete structures for managing criminal justice became overwhelming. Because substance problems are central to the lives of so many offenders, the new specialist criminal justice workers soon developed an expertise in this area of work.

Taken together, these two pieces of legislation ensured the demise of the generic departments and, within a short period, social work in Scotland was reorganised on the basis of three distinct specialisms: children and families, community care and criminal justice. Disembarking at this point in time, our time-travelling social worker would feel at home. New structures tend to solve one set of difficulties but create another. Within social work, people with drug or alcohol problems would no longer be a neglected group. However demarcations of roles led to a situation where, on occasions, practitioners dealing with adults failed to address adequately the risks facing the children of their substance-using clients.

1994 to 2009: An age of strategic plans; an era of controversies

In recent years, successive governments in Scotland have introduced a series of strategic plans aimed at trying to reduce problems at a whole population level and improve services for those who have developed difficulties. These can be seen as attempts both to gain control over shifts in substance use and to streamline the plethora of state funded agencies.

Drug strategies: Crime on the one hand, treatment on the other

Faced with the need to address the significant problems which drug use was causing, the Scottish Office set up a task force which produced its report, *Drugs in Scotland: Meeting the Challenge*, in 1994 (Scottish Office 1994). Demand reduction measures were prominent in this, with calls for an increase in primary prevention initiatives, such as diversionary activities for young people and improved drugs education in schools, and the further development of community based services for people with problems. The value of substitute prescribing was endorsed. An underpinning theme was the importance of multi-disciplinary/multi-agency co-ordination. The report led to the establishment of area based Drug Action Teams to co-ordinate policy initiatives and service provision at the local level. Similar teams already existed regarding alcohol. It was not long before the separate teams for alcohol and drugs began to merge. (Following a review published in 2009, Alcohol and Drug Action Teams were restructured as Alcohol and Drug Partnerships and embedded within the wider arrangements for community planning.)

Collaborative working was again the essence of the next strategy (*Tackling Drugs in Scotland: Action in Partnership*, Scottish Office 1999) and the subsequent action plan (*Scottish Executive's Drugs Action Plan: Protecting Our Future*, Scottish Executive 2000). Responses to the situation were given added urgency by a number of indicators. Statistics showed that there had been, since the Task Force report, an increase in Scotland in reported current drug use by young people, in the number of drug related deaths and in injecting heroin use amongst those seeking treatment, particularly amongst 15–24 year olds (Scottish Office 1999). Actions in the new plan were structured around four themes which had been agreed by the UK Government:

- helping *young people* to resist drug use
- protecting *communities* from drug related crime
- supporting *treatment*
- stifling the *availability* of illegal drugs

Whilst the plan sought to build on the Task Force's work by sharpening delivery with a focus on outcomes, it can also be seen as heralding the swing of the pendulum to a more penal approach. This was just one part of a wider shift, which had begun under the Conservative Government and continued, unquestioned, under New Labour, of increasingly using legislation to deal with social ills. Drug Treatment and Testing Orders and Anti-Social Behaviour Orders (ASBOs), introduced under the Crime and Disorder Act 1998, were becoming operational. Whilst treatment was not ignored, there was an emphasis on supply reduction in *Tackling Drugs in Scotland: Action in Partnership*, with significant funding being made available for the establishment of a Scottish Drug Enforcement Agency to address the organised crime side of supply. Community safety initiatives were strongly endorsed.

In the early years of the new millennium Scotland had the unenviable reputation of having one of the higher rates of opiate users in the developed world (United Nations Office on Drugs and Crime 2009: 238). Efforts continued to try to get more people into treatment both on a voluntary basis and via the criminal justice system by way of initiatives such as Drug Treatment and Testing Orders (Crime and Disorder Act 1998) and mandatory drug testing of arrestees in certain circumstances (Police, Public Order and Criminal Justice (Scotland) Act 2006). However, mandatory drug testing pilot projects were abandoned in 2009 after an evaluation questioned their cost effectiveness. A range of indicators began to emerge which suggested that the increase in problematic use had levelled off. Whilst deaths have continued to rise (General Register Office for Scotland 2009), research suggests that, in the first part of the decade, the numbers of people with heroin and/or benzodiazepine problems reached a plateau (Hay et al. 2009). There is also evidence that the number of younger teenagers using drugs has declined (ISD Scotland/Ipsos MORI 2009). However, it is not possible to say how far these modest gains have occurred because of the impact of the initiatives taken or have been due to broader cultural forces. As the decade draws towards its close, a new debate has begun to tax both practitioners and politicians. Politicians regularly become embroiled in the funding of medical treatments but usually leave judgements regarding their efficacy to clinicians. Drug treatment is, however, different and an increasing number of voices were heard questioning Scotland's use of methadone. A report in 2007 (Scottish Government 2007b) stated that 22,000 people were being prescribed methadone and there have been concerns that the numbers coming off methadone have been very low, although lack of data prevents a clear picture being obtained (Scottish Advisory Council on the Misuse of Drugs 2007). Underneath the rhetoric is a complex debate which has simmered for many years. It involves questions such as how consistently methadone has been prescribed in Scotland, whether it has been prescribed at optimum doses and why it had been used in some areas as a 'stand alone' treatment rather than part of a package of pharmacological and psycho-social interventions aimed at helping people move beyond care to a fulfilling life without drugs, prescribed or otherwise. It erupted into the public domain as a simplistic, and unhelpful, polarisation – harm reduction versus abstinence from all drugs, including prescribed substitutes, as if these two were unconnected objectives rather than parts of the same complex continuum.

The SNP Government took the opportunity this presented to develop a new drug strategy, *The Road to Recovery: A New Approach to Tackling Scotland's Drug Problem* (Scottish Government 2008f). This sought to find a way through these tensions by borrowing concepts from the mental health recovery movement. Substitute prescribing continues to be supported but as part of a more aspirational approach based on the idea of 'treatment' as being an individual's personal journey towards a new identity. Whilst few would argue with this vision, it masks continuing tensions. Hard-line harm reductionists and those dubbed the 'New Abstentionists' by Ashton (2008) can both use such a definition as supporting their opposing cases. In addition, there are dangers that a shift in emphasis towards those more able to make sustained progress could lessen efforts to help those struggling to stabilise their use at a time when many people are still waiting lengthy periods to even access treatment (ISD Scotland 2009).

This whole debate may become less relevant if interest in opiates wanes. There is some evidence, albeit anecdotal, which suggests that heroin may be losing its appeal in the social enclaves in which it has thrived and that the emerging generation may be more interested in mixing alcohol with cocaine or tranquillisers (Roberts 2009a; Scottish Drugs Forum 2009b; McKinlay, Forsyth and Khan 2009). If this proves to be the case, a re-orientation of treatment services will be required.

The Road to Recovery reaffirms the Government's commitment to supply reduction but the main thrust of the document concerns the nature of treatment (harm and demand reduction). Ironically, at the same time, supply reduction has risen to dominate the discourse regarding alcohol.

A further controversy relates to certain measures in the Welfare Reform Act 2009. These require Department of Work and Pensions staff to ask claimants of particular benefits about their drug use and, in certain circumstances, require them to undergo assessment or drug testing. Claimants with substance problems unwilling to enter treatment can be required to comply with a 'rehabilitation plan' which may include educational and motivational sessions. Benefits sanctions can follow non-compliance with these measures. The original Bill included a requirement for people to engage with drug treatment in particular circumstances, although this idea was abandoned and undertaking treatment will now only be with consent. Initially the Act will apply to heroin and/or crack cocaine users only but it allows for extension to people who use other drugs and also to those with alcohol problems. Pilot schemes are being established. Supporters of the Act claim that it will encourage drug users not already in treatment to access services and help them move towards employment. Critics have argued that coercive measures such as these reinforce stigma and could increase crime (DrugScope 2009). Whilst responsibility for the benefits system lies with Westminster, provision of services for people with substance problems is a devolved matter and, to date, the Scottish Government has shown little enthusiasm for these sections of the Act. The implications of this for Scotland are unclear.

Emerging issues include 'legal highs', designer drugs (synthetically manufactured substances often produced because their chemical structures mean that they do not contravene drug laws) and purchase via the internet. Current drug legislation may prove to be inadequate to meet these challenges.

Alcohol strategies: Too much of a good thing

Throughout the 1990s, alcohol slipped off the political agenda. Did this mean that the Licensing (Scotland) Act 1976 and the subsequent Law Reform (Miscellaneous Provisions) (Scotland) Act 1990, which further consolidated the liberalisation of opening hours, had undermined Scotland's binge culture? Duffy states that what evidence there is, and there is a paucity of it, suggests that the changes brought about by the 1976 Act had 'no notable beneficial or adverse effects on levels of alcohol related harm', at least during the seven years following its implementation (Duffy 1992: 96). This perhaps confirms Clayson's opinion (quoted by Duffy 1992: 95) that licensing law, on its own, has a limited role in reducing harm. Whether or not this is true, the picture that has been emerging over the last 15 years or so is of a country blighted by social disorder following intoxification and health problems caused by excessive consumption. A cursory glance at the evidence makes grim reading. There have been very significant increases in a range of health indicators including chronic liver disease and alcohol related mortality and ongoing evidence of the complex but manifest association between alcohol and a wide range of offending, including a significant proportion of incidents of domestic aggression and crimes of violence (Scottish Government 2008a). In 2008, for the first time, the Scottish Government accepted unequivocally the research evidence which links price, per capita consumption at the population level and the extent of a wide range of alcohol related harms. Put simply, the cheaper alcohol is, the more a society will drink and the more it will suffer (Scottish Government 2008a). The price of alcohol, relative to income, has dropped radically since the 1960s (Scottish Government 2008a) and cultural acceptance has fostered its availability at most social gatherings, encouraged by relentless promotion from the drinks industry and liberal licensing laws. Perhaps the latter do have a more central role to play after all. Based on these suppositions, the latest alcohol strategy, *Changing Scotland's Relationship with Alcohol: A Framework for Action* (Scottish Government 2009), proposes the introduction of both supply and demand reduction measures including:

- ending 'irresponsible promotions' and below cost selling in off sales
- minimum pricing per unit
- reviewing advice to parents
- placing a duty on Licensing Boards to consider restricting off sales to people aged 21 and over in specific areas where there are particular concerns

Unit pricing and the increase in age regarding off sales have sparked considerable debate. The Conservatives and, unsurprisingly, the alcohol producers have argued that whole population approaches place impositions on the majority rather than addressing the habits of a minority (Portman Group 2009; Aitken 2009). Some of the proposals in the strategy are contained in the Alcohol Etc. (Scotland) Bill currently before the Scottish Parliament. Most of the opposition parties are opposing unit pricing and it will be surprising if this measure now reaches the statute book.

Whilst taking a more robust and radical approach than the previous Labour/Liberal administration, the SNP Government is building on initiatives started earlier in the decade. Two previous alcohol action plans (Scottish Executive 2002; Scottish Executive 2007) made reducing binge drinking, harmful drinking by children and young people and encouraging culture change central priorities. These earlier plans can be criticised for avoiding advocating any actions which might damage the interests of the drinks industry, including ignoring the role of pricing in reducing demand. The previous administration also introduced the Licensing (Scotland) Act 2005, which came into force in 2009. Under this Act, each licensed premise has an individualised 'operating plan' governing such matters as hours of opening and access by children. Decisions by licensing boards, including the endorsement of operating plans, must, for the first time, be consistent with five 'licensing objectives':

- prevention of crime and disorder
- promotion of public safety
- prevention of public nuisance
- promotion of public health
- protection of children from harm

Children and the damage done

The turn of the millennium heralded a growing awareness that the implications of parental or carer drug or alcohol problems for children had been disregarded. Given prominence by a number of high profile cases of children harmed or neglected by adults with substance problems, this is now an issue of significant political importance. *Getting Our Priorities Right* (Scottish Executive 2003) is a seminal document in which it is estimated that 40,000 to 60,000 children in Scotland are adversely affected by parental drug problems and a greater number by parental drinking. Its central tenets are that all services for adults, whether they are in the health, local authority or voluntary sectors, must ensure that the risks to, and needs of, their service users' children are continuously considered. It stresses the importance of adult and children's services working together and of the dismantling of the barriers which have, historically, hindered such multi-agency working, including disparate assumptions regarding confidentiality. This report was followed by *Hidden Harm* (Advisory Council on the Misuse of Drugs 2003), a UK wide document which took a strategic view of the issues related to parental drug use. The current Scottish drug strategy (*The Road to Recovery*) integrates this agenda with the developments taking place to both improve and unify services for vulnerable children under the banner of *Getting it Right for Every Child* (Scottish Executive 2006a). Adapting to having a role in the protection of children continues to pose significant challenges for services for adults with substance problems. Adult services can screen for the risks to children but cannot be expected to undertake full child-focused assessments and the Government has, so far, stopped short of saying that the latter should take place for every child affected by a parental drug or alcohol problem. However, one MSP, Duncan McNeill, has recently stated: 'Every child living with a parent with an addiction needs to be identified and have the right to have a risk assessment, and ongoing support. Every parent or parents with an addiction should be assessed as to their parenting capacity' (McNeil quoted in Scottish Drugs Forum 2009a).

Growing awareness of the risks to children has been paralleled by the recognition that a significant number of children affected by parental substance problems are being looked after by other family members and that support in such circumstances has been inadequate. Kinship care can be formal (where a child is officially 'looked after' and living with relatives) or informal (arrangements made without involvement of the local authority). The Scottish Government established task groups to consider how best to support such arrangements. At the time of writing, efforts are being made to resolve the anomalies related to financial support and its conflict with the benefits system (Scottish Government 2008d).

Smoking: A success story?

It is estimated that around 13,000 deaths a year in Scotland are attributable to smoking (Scottish Government 2008e). This is almost a quarter of all deaths and many times more than the deaths credited to alcohol and drugs combined. It may, therefore, seem premature to label tobacco control policy as a success but major shifts in patterns of use suggest that the health-related harms will decline significantly in years to come. In 1978, 45 per cent of Scottish adults smoked (Office for National Statistics 2004); by 2007 this had declined to 25 per cent (Scottish Government 2008b). Smoking amongst teenagers has decreased significantly since the mid 1990s (ISD Scotland/Ipsos MORI 2009). Smoking habits do, however, remain resistant to change amongst people in lower income groups (Scottish Executive 2006c). Despite this ongoing challenge, the overall modification in behaviour at the population level is nothing short of remarkable. How has this been achieved?

Since research in the 1950s, which proved beyond doubt that smoking causes numerous health problems, successive governments have acted consistently and unambiguously across a range of fronts and, overall, there has been broad agreement between the political parties. Steps taken have included:

- the unchanging message that smoking causes ill health (demand reduction);
- utilising taxation as a method of discouraging use (demand reduction);
- systematically reducing the profile of tobacco through banning its advertising (Tobacco Advertising and Promotions Act 2002). The Tobacco and Primary Medical Services (Scotland) Act 2010, scheduled to be fully implemented by 2013, will take this element of demand reduction further by removing tobacco products from view in places of sale (demand reduction);
- protecting workers from the effects of passive smoking through banning smoking in enclosed public places. The Smoking, Health and Social Care (Scotland) Act 2005, which introduced this harm reduction measure, led the way in the United Kingdom;
- bringing in supply reduction measures such as raising to 18 the age at which tobacco can be sold to young people (Smoking, Health and Social Care (Scotland) Act 2005) and the banning of vending machines (Tobacco and Primary Medical Services (Scotland) Act 2010, scheduled to be fully implemented by 2013).

Public understanding of the risks has meant that high levels of taxation and the inexorable tightening of restrictions on use and availability have met with little resistance. Even the banning of smoking in enclosed public spaces, initially a controversial idea, is now widely accepted.

Could tobacco strategy act as a template for alcohol and drugs policies? Ambivalence has characterised our attitudes towards alcohol and recent attempts to develop more logical approaches do not entirely eliminate this. We want to continue to enjoy the one drug which still meets with widespread approval but hope to lessen the problems associated with it. This is a more complex idea to communicate than the message that smoking is a dangerous pursuit. Regular heavy drug taking is not a population wide activity and therefore the lessons which can be learned from smoking policy are more oblique. The challenges which illicit and other drugs present may, therefore, be more similar to those posed by reducing smoking in disadvantaged socio-economic groups. Nevertheless the consistency and clarity of smoking strategies contrast sharply with the shifts and uncertainties in drug and alcohol policies.

Exercise 16.2

Develop a comprehensive plan to reduce the harms associated with alcohol use by 14 to 20 year olds. Describe what measures you would propose and outline the reasons for your suggestions. In addressing this, you should consider the following questions amongst others.

- What exactly are the harms experienced by this group which covers an age band stretching from adolescence to early adulthood? Are certain subgroups within this age band more at risk?
- Is current legislation (see Table 16.1) adequate?
- What new initiatives would best be introduced via changes in the law and what actions would best be implemented by less formal means?
- Which of your proposals should be universally targeted and which should be targeted at particular groups of young people?

Table 16.1 describes some of the main legislation in force in Scotland regarding alcohol, drugs, tobacco and volatile substances. This is not the only relevant legislation, however, as there are other Acts which are pertinent to the work of front-line practitioners, particularly those working in the criminal justice system.

Table 16.1 Key legislation applying to Scotland

Drugs
Misuse of Drugs Act 1971 The aim of the Misuse of Drugs Act 1971 is to prevent the non medical use of certain drugs. Drugs subject to the Act are ranked into three classes (A, B and C). These classes stipulate the penalties which can be imposed for the possession for a person's own use or for production/supply. Schedules introduced under the Act specify who can legally possess drugs subject to the Act. Drugs in Schedule 1 are not authorized for medical use and can only be possessed by people (usually researchers) who have a Home Office license. Drugs in Schedule 5 are available over the counter from a pharmacy without prescription. Schedules 2, 3 and 4 cover the prescription of certain drugs and their lawful possession.
Alcohol
Licensing (Scotland) Act 2005 This Act covers all aspects of the sale of alcohol in Scotland including licensing boards, the age of sale and purchase, the issuing of licenses, licensee and server training and licensed hours. The Act lays down the purposes of licensing law.
Tobacco
Children and Young Persons (Scotland) Act 1937 This Act stipulates the age at which young people can be sold tobacco products.
Children and Young People (Protection from Tobacco) Act 1991 The display of warning statements regarding age and the requirement to sell cigarettes only in pre-packed quantities of ten or more are covered in this Act.
Tobacco Advertising and Promotion Act 2002 The Act prohibits advertising of tobacco products and sponsorship which promotes such products.
Smoking, Health and Social Care (Scotland) Act 2005 The ban on smoking in enclosed public places was introduced under this Act. It also allows orders to be made increasing the age at which young people can be sold tobacco products under the Children and Young Persons (Scotland) Act 1937.
Volatile substances
Scottish Common Law Under Common Law it is a crime to 'recklessly' sell substances knowing that they are going to be inhaled.
Consumer Protection Act 1987 Regulations made under this Act make it an offence to supply gas lighter refills to people aged under 18 years.
Children in need of compulsory supervision
Children (Scotland) Act 1995 Under section 52 of the Act, a child can be considered to be in need of compulsory supervision if he/she has 'misused alcohol or any drug, whether or not a controlled drug' or 'has misused a volatile substance by deliberately inhaling its vapour, other than for medicinal purposes'.

Note: Where the word 'Scotland' is contained in the title of an Act, it applies only to that country.

The impact of social policy: A case study

Practitioners will be familiar with the challenges presented by the McDougal family.

Karen (aged 43) and Brian (aged 42) McDougal live with their son, Darren (aged 16). Their daughter, Leanne (aged 20), is a single parent and she has just moved back in with her parents with her son, Jason (aged 3), following their eviction from her flat for non-payment of rent.

Brian

Brian works as a fabricator. He enjoys a drink on Friday evenings with his work mates, consuming around five or six pints of lager. On Saturday afternoons, when at a sports club watching the football and racing, he drinks around four pints. Saturday evenings often involve a meal out with Karen when Brian will drink most of a bottle of wine. He does not drink during the rest of the week. Until recently, Brian gave little thought to his alcohol consumption, which he sees as being in line with that of his peers. However, government adverts on television and the odd comment by Karen, combined with consciousness of an expanding waistline, have begun to make him wonder if he is, indeed, consuming more than is good for his health.

Social policy connections:

- Whilst Brian rarely becomes seriously intoxicated, at the end of both Friday and Saturday evenings those serving him might be charged under the Licensing (Scotland) Act 2005 with the offence of serving a drunk person. Concerns have been expressed that prosecutions for this are rare (The Herald 2007).
- Brian is a binge drinker and his consumption is above recommended Government limits. Government attempts to change cultural attitudes are intended to make people who drink in the way that Brian does aware that health and social risks accrue to regular heavy consumption which is well short of dependent drinking. In addition, measures to reduce demand by preventing types of price discounting in on-sales are contained in the Licensing Scotland Act 2005 and proposals are outlined in the alcohol strategy (*Changing Scotland's Relationship with Alcohol: A Framework for Action*, Scottish Government 2009) and in the Alcohol Etc. (Scotland) Bill to eliminate such discounting in off-sales along with plans to introduce a minimum price per unit of alcohol.
- The alcohol strategy signals the Scottish Government's intention to extend the ability of a range of services to provide brief, opportunist

interventions aimed at encouraging people to reduce their drinking. Brian might well find medical staff, for example, giving him advice.

Karen

Karen only drinks the odd glass of wine when out for a meal. She gets annoyed with Brian for spending so much of the weekend drinking. She is also concerned that Darren might develop similar habits. She is pre-occupied with worries about Leanne and Jason.

Social policy connections:

- Karen's awareness of the risks associated with alcohol have been shaped by Government sponsored television adverts and by leaflets she obtained during Alcohol Awareness Week, an annual event initiated under the Partnership Agreement between the Government and the alcohol industry. The establishment of the Partnership was one of the actions outlined an earlier alcohol strategy (*Plan for Action on Alcohol Problems: Update,* Scottish Executive 2007)
- The Scottish Government funds the Scottish Network for Families Affected by Drugs (SNFAD), a voluntary body which Karen (and Brian) might consider turning to for support.

Leanne

Leanne started to use a variety of drugs when in her mid teens. Jason's father introduced her to heroin when she was 18. Injecting and physical dependence soon followed. After the relationship with Jason's father ended, she approached her GP. He referred her to the local substance problems clinic and she has now been on a methadone programme for six months.

Social policy connections:

- Implementation of the *Getting our Priorities Right/Hidden Harm* agenda has led to services giving high priority to parents with substance problems. If the clinic had a waiting list, Leanne would have been assessed and provided with a service very quickly.
- Leanne has coped well with methadone but there has been the occasional relapse. During these periods, Leanne could be arrested under the Misuse of Drugs Act 1971 for possession of heroin for her own use.
- The aspiration of 'individualised recovery' is the centre piece of the Scottish drug strategy (*The Road to Recovery: A New Approach to Tackling Scotland's Drug Problem,* Scottish Government 2008f). Decisions regarding substitute prescribing lie firmly in the relationship between

the medical profession and the service user, however the expectation is that Leanne will be encouraged to consider opportunities to help her move towards 'a drug-free life as an active and contributing member of society'. The strategy requires that services look beyond the narrow confines of drug 'treatment'. This means that the clinic should not only involve other services to help Leanne with practical issues such as financial and accommodation problems, they should also try to facilitate her engagement in constructive and satisfying activities and support networks.

- Leanne was tested for blood borne viruses, including Hepatitis C, when she first became involved with the clinic. The test was negative but she has asked to be tested again following her last, brief relapse when she shared a spoon and filters. Testing and treatment for Hepatitis C is being further developed under the *Hepatitis C Action Plan for Scotland* (Scottish Government 2008c).
- Services provided for Leanne should meet specific standards laid down in the *National Quality Standards for Substance Misuse Services* (Scottish Executive 2006b).
- If Leanne considered that she needed a period in residential rehab, she could ask the local social work service for an assessment for financial support for the non-medical aspects of this. This assessment would be undertaken under the National Health Service and Community Care Act 1990, normally by a specialist care manager. Funding for her detoxification in residential rehab would need to be approved by the NHS locally.

Jason

Leanne has tried to ensure Jason's safety and meet his needs and Karen and Brian have looked after him from time to time when Karen was not coping. Nevertheless, the nursing staff at the clinic had sufficient concerns at the time that Leanne was referred to advise the social work service.

Social policy connections:

- The referral to social work was made within the context of the inter-agency *Getting our Priorities Right/Hidden Harm* protocols which all areas are required to have in place. Jason was then assessed under the local integrated assessment framework developed as part of the implementation of *Getting it Right for Every Child*. The Scottish Drug Strategy (*The Road to Recovery: A New Approach to Tackling Scotland's Drug Problem*) assimilates arrangements for addressing the risks to, and needs of, children affected by parental substance problems into the development of the *Getting it Right for Every Child* framework

(Scottish Executive 2006a). The assessment did not indicate that Jason needed statutory measures of care under the Children (Scotland) Act 1995 but arrangements were made for him to attend a nursery. The nursery staff are aware that any concerns should be immediately relayed to other services involved (again under the local *Getting our Priorities Right/Hidden Harm* protocols).
- Should Karen and Brian need to look after Jason for any period because Leanne became unable to secure his well-being or because she decided to go into residential rehab, then aspects of the strategy for kinship carers might become relevant (*Getting it Right for Every Child in Foster and Kinship Care: A National Strategy*, Scottish Government 2007a)

Darren

Darren is doing well at school and is presenting no obvious social problems. He does not smoke. He inhaled solvents on two or three occasions with friends in the woods a couple of years ago but there have been no recurrences of this behaviour. He plays for a football team and he, along with other team members, drink on Saturday evenings after a game. They pool their money and one of the 18 year olds buys alcohol from the corner shop, which always has cut price offers. Darren has found that one or two pubs now let him in without questioning his age, although he is still refused at the majority. Darren rarely gets drunk but drinking is now a regular Saturday evening activity as is the norm for many teenagers of his age.

Social policy connections:

- A central plank of legislative changes and policy initiatives has been to discourage young people like Darren from taking up smoking by making it more difficult to gain access to tobacco and by trying to lessen the profile of smoking and making it less glamorous. Actions include keeping the price high through taxation, banning advertising (Children and Young Persons (Protection from Tobacco) Act 1991) and raising the age at which young people can be sold tobacco to 18 (modification of the Children and Young Persons (Scotland) Act 1937 by the Smoking, Health and Social Care (Scotland) Act 2005). The tobacco strategy (*Scotland's Future is Smoke-Free: A Smoking Prevention Action Plan*, Scottish Government 2008e) signalled the government's intention to introduce further measures such as licensing sales, more rigorous enforcement of the law and the restriction of display at the point of sale. Some of these are contained in the Tobacco and Primary Medical Services (Scotland) Act 2010, which is scheduled to be fully implemented by 2013.

- It is not against the law to possess volatile substances in Scotland, nor is there a specific offence of being intoxicated through the use of volatile substances although a person's behaviour might be covered by other offences such as Breach of the Peace. It is an offence under Common Law in Scotland to 'recklessly' sell substances knowing they are going to be inhaled. This has led many retailers to refuse to sell glues and the like to young people. It is an offence to supply gas lighter refills to under-18 year olds (regulations made under the Consumer Protection Act 1987). Misusing a volatile substance by inhaling its vapour is a ground for considering whether a child is in need of compulsory supervision (Children (Scotland) Act 2005).
- Under the Licensing (Scotland) Act 2005, Darren is committing an offence when he buys, or attempts to buy, alcohol in a bar or off-licence as is anyone who sells him alcohol. The 18-year-old team mate who buys alcohol on behalf of the younger players is also in breach of this Act. The introduction of test purchasing of alcohol is an example of one of the measures aimed at reducing underage drinking. Test purchasing allows the authorities to legally use under-18 year olds to try to buy alcohol to ascertain if retailers are adhering to the law. Measures to reduce discounting and proposals to introduce minimum unit price, outlined above in relation to Brian, apply equally to his son.

Exercise 16.3

Identify a service user with a drug or an alcohol problem whose circumstances are known to you. List what legislation and which policy initiatives impact on both this person and those who are dependent on him/her.

Chapter summary: Control conundrums

History teaches us that substance taking is commonplace. Different eras are characterised by widespread or sub-cultural acceptance of particular drugs along with all the benefits and problems they bring. Waves of use reach peaks and then wane. More consistent and logical approaches based on the evidence which exists regarding how harmful particular substances are and the risks associated in how we take them, rather than on fear or historical custom, may be the most productive way of minimising the harms. The disproportionate detriment caused by substances, both licit and illegal, to disadvantaged communities is also a key challenge for policy makers. There are, of course, commentators who condemn current international policy regarding the prohibition of many drugs as an abject failure (Transform Drug Policy Foundation 2009). Their alternative is regulation of availability and taxation. Would the problems caused by such a step be offset by the benefits which would accrue? Might some less radical liberalisation, such as the decriminalisation of possession for personal use, reduce certain difficulties? Does our current struggle to contain the harms caused by the ready availability of cheap alcohol illuminate, in any ways, the prohibition versus licensing debate regarding other drugs? Proposals for major change need to be tested against what the Royal College of Psychiatrists and the Royal College of Physicians (2000: 117) consider to be three truisms:

1. Drugs that give pleasure will be used by some people if they can afford them; if they are prohibited an illicit market will emerge.
2. Greater availability of drugs will lead to more use, and, except where the drugs are relatively innocuous, more health problems will occur.
3. It is almost impossible to keep drugs that are available to adults out of the hands of children and adolescents.

References

Advisory Council on the Misuse of Drugs (2003), *Hidden Harm: Responding to the Needs of Children of Problem Dug Users* (London: Home Office). Available at: http://www.homeoffice.gov.uk/publications/drugs/acmd1/hidden-harm (accessed 27 July 2010).

— (2009), *MDMA (Ecstasy): A Review of its Harms and Classification under the Misuse of Drugs Act 1971* (London: Home Office). Available at: http://www.homeoffice.gov.uk/publications/drugs/acmd1/mdma-report (accessed 27 July 2010).

Aitken, B. (2009), *Speech to Scottish Parliament on 26 March 2009* [Scottish Parliament website]. Available at: http://www.scottish.parliament.uk/business/officalReports/meetingsParliament/or-09/sor0326-02.htm#Col16211 (accessed 18 May 2009).

Ashton, M. (1999), 'The Danger of Warning', *Drug and Alcohol Findings*. Available at: http://www.findings.org.uk/docs/Ashton_M_14.pdf (accessed 14 May 2009).

— (2008), 'The New Abstentionists', *DrugScope*. Available at: http://www.drugscope.org.uk/Resources/Drugscope/Documents/PDF/Good%20Practice/Ashton_M_30.pdf (accessed 18 May 2009).

Barton, A. (2003), *Illicit Drugs: Use and Control* (London: Routledge Falmer).

Berridge, V. (1998), 'AIDS and British Drug Policy: A Post-War Situation', in M. Bloor and F. Wood (eds), *Addictions and Problems Drug Use: Issues in Behaviour, Policy and Practice* (London: Jessica Kingsley).

DrugScope (2009), 'Welfare Reform Bill: Proposed Benefit Regime for Claimants Dependent on or with a Propensity to Misuse Drugs. Second Reading Briefing', *DrugScope*. Available at: http://www.drugscope.org.uk/Resources/Drugscope/Documents/PDF/Policy/welfaresecondreading.pdf (accessed 7 August 2008).

Duffy, J. (1992), 'Scottish Licensing Reforms', in M. Plant, B. Ritson and R. Robertson (eds), *Alcohol and Drugs: The Scottish Experience* (Edinburgh: Edinburgh University Press).

Edwards, G. (2005), *Matters of Substance. Drugs: Is Legalisation the Right Answer or the Wrong Question?* (London: Penguin).

General Register Office for Scotland (2009), *Drug-Related Deaths in Scotland 2008* (Edinburgh: General Register Office for Scotland). Available at: http://www.gro-scotland.gov.uk/files2/stats/drug-related-deaths/j1106200.htm (accessed 17 August 2009).

Gossop, M. (2007), *Living with Drugs* (6th edn) (Aldershot: Ashgate).

Greenwood, J. (1992), 'Services for Problem Drug Users in Scotland', in M. Plant, B. Ritson and R. Robertson (eds), *Alcohol and Drugs: The Scottish Experience* (Edinburgh: Edinburgh University Press).

Hay, G., Gannon, M., Casey, J. and McKeganey, N. (2009), *Estimating the National and Local Prevalence of Problem Drug Misuse in Scotland* (Glasgow: University of Glasgow). Available at: http://www.drugmisuse.isdscotland.org/publications/abstracts/prevalence2009.htm (accessed 18 May 2009).

ISD Scotland (2009), 'Drug Treatment Waiting Times Information Framework Report October–December 2008', *Drug Misuse Information Scotland*. Available at: http://www.drugmisuse.isdscotland.org/wtpilot/reports_revised_octdec08.pdf (accessed 18 May 2009).

ISD Scotland/Ipsos MORI (2009), 'Scottish Schools Adolescent Lifestyle and Substance Use Survey (SALSUS) – 2008 National Report', *Drug Misuse Information Scotland*. Available at: http://www.drugmisuse.isdscotland.org/publications/local/SALSUS_2008.pdf (accessed 7 August 2009).

Karan, P. (2004), *The Non-Western World* (London: Routledge).

McKinlay, W., Forsyth, A. and Khan, F. (2009), *Alcohol and Violence among Young Male Offenders in Scotland (1979–2009)*, Scottish Prison Service Occasional Papers No. 1/2009. Available at: http://www.sps.gov.uk (accessed 18 May 2009).

Merton, R. (1968), *Social Theory and Social Structure* (enlarged edn) (New York, NY: The Free Press).

Murray, B. (2008), 'Tobacco Smuggling in Scotland: A Briefing Paper', *ASH Scotland*. Available at: http://www.ashscotland.org.uk (accessed 20 April 2009).

Newcombe, R. (n.d.), *Ecstasy Deaths*. Available at: http://obsolete.com/ecstasy/russell.html (accessed 14 May 2009).

NHS National Services Scotland Information Services Division (2003), 'Drug Misuse Statistics Scotland 2003', *Drug Misuse Information Scotland*. Available at: http://www.drugmisuse.isdscotland.org/publications/03dmss/03dmss2b.htm (accessed 15 May 2009).

—— (2008), 'Drug Misuse Statistics Scotland 2008', *Drug Misuse Information Scotland*. Available at: http://www.drugmisuse.isdscotland.org/publications/08dmss/08dmss-004.htm (accessed 15 May 2009).

Office for National Statistics (2004), 'Living in Britain: Results of the 2002 General Household Survey. Chapter 8', *UK National Statistics*. Available at: http://www.statistics.gov.uk/lib2002/downloads/smoking.pdf (accessed 15 May 2009).

Portman Group (2009), 'Focus on Irresponsible Minority', *Portman Group*. Available at: http://www.portman-group.org.uk/?pid=26&level=28nid=331 (accessed 18 May 2009).

Release (n.d.), 'Heroin', *Release*. Available at: http://www.release.org.uk/downloads/drugs/Release_heroin.pdf (accessed 15 May 2009).

Roberts, M. (2009a), 'On the Cusp of a New Understanding', *Drink and Drug News*, 6 April 2009.

—— (2009b), 'The Power of Culture', *Druglink* 24(3).

Royal College of Psychiatrists and Royal College of Physicians (2000), *Drugs: Dilemmas and Choices* (London: Gaskell).

The Herald (2007), 'Licensing Chief Warns Over Lack of Pubs Prosecuted for Serving Drunks', *The Herald*, 8 October. Available at: http://www.theherald.co.uk/search/display.var.1742072.0.licensing_chief_warns_over_lack_of_pubs_prosecuted_for_serving_drunks.php (accessed 11 August 2009).

Scottish Advisory Council on the Misuse of Drugs (2007), *Reducing Harm and Promoting Recovery: A Report on Methadone Treatment for Substance Misuse in Scotland*. Available at: http://www.scotland.gov.uk/Publications/2007/06/22094730/2 (accessed 18 May 2009).

Scottish Drugs Forum (2009a), 'Brandon Muir: Issues and Opinions', *Scottish Drugs Forum Bulletin* 219/220: 7.

—— (2009b), Evidence Presented to the *Drugs Trends Conference* on 27 March 2009.

Scottish Executive (2000), *Drugs Action Plan: Protecting our Future* (Edinburgh: Scottish Executive). Available at: http://www.scotland.gov.uk/Publications/2000/05/5815/File-1 (accessed 15 May 2009).

—— (2002), *Plan for Action on Alcohol Problem* (Edinburgh: Scottish Executive).

—— (2003), *Getting our Priorities Right: Good Practice Guidance for Working with Families Affected by Substance Misuse* (Edinburgh: Scottish Executive). Available at: http://www.scotland.gov.uk/Publications/2003/02/16469/18705 (accessed 23 August 2009).

—— (2006a), *Getting it Right for Every Child*. Available at: http://www.scotland.gov.uk/Topics/People/Young-People/childrensservices/girfec (accessed 18 May 2009).

—— (2006b), *National Quality Standards for Substance Misuse Services* (Edinburgh: Scottish Executive). Available at: http://www.scotland.gov.uk/Publications/2006/09/25092710/0 (accessed 23 August 2009).

—— (2006c), *Scotland's People: Annual Report: Results from the 2005 Scottish Household Survey*. Available at: http://www.scotland.gov.uk/Resource/Doc/140387/0034518.pdf (accessed 15 May 2009).

—— (2007), *Plan for Action on Alcohol Problem: Update* (Edinburgh: Scottish Executive). Available at: http://www.scotland.gov.uk/Publications/2007/02/19150222/0 (accessed 11 August 2009).

Scottish Government (2007a), *Getting it Right for Every Child in Foster and Kinship Care: A National Strategy* (Edinburgh: Scottish Government). Available at: http://www.scotland.gov.uk/Publications/2007/12/03143704/0 (accessed 11 August 2009).

—— (2007b), *Review of Methadone in Drug Treatment: Prescribing Information and Practice*. Available at: http://www.scotland.gov.uk/Publications/2007/06/22094632/0 (accessed 18 May 2009).

—— (2008a), *Changing Scotland's Relationship with Alcohol: A Discussion Paper on our Strategic Approach* (Edinburgh: Scottish Government). Available at: http://www.scotland.gov.uk/Publications/2008/06/16084348/0 (accessed 23 August 2009).

—— (2008b), *Health of Scotland's Population: Smoking*. Available at: http://www.scotland.gov.uk/Topics/Statistics/Browse/Health/TrendSmoking (accessed 15 May 2009).

—— (2008c), *Hepatitis C Action Plan for Scotland Phase II: May 2008–March 2011*. Available at: http://www.scotland.gov.uk/Resource/Doc/222750/0059978.pdf (accessed 11 August 2009).

—— (2008d), *Moving Forward in Kinship and Foster Care: Report Prepared by the tFN-BAAF Reference Group and Project Task Groups*. Available at: http://www.scotland.gov.uk/Publications/2009/02/27085637/17 (accessed 13 May 2009).

—— (2008e), *Scotland's Future is Smoke-free: A Smoking Prevention Action Plan*. Available at: http://www.scotland.gov.uk/Publications/2008/05/19144342/0 (accessed 15 May 2009).

—— (2008f), *The Road to Recovery: A New Approach to Tackling Scotland's Drug Problem* (Edinburgh: Scottish Government). Available at: http://www.scotland.gov.uk/Publications/2008/05/22161610/0 (accessed 7 May 2009).

— (2009), *Changing Scotland's Relationship with Alcohol: A Framework for Action*. Available at: http://www.scotland.gov.uk/Publications/2009/03/04144703/0 (accessed 23 August 2009).

Scottish Office (1994), *Drugs in Scotland: Meeting the Challenge* (Edinburgh: Scottish Office). Available at: http://www.scotland.gov.uk/library/documents4/dis-00.htm (accessed 15 May 2009).

— (1999), *Tackling Drugs in Scotland: Action in Partnership* (Edinburgh: Scottish Office). Available at: http://www.scotland.gov.uk/library/documents-w7/tdis-00.htm (accessed 15 May 2009).

Shapiro, H. (2007), *The Essential Guide to Drugs and Alcohol* (London: DrugScope).

Snuff Tobacco (n.d.), 'Snuff in the 20th Century', *Snuff Tobacco*. Available at: http://snufftobacco.co.uk/20c-snuff (accessed 12 May 2009).

Thorley, A. (1980), 'Medical Responses to Problem Drinking', *Medicine* (3rd series) 35: 1816–22.

Transform Drug Policy Foundation (2009), 'A Comparison of the Cost-effectiveness of the Prohibition and Regulation of Drugs', *Transform Drug Policy Foundation*. Available at: http://www.tdpf.org.uk/Transform%20CBA%20paper%20final.pdf (accessed 15 May 2009).

United Nations Office on Drugs and Crime (2008), *World Drug Report 2008*. Available at: http://www.unodc.org/documents/wdr/WDR_2008/WDR_2008_eng_web.pdf (accessed 14 May 2009).

— (2009), *World Drug Report 2009*. Available at: http://www.unodc.org/documents/wdr/WDR_2009/WDR2009_eng_web.pdf (accessed 21 August 2009).

17 Social policy in the criminal justice system

Anne Shirran

Introduction

> Criminal justice social work services are responsible for delivery of all aspects of community based disposals including probation, community service, supervised attendance orders, and bail supervision. It also has responsibility for preparation of Social Enquiry Reports for courts and statutory supervision of offenders on release from custody through the throughcare arrangements. (Scottish Executive 1999: 1)

The aims of criminal justice social work are to identify and deliver community-based programmes which maintain community safety, demonstrate effective practice principles and provide credible alternatives to custody. This should reduce the number of offenders being sent to prison and facilitate opportunities for offenders to tackle their offending behaviour and adopt an offence free life style. In particular young adult offenders with a history of offending should be targeted.

The development and growth of social work within criminal justice services

In order to gain a greater understanding of how criminal justice social work fits into the criminal justice system, the flow chart in Figure 17.1 provides an overview.

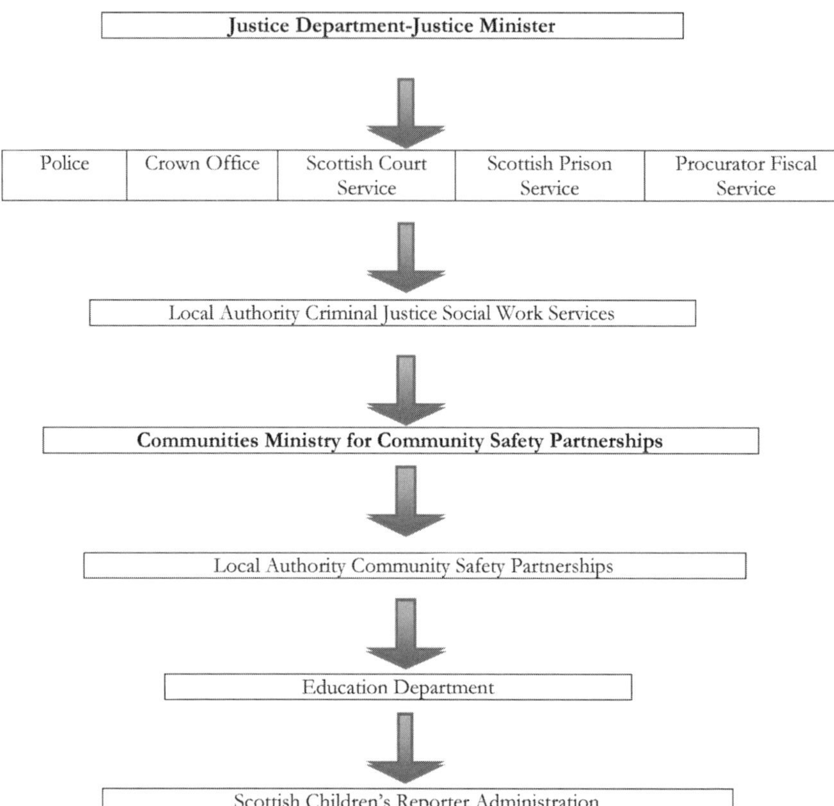

Figure 17.1 Scottish criminal justice agencies

This chapter will focus on social policy developments following the implementation of the Scotland Act 1998, which established the Scottish Parliament. It is important that this is placed in the context of the disbandment of the Probation Service in Scotland and the introduction of criminal justice social work services in the Social Work (Scotland) Act 1968. Instrumental in the development of criminal justice social work were recommendations from the *Children and Young Persons, Scotland* report (Kilbrandon Report 1964). It advocated the merging of child care services and the work of the Probation Service. A key factor was the removal of juvenile offenders from the remit of probation services. Criminal justice social work services at this time were rooted in a welfarist treatment model. The offender was viewed as a person in need. This influenced the sentencing perspective toward rehabilitation of the offender using probation orders. The key legislative framework for supporting this theme was contained within the Social Work (Scotland) Act

1968, section 12 (1): 'by making available advice, guidance and assistance' to promote the welfare of persons within the local authority area.

Further specific provision in relation to the supervision and care of persons placed on probation or released from prison can be found in section 27 of this Act. This particular piece of legislation changed the autonomous role of the probation officer to the role of the criminal justice social worker acting as an agent of the court and accountable through the employing local authority.

The integration of offender services within local authority social work became problematic. This was a direct consequence of funding being diverted toward child protection, and as a result of the development of generic teams, where priority was given to child protection.

The then Scottish Office recognised the difficulties encountered by local authorities in securing funding for criminal justice services as a consequence of the development of generic social work teams. To redress this balance, 100 per cent core funding was introduced through the Law Reform (Miscellaneous Provisions) (Scotland) Act 1990 to enable local authorities to meet their obligations.

The Social Work Services Group (SWSG) was tasked with the development of National Objectives and Standards within the criminal justice system (Social Work Services Group 1991). These standards clearly set out the procedural guidance for activities concerned with offenders from the preparation of reports through to how probation, community service and parole licence should be undertaken. Such standards were introduced to increase the confidence of the courts in the provision of offender services.

Sentencing perspectives within criminal justice

The 1980s saw an increase in the use of custody, to the point of prison overcrowding. The emphasis demonstrates a shift away from treatment and welfarist approaches to that of 'just deserts' in the treatment of offenders. This is consistent with retribution theory whereby the punishment should be proportionate to the seriousness of the offence (Roberts 2008) and the punishment should fit the crime.

Such moves clearly shifted away from the original ethos of the rehabilitation of offenders to protection of the public. The political agenda began to change following the 1979 General Election with law and order becoming a key issue. This was a direct response to 'rising crime, public disorder, political protest and industrial unrest ... merged to form an image of a society under siege from the forces of lawlessness' (Savage and Robins 1990: 89)

Legislative changes were implemented to reflect a move away from the welfarist approach toward offenders. Additional funding was made available to meet the law and order challenge by increasing police pay and the number of police officers.

The 1990s saw legislation introduced to amend criminal justice proceedings and to bring on stream a range of community-based sentences, to provide more suitable alternatives to custody. Significant amongst the legislation was the Criminal Procedure (Scotland) Act 1995, which provides much of the legislative framework for government policy in consolidating Scottish criminal law, evidence and procedure. Research by McGuire (McGuire and Priestley 1995) was published in relation to work with offenders, specifically in what type of interventions worked with offenders and what were the associated pre-requisites. These became known as the 'What Works Principles':

1. 'risk classification' relates to the level of assessed risk posed by the offender being matched with the level of intervention;
2. the identification of criminogenic needs and targeting appropriate interventions to address criminogenic needs and reduce reoffending. Criminogenic needs are factors which contribute to offending behaviour. These include substance misuse, financial problems, accommodation difficulties, poor education, work, social skills, problematic relationships and mental health problems;
3. responsivity, where the learning style of the offender is considered with programmes to develop skills;
4. interventions undertaken in the community fare better than those in custody as offenders are able to practise new learning and skills;
5. 'programme integrity' requires intervention to be delivered as prescribed in the associated programme manual, where the programme has been identified as being effective and accredited for use; and
6. evaluation (McGuire and Priestley 1995).

The development of 'what works', saw a resurgence in the rehabilitative model in the late 1990s. This acknowledged the need to reform offenders and for offenders to take responsibility for their offending behaviour. This included the use of surveillance and greater monitoring, reflecting the political agenda of public protection.

This led to a 'mixed economy' of sentencing approaches, including reparation and restoration. These approaches focused on the notion that the offender should compensate the victim or the community either financially or through undertaking a specific task. Deterrence involves the use of sentences aimed at deterring offending behaviour. Prison and indeed capital punishment were viewed as sentences which would act to deter offending behaviour. It is evident that prison is no more an effective deterrent than other high tariff sentencing options (Doob and Webster 2004). Prison acts to provide an incapacitation effect in line with a public protection agenda.

Table 17.1 sets out the different sentencing perspectives, sentence disposals associated with that perspective and the legislative and policy frameworks.

Table 17.1 Sentencing perspectives, legislation and associated policy

Sentencing perspective	Sentence	Legislation	Policy
Welfarist/ Rehabilitative The offender is seen as a person in need	Probation	Social Work (Scotland) Act 1968	Welfarist
'Just deserts' The punishment is seen to fit the crime	Financial penalty Community service order Imprisonment	Criminal Procedure (Scotland) Act 1995; Crime and Punishment Act 1997	Retribution. 'Twin track' policy regarding re-sentencing. *National Objectives and Standards for Social Work in the Criminal Justice System* (Social Work Services Group 1991)
Restorative Justice The offender is encouraged to take responsibility for their offending	Compensation Order	Criminal Procedure Scotland Act 1995	Social Inclusion through 'reintegrative shaming' (Braithwaite 1989)
	Community Service Order		
	Victim mediation and reparation		Tough on Crime, Tough on the causes of crime
	Probation		
	Diversion from Prosecution scheme (not a sentence of the court: diverted from court process by the Procurator Fiscal for social work intervention)	No legal basis although used under the terms of s. 27 of Social Work Scotland Act 1968	*Smarter Justice, Safer Communities* (Scottish Government 2005a) expansion of alternatives to and the expansion of alternatives to custody

Deterrence	High level Financial penalty	Criminal Procedure Scotland Act 1995	Punishment Social Control
	Community Service Order	Crime and Punishment Act 1997	Incapacitation
	Imprisonment		Retribution. 'Crime doesn't pay'
	Confiscation of property	Proceeds of Crime Act 2002	*Supporting, Safer, Stronger Communities* (Scottish Executive 2004a)
Rehabilitative /Monitoring/ Surveillance	Probation Community Service Order	Social Work Scotland Act 1968	*National Objectives and Standards for Social Work in the Criminal Justice System* (Social Work Services Group 1991).'What Works' (McGuire 1995). *Supporting Safer, Stronger Communities* (Scottish Executive 2004a)
	Restriction of Liberty Order	Criminal Procedure Scotland Act 1995	*Social Inclusion – A Scotland Where Everyone Matters: Our Vision for Social Justice Scottish Office* (Scottish Office 1999b)
	Drug Treatment and Testing Order	Crime and Punishment Act 1997	*Social Inclusion: Opening the Door to a Better Scotland* (Scottish Office 1999c) *Fair, Fast, Flexible Justice* (Scottish Government 2008a)
	Extended Sentence Order for Lifelong Restriction	Crime and Disorder Act 1998	*Multi-Agency Public Protection and Risk Management* (Scottish Government 2008d)

Exercise 17.1

You have read about the different sentencing perspectives and how these have influenced sentencing within the criminal justice system. Try looking at newspaper articles and websites which depict offences, offenders and the sentences imposed. Then consider which sentencing perspective you think is being applied. What similarities if any can be seen between offenders who commit similar offences? What perspectives have you identified?

Comment

Did you identify appropriate material, sentencing perspectives used, factors involved in the sentence imposed? Do you think it will be effective in reducing reoffending? In Scotland the courts currently operate an individualised approach to sentencing, that is, the sentencer considers the individual circumstances of the offender and the offence and imposes an appropriate sentence. Only cases such as murder carry a mandatory life sentence, which demonstrates an equalised sentencing approach.

Supervision following custodial sentences

The Prisoners and Criminal Procedures Act 1993 recognised the need for mandatory supervision of offenders following release from custody after serving sentences of four years or more. This was indicative of the Scottish Office policy shift toward public protection. Subsequent legislation has provided more options, for example the Crime and Disorder Act 1998 s86, which introduced extended sentences. This allows the court to impose a longer period of supervision in the community post release where the usual period is insufficient to manage the risk. The sentence imposed is comprised of a custodial element and a supervision element. The Criminal Justice (Scotland) Act 2003 saw the introduction of the Order for Lifelong Restriction, which could be imposed where the offender is deemed to present an ongoing significant risk to the public.

The introduction of the Crime and Punishment (Scotland) Act 1997 saw a major policy shift away from welfare and treatment to a retribution or 'just deserts' perspective, that is, the punishment should fit the crime. It also acknowledged a growing concern regarding the number of prisoners reoffending after release from custody. This Act initiated provision for vulnerable witnesses to enable them to give evidence.

Victims of crime within the policy context

Services for victims of crime began to develop further with the introduction of the *Scottish Strategy for Victims* (Scottish Executive 2001a). Its key aims were to provide better access to information relating to criminal proceedings regarding the perpetrator, and to increase support from statutory organisations including the Procurator Fiscal's Office. This included extending the Victim Notification Scheme which allows victims to be made aware of when an offender is due to be released. This only applies where the offender has received a custodial sentence of 18 months or more. Other measures included the development of a victim information and advice service and a sense of greater participation within the criminal justice system (Scottish Executive 2001a). It also set out measures for piloting the use of victim statements being put before the court prior to sentencing for serious offences.

Subsequent measures to develop services for victims and to encourage vulnerable witnesses to give evidence in court have been introduced in the Vulnerable Witnesses (Scotland) Act 2004. The Criminal Justice and Licensing (Scotland) Bill (2009) considers ways to provide courts with the power to provide support for victims by allowing them to give evidence anonymously and by developing existing measures for children and vulnerable witnesses.

Other measures are available to victims of crime through Victim Support Scotland, which is operated by volunteers and staff and holds charitable status. The Criminal Injuries Compensation Authority provides a service on behalf of the Scottish Government for those persons who have suffered physical or mental injury as a result of violent crime. This includes ensuring victims are kept informed of proceedings, thus fulfilling the Scottish Government's policy to include victims at all stages.

Exercise 17.2

Please read the following victim statement:

'The actions of Mr. White have impacted greatly on my life. Since the offence I have been unable to sleep, as I am afraid someone will break into the house and sexually assault me again. I find it difficult to go out, maintain daily life and develop and maintain relationships. Due to the stress of coming to terms with what has happened, I have been diagnosed with depression and am currently receiving medication and counselling. As a result I have had a significant period of sickness absence, which has impacted financially.'

If you were acting as the Sheriff in this case, how might this affect the sentence you gave to the offender?
What sentencing perspective would this involve?
What might the court request to assist in sentencing?

Comment

In Scotland sentencing is predominantly based on an individualised approach based on all the circumstances involved in that particular case. These would include the individual characteristics and offending history of the offender, the assessed risk the offender poses to the community and whether the offender pled guilty to the offence or went through trial proceedings. The Criminal Procedure (Amendment) (Scotland) Act 2004 s20 amends the Criminal Procedure (Scotland) Act 1995 through the insertion of s196 to provide for a reduction in sentence where the offender pleads guilty. Should the sentencer not follow this, the reasons must be given.

The sentencer would be aware of the opportunities for the offender whilst in custody. This would include participation in programmes of intervention to address his/her offending behaviour to reduce the propensity to offend following release. A Social Enquiry Report (SER) would be requested to provide background information to the court prior to sentencing. In acknowledging a custodial sentence is inevitable, the author of the SER should identify whether there is an ongoing risk to the public following release. In such circumstances where the offender poses risk, measures required to protect the community such as an extended sentence might be considered. If you recall, this provides for a longer period of supervision once released on licence and could be recommended in the SER.

As criminal justice social workers it is important to maintain a professional value base, using unconditional positive regard (Rogers 1995) as there are times when our professional and personal value bases come into conflict. It is important that good supervision is used in order to allow exploration of these conflicts to facilitate resolution. When considering your response to these questions were you able to step into the shoes of the Sheriff?

Exercise 17.3

Robert is 22 years old and he has three previous convictions for breach of the peace, all of which were committed whilst under the influence of alcohol. Previous court appearances have resulted in financial penalties, all of which he paid. A police report has been sent to the Procurator Fiscal. What options are available to the Procurator Fiscal in this situation?

Comment

The Procurator Fiscal in considering the police report will take the following factors into consideration: the seriousness of the crime, the severity of the crime, the impact upon any victims, any previous convictions (and in this case we are aware of three similar offences) and the possible sentence which could be imposed. The Procurator Fiscal might also take into consideration *Smarter Justice, Safer Communities* (Scottish Government 2005a), which advocates the use of alternatives to prosecution.

We know that the imposition of previous financial penalties have not acted as a deterrent. The Procurator Fiscal could consider taking no further action as it is not in the public interest to prosecute, although this is highly unlikely given Robert's previous offending history. Another option could be to prosecute using summary procedure in either the Justice of the Peace Court or Sheriff Court. A further option which might be appropriate is for the case to be referred to the Criminal Justice Social Work Department for assessment for diversion from the prosecution scheme. This is a low-level crime and assessment might identify underlying criminogenic needs which if addressed during a three-month period could be an effective early intervention and reduce the risk of further offending.

Formation of the Scottish Parliament

In 1998 a devolved parliament was constituted in Scotland in the Scotland Act 1998. *A Safer Scotland: Tackling Crime and its Causes* (Scottish Office 1999a) was published. It laid out the Scottish Parliament's strategy for dealing with crime and the causes of crime. The objectives of this paper were protection of the public, development of partnership arrangements to promote safer communities, increased funding for policing, the development of strategies for dealing with drug using offenders, tackling the causes of crime and working effectively with offenders to raise public confidence regarding the criminal justice system. In order to take this policy forward there was a need to reorganise local authorities. This policy was consistent with New Labour's *Tough on Crime and Tough on the Causes of Crime,* a theme which underpinned the 1997 election campaign (Scottish Executive 1999).

Human rights

The introduction of the Human Rights Act 1998 led to significant legislative changes pertaining to the release of prisoners subject to mandatory life sentences. The Prisoners and Criminal Proceedings (Scotland) Act 1993 as amended by the Convention of Rights (Compliance) (Scotland) Act 2001 made provision for a minimum punishment period to be made before the offender becomes eligible for consideration for release on life licence. Following expiry of the set punishment period the prisoner can apply to the Parole Board for Scotland for release. In such circumstances the Parole Board for Scotland sits as a Life Prisoner Tribunal.

The move toward a single corrections agency

In 2003 the Labour Party in Scotland sought to reconstruct criminal justice social work services through introducing a single correctional agency. This would have resulted in the removal of criminal justice social work services from local authorities and their realignment with the Scottish Prison Service into a single corrections agency. The rationale for such a measure was focused on the increasing re-offending rates and the premise that it would increase the confidence of the judiciary and the public in the use and delivery of community sentences.

As part of this process a consultation was undertaken resulting in the publication of *Re:duce, Re:habilitate, Re:form* (Scottish Executive 2004b) which looked at current service provision within criminal justice agencies. This included seeking the views of service users. It identified key themes, reducing re-offending, roles and responsibilities, purpose of prison, addressing re-offending, integration between agencies and effectiveness in terms of value for money. This resulted in the development of *Supporting Safer, Stronger Communities: Scotland's Criminal Justice Plan* (Scottish Executive 2004a). This set out a number of key interventions in working with offenders, drugs, crime prevention, public protection, improving services for victims and witnesses, sentencing disposals and effective service provision to promote the rehabilitation of offenders

The consultation process highlighted information sharing across agencies as an area of concern and the introduction of a single correctional agency was seen as a way of reducing such problems. A single correctional agency was actively rejected by the Association of Directors of Social Work (ADSW) and the Convention of Local Authority Organisations (CoSLA). Extensive lobbying within the Scottish Office by ADSW led to the introduction of service provision to offenders arrested or in custody within the Criminal Justice (Scotland) Act 2003 s71.

The single corrections agency was eventually abandoned and Community Justice Authorities (CJAs) were introduced in the Management of Offenders etc. (Scotland) Act 2005. The CJAs comprise of local authorities, the Scottish Prison Service, health services, police and key voluntary organisations brought together to ensure the right services are in the right place at the right time. A key objective of CJAs is to provide an integrated approach with a shared duty, to reduce reoffending (Scottish Government 2006a).

Risk Management Authority

The Risk Management Authority was established in 2004 in the Criminal Justice (Scotland) Act 2003 following recommendations in the Mclean *Report into Serious Violent and Sexual Offenders* (Scottish Executive 2000) and *Reducing the Risk: Improving the Response to Sex Offending* (Scottish Executive 2001b). Both reports highlighted the need for robust risk assessment and risk management procedures together with appropriate levels of supervision. The Risk Management Authority has responsibility for promoting public protection by developing professional practice in the management of offenders presenting a serious risk of harm. Its key objectives are to provide an advisory service regarding offender risk assessment, risk management, promote research and oversee accreditation and to approve risk management plans in respect of offenders placed on an Order for Lifelong Restriction.

We can clearly see that public protection and community safety is now the major policy driver. Risk assessment tools providing greater reliability in terms of identifying high-risk offenders utilise actuarial and clinical factors and importantly contain a risk management section. Rigorous and robust risk assessment, development of risk management plans and accredited programmes of intervention employed within the criminal justice system are intended to reduce risk, minimise harm and promote desistance (see

Shirran, Loxton and Hothersall 2010). The role of the criminal justice social worker is clearly as an agent of social control and a key aspect of maintaining successful working relationships with high-risk offenders is the ability to balance the tensions between welfare and social control.

Domestic violence

Domestic violence has a much higher profile within the criminal justice system. Historically it was viewed as a private matter; it is now recognised as a criminal act and as such should be treated accordingly. Domestic abuse is defined by the Association of Chief Police Officers as 'any form of physical, non-physical or sexual abuse which takes place within the context of a close relationship committed either in the home or elsewhere. In most cases this relationship will be between partners (married, co-habiting or otherwise) and ex-partners' (Association of Chief Police Officers n.d.: 2).

In Scotland the development of domestic abuse strategies has prompted the development of local authorities providing specific services for victims of domestic abuse. Within local police forces, specially trained officers lead investigations into domestic abuse. In Scotland the Protection from Abuse (Scotland) Act 2001 provides powers of arrest where an interdict is in place. This is particularly important given that approximately 750,000 children witness domestic abuse each year, and in 2006/7 83 women and 27 men were killed by a partner or ex-partner and 54 per cent of serious assaults were perpetrated by a partner or ex-partner (Howarth 2008).

Women offenders

Concern regarding the suicide of seven female prisoners within a period of 30 months at HMP Cornton Vale (Scotland's only female prison) prompted the Scottish Office to call for a review into community sentences and the use of custody in December 1997. *Women Offenders: A Safer Way* (Scottish Office 1998) identified that very few (about 1 per cent) female prisoners were in prison as a result of the seriousness of their offence. In the main most were imprisoned for non-compliance with community-based sentences. The report concluded that the characteristics surrounding female offending differ to a large extent from that of male offenders. This is in part due to the fact that often women have been, or continue to be, victimised by a male, highlighting issues of power and control.

Harper et al. (2005) identified an increase in criminogenic need for women particularly with regard to relationships and emotional well-being, whereas male offenders demonstrated an increase in criminogenic need in relation to offending behaviour, substance misuse, cognition and attitudes toward offending. Therefore programmes of intervention for male offenders are often not appropriate to address the needs of female offenders.

Similarly, research undertaken by Koons et al. (1997) focused on victimisation and self-esteem in women offenders. They concluded that programmes that addressed previous experiences of victimisation and targeted self-esteem showed encouraging results; however, they acknowledged this required further study.

In 2002 the Scottish Executive published a further report, *A Better Way: The Report of the Ministerial Group on Women Offending* (Scottish Government 2002), to identify the progress made since the publication of *Women Offenders: A Safer Way*. This report found that whilst some progress had been made through improvements to the prison estate, the number of women being sent to custody continued to rise. This was despite the introduction of Supervised Attendance Orders as an alternative to imprisonment for unpaid fines.

A Better Way (Scottish Government 2002) identified that 84 per cent of female offenders were sentenced to custody serving 3 months or less, with high numbers being held on remand and for fine default. The report focused on four areas: breakdown of the female prisoner population, prevention

Table 17.2 Notification for registration periods: Sex Offenders Act 1997

Description of person	Applicable period
A person who, in respect of the offence, is or has been sentenced to imprisonment for life or for a term of 30 months or more	An indefinite period
A person who, in respect of the offence or finding, is or has been admitted to a hospital subject to a restriction order	An indefinite period
A person who, in respect of the offence, is or has been sentenced to imprisonment for a term of more than 6 months but less than 30 months	A period of 10 years beginning with the relevant date
A person who, in respect of the offence, is or has been sentenced to imprisonment for a term of 6 months or less	A period of 7 years beginning with that date
A person who, in respect of the offence or finding, is or has been admitted to a hospital without being subject to a restriction order	A period of 7 years beginning with that date
A person of any other description	A period of 5 years beginning with that date

and effective intervention, community disposals and aftercare for those following release from custody. The report noted that some local authority areas had proposals to set up specific projects to work with female offenders, an example being 'Time Out' in Glasgow (Criminal Justice Scotland 2004).

Despite these efforts, the number of female prisoners continued to increase. The *Gender Equality Scheme* (Scottish Government 2008b) identified that the number of female prisoners had increased over the previous 10 years. It also identified that 98 per cent of female prisoners in HMP Cornton Vale had substance misuse problems, 80 per cent had mental health issues, 70 per cent had a history of abuse and 50 per cent had self-harmed at some point in their lives. One of the actions identified to reduce the number of female offenders being sent to custody was the piloting of mentoring schemes. These schemes would be part of a community-based sentence together with interventions designed to address gender specific needs.

As a result of the work undertaken by the Scottish Parliament's Equality Committee, the Scottish Justice Minister announced that £800,000 of new funding would be made available to the Community Justice Authorities in a bid to address female offending behaviour.

Sex offenders

As a result of increasing public concern regarding offences being committed by known sex offenders, the UK government responded with the introduction of the Sex Offenders Act 1997. For the first time, all sex offenders who were subject to a sentence of the court on 1 September 1997 would become subject to the requirement to register with the police. (Table 17.2 indicates the notification for registration periods according to the Sex Offenders Act 1997.) In addition, offenders were required to provide information including their address and a multi-agency risk assessment would be carried out with appropriate risk management plans developed on the basis of this.

The Sexual Offences Act 2003 saw the introduction of Sexual Offences Prevention Orders which replace the Sex Offender Order established in the Crime and Disorder Act 1998. Sexual Offences Prevention Orders are civil orders which were introduced primarily to protect the public from sexual harm by placing restrictions on the offender's activities. A court may impose a Sexual Offence Prevention Order where an offender has received a conviction for an offence as appears in schedule 3 which relates to sexual offences, or schedule 5 other serious offences, where he or she is assessed as posing a serious risk of harm.

The Protection of Children and Prevention of Sexual Offences (Scotland) Act 2005 provided the legislative framework for the introduction of Risk of Sexual Harm Orders. Such an order can be made where an offender is implicated in sexual activity with a child or in his or her presence, exposing a child to sexual photographic or film material, or using sexual language in any communication with a child.

A key development in identifying internet offenders is the establishment of the Child Protection and Online Protection Centre which is part of the UK police and is involved in identifying offenders, working in partnership with other agencies and international forces.

The use of risk assessment tools when assessing sex offenders has developed significantly over the last 15 years. Currently Risk Matrix 2000 and Stable and Acute 2007 risk assessment tools are being used in Scotland (Scottish Government 2002; 2007).

An important protection element to be considered for sex offenders is appropriate accommodation both to provide effective monitoring of the offender and to safeguard the community. This should also take into account any risk of vigilantism which could put the offender at risk of harm from the public. *Toward a National Accommodation Strategy for Sex Offenders* (Scottish Government 2005c) recognised the need to ensure stable and safe accommodation for sex offenders. It was recognised that this was required to improve the monitoring and supervision of the offender and to facilitate engagement with services to address offending behaviour through the use of cognitive-behavioural programmes of intervention.

Short sentence licence

The Management of Offenders (Scotland) Act 2005 introduced new provisions for sex offenders sentenced to a period of imprisonment of between 6 months and 4 years. This facilitates the supervision of cases where prisoners serving short sentences are released on licence, after completion of half of their sentence. The offender then becomes subject to licence conditions for the duration of the sentence rather than being released unconditionally at the half-way stage of their sentence. This means the offender will serve the latter part of his/her sentence in the community and he or she will be subject to supervision for the licence period. Conditions such as participation in programmes to address offending behaviour and restrictions on certain activities may be applied.

Multi-Agency Public Protection Arrangements (MAPPA)

Where an offender has been deemed to present a serious risk of reoffending following assessment, the case should be referred to a Multi-Agency Public Protection Arrangements meeting. MAPPA draws on a number of agencies involved in protecting the community, including criminal justice social work, probation service, police, health services, housing and voluntary organisations such as SACRO. There are three levels within MAAPA. Level one is for those offenders assessed as presenting a low or medium risk of serious harm to the public and the case is managed under normal agency management policy and procedures. Level two refers to those offenders assessed as posing a high or very high risk of harm; these offenders are managed at an inter-agency risk management level. Level three refers to those offenders who are assessed as presenting a very high risk of causing serious harm or where management is problematic and requires multi-agency co-operation under Multi-Agency Public Protection Panels (MAPPPs). In such cases there may be a requirement for additional resources to be put in place and this requires agency involvement at a senior level.

In order to carry out their function effectively, sharing of information between participating organisations is essential to develop appropriate risk management, monitoring and review. In order to assist MAPPA in its operations ViSOR (the Violent and Sex Offenders Register) was set up to store and share information and intelligence on offenders identified as presenting serious risk of harm. It provides information to police officers on how many registered sex offenders are in their area and for what crimes they have been placed on the register. The system is operated between 'responsible authorities' (police, criminal justice services/probation services and prison services) to facilitate risk management.

Rising prison populations

As in the late 1970s and 1980s, rising prison numbers are a dominant feature of the law and order debate not just in Scotland but elsewhere in the UK. The prison population has been rising steadily since 2001, reaching an average daily population of 7,835 during the year 2008/9. Scotland continues to imprison significantly higher numbers than many other European countries. Indeed it was identified as being twelfth highest, locking up 150 per 100,000 head of population (Scottish Government 2009). One measure to reduce prison overcrowding resulted in the building of two new privately operated prisons, HMP Kilmarnock in 1999, which is run by SERCO, and Addiewell prison in West Lothian, which opened in December 2008 and is run by Kalyx.

An analysis of the prisoners released in 1998 who served three months or less in custody (51 per cent) indicated that a high proportion were imprisoned again within two years of release (48 per cent) (Scottish Executive 2003). Statistics released from a study undertaken in 2005/6 suggest these figures have continued to rise (79 per cent) (Scottish Government 2009). In a press release dated 31 August 2009, the Scottish Justice Minister stated:

> The fact that three out of four offenders who leave prison after a short sentence are reconvicted within two years demonstrates the urgent need for a coherent approach to tackling reoffending. (Scottish Government 2009: 1)

Measures to reduce the prison population

This once again placed law and order high on the political agenda. As in the late 1970s, the drive toward identifying alternative measures to the use of custody became the focus of the Scottish Government's policy on dealing with rising prison populations.

One measure adopted by the Scottish Government was to set up the Scottish Prisons Commission which published its report *Scotland's Choice* in 2008 (Scottish Government 2008c). In this report, consideration was given to court processes, the use of community-based sentences, the current use of imprisonment and sentence management and the open prison estate. The Commission recommended the introduction of *Community Payback*. This encompassed a range of measures including a Community Supervision Sentence which could have a range of conditions imposed. These could include attendance at a training or education programme, undertaking community service and addressing offending behaviour programmes. This is very much based within a restorative/reparation sentencing perspective, where the offender is encouraged to make good the harm caused by his or her offending behaviour (Scottish Government 2008c).

Home detention curfews

The Management of Offenders etc. (Scotland) Act 2005, section 15 introduced Home Detention Curfews (HDC) as a measure to reduce the prison population and promote the reintegration of offenders back into the community. In essence the prisoner is eligible for consideration for a HDC where they may be released early from custody. This measure pertains to those offenders deemed to present a low risk of reoffending. Where a prisoner is being released under this scheme, a risk assessment must be completed. The prisoner once released will be subject to electronic tagging to restrict their movements for up to a maximum period of 12 hours per day. Sex offenders are not eligible for this scheme under the current legislation.

Open prisons

The Scottish Prison Service operates the open prison estate which includes Castle Huntly and Noranside. Transfer to open prison is ordinarily used where a prisoner is assessed as presenting a low risk of absconding and a low risk of harm to the public. As a result of a number of high-profile cases where a prisoner has absconded, including Robert Foye who absconded from Castle Huntly in August 2007 and committed a serious sexual offence, a review was ordered and measures were tightened up. However, following the absconding of another serious offender, Brian Martin, in 2009 a further review was ordered. The conclusion was that information on the risk of absconding had been overlooked in the preparation of the risk assessment by the Scottish Prison Service (Scottish Government 2010).

Youth justice

Public concerns regarding levels of youth offending have shaped negative attitudes toward the treatment of young, persistent offenders. These have shifted between punitive and rehabilitative perspectives and back again.

The Crime and Disorder Act 1998 introduced Anti-Social Behaviour Orders, the so-called ASBOs. ASBOs were viewed as means of preventing or discouraging young people from engaging in criminal activity by addressing the risk factors associated with offending. The main element was that the young person would be held accountable for their behaviour by placing an emphasis on restorative justice and requiring the offender to repair the harm caused by criminal behaviour through challenging apparent deficits in their moral reasoning. Furthermore, reintegration into mainstream society is viewed as an objective, provided that it is accompanied by some means of addressing the risk factors associated with offending. Hannah-Moffat (1999: 88) suggests a 'blurring of needs with risks has taken place'. Risk becomes focused on the failings of the young offender, often arising from poor parental guidance, disruptive behaviour either at school, at home or through their association with an anti-social peer group. The aim of the 1998 Act was to enable young offenders to address risk factors and be reintegrated into their communities as part of the Government's policy on *social inclusion* (see Chapter 5). Further measures were introduced in the Anti-Social Behaviour (Scotland) Act 2004 to support victims of and witnesses to anti-social behaviour through the development of strategies which will allow people to report incidents without fear of intimidation or harassment.

In 2002 the Effectiveness of the Youth Justice Group in 2002 was tasked to improve the youth justice system. *Dealing with Offending by Young People* (Audit Scotland 2002) led to the introduction of National Standards for the Youth Justice System in Scotland. The introduction of Youth Courts in pilot areas where persistent young offenders could be dealt with and Youth Justice Teams to assist the transition from children's services into the criminal justice system would be more effective. An evaluation undertaken in 2006 concluded that the two pilot courts in Airdrie and Hamilton had achieved some of the objectives set, such as reducing reoffending through prompt disposal and provision of appropriate interventions. These were undertaken either through orders of the court or structured deferred sentences. Social workers reported that programmes where employment, training or education were targeted had greater success (Scottish Government 2006b)

Additional measures have been introduced in relation to persistent young offenders including intensive monitoring and supervision. This measure is consistent with the *Getting it Right for Every Child* (Scottish Government 2005b) ethos to support vulnerable young people at high risk of reoffending. These measures include electronic monitoring or movement restriction conditions, structured intervention programmes, provision of educational and training opportunities, respite care and 24-hour support.

Twenty-first century services?

As part of the 21st Century Social Work Review a literature review was commissioned by the Scottish Executive's Social Work Services Inspectorate regarding criminal justice social work (Social Work Inspection Agency 2005). This review considered the skills and knowledge base which criminal justice social workers required in order to work with and manage change effectively. These skills included developing effective working relationships with offenders which support change, identifying and delivering research based interventions. All of these are aimed at reducing reoffending and promoting desistance and supporting the Scottish Government's commitment to social inclusion.

Chapter summary

The criminal justice system will remain prominent within the Scottish policy context. Therefore criminal justice social workers need to be equipped with the knowledge base to be able to carry out effective practice. This can be achieved through participation in relevant training to undertake assessment of risk and use of accredited programmes of intervention. Public protection remains central to the policy agenda, with the expectation that offenders accept responsibility for their offending. The increased use of community-based sentences which are supervised rigorously is central to the Scottish government's commitment to reduce the number of offenders going to custody.

Research into what works with offenders remains critical in terms of informing practice. Bringing about desistance through building family ties, and providing offenders with opportunities to 'tell their own story' in order to develop their sense of identity has been proven to be effective (Maruna 2000).

Partnership working and agency cooperation in assessing and managing risk as set out in *Supporting, Safer, Stronger Communities: Scotland's Criminal Justice Plan* (Scottish Executive 2004a) remains very much in evidence.

References

Association of Chief Police Officers (n.d.), 'In Partnership: Challenging Domestic Abuse', Joint Protocol between Association of Chief Police Officers (ACPOS) in Scotland and the Crown Office and Procurator Fiscal Service (COPFS). Available at: http://www.acpos.police.uk/Documents/Policies/CRIME%20-%20ACPOS%20COPFS%20Domestic%20Abuse.pdf (accessed 15 January 2010).

Audit Scotland (2002), *Dealing with Offending by Young People*. Available at: http://www.auditscotland.gov.uk/docs/central/2003/nr_031106_youth justice.pdf (accessed 12 July 2008).

Braithwaite, J. (1989), *Crime, Shame and Reintegration* (Cambridge: Cambridge University Press).

Criminal Justice Scotland (2004), 'Alternatives to Prison: Glasgow's Women's Project Opens At Last'. Available at: http://www.cjscotland.org.uk/index.

php/cjscotland/dynamic_archives_GET/2004/01/ (accessed 13 February 2010).

Doob, A.N. and Webster, C. (2004), 'Sentence Severity and Crime: Accepting the Null Hypothesis', in M. Tonry (ed.), *Crime and Justice: A Review of Research* (Chicago, IL: University of Chicago Press).

Hannah-Moffat, K. (1999), 'Moral Agent or Actuarial Subject? Risk and Canadian Women's Imprisonment', *Theoretical Criminology* 3: 71–94.

Harper, G., Man, L.H., Taylor, S. and Niven, S. (2005), 'Factors Associated with Offending', in G. Harper and C. Chitty (eds), *The Impact of Corrections on Re-offending: A Review of 'What Works'*, Home Office Research Study No. 291 (2nd edn) (London: Home Office).

Howarth, S. (2008), 'In Figures: Domestic Abuse', National Assembly for Wales. Available at: http://www.assemblywales.org/08-040.pdf (accessed 14 August 2009).

Kilbrandon Report (1964), *Children and Young Persons, Scotland*. Available at: http://www.scotland.gov.uk/Publications/2003/10/18259/26892#246 date (accessed 10 November 2009).

Koons, B.A., Burrows, J.D., Morash, M. and Bynum, T. (1997), 'Expert and Offender Perceptions of Program Elements Linked to Successful Outcomes for Incarcerated Women', *Crime and Delinquency* 43: 512–32.

Maruna, S. (2000), 'Desistance from Crime and Offender Rehabilitation: A Tale of Two Research Literatures', *Offender Programs Report* 4(1): 1–13.

McGuire, J. (ed.) (1995), *What Works: Reducing Reoffending* (Chichester: John Wiley).

McGuire, J. and Priestley, P. (1995), 'Reviewing "What Works": Past, Present and Future', in J. McGuire (ed.), *What Works: Reducing Reoffending* (Chichester: John Wiley).

Roberts, J. (2008), *Punishing Persistent Offenders: Exploring Community and Offender Perspectives*, Clarendon Studies in Criminology (Oxford: Oxford University Press).

Rogers, C. (1995), *A Therapist's View of Psychotherapy: On Becoming a Person* (London: Constable).

Savage, S. and Robins, L. (eds) (1990), *Public Policy under Thatcher* (London: Macmillan).

Scottish Executive (1999), 'Minister Outlines Way Forward for Criminal Justice Social Work', News Release: SE1070/1999, 28/10/99. Available at: http://www.scotland.gov.uk/News/Releases/1999/10/3a2ef89a-0427-4558-8b2d-6481b685b01c (accessed 14 January 2010).

— (2000), *Report into Serious Violent and Sexual Offenders*. Available at: http://scotland.gov.uk/maclean/docs/svso-00.asp (accessed 15 January 2010).

— (2001a), *Scottish Strategy for Victims*. Available at: http://www.scotland.gov.uk/Publications/2001/01/7964/File-1 (accessed 14 January 2010).

—— (2001b), *Reducing the Risk: Improving the Response to Sex Offending*. Availableat:http://www.scotland.gov.uk/News/Releases/2001/06/71b84a73-8a53-4b59-9175-b26d2282da9f (accessed 15 January 2010).
—— (2002), *A Better Way: The Report of the Ministerial Group on Women Offending*. Available at: http://www.scotland.gov.uk/Resource/Doc/158858/0043144.pdf (accessed 16 January 2010).
—— (2003), *Report to the Criminal Justice Forum on Short Term Sentences*. Available at: http://www.scotland.gov.uk/Publications/2003/02/16442/18506 (accessed 25 January 2010).
—— (2004a), *Supporting Safer, Stronger Communities: Scotland's Criminal Justice Plan*. Available at: http://www.scotland.gov.uk/Publications/2004/12/20345/47611 (accessed 15 January 2010).
—— (2004b), *Re:duce, Re:habilitate, Re:form: Reducing Reoffending*. Available at: http://www.scotland.gov.uk/Publications/2004/10/20034/44429 (accessed 14 January 2010).
Scottish Government (2002), *Serious Violent and Sexual Offenders: The Use of Risk Assessment Tools in Scotland*. Available at: http://www.scotland.gov.uk/Publications/2002/11/15734/12665 (accessed 13 February 2010).
—— (2005a), *Smarter Justice, Safer Communities: Summary Justice Reform, Next Steps*. Available at: http://www.scotland.gov.uk/Publications/2005/03/20894/55131 (accessed 15 January 2010).
—— (2005b), *Getting it Right for Every Child*. Available at: http://www.scotland.gov.uk/Resource/Doc/54357/0013270.pdf (accessed 13 February 2010).
—— (2005c), *The National Accommodation Strategy for Sex Offenders*. Available at: http://www.scotland.gov.uk/Publications/2007/03/circjd1506updmar07/Q/Page/15 (accessed 15 January 2010).
—— (2006a), *Reducing Reoffending: National Strategy for the Management of Offenders*. Available at: http://www.scotland.gov.uk/Publications/2006/05/19094327/2 (accessed 15 January 2010).
—— (2006b), *Evaluation of Airdrie and Hamilton Youth Courts*. Available at: http://www.scotland.gov.uk/Publications/2006/06/13155406/7 (accessed 25 January 2010).
—— (2007), *Implementation of the Second Risk Assessment Tool for Use with Sex Offenders, Stable and Acute 2007*, JD Circular No: JD/13/2007. Available at: http://www.scotland.gov.uk/Publications/2007/09/jdcircular132007 (accessed 13 February 2010).
—— (2008a), *Protecting Scotland's Communities: Fair, Fast and Flexible Justice*. Available at: http://www.scotland.gov.uk/Publications/2008/12/16132605/12 date (accessed 15 January 2010).
—— (2008b), *Gender Equality Scheme 2008–11*. Available at: http://www.scotland.gov.uk/Resource/Doc/227413/0061507.pdf (accessed 15 January 2010).

—— (2008c), *Scotland's Choice Report of The Scottish Prisons Commission*. Available at: http://www.scotland.gov.uk/Publications/2008/06/30162955/1 (accessed 15 January 2010).

—— (2008d), *MAPPA Guidance* (Edinburgh: Scottish Government). Available at: http://www.scotland.gov.uk/Topics/Justice/public-safety/offender-management/offender/protection (accessed 28 May 2010).

—— (2009), *Statistical Bulletin: Crime and Justice Series: Prison Statistics: 2008–09*. Available at: http://www.scotland.gov.uk/Publications/2009/11/27092125/4 (accessed 25 January 2010).

—— (2010), *The Scottish Government's Response to Professor Alex Spencer's Report 'Balancing Risk and Need'*. Available at: http://www.scotland.gov.uk/Publications/2010/01/06103357/3 (accessed 25 January 2010).

Scottish Office (1998), *Women Offenders: A Safer Way*. Available at: http://www.scotland.gov.uk/library/documents5/off-01.htm (accessed 16 January 2010).

—— (1999a), *A Safer Scotland: Tackling Crime and its Causes*. Available at: http://www.scotland.gov.uk/library/documents-w6/cp-06.htm (accessed 14 January 2010).

—— (1999b), *A Scotland Where Everyone Matters: Our Vision for Social Justice*. Available at: http://www.scotland.gov.uk/library/documents-w7/sima-00.htm (accessed 15 February 2010).

—— (1999c), *Social Inclusion: Opening the Door to a Better Scotland*. Available at: http://www.scotland.gov.uk/News/Releases/1999/11/e3c12f7b-132d-4f0c-8b57-e2681c088c9e (accessed 15 February 2010).

Shirran, A., Loxton, J. and Hothersall, S.J. (2010), 'Risk', in S.J Hothersall and M. Maas-Lowit (eds), *Risk, Need and Protection in Social Work Practice* (Exeter: Learning Matters): Chapter 2.

Social Work Inspection Agency (2005), *21st Century Social Work* (Edinburgh: Scottish Executive).

Social Work Services Group (1991), *National Objectives for Social Work Services in the Criminal Justice System*. Available at: http://www.scotland.gov.uk/Publications/2004/12/20474/49335 (accessed 10 November 2009).

Legislation

Antisocial Behaviour etc. (Scotland) Act 2004, c. 8. Available at: http://www.opsi.gov.uk/legislation/Scotland/acts2004/asp_20040008_en_1 (accessed 15 January 2010).

Convention Rights (Compliance) (Scotland) Act 2001, asp 7. Available at: http://www.opsi.gov.uk/legislation/scotland/acts2001/asp_20010007_en_1 (accessed 14 January 2010).

Crime and Disorder Act 1998, c. 37. Available at: http://www.opsi.gov.uk/acts/acts1998/ukpga_19980037_en_1 (accessed 14 January 2010).

Crime and Punishment Act 1997, c. 48. Available at: http://www.opsi.gov.uk/acts/acts1997/ukpga_19970048_en_1 (accessed 14 January 2010).

Criminal Justice (Scotland) Act 2003, asp 7. Available at: http://www.opsi.gov.uk/legislation/scotland/acts2003/asp_20030007_en_1 (accessed 14 January 2010).

Criminal Procedure (Scotland) Act 1995, c. 46. Available at: http://www.opsi.gov.uk/Acts/acts1995/ukpga_19950046_en_1 (accessed 10 November 2009).

Criminal Procedure (Amendment) (Scotland) Act 2005, asp 5. Available at: http://www.opsi.gov.uk/legislation/Scotland/acts2004/asp_20040005_en_1 (accessed 10 January 2010).

Human Rights Act 1998, c. 42. Available at: http://www.opsi.gov.uk/ACTS/acts1998/ukpga_19980042_en_1 (accessed 14 January 2010).

Law Reform (Miscellaneous Provisions) (Scotland) Act 1990, c. 40. Available at: http://www.opsi.gov.uk/Acts/acts1990/ukpga_19900040_en_1 (accessed 10 November 2009).

Management of Offenders etc. (Scotland) Act 2005, asp 14. Available at: http://www.opsi.gov.uk/legislation/scotland/acts2005/asp_20050014_en_1 (accessed 15 January 2010).

Prisoners and Criminal Procedures Act 1993, c. 9. Available at: http://www.opsi.gov.uk/ACTS/acts1993/ukpga_19930009_en_1 (accessed 14 January 2010).

Proceeds of Crime Act 2002, c. 29. Available at: http://www.opsi.gov.uk/acts/acts2002/ukpga_20020029_en_1 (accessed 14 January 2010).

Protection of Children and Prevention of Sexual Offences (Scotland) Act 2005, asp 9. Available at: http://www.opsi.gov.uk/legislation/scotland/acts2005/asp_20050009_en_1 (accessed 10 January 2010).

Sex Offenders Act 1997, c. 51. Available at: http://www.opsi.gov.uk/acts/acts1997/ukpga_19970051_en_1 (accessed 28 May 2010).

Sexual Offences Act 2003, c. 42. Available at: http://www.opsi.gov.uk/Acts/acts2003/ukpga_20030042_en_1 (accessed 28 May 2010).

Social Work (Scotland) Act 1968, c. 49 Available at: http://www.opsi.gov.uk/RevisedStatutes/Acts/ukpga/1968/cukpga_19680049_en_1 (accessed 10 November 2009).

Vulnerable Witnesses (Scotland) Act 2004, asp 3. Available at: http://www.opsi.gov.uk/legislation/scotland/acts2004/asp_20040003_en_1 (accessed 14 January 2010).

Web-based resources

BBC News (2007), 'Two Thirds Prisoners Reoffend', Tuesday 9 October. Available at: http://news.bbc.co.uk/1/hi/scotland/7035325.stm (accessed 28 May 2010).

Campsie, A. (2009), 'MacAskill: Justice in Scotland is Sexist', *Herald Scotland*, 12 August. Available at: http://www.heraldscotland.com/macaskill-justice-in-scotland-is-sexist-1.916505 (accessed 15 January 2010).

Scottish Government (2006), *Evaluation of the 218 Centre for Women Offenders*. Available at: http://www.scotland.gov.uk/Publications/2006/04/24161157/0 (accessed 16 January 2010).

Scottish Government (2008), *A Guide to Getting it Right for Every Child*. Available at: http://www.scotland.gov.uk/Publications/2008/09/22091734/0 (accessed 28 January 2010).

Scottish Government (2008), News Release: 'Reconviction Rates 31 August 2009' Available at: http://www.scotland.gov.uk/News/Releases/2009/08/31095423 (accessed 25 January 2010).

18 Asylum and immigration

Clare Swan

Introduction

When this area of practice first came to my attention some years ago I was struck by two things: firstly how little I knew about the subject and secondly how it seemed to be the norm, and even acceptable, for social workers to have no real understanding of even the most fundamental aspects of law and policy that affect asylum seekers and economic migrants.

A few years down the line and it seems to me that there are a number of possible reasons for this 'sanctioned' gap in practice knowledge and expertise. It could be argued that much of the work with displaced persons involves a direct conflict between the needs of the individual and the policies and legislation that are in place to safeguard the perceived needs of society. This is not a comfortable position for the social work profession to find itself in. There would also appear to be a level of structural and cultural racism that is clearly in complete contradiction to social work values and would be exposed as such, if practice issues with regard to asylum seekers and migrants were to be put under the spotlight.

A particular feature of immigration in the UK is that it is a highly legislated and *reserved* area (meaning that control of all aspects of immigration are controlled by the Westminster Parliament; these powers are not *devolved* to the Scottish Parliament or any of the other Regional Assemblies). A useful analogy for the relationship between law and policy is that the two are like rail tracks, running parallel to each other; legislation providing the authority and legal basis for action and policy being the means by which it is interpreted and implemented. However, when it comes to asylum and immigration, the analogy is more like a monorail, in that law and policy are difficult to separate. Due to the amount of control that the UK Government exercises in this area of public life, law is the predominant factor. Therefore any study on asylum and immigration policy will necessarily look more at legislation and the philosophy behind it, rather than at specific Government policy.

Some definitions and interpretations

Any discussion on asylum and immigration must start with an examination of the terminology used. By gaining an accurate understanding of some of the key terms, much of the basic information needed to understand the legislative and policy context will be clarified.

Asylum seeker

An asylum seeker is a person who has left their country of origin and formally applied for asylum in another country, but whose application has not yet been decided (Confederation of Scottish Local Authorities 2010).

Economic migrant

An economic migrant is someone who has moved to another country to work. Particular rules and conditions apply depending on which country the applicant comes from (UK Border Agency 2010a).

Immigrant

This is an all-encompassing term, often used by the media, but it actually means very little. In essence, an immigrant is someone who migrates to another country, usually for permanent residence. There is no reference to the term in current asylum and immigration legislation.

Refugee

A refugee is someone whose asylum application has been successful and who is allowed to stay in another country having proved that they would face persecution back home. The term refugee is defined under The United Nations Convention on Refugees 1951. Article 1 of the Refugee Convention defines a refugee as

> A person who is, owing to a well-founded fear of being persecuted for reasons of race, religion, nationality, membership of a particular social group, or political

> opinion, is outside the country of his nationality, and is unable to, or owing to such fear, is unwilling to avail himself of the protection of that country …. (UN Refugee Agency 2007)

Humanitarian protection

In some instances a person's claim for asylum may not have been successful and they are therefore not given refugee status but are instead awarded *humanitarian protection* as it is believed that they would face serious risk to life or person, or suffer inhuman or degrading punishment or treatment if they were to return home. Being awarded humanitarian protection enables someone to stay in the UK for a period of five years, at which time they can then apply for settlement and indefinite leave to remain (UK Border Agency (2010a).

Indefinite leave to remain

Indefinite leave to remain can be granted for a number of reasons, but is rarely given as an initial decision in asylum cases. It enables recipients to remain and work indefinitely in the UK (UK Border Agency 2010a).

Discretionary leave

Discretionary leave is sometimes awarded to people who have not qualified for refugee status or humanitarian protection. This form of leave is rarely conferred and tends to be applied to unaccompanied asylum seeking children on a time-limited basis (UK Border Agency 2010a).

Illegal immigrant

This is someone whose entry into, or presence in the UK contravenes immigration laws – for example, people who haven't claimed asylum, or registered as a migrant worker or have been refused asylum and haven't left the country (Scottish Refugee Council 2010a: 14).

By briefly considering a few of the basic terms used in the immigration debate, it is evident how much misinformation is presented in the media. A clear example of this is the frequent use of the term 'bogus asylum seeker'. Anyone seeking asylum from a country not listed as 'safe' by the UK (as defined by the UK) has the right to do so, and though they may not be successful and ultimately may have to leave the UK, this does not mean that they are breaking any immigration laws when in the process of making their application. When considered in the context of current UK legislation, this term becomes nonsensical, but still frequently appears as a headline in certain newspapers. This is despite the Press Complaints Commission stating in its guidance that this term should not be used, as it is misleading and inaccurate.

This chapter will focus specifically on issues affecting asylum seekers but with some reference to economic migrants and others subject to immigration controls.

A history of British immigration controls

As previously discussed in Chapter 3, legislation and policy developments reflect the political ideology of successive governments. However in the field of immigration they also reflect the need for labour, a perceived need for security, and protection of what are viewed as limited resources.

Much as the media would like us to believe otherwise, the movement of people across the globe is not a new phenomenon. Over the last century in particular, people have moved from country to country, continent to continent in search of better opportunities and to escape poverty, starvation, civil war and persecution.

Migration is generally categorised by both 'push' and 'pull' factors. People leaving a country due to extreme hardship, such as persecution, would be seen to be pushed out of their countries of origin, for example the wave of Ugandan Asians that came to the UK in the early 1970s (BBC Inside Out 2003), whereas people that are drawn to another country in search of better employment opportunities would be seen to be pulled towards that country. In reality of course it is not always easy to make a clear-cut distinction between these factors. The recent migration of people from eastern European countries to the UK would generally be seen to be one characterised by the 'pull' of a higher standard of living, but some may be escaping extreme hardship and discrimination within their own country, for example the Roma people of Eastern Europe (Amnesty International 2009).

It is not easy to reconcile the historical picture of the long-term patterns of migration with the current picture portrayed in the media of the 'new phenomenon' of growing numbers of people arriving in Western Europe, whether from the war-torn and starving nations of the developing world, or the more recent wave of economic migrants from Eastern Europe. What has changed significantly in recent history is the way in which the more developed countries have chosen to legislate in an attempt to *control* immigration. Underpinning this desire to restrict the movement of people is the view that migrants of whatever sort are a burden. These concerns and opinions have framed developments in policy and legislation and have caused immigration laws to become increasingly restrictive to those wishing to enter the UK, especially people from Africa, the Indian subcontinent and the Caribbean.

Cohen (2001) believes that the twentieth century can be divided into three main phases of immigration controls: the first consisted of restrictions against Jewish refugees, the second witnessed controls against black people, whilst the 1990s and the early part of the twenty-first century have seen controls against anyone fleeing war, disaster or economic mayhem (Cohen 2001: 33).

Control through legislation

The first major piece of immigration legislation in the UK came in the form of the Aliens Act 1905. Though aimed at denying access to 'undesirable foreigners' from outside the British Empire, the law was specifically intended to limit Jewish immigration to the UK. Newspaper headlines of the day raised concerns about Jewish immigrants bringing disease to the UK as well as taking jobs and therefore causing unemployment and poverty amongst UK nationals (Mynott 2002: 13). It is not too difficult to draw comparisons with more recent newspaper headlines, particularly in relation to the wave of migrants from countries such as Romania in the late 1990s. Not only are patterns of migration cyclical, the concerns of the indigenous population have also been repeated throughout history.

Subsequent to the passing of the 1905 Act, immigration rules became progressively more restrictive, limiting access to the UK for some groups and nationalities, whilst allowing relatively free access for others.

In post-war Britain the introduction of the concept of 'universal welfare' arose as a result of the war effort, which had emphasised the need for and the value of a collective approach in responding to common problems (see Chapter 2). This coincided with the first wave of black immigration from the West Indies. These immigrants, during the 1950s and 1960s, were constructed as 'migrant workers', not citizens. Their role was to ease the shortage of labour, particularly manual labour, and to work on the rapidly expanding public transport system. It was not envisaged that these workers would settle permanently in the UK and they were therefore not afforded full rights as citizens. As a result they were unable to access the full range of services and resources available to UK citizens. An example of this is that these migrant workers were not entitled to public housing but were left to the private market (Hayes 2002) and all its vagaries. This housing tended to be substandard and even then proved difficult to access with the now infamous signs of 'No blacks, no dogs, no Irish' routinely displayed. Access was given to health services but implicit barriers were constructed whereby immigrants would often be asked for passports and proof of residency before they received treatment. Structural and individual racist attitudes ensured that black immigrants in this country were not able to integrate fully into British society or receive the full range of benefits accorded to white UK citizens.

During the 1960s and 1970s the immigration debate continued to be about citizenship rights accorded to people who came to the UK to work. In 1962 the Commonwealth Immigrants Act took away the automatic right of entry to Commonwealth citizens by introducing work vouchers (Sales 2007). This was followed by the 1968 Commonwealth Immigrants Act which systematically removed citizenship rights overnight to UK passport holders, unless they, a parent, or a grandparent had been born, adopted or naturalised in the UK (Sales 2007). Next came the 1971 Immigration Act, which remained the cornerstone of immigration law until 2009. Under the newly elected Conservative Government of the time, the 1971 Act effectively ended immigration for settlement for people from the Caribbean, the Indian subcontinent and Africa (Hayes 2004).

Further restrictions were introduced with the 1981 British Nationality Act. Amongst other things, this abolished the automatic right to citizenship to those born on British soil. This effectively established 'the bloodline' as the key factor in determining someone's eligibility for residency and citizenship (Hayes 2004).

Since the 1980s, migration for permanent settlement in the UK has been even more difficult to obtain, as entry requirements have become increasingly restrictive. This is a pattern that is repeated throughout the developed countries of the Western world. One of the effects of these policy developments is that the families of those seeking a new life in the Western world become divided. Developed countries are always keen to take temporary, migrant labour when it is needed (and therefore suits *them*), but don't want the added responsibility of families and the resultant impact on resources such as housing, health and education. This clearly has major implications for social workers and other professionals supporting these divided families.

Since the end of the 1990s a number of major pieces of legislation regarding immigration have been introduced. These increasingly restrictive pieces of legislation are aimed specifically at controlling the numbers of those seeking asylum in the UK as well as their access to resources whilst they are here. These restrictions include the creation of a separate welfare system, forced dispersal, the increased use of detention, deportation and what is viewed by many as forced destitution for those people whose claims for asylum have failed (Refugee Action 2010).

The Immigration and Asylum Act 1999 removed entitlement to a range of non-contributory family and disability benefits for asylum seekers.

This effectively set them apart from UK citizens in that their needs were no longer assessed by the same criteria as the general population. A very clear message was being given that asylum seekers did not have the same rights as UK citizens and that their needs were not deemed as important as the rest of the population. The 1999 Act also extended the use of vouchers instead of money for basic subsistence payments (Harvey 2002: 188). Those that support the most vulnerable in our society are only too aware of the stigma that is attached to the use of vouchers, whereby people are readily identified by their use as being not quite a full member of society that is in need of support.

Alongside this, a system of compulsory dispersal was introduced. This was intended to relieve the pressure from certain parts of the country, particularly the south east of England, which had a very high number of asylum seekers in need of accommodation and support. Though few would argue with the fact that the geographical concentration of those seeking asylum in the south of England needed to be reviewed, the system of *forced dispersal* meant that asylum seekers could be sent to any one of the dispersal centres in the UK, the primary one in Scotland being located in Glasgow. To administer this new asylum support system, a centralised agency, the National Asylum Support Service (NASS) was created. NASS entered into arrangements with voluntary organisations and local authorities regarding the support of asylum seekers in the dispersal areas. Subsistence was given through money or vouchers and was set at *70 per cent* of income support levels, and housing was provided on a 'no choice' basis. Essentially, the 1999 Act created a distinct welfare system for asylum seekers that was separate and inferior, not even offering subsistence levels of support and a system of relocation that moved people around the country without consideration of individual choice or individual need (Fell and Hays 2007: 130 in Adams, Dominelli and Payne 2009: 120).

Continuing restrictions for those wishing to enter the UK have been introduced with each subsequent piece of legislation. The Nationality Immigration and Asylum Act 2002 brought in the requirement for applicants to pass an English test along with the introduction of a citizenship ceremony. Of more concern was the punitive and notorious section 55 of the 2002 Act (Save the Children 2004). This section of the Act allowed support to be refused to any single asylum seeker on the grounds that they had not made their claim for asylum as soon as 'reasonably practicable'. There are some particular problems with this aspect of the asylum process and how it is managed. For example, victims of sexual violence, particularly women who have been trafficked, are an extremely vulnerable group who may need time to process the traumatic events that they have experienced and to build up sufficient trust and confidence in order to feel able to disclose the details of those traumatic events. However the process of claiming asylum requires that these details be disclosed immediately and failure to do so can be treated as sufficient grounds for the rejection of a claim and the denial of any form of support (Ceneda 2003).

Many asylum seekers have a great fear of those in authority, based on experiences in their home countries and are often reluctant to make themselves known to immigration authorities. There are many well-documented cases where people have been denied support after attempting to register with the authorities only one or two days after arriving in the country (Gerrard 2004). The only avenue of support for this group of people has been charities and voluntary organisations who have often stepped in to feed and clothe them. However, as a result of recent financial restraints in public spending, much of the voluntary sector provision has all but disappeared, which has resulted in some people being left completely destitute with no support available to them from any source at all.

Even when voluntary organisations are still able to provide basic levels of support it is often at a price. The voluntary sector has had to chase money and resources for their own future survival, so it is not surprising that monies have sometimes been accepted with conditions. Conditions for voluntary organisations concerning surveillance, control and co-operation with the UK Border Agency (UKBA) are not uncommonly attached to funding streams (Cohen 2001: 306).

The 2004 Asylum and Immigration (Treatment of Claimants) Act introduced further penalties for those entering the UK unlawfully. The term 'unlawfully' could cover a wide range of situations; for some this could mean not having the correct papers, or as previously discussed, not making a formal application for asylum within the required timescale. Most importantly though, under section 9 of the Act was added 'asylum seeker with family' to the list of those who could become *ineligible* for Government support, and this now infamous section of the 2004 Act was piloted in Leeds, London and Manchester.

This piece of legislation created situations where families that failed to take steps to comply with removal directions could have all supports withdrawn, with the possibility of children being taken into the care of the local authority for their own protection (sic) as a result of their parents becoming destitute and therefore no longer able to care for them. In many ways this is another example of tensions not only between different pieces of legislation, but also between fundamental principles underpinning broad policy objectives relating, for example, to children (see Chapter 14), a point raised by the Chair of the Asylum and Refugee Task Group of the Association of Directors of Social Work in England and Wales, who said in November 2005, 'I am greatly concerned that Section 9 has apparently encouraged so many families to disappear … It is ironic that at the same time the government is working hard to implement Every Child Matters, national policy appears to be encouraging families to disappear' (Refugee Council Action 2006: 6).

The pilot scheme was in operation for over a year and involved 116 families (Refugee Council 2006). There was widespread public outrage on a local and a national level about this change in legislation. The Home Office eventually admitted in June 2007 that the exercise had not gone according to plan and that there was no real evidence to support a claim that there had been any significant increases in the number of voluntary returns or removals of unsuccessful asylum-seeking families (Refugee Council 2006).

Another significant piece of legislation is the Immigration, Nationality and Asylum Act 2006. This Act implemented the key legislative aspects of the Home Offices' five-year strategy for asylum and immigration – *Controlling our Borders: Making Migration Work for Britain* (Home Office 2005). The 2006 Act focused mainly on economic migration (rather than asylum) and included restrictions on appeal rights, sanctions on employers of unauthorised labour, and a tightening of citizenship rules. The last significant piece of legislation prior to the current 2009 Act was the UK Borders Act 2007. This provides immigration officers with statutory powers to detain anyone at a *point of entry* for the purposes of obtaining personal details, including biometric information, on demand. There are penalties for a refusal to comply with any request made.

The current picture

As has been discussed in the previous section, the legal context with regard to immigration and asylum is complex and it changes frequently, and the battle is still raging between the main political parties as to who can be seen to be the 'toughest' on asylum seekers. The overall picture though, is that there has been a continual effort by the UK government to reduce the number of asylum applications being made, and an increase in the number and type of restrictions placed upon the means to support them.

An important starting point in any discussion of current policy and legislation in Scotland must centre on the issue of devolution. As we mentioned earlier, asylum and immigration continue to remain 'reserved' matters, responsibility for which lies with the UK Parliament at Westminster. Therefore decisions about someone's status in terms of residency, where they can live and the support that they are entitled to are dictated by reserved legislation and the provision of the support that they are entitled to is organised by the United Kingdom Borders Agency (UKBA). However, other significant aspects of legislation in the fields of social work, education and health are *devolved to the Scottish Government*; it is therefore not too difficult to envisage the potential conflicts that can occur when a family is subject to immigration controls and also has, for example, child care and health needs.

The European dimension of immigration policy is also of increasing importance. European Union immigration policy focused initially on controls on entry, particularly of asylum seekers. With the 1997 *Amsterdam Treaty*, the *Schengen Convention* became part of the EU legal framework. This brought about both a strengthening of the EUs external border and increased internal surveillance of migration status (EU Facts: Civitas EU Facts 2009). The term 'fortress Europe' has commonly been used to describe the ever-increasing physical and legal controls that have been used to police entry into Europe (Sales 2007). When considering the European perspective, the *Dublin Convention* is also central to asylum policy. The Dublin Convention provided an agreed framework to determine which EU member state is responsible for those seeking asylum and introduced the 'safe' third country rule, allowing EU countries to return applicants to other 'safe' EU countries that they had travelled through. EU countries continue to work together to harmonise asylum systems across EU member states (common European asylum system at www.ecre.org) but the enforcement of EU initiatives depends to a large extent on the will of national governments. EU policymaking is highly complex, involving both binding and non-binding regulations on member states (Sales 2007: 122). It is perhaps interesting to note that the terms of the Dublin Convention mirror the broad principles and practices of the old Poor Laws and the Act of Settlement of 1662 (see Chapter 2) that aimed to address very similar issues but at that time, on a more parochial level.

International Human Rights legislation also plays a central role in UK immigration legislation and policy. These rights are enshrined in the European Convention on Human Rights and were passed into UK Law by the 1998 Human Rights Act (OPSI 1998). It is important to remember though that whilst asylum seekers may have the same human rights as any other person, they do not have the same *citizenship rights*. There may be situations where this could mean that resources denied to an asylum-seeking family in accordance with UK immigration law could lead to a break up of the family unit and therefore contravene their right to a family life under Article 12 of the ECHR. Here we have a clear example of a distinct *lack of integration* across policy areas and an apparent conflict of principles (see Chapter 1).

In 2007 the then Labour Government announced plans to break up the Home Office into two separate departments, a Ministry of Justice, and a new, streamlined Home Office focused on crime, immigration, and terrorism.[1] In

---

1 Whilst it may well be a coincidence, it is interesting to note the juxtaposition of immigration with crime and terrorism in the configuration of the new Home Office.

April of 2007, the new UK Border and Immigration Agency (UKBIA) was formed. Further reorganisation in April 2008 brought about the formation of the UK Border Agency (UKBA). This Agency brings together the work previously carried out by the UKBIA, customs detection work and UK Visa Services. The UKBA considers applications for permission to enter or to stay in the UK and applications for citizenship and asylum. UKBA's responsibilities now also include the provision of asylum support in terms of accommodation and financial help for asylum seekers while their claim is being considered, support previously provided through NASS. The UKBA is also responsible for the management of Immigration Removal Centres (detention centres) such as Dungavel near Glasgow, which can be used to house people whose asylum claim has been unsuccessful and who await deportation or for those that the UKBA believe will not comply with asylum regulations (Scottish Government 2010).

Until now the Immigration Act 1971 has remained the main statutory source of modern immigration law. Secondary legislation relevant to immigration has been introduced under the authority of this Act (see Chapter 1). At the time of writing, the Borders, Citizenship and Immigration Act 2009 has just been enacted and will form and frame all new developments in the field of immigration.

The previous Labour Government had clearly stated that the 2009 Act was designed to simplify immigration law, strengthen borders and extend the time it takes to gain citizenship. There appears to be, though, a lack of emphasis on *protection* for those fleeing persecution or war and seeking asylum in a place of safety. One way in which the previous Labour Government stated that it has prioritised the needs of asylum seekers, though was through the *One Gateway Protection Programme*. This programme is operated by the UKBA in partnership with the United Nations High Commissioner for Refugees and offers a legal route for up to 750 refugees to settle in the UK each year. This is completely separate from the standard procedure of claiming asylum in the UK (UK Border Agency 2010b; Refugee Council 2004).

A uniquely Scottish perspective

Political discourse surrounding immigration in Scotland has generally been more favourable than in the rest of the UK. This has contributed to better media and public attitudes towards asylum seekers and refugees (Scottish Refugee Council 2006). The Scottish National Party (SNP) administration, which came to power in 2007, has stated its commitment to the integration of refugees and has continued to put pressure on the Home Office to rethink some of the more restrictive and punitive aspects of immigration law.

An example of Scotland's differing views on asylum and refugee policy is demonstrated by the ongoing debate on enforced removals. In 2005 the then Scottish Executive raised concerns with the Home Office over immigration policy, particularly around the impact that enforced removals, often facilitated by 'dawn raids', was having on children. Unison Scotland, along with other organisations and individuals, has also condemned the treatment of failed asylum seeker families by the immigration authorities. The First Minister has stated that where a family with children under 16 is to be deported, best practice should be established that involves education and social work services *in advance of any action being taken by the immigration authorities,* to ensure that the rights of the children and concerns of relevant professionals are taken into account (Unison Scotland 2010). The agenda for the integration of refugees has been driven through the Scottish Refugee Integration Forum (SRIF). SRIF was set up in 2002 by the Scottish Executive to allow Scotland's statutory and voluntary agencies to work in partnership to support refugees more effectively. The Forum has continued to address new and emerging issues affecting integration for asylum seekers and refugees (Scottish Refugee Integration Forum 2003; Scottish Executive 2005). These include areas such as housing, access to justice, employment and training, health and social care, community development and children's issues (Confederation of Scottish Local Authorities 2007).

Addressing these issues has not been purely for the benefit of refugees, but also for the benefit of local people in the communities they live in. Most of the allocated funding for SRIF has been targeted at areas such as Sighthill in Glasgow where high numbers of asylum seekers and refugees live. Between 2001 and 2008 over £12.5 million was invested through SRIF.

Through these initiatives and policy developments, the Scottish Government has stated its aim to welcome and promote diversity in Scottish culture and society. Alongside this is also the impact of current demographic trends that involve a falling and ageing population and a continuing out-migration of younger people and of skilled people (General Register for Scotland 2005). It is within this context that the Scottish Government has highlighted a need to encourage more people to choose to live and work in Scotland and to recognise that refugees (and potentially asylum seekers if work restrictions are lifted) have much to contribute to Scotland's economic and social development.

What does this mean in practice?: What is the actual process of seeking asylum in the UK?

The flow chart in Figure 18.1 helps to explain the current process for seeking asylum in the UK.

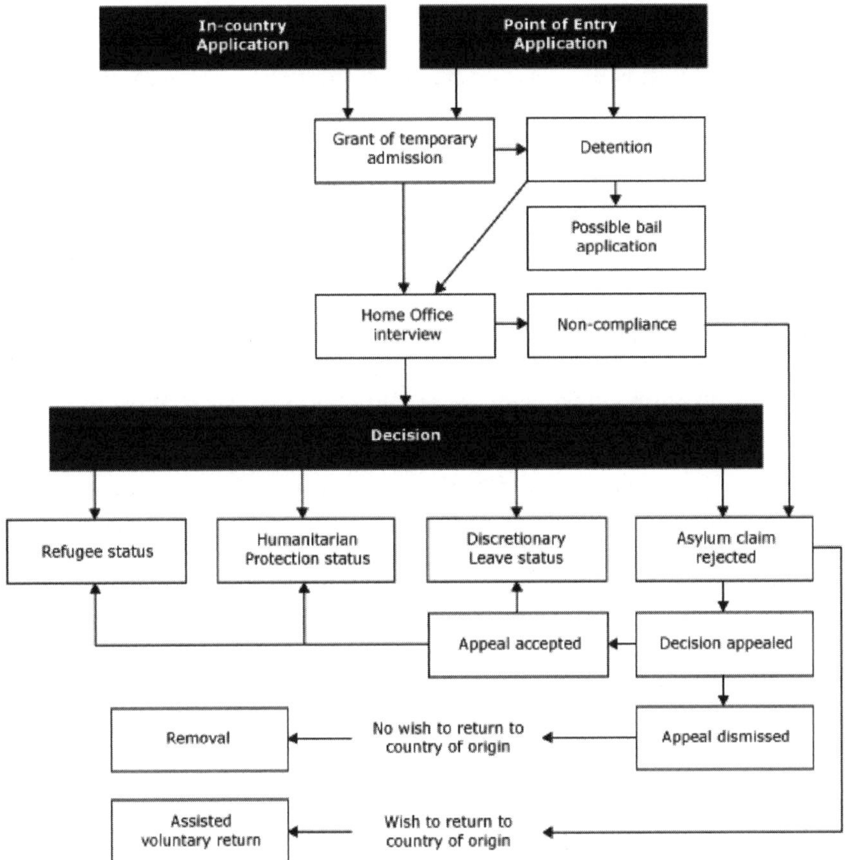

Figure 18.1 The process for seeking asylum in the UK

Source: Reproduced with permission of CoSLA.

This section will look at the key stages in the asylum process. However, due to the complexity of the law and the way in which it is constantly evolving, this can only be seen as an outline at the time of writing and not a definitive account of the legal process.

To apply for asylum, people need to *present themselves* to an immigration officer upon arrival at a 'port of entry', that is, the airport or seaport or by visiting the nearest UKBA Asylum Screening Unit; in Scotland this is in Glasgow, but as things stand, only families and vulnerable adults can claim asylum there; other people must travel to Liverpool or Croydon. When claiming asylum in the UK, people can also apply for asylum support. If they are successful in this they will be placed in 'induction accommodation' and subsequently moved to dispersal accommodation anywhere across the UK, including Glasgow.

The next part of the process is the *screening interview*, where information is gathered to establish identity, nationality and number of dependents. Fingerprints are taken, as are photographs and biometric data. At this stage in the process the applicant is assigned a 'case owner' who deals with the asylum claim from start to finish. The case owner has a wide range of responsibilities from interviewing the client, gathering evidence to support their claim, deciding whether to grant asylum or not, presenting appeals in court, providing and managing asylum support, responding to queries from the asylum seeker, and organising the applicants integration into the UK if their claim is successful or arranging voluntary return or removal back home if the claim is unsuccessful. Asylum applicants have to report to their case owner on a regular basis whilst their application is being considered. The frequency of reporting is decided on a case-by-case basis but can be as frequently as weekly.

After the case owner has considered information from the asylum interview and any supporting evidence, they inform the asylum seeker of the decision in person. If the claim is successful and the asylum seeker is granted refugee status, the applicant is granted five years *Limited Leave to Remain* in the UK, or alternatively they may be granted *Discretionary Leave to Remain* or *Humanitarian Protection*. If granted refugee status, they have the right to work, apply for travel documents and for family reunion. If the claim is unsuccessful the case owner will explain rights of appeal and time limits. If the claim is unsuccessful at appeal, the asylum seeker will be encouraged to return home voluntarily.

It is expected that anyone who has received a negative decision (and has therefore had their temporary access to the UK revoked) should take steps to leave the UK. If appeal rights have been exhausted, single or childless applicants will no longer be entitled to Government support and will be removed from the country if they do not leave voluntarily. In some circumstances it is possible for a person to apply for support under the terms of section 4 of the Immigration and Asylum Act 1999, which is paid to persons who are making arrangements to leave, or who are unable to return home at that time (Asylum Support Appeals Project 2007). This support consists of shared accommodation and vouchers to cover subsistence. Those with children aged under 18 will currently continue to be supported by the Government until such time as they leave the country. If they fail to make their own arrangements to go home or to participate in the Assisted Voluntary Return Programme they may be forcibly removed (see Confederation of Scottish Local Authorities 2010), although appeals are sometimes made and become newsworthy because of their potential to generate positive change (Twinch 2010).

The use of detention or removal centres

Immigration detention centres, or removal centres as they are currently known, are holding centres for foreign nationals, some of whom are awaiting decisions on their asylum applications whilst others are awaiting deportation. *People seeking asylum are liable to detention at any time throughout the asylum process.*

The use of detention is controversial. Critics would argue that people who have committed no crime, serious or otherwise, and in many cases who have come to the UK to escape persecution, are effectively imprisoned and treated as criminals. There have also been concerns raised about conditions in the detention centres, with reported high incidences of mental health problems amongst detainees and concerning levels of self-harm and suicide (Institute of Race Relations 2006). The detention centre in Scotland is Dungavel House in North Lanarkshire. It was opened in September 2001 and currently has the capacity to hold 190 people including families (UK Border Agency 2010c).

Dispersal

As already mentioned, the system of dispersal was introduced under the Immigration and Asylum Act 1999. It was introduced to share the perceived burden of asylum seekers across the UK. It is also viewed by many as a potential deterrent to those planning on seeking asylum in the UK (Sales 2007: 148). Opponents of the scheme would claim that enforced dispersal is a major contributory factor to the increased social exclusion of this already vulnerable group. Asylum seekers have been dispersed to Scotland since April 2000 under the UK Government dispersal programme.

In Scotland, Glasgow City Council was the only local authority to agree to receive asylum seekers and, with little in the way of preparation, thousands began arriving there in 2000. Glasgow now houses the largest number of asylum seekers in the UK. In 2007 over 5,500 people were living in UKBA contracted accommodation which is provided through Glasgow City

Council, the YMCA and The Angel Group (a private housing organisation) (Scottish Refugee Council 2010b).

Essentially this has resulted in some of the most vulnerable people in our society, often suffering trauma, and at the very least extreme anxiety due to the uncertainty of their future, being sent to parts of the UK that they had often never heard of, and where there is possibly no local community support available. This policy has served to increase the divide between asylum seekers and the rest of the UK population and has in turn increased their sense of isolation and uncertainty.

Rights and responsibilities

Whilst an asylum applicant is in the UK there are a number of rights and responsibilities relevant to them. *Rights* include such things as being treated fairly and lawfully regardless of race, gender, age, religion, sexual orientation or any disability, and to have their application considered fairly and accurately. Asylum seekers also have the right to free NHS treatment, involving both primary and secondary care and asylum-seeking children aged between five and 16 are entitled to free statutory school education.

Responsibilities include staying in regular contact with their case owner and keeping all appointments and obeying the law. If an asylum seeker is found to be non-compliant with these responsibilities, their claim for asylum will in all probability be decided unfavourably, and in most instances they will be moved to a detention centre (UK Border Agency 2010d).

On being granted *Leave to Remain*, a refugee has the same housing and social security entitlements as a UK citizen. Refugees also have an automatic right to work.

The rights and responsibilities of refused asylum seekers are, however, limited and subject to constant review under new legislation and policy. It is not always clear whether or not an asylum seeker has fully exhausted all of their legal options and therefore legal advice should always be sought. Asylum seekers who are single or have no children and are no longer eligible for accommodation or financial support will be evicted from their property. As previously discussed, one option that may be available to them at this stage is section 4 support. This consists of full board accommodation but is subject to the claimant meeting certain criteria, such as demonstrating that they are taking all reasonable steps to leave the UK, or that they are unable to travel because of a physical impairment, or if there is no safe route of return available.

Children

Any discussion of asylum and immigration must include consideration of the needs of unaccompanied children. This is of particular relevance when considering the social work role in this field of practice (Kohli and Mitchell 2007). An 'Unaccompanied Child' is 'Anyone who is under the legal age of majority and is not accompanied by a parent, guardian, or other adult who, by law or custom, is responsible for him or her' (Unison Scotland 2006a). Clearly this is a fairly broad definition that gives responsibility for the welfare of a child entering the UK to any number of people who may or may not have the best interests of the child at heart. The UKBA also states though, that it will involve social services in any case where there is any concern about the child's relationship with the 'responsible' adult (Unison Scotland 2006a).

Children are not included in the definition of 'asylum seeker' while they are under 18, so by law there should be no limitation on their entitlement to support under the Children (Scotland) Act 1995. Local authorities therefore have the same responsibilities to young unaccompanied asylum seekers (or separated children) as they would have to any other children in their area. Unaccompanied or separated asylum-seeking children face particular difficulties though when they reach the age of 18. If they have been looked after and accommodated by the local authority, they should be offered *throughcare support* (Hothersall 2008), but this will depend on a number of individual factors. If this is not deemed appropriate, they may have to find their own accommodation, be dispersed to another area, or have their Leave to Remain reassessed (Unison Scotland 2006a).

The Children (Scotland) Act 1995 states in its overarching principles that the welfare of the child must be paramount and that the child's views must be taken into account in all matters affecting him or her. These principles are underpinned by the UN Convention on the Rights of the Child and apply to all children living in Scotland. Guidance provided by BASW and Unison considers that because of their particular circumstances and vulnerabilities, asylum-seeking children, whether unaccompanied or living with their families can be considered as 'children in need' under S93(4) of the Children (Scotland) Act 1995. These children should therefore be entitled to all the rights and services accorded to 'children in need' under the Act. This is an area of social work practice that requires special consideration because of the legal complexities as well as the extreme vulnerability, particularly, of unaccompanied asylum-seeking children (Knight, Chase and Statham 2008).

Facts and figures: Myths and reality

There is a vast amount of misinformation presented by the media around immigration issues. Without the accurate dissemination of accurate information, the asylum debate becomes based on discriminatory and all too

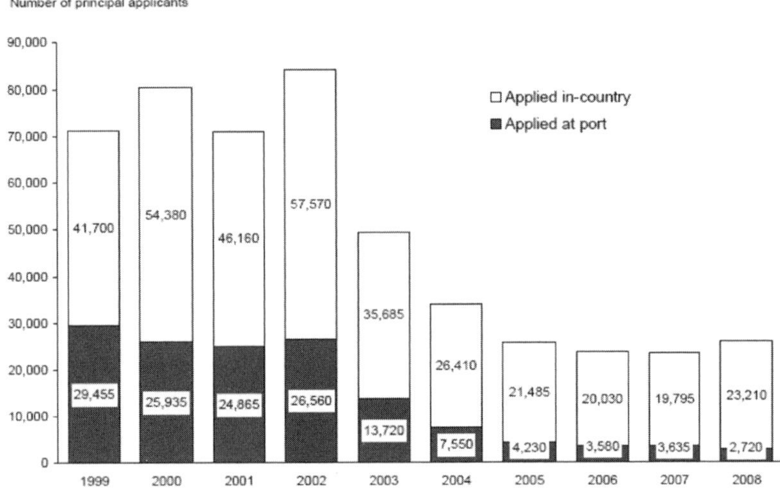

Figure 18.2 Applications for asylum in the UK

Note: May exclude some cases lodged at Local Enforcement Offices between January 1999 to March 2000.

Source: Home Office 2009: Fig. 2.1. Reproduced under the terms of Crown Copyright guidance issued by HMSO.

frequently racist views. The next section of this chapter will aim to present some factual information, challenging popular myths and misinformation.

The business of collecting and producing statistical data relating to asylum is necessarily complex. This is due mainly to the amount of time that it can take for decisions to be reached and appeals to be heard. Most statistics drawn on come from the annual and quarterly (2008–2009) statistical bulletins, published by the Research Development Statistics (RDS) unit (Home Office 2010).

So what are the numbers of people applying for asylum in the UK each year?

The graph in Figure 18.2 shows the decline in applications for asylum received, between its peak in 2002 through to 2008. In terms of outcomes, the proportion of successful outcomes has also decreased significantly between 2001 and 2008. It is important to note though that these figures do not include decisions made after appeal.

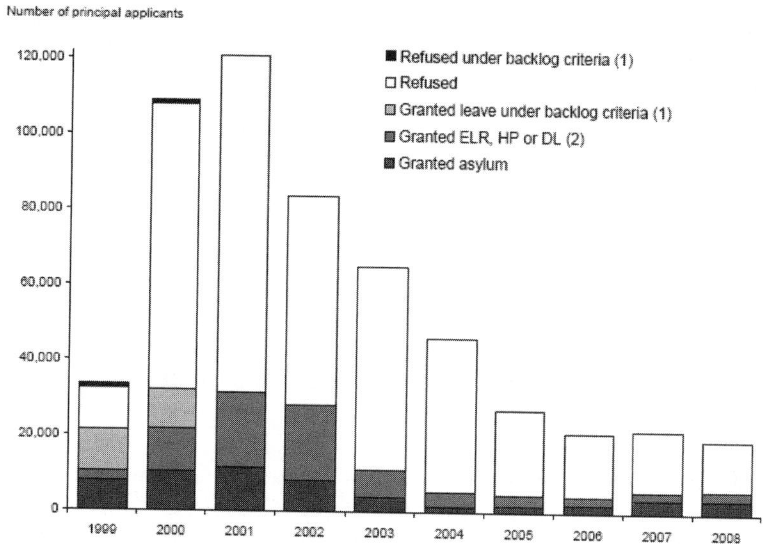

(1) Cases decided under measures aimed at reducing the pre-1996 asylum backlog.
(2) Humanitarian Protection and Discretionary Leave replaced Exceptional Leave to Remain from 1 April 2003.

Figure 18.3 Asylum settlement figures 1999–2008

Source: Home Office 2009: Fig. 2.2. Reproduced under the terms of Crown Copyright guidance issued by HMSO.

How many asylum seekers are actually granted settlement in the UK?

The settlement figures (see Figure 18.3) indicate the number of asylum applicants that are given Indefinite Leave to Remain in the UK. As was previously discussed, since August 2005, all refugees, other than those arriving in the UK under managed migration resettlement schemes such as the *Gateway Programme*, have been granted five years *Limited Leave* rather than *Indefinite Leave to Remain*. At the end of this period they are entitled to apply for settlement. *Humanitarian Protection* has also been brought in line with refugee leave, and as such those granted Humanitarian Protection may also apply for settlement after five years, though the time limit for those given *Discretionary Leave to Remain* to apply for settlement remains at six years (Home Office 2009: 22).

How does Britain compare with the rest of Europe in terms of numbers of asylum seekers?

The most recent annual asylum application figures for European countries show that the UK received 0.51 asylum applications per 1,000 people in 2008, just above the European average at 0.48. France received more asylum applications than any other EU country in 2008, followed by the UK. However, when the relative size of the domestic population is taken into account, the UK ranks 15th amongst European Union countries in terms of asylum seekers per head of population (Home Office 2009: 60).

What are the main nationalities of those seeking asylum in the UK?

The main countries of origin of asylum seekers in 2008 were: Afghanistan, Zimbabwe, Iran, Eritrea, Iraq, Sri Lanka, China, Somalia, Pakistan and Nigeria. Many of these nationalities have featured consistently in the top ten for the last five years (Unison Scotland 2006b: 14).

Exercise 18.1

Using on-line resources find out more about asylum seekers in your area. What country are they from? What is their religion, and what languages do they speak? It would also be useful to identify any support services that are available.

People may be forced to flee their country for a number of reasons. Seeking refuge is a last resort for people who cannot find protection in their own country. In fact the majority of people seeking refuge do so in developing nations (Unison Scotland 2006b: 11).

Do asylum seekers receive enhanced financial benefits and jump the housing queue?

As already discussed, to qualify for support, a person must have applied for asylum, be destitute and make their claim for asylum in the UK 'as soon as reasonably practical' after arrival. At the time of writing 'reasonably practical' is currently defined as within three days. If a person is successful in their application for support they will be dispersed to accommodation to any one of a number of regions in the UK. Accommodation is allocated dependent on need and on a 'no-choice' basis. Sometimes people need to share accommodation with other asylum seekers. The UKBA also provides for essential living needs, including cash support (Unison Scotland 2006b).

What skills and qualifications do asylum seekers in Scotland have?

Refugees and asylum seekers in Scotland are, for the most part, well qualified. More than 75 per cent of respondents to a study conducted by the Scottish Executive in partnership with the Scottish Refugee Council said they had completed secondary school education or its equivalent. Over half said they had completed college education (or an equivalent) and approximately 21 per cent of respondents said they had completed a course at university. However, demonstrating their qualifications was problematic as few had their certificates with them (Scottish Executive 2004).

Of those respondents with refugee status, Exceptional Leave to Remain or Indefinite Leave to Remain, under 7 per cent were either in paid employment or self-employed. Those refugees in paid employment were mainly working in the service industries, in jobs that were not commensurate with their experience and skills. Lack of English language skills and training opportunities were identified as being key barriers for refugees to gaining employment in the UK (Scottish Executive 2004).

What does all of this mean for social work and other professions?

A starting point for any discussion on the role of social work and other professions in Scotland in the area of asylum and immigration must be to consider policy and practice issues in relation to those professions' Codes of Practice. These require practitioners to work to a set of professional standards when providing a service, some being of particular relevance when working with asylum seekers.

Similarly, and in addition to these Codes are underpinning professional Codes of Ethics, all of which offer comprehensive frameworks for ethical practice. In relation to social work, its five basic values state that the profession should promote respect for human dignity and pursue social justice through service to humanity, integrity and professional competence (British Association of Social Workers 2010).

In terms of anti-discriminatory practice the first point of consideration is the fact that asylum seekers are discussed as just that – but of course asylum seekers are not just that, they are first and foremost human beings with roles: mothers, fathers, children, members of families who carry with them the range of human attributes as we all do, but they may also have some very *specific needs* in terms of mental health problems, a range of differing disabilities and problems associated with increasing age and these must not be overlooked. '*Asylum seeker*' is but one specific social construction and in and of itself does not define who a person is.

As professionals it is essential that we should be able to discuss and examine the subject in an informed way and be able to see through (often stereotypical) media representations and to challenge misinformation when it is presented. Education is a central part of the social work role, as we know that misinformation supports prejudice. Social workers and other professionals need to challenge misleading media images. Some people are motivated by compassion and see asylum seekers as victims whilst others see them as dangerous and as a burden. All of these preconceptions need to be challenged on an individual and a structural level.

As previously discussed, there are varying levels of assistance, financial and otherwise, that can be offered to people depending on their immigration status. The question must be asked though as to how relevant it is to determine someone's status with regard to immigration controls when faced with a person in need?

What is also evident is that issues of policy and practice are matters for which politicians, policy makers and managers have to take responsibility. Most would agree that it is bad practice to expect individual workers to decide on these issues on a case-by-case basis. As Cohen reminds us:

> At the moment many workers are either ignorant of, or are turning a blind eye to immigration matters because they have received no management guidelines. Alternatively they are attempting to deal with these issues without the support of management and sometimes behind the back of management. None of this is professionally tenable. (Cohen 2001: 61)

When considering the role that social workers and other professionals have in supporting asylum seekers and others subject to immigration controls, the question must be asked whether social work and other professions have become too uncritical of immigration policy and therefore unquestioningly complicit in its delivery? This area of practice is surely one where social work has the clearest of roles – to advocate for and uphold fairness for the most marginalised in society.

Chapter summary

In this chapter we have looked at the range of legislation and policy that currently shapes practice in and around the whole area of asylum and migration. We have seen how different definitions are applied to different people at different times during the asylum process and that these definitions confer a particular status on people which in turn determines the rights they have at that time. We have also seen how *ideology* appears to play a large part in this area and we have concluded by reminding ourselves that social work, and other caring professions have a significant role to play in relation to asylum and migration.

References

Adams, R., Dominelli, L. and Payne, M. (2009), *Practising Social Work in a Complex World* (Basingstoke: Palgrave Macmillan).

Amnesty International (2009), 'Europe's Roma Community Still Facing Massive Discrimination', *Amnesty International*. Available at: http://amnesty.org/en/news-and-updates/feature-stories/europe-roma-community-still-facing-massive-discrimination-20090408 (accessed 30 November 2009).

Asylum Support Appeals Project (2007), *Section 4 Support for Failed Asylum Seekers: Factsheet 2* (London: ASAP). Available at: http://www.asaproject.org/web/index.php (accessed 28 May 2010).

BBC Inside Out (2003), *Ugandan Asians*. Available at: http://www.bbc.co.uk/insideout/west/series2/ugandan_asians.shtml (accessed 30 November 2009).

British Association of Social Workers (2010), *Code of Ethics*. Available at: http:// www.basw.co.uk/about/codeofethics/ (accessed 5 March 2010).

Ceneda, S. (2003), *Women Asylum Seekers in the UK: A Gender Perspective*, Information Centre about Asylum and Refugees. Available at: http://www.icar.org.uk/3771/research-directory/women-asylum-seekers-in-the-gender-perspective-html (accessed 30 November 2009).

Civitas EU Facts (2009), *Schengen Convention*. Available at: http://wwwcivitas.org.uk/eufacts/FSEXR/EX2.htm (accessed 29 October 2009).

Cohen, S. (2001), *Immigration Controls, the Family and the Welfare State* (London: Jessica Kingsley).

Confederation of Scottish Local Authorities (CoSLA) (2007), *The Role of the Scottish Executive*. Available at: http://www.asylumscotland.org.uk/scottishexecutive.php (accessed 25 February 2010).

—— (2010), *Strategic Migration Partnership* (Glasgow: CoSLA). Available at: http://www.asylumscotland.org.uk/index.php (accessed 28 May 2010).

General Register for Scotland (2005), 'Population Expected to Rise and Age', News Release. Available at: http://www.gro-scotland.gov.uk/press/news2005/04-pop-proj-press.html (accessed 25 February 2010).

Gerrard, N. (2004), *Section 55 of the Nationality, Immigration and Asylum Act 2002*. Available at: http://www.neilgerrard.co.uk/Old%20Press/section_55.htm (accessed 25 January 2010).

Harvey, A. (2002), 'The 1999 Asylum and Immigration Act and How to Challenge it: A Legal View', in S. Cohen, B. Humphries and E. Mynott (eds), *From Immigration Controls to Welfare Controls* (London: Routledge).

Hayes, D. (2002), 'From Aliens to Asylum Seekers: A History of Immigration Controls and Welfare in Britain', in S. Cohen, B. Humphries and E. Mynott (eds), *From Immigration Controls to Welfare Controls* (London: Routledge).

—— (2004), 'History and Context: The Impact of Immigration Control on Welfare Delivery', in D. Hayes and B. Humphries (eds), *Social Work, Immigration and Asylum* (London: Jessica Kingsley).

Home Office (2005), *Controlling our Borders: Making Migration Work for Britain*. 7 February. Available at: http://presshomeoffice.gov.uk/press-releases/Controlling_Our_Border_Markers_.html (accessed 25 February 2010).

—— (2009), *Home Office Statistical Bulletin. Control Of Immigration: Statistics. United Kingdom*. Available at: http://www.homeoffice.gov.uk/rds/pdfs09/hosb1409.pdf (accessed 25 February 2010).

—— (2010), *Research Development Statistics*. Available at: http://www.homeoffice.gov.uk/rds/index.html (accessed 25 January 2010).

Hothersall, S.J. (2008), *Social Work with Children, Young people and their Families in Scotland* (2nd edn) (Exeter: Learning Matters).

Institute of Race Relations (2006), *Driven to Desperate Measures*. Available at: http://www.irr.org.uk/2006/September/ha00013.html (accessed 25 October 2009).

Knight, A., Chase, E. and Statham, J. (2008), *The Emotional Well-Being of Unaccompanied Young People Seeking Asylum in the UK* (London: BAAF).

Kohli, R.K.S. and Mitchell, F. (eds) (2007), *Working with Unaccompanied Asylum Seeking Children: Issues for Policy and Practice* (Basingstoke: Palgrave Macmillan).

Mynott, E. (2002), 'Nationalism, Racism and Immigration Control: From Anti-Racism to Anti-Capitalism', in S. Cohen, B. Humphries and E. Mynott (eds), *From Immigration Controls to Welfare Controls* (London: Routledge).

OPSI (1998), *Human Rights Act 1998*. Available at: http://www.opsi.gov.uk/acts/acts1998/ukpga_19980042_en_1 (accessed 12 October 2009).

Refugee Action (2010), *What is the Destitution Trap?* Available at: http://www.refugee-action.org.uk/campaigns/destitution/intro.aspx (accessed 5 January 2010).

Refugee Council (2004), *Resettling to the UK: The Gateway Protection Programme*, Refugee Council Briefing (October 2004) (London: Refugee Council).

— (2006), *Section 9 Inhumane and Ineffective – Section 9 in Practice; A Joint Refugee Council and Refugee Action Report on the Section 9 Pilot*. Available at: http://www.refugeecouncil.org.uk/policy/position/2006/section9 (accessed 10 September 2009).

Sales, R. (2007), *Understanding Immigration and Refugee Policy Contradictions and Continuities* (Bristol: Policy Press).

Save the Children (2004), *Child Asylum and Refugee Issues in Scotland*. Available at: http://www.savethechildren.org.uk/caris/legal/asylumproc/ap_sl_06.php (accessed 8 January 2010).

Scottish Executive (2004), *Refugees and Asylum Seekers in Scotland: A Skills and Aspirations Audit: Research Findings*. Available at: http://www.scotland.gov.uk/Publications/2004/03/19165/355249 (accessed 25 February 2010).

— (2005), *SRIF Action Plan: Progress Report* (Edinburgh: Scottish Executive).

Scottish Government (2010), *Government Responsibility. The Role and Responsibilities of the UK Home Office and the Scottish Government*. Available at: http://www.scotland.gov.uk/Topics/People/Equality/Refugees-asylum/responsibility (accessed 10 January 2010).

Scottish Refugee Council (2006), *Warm Welcome? Understanding Public Attitudes to Asylum Seekers in the UK*. Available at: http://www.scottishrefugeecouncil.org.uk/pub/warm_welcome (accessed 10 September 2009).

— (2010a), *Asylum: The Facts*. Available at: http://www.scottishrefugeecouncil.org.uk/info/ (accessed 3 March 2010).

— (2010b), *About Us*. Available at: http://www.scottishrefugeecouncil.org.uk/about/History (accessed 25 February 2010).

Scottish Refugee Integration Forum (2003), *SRIF Action Plan* (Edinburgh: SRIF).

Twinch, E. (2010), *High Court to Rule on Section 4 Support Changes*. Available at: http://www.insidehousing.co.uk/story.aspx?storycode=6508694 (accessed 5 March 2010).

UK Border Agency (2010a), *Working in the UK*. Available at: http://www.ukba.homeoffice.gov.uk/workingintheuk/ (accessed 4 March 2010).

— (2010b), *One Gateway Protection Programme*. Available at: http://www.bia-homeoffice.gov.uk/asylum/gateway/ (accessed 4 March 2010).

— (2010c), *Dungavel Immigration Removal Centre*. Available at: http://www.bia.homeoffice.gov.uk/managingborders/immigrationremovalcentres/dungavel (accessed 10 September 2010).

— (2010d), *Rights and Responsibilities*. Available at: http://www.bia.homeoffice.gov.uk/asylum/rights/ (accessed 25 February 2010).

UN Refugee Agency (2007), *The 1951 Refugee Convention: Questions and Answers, 2007 Edition*. Available at: http://www.unhcr.org/3c0f495f4.html (accessed 5 January 2010).

Unison Scotland (2006a), *Asylum in Scotland: Child's Welfare Paramount?* Available at: http://www.unison-scotlandorg.uk/socialwork/asylum booklet/asylumchild2html (accessed 11 November 2009).

— (2006b), *The Asylum Myths*. Available at: http://www.unison-scotland.org.uk/activists/asylummyths2ndedition.pdf (accessed 5 March 2010).

— (2010), *Social Work. Asylum Seeker. Children Briefing Paper*. Available at: http://www.unison-scotland.org/socialwork/asylumbrief.html (accessed 10 January 2010).

Web-based resource

Scottish Government (2010), *Support*. Available at: http://www.scotland.gov.uk/Topics/People/Equality/Refugees-asylum/support (accessed 10 January 2010).

19 Housing and homelessness

Pedro Morago

Introduction

The present chapter begins by providing a brief introduction to the policy area of housing and examining how the structure of tenure has evolved in the UK over the last decades. The discussion then focuses on the phenomenon of homelessness, the most severe form of housing needs and one that heavily affects many users of social services. Contributing factors to as well as effects of homelessness are analysed, following which the chapter ends with an overview of the main policy developments and strategies developed in the UK in order to tackle homelessness and some considerations about their implementation.

Housing policy: Concept and relevance

Housing policy generally refers to government action aimed at ensuring – mainly through public investment and public regulation – that everyone has access to adequate and affordable housing (Alcock 2003). However, this area is also influenced by socio-economic, political and demographic factors as well as by market forces – like housing corporations, banks and building societies – which, through principles of supply and demand, may make a considerable impact on the housing system (Mullins and Murie 2006).

The role of housing policy as a core element of the welfare state is evident since housing arrangements are closely associated to people's well-being and quality of life: while adequate, good quality housing is an important contributor to individuals' physical and mental health (Lawrence 2002;

Smith 1989), self-esteem and social integration (Dunn 2002; Henderson and Karn 1987; Power 1987), poor housing is often related to other dimensions of disadvantage, such as poverty and social exclusion (Pawson and Kintrea 2002). Dwellers of deprived areas also suffer from stigma and poor reputation (Dean and Hastings 2000). In addition, the lack of adequate housing is a major risk to health, for example:

- Crowded households increase the risk of infectious diseases (Baker et al. 2000; Coetzee et al. 1988; Milne et al. 1987), have an impact on mental health (Entner Wright et al. 1998) and contribute to premature mortality (Kellet 1993).
- There is a strong relationship between damp housing and respiratory problems (Haverinen et al. 2001; Peat et al. 1998; Zock et al. 2002).
- Insufficient heat in homes is linked to excess winter mortality (Aylin et al. 2001).
- Overall, multiple housing deprivation experienced by individuals over the lifecourse is a significant determinant of poor health and health inequalities between different socio-economic groups (Marsh et al. 1999).

Within the UK housing system, differential status and levels of quality of life have traditionally been associated to the concept of tenure, as we will examine in the next section.

Tenure structure in the UK

The term *tenure* refers to the legal status in which a person or household occupies a home. In the UK, housing is commonly classified according the following types of tenure or residential settings:

- properties that are occupied by their owners;
- privately rented housing, occupied by tenants who rent the property from a private landlord;
- social housing renting, occupied by tenants who rent the property either from the local authority (council renting) or from a housing association (housing association renting).

Since the early 1900s, the structure of tenure in the UK has evolved dramatically: in 1914, 90 per cent of homes were rented while the remaining 10 per cent were owner-occupied properties; however, in 2008, 69 per cent of households were living in their own house or flat, with 18 per cent of dwellings being rented from the social housing sector and only 13 per cent from private landlords (Malpass and Murie 1999; Richards et al. 2003; Office for National Statistics 2010). Such a significant change in tenure is the result of a range of factors like an overall increase in income coupled with more favourable attitudes towards home ownership, incentives in the mortgage market – such as low interest rates and the introduction of tax relief on mortgage interest – and the establishment of measures like the tenant's right to buy, which gave millions of tenants the opportunity to buy their council house or flat. On the other hand, the council housing stock fell, not only in quantity – from 31.7 per cent of all UK housing in 1978 to 14.4 per cent in 2001 – but also in quality, as the housing remaining after 'right-to-buy' sales was mostly made up of flats located in deprived areas. In fact, council house dwellings are now largely occupied by tenants from low socio-economic groups (Murie 2003; Pickvance 2003)

In Scotland, the proportion of owner-occupied dwellings in 2008 was almost 66 per cent – lower than the UK average. 24 per cent of households were living in social housing (above the UK average), 9 per cent in private renting and 1 per cent in other types of residential setting (MacDonald et al. 2009), figures which suggest higher levels of deprivation in Scotland compared to the rest of Britain.

Housing needs and homelessness

There are different levels of housing needs: for instance, older people who are home owners but experience low income and deprivation are often unable to make the arrangements necessary to have a home warm and secure enough. In addition, the stock of the social housing sector still includes accommodation which – due to small dwelling size, location, and lack of renovation – is inadequate for the tenants' housing needs. But the most extreme manifestation of housing need is homelessness, which will be the main focus of the present chapter.

In the UK, a person or household are legally considered homeless if they have no home or if, having it, it would be unreasonable for them to occupy that home. As examined below, also those who are threatened with homelessness are covered by the legislation in this area. While homelessness is frequently associated with rough sleeping, the reality is that the vast majority of people who are homeless are not living on the streets but with relatives, friends, or in temporary or emergency accommodation. For example, although over 130,000 households were officially considered homeless in the UK, only fewer than 500 people were sleeping rough any single night in that period (Crisis 2010).

In Scotland, more than 40,000 persons or households were recognised as homeless by their local authority between April 2008 and March 2009. Amongst those who made a homeless application, a significant proportion (40 per cent) were single men. Single women accounted for 21 per cent and lone mothers for 18 per cent, while the rest of applicants were male lone parents (6 per cent), couples with children (5 per cent) and couples without children (5 per cent) (Shelter Scotland 2010). What are the causes of this phenomenon? Why do people become homeless? This issue will be analysed in the next section.

Contributing factors to homelessness

Until the late 1990s, homelessness was mainly seen as a housing problem, namely, as the result of a lack of sufficient supply of adequate and affordable housing. However, a large body of research has led in the last years to more complex explanations which, rather than on single causes, focus on the interaction of structural and personal factors. In particular, the latest research literature identifies the following factors contributing to homelessness:

Structural/societal factors

- *Demographic trends.* Family fragmentation, greater residential mobility and the sharp rise of single-person and lone-parent households have contributed to a significant increase in the demand for housing (Harvey 1999).
- *Insufficient supply of social housing.* As noted above, policies encouraging the sale of council housing, while giving a high number of tenants the opportunity to buy their homes, also led to a decline in the availability of social housing.
- *Economic processes.* There is a strong link between adverse economic factors such as poverty, structural inequality, unemployment and insufficient social security protection and homelessness (Anderson and Christian 2003; Caton et al. 2005; Fitzpatrick et al. 2000; Foord et al. 1998; Oldman 1997).
- *Social exclusion.* Exclusion from the opportunities and resources of mainstream society is a major risk for homelessness (MacKenzie and Chamberlain 2003). Furthermore, homelessness can be seen as the most severe dimension of social exclusion, one which leaves the individual with little or no chance for a better life (Talbot 2003).

While having a strong impact on the overall levels of homelessness, the above structural and societal factors and processes may have different effects on different individuals. In other words, individuals' vulnerability to structural contributors to homelessness is not equal. This is another key finding of the research studies conducted over the last two decades, which have found that the risk of becoming homeless is significantly higher among those individuals exposed to the following personal risk factors.

Personal risk factors

- *Poverty and unemployment* are the commonest risk factors among individuals who experience homelessness (Anderson et al. 1993; Caton et al. 2005; Fitzpatrick et al. 2000). As Fitzpatrick and colleagues highlight, it is often the lack of adequate income and employment opportunities that prevents homeless people – either long-term or those experiencing personal crises – from avoiding such an adverse situation.
- *Sexual or physical abuse*, particularly when experienced in childhood or adolescence, is likely to lead to detachment from family and community networks which, in turn, is related to increased vulnerability to homelessness (Lawrenson 1997; Stiffman 1989).
- *Institutionalisation.* Institutional background in local authority care, the armed forces or prison are linked to homelessness through mechanisms such as lack of independent living skills and support networks (Anderson et al. 1993; Gunner and Knott 1997; Randall and Brown 1999).
- *Offending behaviour.* Research studies among the homeless population show a high prevalence of individuals with a history of offending, particularly when in combination with other risk factors like low basic and social skills (Carlisle 1996; Homeless Network 1997; Housing Services Agency 1998).
- *Low educational attainment and poor basic skills* increase the risk of unemployment and lack of opportunities and, therefore, the likelihood of becoming homeless (Anderson et al. 1993; Randall and Brown 1999).
- *Lack of adequate support.* The lack of a family or social support network as well as of appropriate services make people more vulnerable to homelessness and more likely to become institutionalised as homeless (Randall and Brown 1999; Vostanis et al. 1998).
- *Alcohol and/or substance misuse.* A high proportion of homeless people report alcohol- and drug-related problems and cite them as the main reason for becoming homeless (Anderson et al. 1993; Fountain and Howes 2002; Gill et al. 1996).

- *Poor health,* in particular addiction and mental health problems, is strongly associated with homelessness (Connelly and Crown 1994; Gill et al. 1996; Pleace and Quilgars 1996).

The research literature has found that it is often a combination of the above risk factors – which are linked and mutually reinforcing – that puts individuals at high risk of becoming homeless. In addition, research studies have also identified a range of factors or events that can trigger homelessness.

Triggering factors

Family disputes and breakdown, debts and eviction, discharge from institutions, deterioration in physical or mental health and widowhood can trigger homelessness – and even rooflessness – especially among highly vulnerable individuals (Anderson et al. 1993; Evans 1996; Randall and Brown 1999). Therefore, rather than speaking of direct causes of homelessness, it is probably more accurate to argue that a combination of structural and personal factors puts individuals in a situation of high vulnerability to adverse events that can operate as triggers of homelessness (Swärd 1999).

Effects of homelessness

Homelessness has a strong impact on the lives of those individuals who experience it. In particular, the research literature has identified the following effects of homelessness:

- *Poorer health.* Homeless people suffer from worse health compared to the general population and are especially vulnerable to develop physical disorders like respiratory, skin, digestive, dental and musculoskeletal conditions (Connelly and Crown 1994; Pleace and Quilgars 1997). Homelessness is also a major risk factor for mental health problems like schizophrenia, depression and anxiety (Bines 1994; 1997; Connelly and Crown 1994), and significantly high rates of mortality and suicides among homeless people have been consistently reported by research studies (Baker 1997; Connelly and Crown 1994; Grenier 1996; Nordentoft and Wandall-Holm 2003).
- *Increased drug and alcohol misuse.* Substance misuse and/or heavy drinking are serious contributors to, but also exacerbated by, homelessness (Fitzpatrick et al. 2000; Morrish 1993; Wake 1992). For example, it has been found that an increasing proportion of young homeless people use a variety of drugs, often in conjunction with

alcohol, as a way to cope with the stress derived from homelessness (Klee and Reid 1998).

- *Stigma and discrimination.* Homelessness is often associated with a number of stereotypes and stigmas which, among other consequences, prevent homeless individuals from gaining appropriate access to employment and training opportunities, health care services, social housing, and other mainstream services like, for example, opening a bank account (Fitzpatrick et al. 2000; Lowry 1990; Stern 1994; Williams 1995).
- *Institutionalisation.* In addition to the stigma attached to homelessness, charges for temporary accommodation and support care are so high that they can create a strong disincentive to take up paid work, with which homeless people may remain indefinitely institutionalised within the homelessness welfare system (Fitzpatrick et al. 2000).
- *Offending and victimisation.* Homeless people, particularly rough sleepers, are at high risk of getting involved in criminal and anti-social activities, but also of being abused, sexually harassed and assaulted (Carlen 1996; Randall and Brown 1999; Reid et al. 1997).

As can be noted, there are considerable similarities between factors contributing to, and effects of homelessness. Certainly, not only do adverse factors such as ill health, drug and alcohol misuse, poverty and unemployment, sexual or physical abuse, poor basic skills, institutionalisation and offending behaviour put individuals at risk of becoming homeless, but they are also exacerbated by homelessness. In other words, the two-way interaction between homelessness and other dimensions of disadvantage and social exclusion is likely to create a trap or cycle of disadvantage from which it is extremely difficult to escape. This is a pattern that can be observed across most areas of social policy and which is summarised by one of the major assumptions of the social exclusion approach, namely, that deprivation leads to more deprivation. How has the problem of homelessness been tackled? The next section will examine the evolution of housing and homelessness policies in the UK over the last decades.

Policy developments and strategies

As noted above, over the twentieth century – and especially from 1945 – dramatic changes in tenure took place in the UK, with a sharp increase in owner-occupied homes, a significant decline in private renting and varying trends in the social housing sector. Such changes are, to a large extent, the result of socio-economic, demographic and market-related factors, but are also connected to the way in which policies in this area have evolved over time. For example, in the post-war period, along with steady growth in owner occupation, there was also a strong government focus on council housing, the importance of which grew until reaching its peak in the late 1970s, when publicly rented houses and flats represented 32 per cent of total tenure. However, from 1979 private ownership was particularly encouraged with strategies such as the 'right to buy' policy, which enabled around two million council tenants to buy their flat or house. The downside of the privatisation process was a decline in the quantity and quality of the council housing stock.

Simultaneously, housing associations – non-profit organisations which rent affordable social housing to different groups of people with specific needs – have grown to the extent that, since 1991, they have been building more new social housing than local authorities. Housing associations, which now own nearly 1.5 million homes in the UK, are companies that reinvest any profit in maintaining existing properties as well as in financing new ones.

Thus, the last 25 years have witnessed a dramatic shift in housing policy in the UK whereby dominant state intervention – through provision of council housing – has been replaced by a mixed economy of welfare which largely operates as a private or liberal market and, residually, provides means-tested benefits to those who cannot afford their housing costs. While a high number of households have seen their housing situation substantially improved, the property market has also generated negative outcomes: the housing boom and subsequent rising prices makes it virtually impossible for low-income households to buy a property so that they are becoming increasingly concentrated in deprived areas, often in unpopular council flats remaining after 'right-to-buy' sales. This phenomenon is known as the '*housing divide*', namely, the gap between those who can access the property ladder and those who cannot. For example, the average income – including benefits – of households living in social housing is around a quarter of the income of those buying a property with a mortgage. In Scotland, around 54 per cent of households living in social housing contain a non-working single adult while the proportion among those households that are buying a property is only 5 per cent (Martin et al. 2004).

When New Labour came to office in 1997, one of its first goals was to reduce street homelessness, for which purposes the Government established the Rough Sleepers Unit – formally integrated within the Social Exclusion Unit. The Rough Sleepers Unit published in 1999 *Coming in from the Cold* (Rough Sleepers Unit 1999), a report setting out the Government's strategy to tackle street homelessness as well as the target of reducing the problem by two-thirds by March 2002.

After the apparent success of its strategy, the Government took action in relation to other, wider forms of homelessness through the Homelessness Act 2002. Largely as a result of the findings reported by the research literature of the 1990s, the Homelessness Act requires local authorities to adopt a strategic, long-term approach to tackling homelessness, with special emphasis on preventative support to those at risk of becoming homeless. For such purposes, housing services are expected to develop a multi-agency approach, working in partnership with all other appropriate agencies and groups involved in addressing risk factors contributing to homelessness (for example health services, social and welfare services, education services, the police, the voluntary sector and so on). Another main change introduced by the Act is that the previously existing categories of priority need for housing (pregnant women, people responsible for dependent children, people who have become homeless by any disaster or emergency and especially vulnerable people) are expanded to include new groups such as most of 16 and 17 year olds, care leavers aged 18 to 21, people who are vulnerable due to an institutionalised background and people having to leave their homes because of violence or threats of violence.

A new set of housing reforms has been implemented in England and Wales by the Housing Act 2004, which introduces greater protection for tenants against hazards in properties, the possibility to bring long-term empty homes back into use, better protection for gypsies and travellers in relation to their accommodation needs, and measures for tackling the activities of anti-social tenants.

Also in Scotland recent years have seen major developments in housing and homelessness policy. For instance, the Scottish Office set up in 1997 a Rough Sleepers Initiative and a budget of £16 million was allocated to local authorities to meet the needs of individuals living on the streets. When responsibility for this area was transferred to the Scottish Executive in 1999, subsequent funds were provided in order to eradicate rough sleeping by the end of 2003. Whilst the Rough Sleepers Initiative has led to a sizeable reduction in the number of people who sleep rough in Scotland, this is still a significant problem in some parts of the country, like Glasgow.

Another initiative of the Scottish Executive in the area of homelessness was the creation in August 1999 of the Homelessness Task Force (HTF), made up of agencies from the statutory and voluntary sectors. The recommendations formulated by the HTF in 2000 resulted in the Housing (Scotland) Act 2001, which requires local authorities to assess the extent of homelessness in their area and develop a strategic approach to combating homelessness. In addition, the Act expands the rights of those individuals that may be affected by homelessness. For example, while homelessness is defined – like in the rest of the UK – as the situation in which someone lacks a home or is threatened to lose it, the period in which threatened homelessness may occur varies from 28 days in England and Wales to two months in Scotland. Another major change brought in by the Act is that local authorities must provide temporary accommodation to all homeless applicants, and not only to those in priority need like in England and Wales. Further initiatives were passed into Law with the Homelessness (Scotland) Act 2003, which sets the target that by 2012 everyone in Scotland will have a permanent home. For such purposes, the Act considerably broadens the population groups that are in priority need for permanent housing, criteria to be definitely abolished in 2012, when the right to permanent accommodation will apply to everyone – with the exception of some cases of intentional homelessness.

Finally, the Housing (Scotland) Act 2006 sets out a number of measures to ensure that privately owned properties are maintained to a reasonable standard as well as to raise standards in the private rented sector, with wider rights for tenants if necessary repairs are not carried out by their landlords and for tenants with disabilities to adapt the home to their specific needs. The Act also strengthens the rights of owners of mobile homes when deciding whether a home of this type is detrimental to a site and provides them with increased protection against harassment.

Implementation of the above measures is the responsibility of the Scottish Executive Development Department (SEDD), which – through Communities Scotland, its housing and regeneration agency – aims to ensure the supply of adequate and affordable housing across Scotland, with particular attention to disadvantaged communities.

Implications for social work

We now know, from a considerable body of research evidence, that homelessness is a phenomenon of complex nature and often associated to a range of contributing factors. Implications of this for social work professionals include, certainly, a non-judgmental approach towards people affected or threatened by homelessness, but also a broad, holistic understanding of their various – and often multiple – areas of need. All those needs have to be identified through a comprehensive assessment process which, in turn, will form the basis of a strategic action plan. Within such process, it is important to listen to and take into account the service user's perspectives, which not only will help us in producing a more informed assessment of needs, but is also an empowering mechanism likely to result in better outcomes.

Another consequence of the multi-dimensional nature of homelessness is that those affected by or at risk of homelessness may require support in relation to different areas of need and provided by a wide range of agencies or services. In fact, homelessness strategies often involve multi-agency work across areas such as accommodation, benefits, health care, practical, emotional, legal and social support, training and employment, and advocacy. Therefore, social workers need to liaise effectively and work in close partnership with all those key agencies involved in service provision for homeless people.

Finally, social workers working with this service-user group should be encouraged to: (i) adopt an evidence-based approach whereby programmes of proven efficacy in preventing and alleviating homelessness are implemented – or its use increased; (ii) undertake studies of qualitative research amongst service users in order to gain a better understanding of the trajectories, mechanisms and interactions of factors through which people become homeless.

Chapter summary

Despite housing being an essential contributor to people's well-being, there are still significant sectors of the UK population whose housing needs are not adequately met. Amongst such needs, homelessness is the most extreme one. A large body of research studies conducted in the 1990s shows that homelessness is not merely a problem of lack of housing supply. Rather, it is a combination of structural, societal and personal adverse factors that puts individuals and households in a situation of increased vulnerability to homelessness. Therefore, tackling homelessness requires strategic solutions that take the multi-dimensional nature of homelessness into account. Such an approach has informed the most recent homelessness initiatives in the UK. In particular, the Housing (Scotland) Act 2001 requires local authorities to develop articulated strategies aimed at preventing and combating homelessness. Another major piece of legislation passed by the Scottish Parliament, the Homelessness (Scotland) Act 2003, introduces further measures to protect those at risk of homelessness and sets the target that by 2012 everyone in Scotland will have a permanent home. Although such initiatives have received, in general, a good response from the housing sector, concerns have also been raised that the objective of ending homelessness by 2012 might not be achieved (Scottish Executive 2005). In fact the new pieces of legislation ask local authorities to undertake additional duties, which is likely to further stretch their already overwhelmed resources. Therefore, local authorities need to be provided with sufficient material and financial assistance if the 2012 target is to be met.

References

Alcock, P. (2003), *Social Policy in Britain* (2nd edn) (Basingstoke: Palgrave Macmillan).

Anderson, I. and Christian, J. (2003), 'Causes of Homelessness in the UK: A Dynamic Analysis', *Journal of Community and Applied Social Psychology* 13: 105–18.

Anderson, I., Kemp, P. and Quilgars, D. (1993), *Single Homeless People* (London: Her Majesty's Stationery Office).

Aylin, P., Morris, S., Wakefield, J., Grossinho, A., Jarup, L. and Elliott, P. (2001), 'Temperature, Housing, Deprivation and their Relationship to Excess Winter Mortality in Great Britain, 1986–1996', *International Journal of Epidemiology* 30: 1100–108.

Baker, L. (1997), *Homelessness and Suicide* (London: Shelter).

Baker, M., McNicholas, A., Garrett, N., Jones, N., Stewart, J., Koberstein, V. and Lennon, D. (2000), 'Household Crowding a Major Risk Factor for Meningococcal Disease in Auckland Children', *Pediatric Infectious Disease Journal* 19: 983–90.

Bines, W. (1994), *The Health of Single Homeless People* (York: Centre for Housing Policy, University of York).

— (1997), 'The Health of Single Homeless People', in R. Burrows, N. Pleace and D. Quilgars (eds), *Homelessness and Social Policy* (London: Routledge).

Carlen, P. (1996), *Jigsaw: A Political Criminology of Youth Homelessness* (Buckingham: Open University Press).

Carlisle, J. (1996), *The Housing Needs of Ex-Prisoners*, Housing Research Findings 178 (York: Joseph Rowntree Foundation).

Caton, C.L., Dominguez, B., Schanzer, B., Hasin, D.S., Shrout, P.E., Felix, A., McQuistion, H., Opler, L.A. and Hsu, E. (2005), 'Risk Factors for Long-Term Homelessness: Findings from a Longitudinal Study of First-Time Homeless Single Adults', *American Journal of Public Health* 95(10): 1753–9.

Coetzee, N., Yach, D. and Joubert, G. (1988), 'Crowding and Alcohol Abuse as Risk Factors for Tuberculosis in the Mamre Population: Results of a Case-Control Study', *South African Medical Journal* 74: 352–4.

Connelly, J. and Crown, J. (eds) (1994), *Homelessness and Ill Health* (London: Royal College of Physicians).

Crisis (2010), *Official Homelessness Statistics. England: Trends over Time*. Available at: http://www.crisis.org.uk/policywatch/pages/england_trends_over_time.html (accessed 5 February 2010).

Dean, J. and Hastings, A. (2000), *Challenging Images: Housing Estates, Stigma and Regeneration* (Bristol: Policy Press).

Dunn, J.R. (2002), 'Housing and Inequalities in Health: A Study Of Socioeconomic Dimensions of Housing and Self Reported Health from a Survey of Vancouver Residents', *Journal of Epidemiology and Community Health* 56: 671–82.

Entner Wright, B.R., Caspi, A., Moffit, T.E. and Silva, P.A. (1998), 'Factors Associated with Doubled-Up Housing: A Common Precursor to Homelessness', *Social Service Review* 72(1): 92–111.

Evans, A. (1996), *We Don't Choose to be Homeless: Report of the National Inquiry Into Preventing Youth Homelessness* (London: CHAR).

Fitzpatrick, S., Kemp, P.A. and Klinker, S. (2000), *Single Homelessness: An Overview of Research in Britain* (Bristol: Policy Press).

Foord, M., Palmer, J. and Simpson, D. (1998), *Bricks without Mortar: 30 Years of Single Homelessness* (London: Crisis).

Fountain, J. and Howes, S. (2002), *Home and Dry? Homelessness and Substance Use in London* (London: Crisis and the National Addiction Centre).

Gill, B., Meltzer, H. and Hinds, K. (1996), *The Prevalence of Psychiatric Morbidity among Homeless Adults* (London: Office of Population, Censuses, and Surveys).

Grenier, P. (1996), *Still Dying for a Home* (London: Crisis).

Gunner, G. and Knott, H. (1997), *Homeless on Civvy Street: Survey of Homelessness amongst Ex-Service-Men in London* (London: PS Opinion Research).

Harvey, B. (1999), 'The Problem of Homelessness: A European Perspective', in S. Hutson and D. Clapham (eds), *Homelessness: Public Policies and Private Troubles* (London: Cassell).

Haverinen, U., Husman, T., Pekkanen, J., Vahteristo, M., Moschandreas, D. and Nevalainen, A. (2001), 'Characteristics of Moisture Damage in Houses and their Association with Self-Reported Symptoms of the Occupants', *Indoor Built Environment* 10: 83–94.

Henderson, J. and Karn, V. (1987), *Race, Class and the Allocation of State Housing* (Aldershot: Gower).

Homeless Network (1997), *Central London Street Monitor* (London: Homeless Network).

Homelessness Act 2002 (London: Her Majesty's Stationery Office).

Homelessness (Scotland) Act 2003 (Edinburgh: Stationery Office).

Housing Act 2004 (London: Her Majesty's Stationery Office).

Housing (Scotland) Act 2001 (Edinburgh: Stationery Office).

Housing (Scotland) Act 2006 (Edinburgh: Stationery Office).

Housing Services Agency (1998), *The Outreach Directory Annual Statistics 1996–7* (London: Housing Services Agency and Homeless Network).

Kellet, J.M. (1993), 'Crowding and Mortality in London Boroughs', in R. Burridge and D. Ormandy (eds), *Unhealthy Housing* (London: Chapman and Hall).

Klee, H. and Reid, P. (1998), 'Drug Use among the Young Homeless: Coping through Self-Medication', *Health* 2(2): 115–34.

Lawrence, R. (2002), 'Healthy Residential Environments', in R. Bechtel and A. Churchman (eds), *Handbook of Environmental Psychology* (New York, NY: John Wiley).

Lawrenson, F. (1997), 'Runaway Children: Whose Problem?', *British Medical Journal* 314: 1064.

Lowry, S. (1990), 'Housing and Health: Health and Homelessness', *British Medical Journal* 300: 32–4.

MacDonald, E., Cairns, P., Cormack, D., Máté, I. and McLaren, D. (2009), *Scottish House Condition Survey: Key Findings for 2008*. Available at: http://www.scotland.gov.uk/Resource/Doc/292876/0090383.pdf (accessed 5 February 2010).

MacKenzie, D. and Chamberlain, C. (2003), *Homeless Careers: Pathways in and out of Homelessness, Counting the Homeless 2001 Project* (Hawthorn, Victoria: Swinburne University of Technology and RMIT (Royal Melbourne Institute of Technology) University).

Malpass, P. and Murie, A. (1999), *Housing Policy and Practice* (5th edn) (Basingstoke: Macmillan Press).

Marsh, A., Gordon, D., Pantazis, C. and Heslop, P. (1999), *Home Sweet Home? The Impact of Poor Housing on Health* (London: Policy Press).

Martin, C., Dudleston, A., Harkins, J., Hope, S., Littlewood, M., Murray, L. and Ormston, R. (2004), *Scotland's People: Results from the 2003 Scottish Household Survey. Annual Report* (Edinburgh: Scottish Executive National Statistics, TNS Social Research and Mori Scotland).

Milne, A., Allwood, G.K, Moyes, C.D., Pearce, N.E. and Newell, K. (1987), 'A Seroepidemiological Study of the Prevalence of Hepatitis B Infection in a Hyperendemic New Zealand Community', *International Journal of Epidemiology* 16: 84–90.

Morrish, P. (1993), *Living in the Shadows: The Accommodation Needs and Preferences of Homeless Street Drinkers* (Leeds: Leeds Accommodation Forum).

Mullins, D. and Murie, A. (2006), *Housing Policy in the UK* (Basingstoke: Palgrave Macmillan).

Murie, A. (2003), 'Housing', in P. Alcock, A. Erskine and M. May (eds), *The Student's Companion to Social Policy* (2nd edn) (Oxford: Blackwell).

Nordentoft, M. and Wandall-Holm, N. (2003), '10 Year Follow Up Study of Mortality among Users of Hostels for Homeless People in Copenhagen', *British Medical Journal* 327: 81.

Office for National Statistics (2010), *Housing Tenure*. Available at: http://www.statistics.gov.uk/cci/nugget.asp?id=1105 (accessed 5 February 2010).

Oldman, J. (1997), 'Beyond Bricks and Mortar', in J. Roche and S. Tucker (eds), *Youth in Society* (London: Sage Publications).

Pawson, H. and Kintrea, K. (2002), 'Part of the Problem or Part of the Solution? Social Housing Allocation Policies and Social Exclusion in Britain', *Journal of Social Policy* 31(4): 643–67.

Peat, J.K., Dickerson, J. and Li, J. (1998), 'Effects of Damp and Cold on Respiratory Health', *Allergy* 53: 120–28.

Pickvance, C. (2003), 'Housing and Housing Policy', in J. Baldock, N. Manning and S. Vickerstaff (eds), *Social Policy* (2nd edn) (Oxford: Oxford University Press).

Pleace, N. and Quilgars, D. (1996), *Health and Homelessness in London* (London: King's Fund).

— (1997), 'Health, Homelessness and Access to Health Care Services in London', in R. Burrows, N. Pleace and D. Quilgars (eds), *Homelessness and Social Policy* (London: Routledge).

Power, A. (1987), *Property before People* (London: Allen and Unwin).

Randall, G. and Brown, S. (1999), *Prevention is Better than Cure: New Solutions to Street Homelessness from Crisis* (London: Crisis).

Reid, P., Klee, H. and Lewis, S. (1997), 'Danger', *Community Care* 16–22 January: 28–9.

Richards, L., Fox, K., Roberts, C., Fletcher, L. and Goddard, E. (2003), *Living in Britain: Results from the 2002 General Household Survey* (London: National Statistics).

Rough Sleepers Unit (1999), *Coming in from the Cold: The Government's Strategy on Rough Sleeping* (London: Department of the Environment, Transport and the Regions).

Scottish Executive (2005), *Helping Homeless People: Homelessness Consultation Responses: Ministerial Statement on Abolition of Priority Need by 2012. A Summary of Responses to the Consultation on Ministerial Statement Required by Section 3 of the Homelessness etc. (Scotland) Act 2003 Homelessness Consultation Responses* (Edinburgh: Scottish Executive).

Shelter Scotland (2010), *Homelessness Statistics*. Available at: http://scotland.shelter.org.uk/housing_issues/research_and_statistics/key_statistics/homelessness_facts_and_research#1 (accessed 5 February 2010).

Smith, S.J. (1989), *Housing and Health: A Review and Research Agenda* (Glasgow: Centre for Housing Research, University of Glasgow, Economic Social Research Council).

Stern, R. (1994), 'Homelessness People and the NHS: Are We Discriminating Enough?', *Journal of Interprofessional Care* 8(2): 173–81.

Stiffman, A.R. (1989), 'Physical and Sexual Abuse in Runaway Youths', *Child Abuse and Neglect* 13(3): 417–26.

Swärd, H. (1999), 'Homelessness in Sweden: Discussion, Patterns, and Causes', *European Journal of Social Work* 2(3): 289–303.

Talbot, C. (2003), *Social Exclusion and Homelessness: Everyone's Responsibility* (Adelaide: Uniting Care Wesley).

Vostanis, P., Grattan, E. and Cumella, S. (1998), 'Mental Health Problems of Homeless Children and their Families: A Longitudinal Study', *British Medical Journal* 316: 899–902.

Wake, M. (1992), *Homelessness and Street Drinking* (Arlington: Arlington Housing Association).

Williams, S.A. (1995), *Review of Primary Care Projects for Homeless People* (London: Department of Health).

Zock, J.P., Jarvis, D., Luczynska, C., Sunyer, J., Burney, P. and European Community Respiratory Health Survey (2002), 'Housing Characteristics Reported Mould Exposure, and Asthma in the European Community', *The Journal of Allergy and Clinical Immunology* 110: 285–92.

20 Conclusions: Onwards and upwards?

Steve J. Hothersall and Janine Bolger

> Uncertainty is the only certainty there is, and knowing how to live with insecurity is the only security.
>
> John Allen Paulos

Perhaps one of the key themes to emerge from this book is that we all live in an uncertain world. One of the aims of social policy has been, and continues to be, to try and address this. As we saw in Part I, perhaps one of the major achievements of recent social policy was the creation of the welfare state. Whether this arrangement for the public provision of welfare is now the best or the only way to maintain, enhance and ensure well-being and ontological security (Kraemer and Roberts 1996; Marris 1996) is certainly a contested issue (Rodger 2000) and one that will continue to be debated for some time to come. The provisions of the welfare state have clearly brought benefit to many and this claim would, we think, be difficult to dispute even in the knowledge that its effectiveness can be brought into question at a number of levels. Many of you would not be reading this today if, for example, you had not had access to health care, free at the point of delivery. Similarly, it could be argued that many of you might also not be able to read and understand this book if you had not had the benefits of free education that helped you develop the capacity to read. Whilst these are perhaps simplistic arguments, they do highlight some of the broad benefits that millions of people have enjoyed because of some of the provisions of the Beveridge welfare state. And even though critics of the welfare state might argue that such provision is nothing short of a capitalist conspiracy to subvert the population to the ends of the ruling classes, this is but one (persuasive) view (Ferguson, Lavalette and Mooney 2002) but even it cannot detract we feel from the realities of those claims we mention.

As time has passed and society has evolved, the ways in which welfare is conceived of, delivered and paid for have been subjected to (necessary) scrutiny. As a result, various attempts to 'reform' the welfare state have taken effect and whether these have added to or subtracted from the general good is often a matter of opinion in spite of governments and academics making their own claims in one direction or the other. At the time of writing, this debate in various forms still goes on so we cannot say absolutely whether what *is* represents that which *ought to be*; this book has provided you with the detail of what *is* whilst offering our views on whether this is how it perhaps *ought to be*, but these are our views and may well differ from the views of others. Such is the nature of opinion.

What is clear though is that social policy in Scotland, as in the rest of the UK, Europe and across differing parts of the rest of the world, is now more enmeshed than it perhaps ever was. The effects of globalisation cannot be ignored (Ritzer and Atalay 2010; George and Wilding 2002) and social protection for the poorest and most vulnerable in the world is now very much a 'local' issue (Barrientos and Hulme 2010), so our frame of reference in terms of welfare is becoming much broader and there is an increasing focus upon the need for comparative welfare studies (Cochrane, Clarke and Gewirtz 2001; Clarke 2004). As a result, our conceptions and understandings of best practice in social work, social care and related professions requires expansion (Hugman 2010) to take account of increased diversity, changing cultural patterns and the continuing phenomena of asylum and migration, not to mention the effects of war and terrorism on all of us; in essence, 'global conditions and local practice' (Lyons, Manion and Carlsen 2006).

As practitioners in the field of what we will refer broadly to as 'welfare', you will experience firsthand the many uncertainties and insecurities of modern-day life in your contacts with service users and part of your professional task will be to utilise your knowledge and understanding of policy (amongst many other things) in order to make practice *meaningful* for those on the receiving end. Understanding policy is *absolutely essential* for good practice. If you don't know what's out there and what the parameters for your practice are, then you can't realistically be safe to practice. This does not mean that every practitioner has to know everything there is to know about the law and policy, but what it *does mean* is that you have to be able to make what is available *work* for those people concerned and that requires knowledge and understanding on your part, particularly when nowadays many practitioners complain bitterly about feeling 'distanced' from the people they feel they should be working with and that they are not allowed to use their professional judgement or discretion in relation to their practice because policy makes what they do and how they do it far too prescriptive.

We are not wholly convinced by this line of argument. We believe that professionals can and should act as *'street-level bureaucrats'* (Lipsky 1980; and see Chapter 4) in spite of contemporary claims that the use of discretion in professional practice is being curtailed, although this would run counter to the expressed aims of governments in both Scotland and the UK for social work and related professions in relation to their role as 'autonomous professionals'.

It is unclear as to how the ongoing debates on welfare will develop, although there is no doubt in our mind that there will always be a need for some form of state and therefore *centralised* involvement in private life; the spheres of private and public are intimately connected and so it seems that it is more a case of *how* public (and therefore, social) policy will develop and *how* the role of the state will evolve in relation to that of its citizens, rather than thinking in terms of the abandonment of such notions.

In relation to you and your practice, knowledge of policy is essential and we hope that this book has given you a clearer appreciation of the important relationship that exists between politics, policy, people and practice. After all, we are all in this together.

References

Barrientos, A. and Hulme, D. (eds) (2010), *Social Protection for the Poor and the Poorest: Concepts, Policies and Politics* (Basingstoke: Palgrave Macmillan).

Clarke, J. (2004), *Changing Welfare, Changing States: New Directions in Social Policy* (London: Sage).

Cochrane, A., Clarke, J. and Gewirtz, S. (eds) (2001), *Comparing Welfare States* (2nd edn) (London: Sage).

Ferguson, I., Lavalette, M. and Mooney, G. (2002), *Rethinking Welfare: A Critical Perspective* (London: Sage).

George, V. and Wilding, P. (2002), *Globalization and Human Welfare* (Basingstoke: Palgrave Macmillan).

Hugman, R. (2010), *Understanding International Social Work: A Critical Analysis* (Basingstoke: Palgrave Macmillan).

Kraemer, S. and Roberts, J. (eds) (1996), *The Politics of Attachment: Towards a Secure Society* (London: Free Association Books).

Lipsky, M. (1980), *Street-Level Bureaucracy: The Dilemmas of Individuals in Public Service* (New York, NY: Russell Sage Foundation).

Lyons, K., Manion, K. and Carlsen, M. (2006), *International Perspectives on Social Work* (Basingstoke: Palgrave Macmillan).

Marris, P. (1996), *The Politics of Uncertainty: Attachment in Private and Public Life* (London: Routledge).

Ritzer, G. and Atalay, Z. (eds) (2010), *Readings in Globalization: Key Concepts and Major Debates* (Oxford: Wiley-Blackwell).

Rodger, J.J. (2000), *From a Welfare State to a Welfare Society: The Changing Context of Social Policy in a Post Modern Era* (Basingstoke: Palgrave Macmillan).

Index

Aberdeen City Council 111
Aberdeen University 317
Acheson Report 209, 214
Act of Settlement 1662 35, 402
Act of Union 1707 16–17, 38
Addiewell prison 383
Adoption and Children (Scotland) Act 2007 21, 24, 297
Adult Support and Protection (Scotland) Act 2007 116, 242, 261
Adults with Incapacity (Scotland) Act 2000 24, 116, 242, 261, 263
Age UK 249
ageism 247, 248, 259
  see also older people
agricultural policy 72–3
AIDS 345, 346
Airdrie 385
alcohol 337, 338, 341, 348, 350
  case study 357–61
  historical perspective 343–7
  legislation 356
  strategies 351–3
Alcohol Awareness Week 358
Alcohol and Drug Action Teams/Partnerships 348
Alcohol etc. (Scotland) Bill 352
Alcoholics Anonymous 346
Aliens Act 1905 397
Amsterdam Treaty 1997 402
anarchism 62
Angel Group 408
anti-social behaviour 308, 309, 348, 385, 386, 423, 424, 425, 427
Anti-Social Behaviour etc. (Scotland) Act 2004 308, 386
Anti-Social Behaviour Orders (ASBOs) 348, 385
Applied suicide intervention skills training (Asist) 235
apprentices 35, 328, 329
Arrangements to Look After Children (Scotland) Regulations 1996 14
Assisted Voluntary Return Programme 407
Association of Carers (UK) 135
Association of Directors of Social Work in Scotland (ADSW) 194, 263, 377
asylum 93, 98, 163, 185, 393–415
Asylum and Immigration (Treatment of Claimants) Act 2004 400
Asylum and Refugee Task Group, Association of Directors of Social Work in England and Wales 400
Asylum Screening Unit 406
asylum seekers *see* asylum
attendance allowance 156, 158
Audit Scotland 2005 142

Baby Peter 111, 112–13, 114
Beattie Committee 285, 322
Beck Depression Inventory 78
Beck, Ulrich 113–14
Beckford, Jasmine 296
'bed-blocking' 142
benefits 36, 52, 77, 151–70
  table 155
  see also specific allowances
Bethnal Green 91
Better Health, Better Care Action Plan 2007 216
A Better Way: The Report of the Ministerial Group on Women Offending 379
Beveridge Report 1942 46–7, 54, 60, 66, 67, 85, 254, 280
Beveridge, Sir W.H. 46
Black Death 113
Black Report 209
Blair, Tony 92, 102, 136, 169, 190
'Boarding Out' schemes 294
Booth, Charles 43, 279

Borders, Citizenship and Immigration Act 2009 403
Borders Inquiry 114–16
Bowlby, John 294
Breaking the Cycle 103
British Association of Social Workers (BASW) Code of Ethics 185
British Nationality Act 1981 398
broadband internet access 82
Bronfenbrenner, U. 295, 299
Brown, Gordon 190
Building a Better Scotland 2004 216
Building Our Future: Scotland's School Estate 324

Camphill Communities 289
capitalism 39, 40, 55–9, 64, 85, 253
Cardiff, Ely Hospital 126
care 125–45, 189, 197, 261
  funding 141–2
Care 21 137, 138, 139
Care Commission 289, 323
care homes *see* residential care
carers 134–8, 260
carers' allowance 155, 156, 159
Carers National Association 135
Carers (Recognition and Services) Act 1995 135–6, 139, 142
Carers Rights Charter 138
Carers Scotland 285
Carers Strategy 2008 192
Caring for People: Community Care: Into the Next Decade and Beyond 128, 188, 283
case studies
  care 133–4
  disability 288–90
  education and training 320–1, 324–6
  mental health 239–41
  older people 258–9
  welfare rights 156–61
Castle Huntly open prison 385
Chalmers, Thomas 41
Changing Children's Services Fund 299
Changing Lives: Report of the 21st Century Social Work Review Group 41, 131, 143, 192, 263, 287, 295, 301, 385–6
Changing Scotland's Relationship with Alcohol: A Framework for Action 351–2
charitable organisations 40–2
Charity Organisation Society (COS) 41, 279
child abuse and neglect 16, 294–5
The Child at the Centre 323
child benefit 155, 156, 159
child care policy 10
child labour 43, 318
Child Maintenance and Enforcement Commission (formerly Child Support Agency) 155
Child Poverty Action Group (CPAG) 153
child protection 293, 305, 382
Child Protection Committees 305
Child Protection and Online Protection Centre 382
Child Strategy Statement: Working Together for Scotland's Children 304
Child Support Agency (now Child Maintenance and Enforcement Commission) 155
Childcare Information Services 322
Childcare Partnerships 322
children
  asylum seekers 408
  deprivation, and health 213
  and drugs 352–3
  legislation 356
  poverty 164–5, 183, 196–7
  and their families 293–310
  young carers 136, 138–40
Children Acts
  1908 293
  1948 47, 294
  1975 296
Children (Scotland) Act 1995 14, 15, 21, 22, 24, 26, 136, 180, 185, 186, 297, 320, 360, 409
Children and Young Persons (Protection from Tobacco) Act 1991 360
Children and Young Persons (Scotland) Act 1937 294, 360

Children and Young Persons, Scotland (Kilbrandon Report) 368
Children's Departments 294
Children's Hearing System (Scottish Children's Reporter Administration (SCRA)) 305
Children's Panels 294
Children's Services (Scotland) Bill 2009 303
children's tax credit (CTC) 101, 159, 160
Choose Life 234–5, 236
Choosing Health: Making Healthy Choices Easier 2004 215–16
Churchill, Winston 44
Citizens' Advice Bureaux (CABs) 153
citizenship rights 398, 402
civil liberties 113
Clayson Committee 345, 351
Cleveland Report 1988 296
Clyde Committee on Child Care 294
Co-ordinated support plan (CSP) 325, 326
coca 339
Codes of Ethics 413
Codes of Practice 413
collectivism 51, 52, 54, 55, 75
Commissioner for Children and Young People (Scotland) Act 2003 181
commodification, welfare 52
Commonwealth Immigrants Act 1968 398
community care 126–34, 255, 283
Community Care: Agenda for Action (Griffiths Report) 128, 129, 188
Community Care (Direct Payments) Act 1996 142, 260, 262
community care grant (CCG) 160, 161
Community Care and Health (Scotland) Act 2002 48, 137, 140, 141, 142, 144, 255, 262, 285
Community Care (Joint Working etc.) (Scotland) Regulations 2002 144
Community Health Partnerships (CHPs) 142
Community Justice Authorities (CJAs) 377
Community Payback 383
Community Supervision Sentence 383
Confederation of Scottish Local Authorities (COSLA) 262
conservatism 57–8
Consumer Protection Act 1987 361
consumerism 64, 178, 188–90
'contract culture' 58, 189
Controlling our Borders: Making Migration Work for Britain 401
Convention of Local Authority Organisations (CoSLA) 377
Convention of Rights (Compliance) (Scotland) Act 2001 376
Cornton Vale, HMP 379, 380
council tax benefit 166
Count Us In: Improving the Education of our Looked After Children 329
courts 15–16
Crime and Disorder Act 1998 348, 349, 373, 380, 381, 385
Crime and Punishment (Scotland) Act 1997 373
Criminal Injuries Compensation Authority 374
Criminal Justice and Licensing (Scotland) Bill 2009 374
Criminal Justice (Scotland) Act 2003 373, 377
criminal justice system 15, 16, 367–87, 390–1
Criminal Procedure (Amendment) (Scotland) Act 2004 375
Criminal Procedure (Scotland) Act 1995 370, 375
crisis loan (CL) 160
Crown Office and Procurator Fiscal Service 18–19
Curriculum for Excellence 140, 299, 327
A Curriculum Framework for Children in their Pre-School Year 321
Curtis Committee 294

Dealing with Offending by Young People 386
decision network 10
Defence of the Realm Act 1916 343
'Delivering for Mental Health' 2006 238
demographics 96–7, 140, 252–3, 275, 404, 422

Department for Work and Pensions (DWP) 92, 93, 155, 158, 162, 163, 166, 170, 350
deprivation
  disability 179
  health 210, 212, 213, 214, 217, 218
  homelessness 420, 421, 425
  older people 250, 252, 266
  poverty and social exclusion 93, 99, 100, 104, 164
detention centres (immigration removal centres) 403, 407
Determination of Needs Act 1941 45
Direct Payments 192, 193, 197
disability, *see also* impairment
Disability and Carers Service 155
Disability Discrimination Act 1995 282, 283, 331
disability living allowance 155, 156, 158
Disabled Persons Act 1986 (UK) 135
Disablement Incomes Group (DIG) 281
discrimination
  care 138
  disability 273, 282, 283, 284
  education 331
  empowerment 176, 177, 185
  health 214, 217
  homelessness 425
  immigration 396
  mental health 228
  older people 247, 248, 254, 258, 259
  poverty 96, 99, 103
  welfare rights 164, 165
Disraeli, Benjamin 58
domestic violence 304, 379
domiciliary care 127–8, 134, 143, 261
Drug Action Teams 348
Drug Treatment and Testing Orders 348, 349
drugs 16, 337–62, 424
  and children 352–3
  and crime 348–51
  and gender 340
  legislation 356
  treatment 348–50
Drugs in Scotland: Meeting the Challenge (1994) 348
Dublin Convention 402
Dungavel House, North Lanarkshire 403, 407
Dunning Report 319

Early Learning Forward Thinking: The Policy Framework for ICT in Early Years 322
Early Years and Early Intervention: A Joint Scottish Government and COSLA Policy Statement 307
Early Years Framework 307
ecological representation of the relationship between society, law, policy and professional practice (fig) 22
ecstasy 339
education 2, 40, 43, 46, 52, 54, 75, 317–30
Education Act 1944 (Butler Act) 47
Education (Additional Support for Learning) (Scotland) Act 2004 180, 324
Education Amendment (Scotland) Act 1981 319
Education (Disability Strategies and Pupils' Educational Records) (Scotland) Act 2002 331
Education (Ministerial Powers of Direction) Bill 2003 324
Education (Scotland) Acts 317–19
  1872 318
  1936 319
  1996 321
Education and Skills Bill (England and Wales) 331
Effectiveness of the Youth Justice Group 385
efficiency savings 111
Ely Hospital, Cardiff 126
employment
  and criminal justice 386
  and disability 273, 279, 280, 285, 287, 288
  and empowerment 177, 182
  and mental health 239
  older people 250, 262
  poverty and social exclusion 95–7, 100–2, 104

refugees 404, 413
and substance use 350
training 329, 330
welfare rights 151, 153, 161, 165, 167
young people 300, 306
see also unemployment
employment and support allowances (ESA) 156, 159, 170
empowerment 142, 175–98
environmentalism 62–3
Equality Bill 288
Erskine, John 15
ethnic minorities 93, 96, 100, 102, 165, 273, 288
ethnicity 61, 177, 183, 209
and education 2, 317, 330–1
eugenics 277, 278
European Convention on Human Rights (ECHR) 20, 130, 184, 233, 402
European Union Law 20
Every Child Matters 400

Fabian Society 44, 279, 298, 301
Factory Acts 43
1802 318
1878 318
family 52, 260–1, 300, 308–10
see also children
Family Allowances Act 1945 47
Family Mediation in Scotland 102
Family Resource Survey 94
fascism 60, 61
feminism 62
feudalism 15, 57
For Scotland's Children 303
Forensic Network 119
foster care 14, 26, 294, 306
Fostering of Children (Scotland) Regulations 1996 14
Foucault, Michel 176
Foye, Robert 384
Framework for Mental Health Services in Scotland 1997 237
France 52
free school meals 46, 324
free television licences 101

Galbraith, John Kenneth 249
Galbraith, Sam 323
Galton, Francis 277
Gateway Programme see One Gateway Protection Programme
Gemeinschaft 61
gender 329–30, 340, 379
Gender Equality Scheme 379
Germany 52, 61
Getting it Right for Every Child in Foster Care and Kinship Care 306, 360
Getting it Right for Every Child (GIRFEC) 117–18, 120, 139, 140, 297, 299–300, 303, 304, 305–6, 329, 353, 359, 385
Getting Our Priorities Right 353, 358, 359, 360
GIRFEC *see Getting it Right for Every Child*
Glasgow City Council, asylum seekers 407–8
Glasgow University 317
globalisation 11, 64, 308
Government Economic Strategy 300
Griffiths Report *see Community Care: Agenda for Action*
Griffiths, Sir Roy 128, 283
guardian's allowance 155
Guidelines for the Development of National Strategies for the Prevention of Suicidal Behaviours 1993 234

Hamilton court 386
Haringey Council 112–13
Hawking, Stephen 77
HCR20 119
health 74, 112, 144–5, 168, 205–18, 423, 424
see also mental health; public health
The Health Divide 209
Health Efficiency Access and Treatment (HEAT) 235
Hepatitis C Action Plan for Scotland 359
Her Majesty's Revenue and Customs (HMRC) 155
Hidden Harm 308, 353, 358, 359, 360
Higher Aspirations, Brighter Futures 303

Hills, John, *Inequality and the State* 162
HIV 99, 218, 346
Home Detention Curfews (HDC) 384
home help service 46, 143
see also domiciliary care
homelessness 419–37
Homelessness Act 2002 427
Homelessness (Scotland) Act 2003 428, 429
Homelessness Task Force (HTF) 427
Household Means Test 45–6
households below average income (HBAI) 92
houses of correction 35, 152
see also workhouses
housing 10, 40, 43, 47, 73, 75, 167, 255, 419–37
benefit 155, 159, 166, 169
and health 213–14
Housing Act 2004 427
Housing (Scotland) Acts
2001 427–8, 492
2006 428
human rights 20, 85, 130, 138, 184–7, 195, 197, 232–4, 242, 338, 377–8, 402
Human Rights Act 1998 20, 130, 185, 233, 377–8, 402
Hume, David 15

ideology 12, 51–68
immigration 165–6, 393–415
controls 396–401
terminology 394–6
Immigration Act 1971 398, 403
Immigration and Asylum Act 1999 398–9, 407
Immigration, Nationality and Asylum Act 2006 401
immigration removal centres (detention centres) 403, 407
impairment 271–90, 331
see also disability living allowance
Implementing Inclusiveness, Realising Potential 285
Improving Health in Scotland: The Challenge 2003 216
Improving Scottish Education 2002-2005 327
incapacity benefit 156, 158, 170
income support 92–3
InControl 192
Independent Inquiry into Inequalities in Health (Acheson Report) 209, 214
Independent Living 193, 197
Individual Budget Evaluation Network 194
individualism 52, 57, 64, 308
industrial disablement benefit 156
industrialisation 31, 36, 39–40, 42
information communication technology (ICT) 321–2
Ingleby Committee 295
Ingram, Adam 307
Institute of Fiscal Studies (IFS) 159
institutionalisation 125–7, 423, 424
Integrated Assessment, Planning and Recording Framework (My World Framework) 306
Integrated Children's Service Planning Guidance 303
Integrated Community Schools network 323, 329, 332
Integrated Strategy for the Early Years 307
Interdepartmental Committee on Social Insurance and Allied Service 46
It's Everyone's Job to Make Sure I'm Alright: Report of the Child Protection Audit and Review 304, 305

Jobcentre Plus 155
Jobseeker's Allowance (JSA) 156, 158, 160, 161
Joint Future 131, 132
Joseph Rowntree Foundation 165, 210, 249, 258
juvenile delinquency 295–7

Kalyx 383
The Key Capabilities in Child Care and Protection 118
khat 339
Kilbrandon Committee 294, 295, 368

Kilmarnock, HMP 383
The Kirk's Care of the Poor 276
Knox, John 317

Labour of Children in Factories Act 1833 318
Labour Exchanges 44, 47
Lapper, Alison 278
law, and policy 12–16, 22–7
Law Officers 18–19
Law Reform (Miscellaneous Provisions) (Scotland) Act 1990 347, 351, 369
Leave to Remain 408
legal aid scheme 153
legislation 13–22, 356
  alcohol 356
  community care 130
  criminal justice system 371–2
  older people 256–7
  public health 43
  substance use 356
Levitas, Ruth 285
liberalism 43–4, 52–3, 55–7, 64
Licensing (Scotland) Acts
  1976 351
  2005 342, 345, 352, 361
Life Prisoner Tribunal 377
Lloyd George, David 44
local enterprise companies (LEC) 328
Local Government in Scotland Act, 2003 303
Local Government (Scotland) Acts
  1889 152
  1929 152
Looked After Children (Scotland) Regulations 2009 (SSI 2009/210) 14, 26
Looked After Children and Young People: We Can and Must Do Better 298
Lord Advocate 18–19
Low Pay Unit 96
Lunacy (Scotland) Act 1857 229

McCrone Report 323
MacLean Committee 119, 377
McNeill, Duncan 353
Making a Reality of Community Care (Audit Commission Report) 128
Management of Offenders (Scotland) Act 2005 377, 381, 384
Mandatory Committees 19–22
MAPPA (Multi-Agency Public Protection Arrangements) 120
Martin, Brian 384
Marxism 59
Maslow, Abraham 75, 76, 83, 263
'Material Resources and Well-Being of Older People' 249
maternity allowance (MA) 159–60
Maternity and Child Welfare Act 1918 46
means-testing 45–6, 53, 92, 143, 153, 155, 156, 161–3, 263, 426
Measuring Severe Child Poverty 196
Meeting the Childcare Challenge: A Childcare Strategy for Scotland 322
Meeting the Needs of Children from Birth to Three 323
mental health 10, 127, 227–43, 424
Mental Health Act 1959 126
Mental Health (Care and Treatment) (Scotland) Act 2003 18, 21, 23, 24, 180, 230–4, 242, 261
The Mental Health of Children and Young People: A Framework for Promotion, Prevention and Care 306
Mental Health Commission (New Zealand) 236
Mental Health Officers 232
Mental Health (Scotland) Act 1984 231–3, 242
Mental Health Tribunal 23, 242
Mental Welfare Commission 23, 116
migration *see* immigration
Milan Report 231
Ministerial Strategic Group on Health and Community Care 250
Ministerial Task Force on Health Inequalities 216
Ministry of Labour 44
Misuse of Drugs Act 1971 342, 343, 358
Modern Apprenticeships 328, 329
Modernising Community Care: An Action Plan 131, 284

modernity 65–6
monetarist policies 95
Monitoring Poverty and Social Exclusion in Scotland 103
mortality rates 168
Multi-Agency Public Protection Arrangements (MAPPA) 382
Munn Report 319
My World 120, 306

National Assistance Act 1948 (UK) 47, 129, 152–3, 263
National Asylum Support Service (NASS) 399, 403
National Care Standards Committee 323
National Care Standards for Early Education and Childcare up to the Age of 16 323
National Carers Strategy for Scotland 139
National Child Care Strategy 101, 102
National Council for Carers and their Elderly Dependents (NCCED) 135
National Council for the Single Woman and Her Dependents 135
National Domestic Abuse Delivery Plan for Children and Young People 306–7
National Equality Panel 183
National Grid for Learning (NGFL) 322
National Health Service 45, 46, 54, 167, 206, 207–8, 215, 254
National Health Service Acts
  1946 47
  1977 135
National Health Service and Community Care Act 1990 (NHSCCA) 18, 48, 129, 140, 188, 207, 229, 255, 261, 263, 283, 296, 346–7
National Health Service Reform (Scotland) Act 2004 142
National Health Service Trusts 207
National Implementation Support Team (NIST) 236
National Insurance Act 1946 47
National Insurance (Industrial Injuries) Act 47
National Minimum Wage 101
National Plan for Gaelic (2007-2012) 327–8
National Programme for Improving Mental Health and Wellbeing (NPIMHW) 234, 236, 237
National Quality Standards for Substance Misuse Services 359
National Residential Child Care Initiative 303
National Unemployed Workers Movement 153
nationalisation 47
nationalism 60–1
Nationality Immigration and Asylum Act 2002 399
needs 73–4, 77–86, 234
Neighbourhood Renewal 332
neo-liberalism 57
neoconservatism 57
Ness, Caleb 117–18
New Deal for Lone Parents 164
A New Deal for Welfare: Empowering People to Work 285
New Deal for Young People (NDFYP) 101, 164, 182, 328
New Freedom Commission on Mental Health (USA) 237
New Futures Funds 101
New Labour 48, 67, 100, 153–4
New Policy Institute 210
New Right 57, 58
New Social Democracy (NSD) 60
new vocationalism 321
The NHS Plan 2000 215
nicotine 339, 342
Noranside open prison 385
Nordic countries 52
nursing and residential care services 143–4
Nutritional Guidance for Early Years 324

Obama administration 52–3
older people 127, 166–7, 247–66
  family care 260
  social policy 254–7

legislation in Scotland, table 256–7
One Gateway Protection Programme 403, 411
O'Neill, Denis 294
open prisons 385
opium 343
Order for Lifelong Restriction 373, 378
Outdoor Labour Test Order (1842) 39
outdoor relief 36–7, 152
Outdoor Relief Prohibitory Order 1844 37

Panels of Justices 294
Parent Councils 327
Parental Responsibilities Orders 21
parenting 21, 165, 213, 308–9, 310, 319, 327
Parent's Charter 319
parks *see* public spaces
Parliament 14–22
Parochial Boards 152
Parole Board for Scotland 376
PCS Analysis (personal, cultural, structural) 177, 248
Peacock, Peter 117
pension credit 101, 164, 166
Pension Reform, White Paper 2006 249
Pension Service 155
pensions 43, 157, 251, 254–5
people, and policy 71–86
People First 197
People and Society 250
'People's Budget' 1909 45
personal care 134, 140, 141, 142–3, 254, 255, 260, 261–3
personalisation 142, 165, 170, 175, 190–4, 197, 252, 261, 264, 266, 287
Police, Public Order and Criminal Justice (Scotland) Act 2006 349
political and policy-making process, Scotland 19–22
Poor Law Acts 402
1579 (Scots) 33–4, 151
1601 (43rd of Elizabeth) 34–6, 40
1834 31, 36–8, 39
Poor Law (Scotland) Act 1845 33, 38–9, 276
poorhouses *see* workhouses
poverty 35, 36, 38–9, 40, 42–3, 80–1
and health 213
and homelessness 422, 423
and old age 249, 250
and social exclusion 91–104
Poverty and Social Exclusion Survey 249
Press Complaints Commission 396
'The Primary Memorandum' 319
prison populations 383–4
Prisoners and Criminal Proceedings Act 1993 373, 377
privatisation 48, 188, 190, 254
probation orders 16, 368
Protection of Children and Prevention of Sexual Offices (Scotland) Act 2005 381
Protection from Abuse (Scotland) Act 2001 378
Public Assistance Institutions 152
public health 40, 43, 47, 208
Public Health Institute of Scotland 209

Qualifications and Curriculum Authority 330

Re:duce, Re:habilitate, Re:form 377
Reagan, Ronald 57, 58
Record of Needs (RON) 331
Reducing Dependency, Increasing Opportunity: Options for the Future of Welfare to Work 170
Reducing Health Inequalities: An Action Report 215
Reducing the Risk: Improving the Response to Sex Offending 378
Regulation of Care (Scotland) Act 2001 323
Regulations and Guidance 21
religious fundamentalism 63
Report of the 21st Century Social Work Review see 'Changing Lives'
Report into Serious Violent and Sexual Offenders 378
Report of the Royal Commission on Long Term Care for the Elderly 141
Reshaping Services 250
residential care 127, 143–4, 264–5

Residential Establishments - Child Care (Scotland) Regulations 1996 14
retirement 167, 251, 258
risk 109–21, 378–9, 380
Risk Assessment Guidance Framework 120
Risk Management Authority 378–9
Risk Matrix 2000 381
The Road to Recovery: A New Approach to Tackling Scotland's Drug Problem 139, 350, 353, 358
Road Traffic Act 1988 338
Rough Sleepers Initiative 427
Rough Sleepers Unit 426
Rowntree, Benjamin Seebohm, *Poverty: A Study of Town Life* 43, 279
Rowntree (Joseph) Foundation 165, 210, 249, 258
Royal Commission on the Poor Laws 1905-1909 44–5, 279
Russian Revolution 61

SACRO 382
A Safer Scotland: Tackling Crime and its Causes 376
SafeTALK 235
St Andrews University 317
Saint-Simon, Henri de 58
Same as You report 2000 284, 285
Saving Lives: Our Healthier Nation 214–15
Scandinavian countries 52
Schengen Convention 402
Scotch (Scottish) Education Department 318
Scotland Act 1998 13, 16, 19, 137, 338, 368, 376
Scotland's Children: Regulations and Guidance 26
Scotland's Choice 384
Scotland's Future is Smoke-Free: A Smoking Prevention Action Plan 360
Scottish Association for the Care and Rehabilitation of Offenders (SACRO) 233
Scottish Criminal Cases Review Tribunal 15
Scottish Development Group 194
Scottish Drug Enforcement Agency 349
Scottish Education Department 317
Scottish Enterprise 100
Scottish Executive Care Development Group 263
Scottish Executive Development Department (SEDD) 428
Scottish Executive's Drugs Action Plan: Protecting Our Future (2000) 348
Scottish and Highland and Island Enterprise 328
Scottish Homes 100
Scottish Institute for Excellence in Social Work Education 118
Scottish Nationalist Party (SNP) 59
Scottish Network for Families Affected by Drugs (SNFAD) 358
Scottish Office 17, 304, 321, 347, 348, 369, 373, 377, 378, 427
Scottish Poor Law Act 1845 152
Scottish Prison Service 120, 376, 384
Scottish Prisons Commission 383
Scottish Qualifications Authority (SQA) 321
Scottish Recovery Network 237, 238–9
Scottish Refugee Council 413
Scottish Refugee Integration Forum (SRIF) 404
Scottish Royal Commission, 1843 33
Scottish Schools (Parental Involvement) Act 2006 327
Scottish Social Inclusion Network 100–1, 103
Scottish Strategy for Victims 374
Scottish Young Parliament 186
Second World War 45–6, 72, 184, 294
Self-Directed Support 193
SERCO 384
Sewel Convention 21
Sex Offenders Act 1997 381
Sexual Offences Act 2003 381
Sexual Offences Prevention Orders 381, 382
SHANARRI (Safe, Healthy, Achieving, Nurtured, Active, have Responsibility, be Respected, and be Included) 306

Single Outcome Agreements (SOAs) 235
Single Shared Assessment (SSA) 131, 132
Skill-seekers 328
Skills for Life 332
smoking *see* tobacco
Smoking, Health and Social Care (Scotland) Act 2005 354, 360
social democracy 52
Social Enquiry Report (SER) 375
social exclusion 98–101, 177
  asylum seekers 319
  and homelessness 422
  and poverty 91–104
  see also social inclusion
Social Exclusion Unit 98, 102–3, 166, 177, 181
Social Fund (SF) 160
social inclusion 19, 103, 176, 181–4, 196, 217, 273, 285–8, 300, 323, 385
  see also social exclusion
Social Inclusion – Opening the Door to a Better Scotland: Strategy 103
Social Inclusion Network 100, 103, 181
Social Inclusion Partnerships (SIPs) 102
social insurance 44–5, 46, 60, 66–7, 85, 254
social justice 59, 67, 85–6, 181, 184–5, 198, 217, 297, 299–302, 413
Social Justice: A Scotland Where Everyone Matters 182, 304
social policy
  defined 8–12
  history 31–48
Social Role Valorisation (SVR) 283, 284
Social Security Act 1986 160
social work, origins 40–2
Social Work at its Best 295
Social Work Inspection Agency 116
Social Work (Scotland) Act 1968 295–6, 368, 369
Social Work Services Group (SWSG) 369
socialism 58–60
Special Educational Needs and Disability Act 2001 331
Stable and Acute 2007 382
Stair, James Dalrymple, 1st Viscount 15
Standards in Scotland's Schools (Scotland) Act 2000 323
statutory maternity pay (SMP) 156, 159–60
statutory sick pay (SSP) 156, 160
STORM 235
Strategy for Carers 1999 139
substance use 337–62, 423
  legislation, table 356
suicide 234–6
Suicide Talk 235
supplementary benefits 36
Support and Assitance of Young People Leaving Care (Scotland) Regulations 2003 14
'Supporting Families' 102
Supporting, Safer, Stronger Communities: Scotland's Criminal Justice Plan 377, 386
Sure Start 102, 155, 160, 307, 332
swine flu pandemic (H1N1) 113, 114

Tackling Drugs in Scotland: Action in Partnership (1999) 348, 349
Tackling Health Inequalities: A Programme for Action 2003 215, 216
Tawney, R.H. 298
tax avoidance 163
tax credits 155–6, 169
temazepam 341
Thatcher, Margaret 47, 48, 57, 58, 67, 128
'third way' 59–60, 67
'Time Out', Glasgow 379
tobacco 337, 338, 341, 342, 343, 353–5
  legislation 356
Tobacco Advertising and Promotions Act 2002 354
Tobacco and Primary Medical Services (Scotland) Act 2010 354, 360
Tough on Crime and Tough on the Causes of Crime 376
Toward a National Accommodation Strategy for Sex Offenders 381
Towards a Healthier Scotland 216
Towards a Mentally Flourishing Scotland 2007 227, 230, 231, 236

Townsend Deprivation Index 93
Toynbee, Arnold 42
training 328–9
Transform Drug Policy Foundation 362
Transforming Public Services 301
Tressell, Robert, *The Ragged Trousered Philanthropist* 41
Tribunals Service 155
Tronto, Joan 286

UK Border Agency (UKBA) 400, 401, 403
UK Border and Immigration Agency (UKBIA) 403
UK Borders Act 2007 401
UK Visa Services 403
Unemployed Workman's Act, 1905 43
unemployment 45, 47, 95–7, 213, 329, 422, 432
  youth 328
Union of the Physically Impaired Against Segreation (UPIAS) 281–2
Unison Scotland 404
United Nations Convention on Refugees 1951 394
United Nations Convention on the Rights of the Child (UNCRC) 181, 184, 185, 320, 323
United Nations High Commissioner for Refugees 403
Universal Declaration on Human Rights 1948 85, 184, 197
Users and Carers Panel 137

Victim Notification Scheme 374
Victim Support Scotland 374
Violent and Sex Offenders Register (ViSOR) 382
'The Voice of Carers' 137
volatile substances, legislation 356
Vulnerable Witnesses (Scotland) Act 2004 374

Warnock Report 319, 320, 331
We Can and Must Do Better 329
Webb, Beatrice and Sydney 44
Weber, Max 113
welfare 43–8, 51–4, 64, 66–8, 151–70, 279
Welfare Reform Act 2009 350–1
welfare-to-work initiatives 37, 101, 153, 164
Wellness Recovery Action Planning (WRAP) 239
'What Works Principles' 370
Who Cares? Scotland, Charter of Rights 180
Winnicott, David 294
winter fuel payments 101
Wollstonecraft, Mary, *A Vindication of the Rights of Women* 62
women, trafficked 399
women offenders 379–81
Women Offenders: A Safer Way 379
Work Capability Assessment 170
workhouses 35, 36, 37, 318
  see also houses of correction
working tax credit 101
'Working Together for a Healthier Scotland' 102
World Health Organisation (WHO) 205–6, 234

YMCA 408
young carers 136, 138–40
Youth Courts 386
youth justice 385–6
Youth Training Schemes (YTS) 328
youth unemployment 328